CYBERSECURITY
FOR SCADA SYSTEMS

CYBERSECURITY
FOR SCADA SYSTEMS

WILLIAM T. SHAW, PHD, CISSP

Disclaimer

The recommendations, advice, descriptions, and the methods in this book are presented solely for educational purposes. The author and publisher assume no liability whatsoever for any loss or damage that results from the use of any of the material in this book. Use of the material in this book is solely at the risk of the user.

Copyright © 2006 by
PennWell Corporation
1421 South Sheridan Road
Tulsa, Oklahoma 74112-6600 USA
800.752.9764
+1.918.831.9421
sales@pennwell.com
www.pennwellbooks.com
www.pennwell.com

Director: Mary McGee
Managing Editor: Steve Hill
Production/Operations Manager: Traci Huntsman
Assistant Editor: Amethyst Hensley
Production Editor: Tony Quinn
Cover Designer: Karla Pfeifer
Book Designer: Brigitte Pumford-Coffman

Library of Congress Cataloging-in-Publication Data

Shaw, William T.
  Cybersecurity for industrial scada systems / William T. Shaw.
      p. cm.
  Includes index.
  ISBN-13: 978-1-59370-068-3 (hardcover)
  ISBN-10: 1-59370-068-7 (hardcover)
  1. Supervisory control systems. 2. Automatic data collection systems. 3. Data protection.
4. Computer security. I. Title.
  TJ222.S53 2006
  620'.46028558--dc22

                                                                              2006013261

Printed in the United States of America

1 2 3 4 5 10 09 08 07 06

Contents

Preface

In the 1960s, when the first computer-based supervisory control and data acquisition (SCADA) systems were being developed, there was no cultural concept of the need for particular protective measures to keep such systems safe from intentional attacks. After all, why would someone want to disrupt the operation of such systems? The world was a different place, and the computer expertise to work on or with such systems was a rare commodity. The only protective considerations built into those systems were instituted to minimize or eliminate the impact of user errors.

Not so today. Computers have become commodity appliances, and computer expertise is far more commonplace. In addition, there are people who have technical expertise and, for a variety of reasons, choose to use it to inflict damage. Worse still, there are those who wish to use such expertise to cause serious harm to the government and citizens of the United States. The Internet, a world-spanning communications technology that should be a positive force to unite cultures and peoples, is being used also as a means to reach into our computer systems by such ill-intentioned people. Much of our critical industrial infrastructure is managed and controlled by SCADA systems, and thus, it is now essential that we place protective measures within and around these systems. This book is intended to provide a general background of SCADA system technology and of cybersecurity concepts and technologies and to explain how the two can be brought together to safeguard our infrastructure and computer automation systems.

Acknowledgments

I would like to acknowledge all of the people who assisted in the writing of this book and, in particular, my wonderful and understanding wife, who put up with the long nights and weekends spent writing, editing, and proofreading this manuscript. In addition, I would like to acknowledge the assistance of all of the friends and associates who let me bounce ideas off of them or who read and reviewed some of the early scribbling.

Introduction — Industrial Automation in the Aftermath of 9/11

Without the events of September 11, 2001, there might not have been a need for this book—or at least not this soon. Until the events of that day, the people and government of the United States held the belief that we were insulated from those foreign governments and "true believers" that might wish us harm. It is true that for many years, computer hacking and the periodic introduction of computer worms, viruses, and other forms of malware over the Internet have represented a growing problem. Nevertheless, these activities were not perceived as serious, intentional attacks on our country or its infrastructure. After 9/11 everything changed. We now know that there are people and groups that will spend the time and money to create havoc and terror to advance their political, social, or religious agendas.

In response to the events of 9/11, the Department of Homeland Security (DHS) was formed and given the responsibility for protecting us from these people and organizations. One of the results of the early work of the DHS was the recognition that the vast majority of our industrial and manufacturing facilities, technological and energy infrastructure, and transportation systems are run and controlled by computer-based systems and that these systems (mainly SCADA systems, distributed control systems [DCS], and programmable logic controller [PLC] systems) were not designed with any intrinsic protective mechanisms. This is not to imply that such systems are fragile or even readily accessible to an attacker. Rather, the vendors of these systems generally designed them to be robust and capable of continued full or partial operation, even with some level of component failures or damage. This was essential because of the critical or essential nature of the processes controlled by such systems. Designers of computer-based automation and control systems have always known that computers—and electronic devices in general—can and will fail. Thus, system designs have long accounted for this possibility through redundancy schemes and architectures that permitted graceful degradation.

In the early years of computer-based automation systems, these systems were typically employed in a stand-alone configuration without any communication with or interfaces to other computer systems. The only way a remote cyber attacker/hacker could access such systems would have been if a dial-in telephone circuit had been supplied with the system, for the purpose of providing remote support by the system vendor. However, as computer and networking technology became pervasive and ubiquitous in all aspects of modern business enterprises, these automation systems started to be interfaced with corporate networks, business systems, and eventually, even to the Internet itself. This evolutionary process has provided cyber attackers with much greater access to these critical automation systems.

The world of computer-based automation systems can be divided into two broad classes: those systems used with processes that are spread over a large geographic area (and thus require the use of wide area communications technology); and those systems that manage processes that are geographically constrained (and thus can use local area communications technology). The first type of system is considered a SCADA system and is used in applications such as gas and liquid pipelines, electric power transmission and distribution, and water distribution systems. The second type of system is called a DCS and is used in plant automation applications—such as refining, steel production, paper and pulp, food and beverage, and bulk and fine chemicals. A variation of this second type of system is based on PLC technology. Almost every high-volume manufacturing facility is automated using PLC technology. The DHS has initially focused its efforts on cybersecurity for SCADA systems; therefore, that is the focus of this book, although many of the issues and principals will be directly relevant and applicable to DCS as well.

SECTION 1:
INTRODUCTION TO SCADA SYSTEMS

The Technological Evolution of SCADA Systems

The Early History of SCADA—Mainframes

Supervisory control and data acquisition (SCADA) systems are used to monitor and remotely control critical industrial processes, such as gas pipelines, electric power transmission, and potable water distribution/delivery. As such, SCADA systems are important to our daily lives, even though most people never see them or even know of their existence.

To properly understand what SCADA systems are, how they came to be, and why they are designed the way they are, one needs a basic understanding of the history of SCADA system development. It is also helpful to know why things have evolved and what factors have pushed this evolution. Computer-based supervisory control systems were introduced in the 1960s, and the first such systems were based on the mainframe computer technology available at the time. These systems were not yet called SCADA systems, as that particular acronym did not come into general use until the 1980s. SCADA systems were developed to replace older technologies (e.g., tone telemetry) and to provide features and functions that required computational and logical capabilities. The incorporation of a computer into telemetry systems provided a means for manipulating, processing, storing, and presenting data that could not be provided with previous technologies.

In the late 1960s, the integrated circuit had been invented, making it possible to build complex and sophisticated (for the time) electronic devices, including mainframe computers. By their nature and purpose, SCADA systems are intended to provide a human *operator* with updating *real-time* information about the current state of the remote process being monitored, as well as the ability to manipulate the process remotely. There were four basic components in a 1960s SCADA system (fig. 1–1): the central computer (also called the *host* computer), the field-based remote measurement and control equipment (called *remote terminal units* [RTUs]), the wide area telecommunications system to connect them, and the operator interface that provided user/operator access to the system (also called the *operator console*, man-machine interface [MMI], and in the politically correct age, human-machine interface [HMI]). Although computer and communications technology have advanced since the 1960s, even modern SCADA systems have a similar architectural basis.

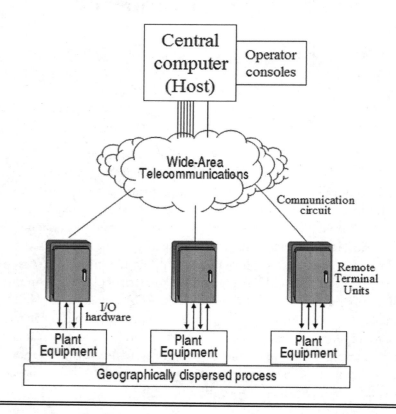

FIG. 1–1. *Simplified component diagram of a SCADA system*

To provide real-time data updates from the field, a SCADA system needs remote sensory and communications capabilities. Electronic devices called RTUs are located at each point where measurements are to be taken or where process equipment is to be controlled. The central computer continuously polls the field-based RTUs to fetch their current measurement values. Polling is the process of sending a message to an RTU, to elicit a response message containing updated values, and repeating that operation with subsequent RTUs, until all have been processed. Then, that sequence is repeated over and over, without end.

The RTUs designed in the 1960s, many of which remain in use, are very simple electronic devices with a severely limited set of hardwired functions. Normally, RTUs are equipped with input/output (I/O) hardware circuitry that enabled the measurement of electrical signals generated by devices that produce voltages or currents in proportion to a physical process parameter such as pressure, flow rate, level, or temperature. (The term *transmitter* is often used for the device that produces an electrical signal proportional to the value of a physical property.) RTUs are also able to generate control outputs, either as voltage or current signals, or in the form of switch/contact signals. Output control signals are initiated or adjusted on receipt of a command from the central computer, usually initiated by a human operator. In order for the RTUs and the central host computer to exchange data and control commands, there needs to be a communications system to allow messages to be sent/received over large distances, as well as an agreed-on message format and predefined set of messages and responses.

SCADA system designers in the 1960s had to use the currently available long-distance telecommunications technologies of the time, and that meant either the telephone company ("Ma Bell") technology or radio technology. Frequently, the RTU equipment (and the process being monitored and controlled) was located in remote areas where no telephone service was available. In those instances, the equipment owner (e.g., a pipeline company or an electric utility) would build their own telephone system, using the same equipment that the telephone company would have employed (microwave relay towers, signal multiplexers, etc.).

Telephone and radio technologies are designed for voice (sound) communications. Thus, SCADA systems required the use of *modems* to turn computer and RTU electrical signals into sound. In the late 1960s, modem technology was restricted to very low data transmission rates, typically 110–300 bits per second. The RTUs in the 1960s were electronic, but not computer based, so they had to be hardwired to support a simple set of messages for exchanging data with the central host computer.

Further, since most communications would take place at 300 bits per second (bps) or less, keeping messages short was essential. The set of messages that could be sent to the RTUs and the set of messages that the RTUs could generate together define a *communications protocol*. In the 1960s, vendors of SCADA systems had to design and build their own RTUs and thus also defined their own (proprietary) communications protocol(s). In certain industries today (primarily the electric utilities), there are still RTUs utilizing some of these old, obsolete protocols—often referred to as *legacy* protocols.

In the 1960s, the *universal asynchronous receiver transmitter* (UART) chip had not yet been invented, so it was up to each vendor to decide the format of their protocol messages (i.e., how many bits in a message). To simplify the electronic design of the RTUs, most vendors elected to send all available numeric (analog) or binary (status) data in single messages (fig. 1–2). This would mean messages of 30, 48, 64, or some other extended number of bits. In essence, a response to a polling message from the SCADA host was the transmission of the current values of the inputs, sent as one long message.

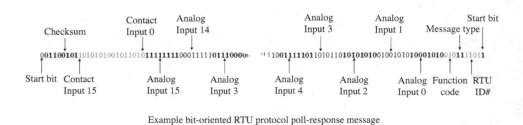

Example bit-oriented RTU protocol poll-response message

FIG. 1–2. *Example bit-oriented message format (starting and ending bits only, owing to actual number of bits required in a full-length message)*

These *bit-oriented* protocols fell out of favor with the invention of the UART chip (and microprocessors), but as previously mentioned, some of these legacy bit-oriented protocols remain in limited use. Most RTU protocols used today are based on the breaking of long messages into some integral number of eight-bit octets suitable for asynchronous serial transmission via UART circuits, which all modern computers employ in their serial ("COM:") ports. These are generally called *character-oriented* protocols. You will also hear these two types of protocols called *synchronous* and *asynchronous* protocols, but this is not technically accurate. In fact, both are asynchronous, but one uses 8-bit frames and the other some vendor-defined number of bits (usually many more than eight.) The differences between these two categories of protocols will be discussed in more detail in a later chapter.

A SCADA system is used to fetch and present current data values to a human operator. The time required to refresh the measurement data in a SCADA system that represent the *current state* of the remote process, through the polling of RTUs, depends on several factors:

- The bit rate (110, 300, or 1,200 bps) of the communication circuit(s)

- The number of RTUs sharing a given communications circuit

- The length (in bits) and number of messages exchanged in the polling process

- The number of communication circuits being used sequentially or concurrently

- The time delay characteristics of the communication circuits

The protocol used by an RTU can be designed to permit multiple RTUs to share a common communication circuit, much like a party-line telephone. This means that the protocol incorporates some mechanism (usually an RTU identification number [ID] in the message) that allows a given RTU to identify which messages are intended for that RTU and to ignore messages addressed to other RTUs. Placing multiple RTUs on communication circuits reduces the required number of such circuits, but it can lengthen the time required in order to poll all RTUs for current data values. Most SCADA systems that support multiple polling circuits are designed to poll RTUs on all of these circuits concurrently. Thus, if there are x circuits, the SCADA host can be polling x RTUs concurrently (i.e., one on each circuit).

In some industries, the process dynamics are such that a human operator (or supervisory application program) monitoring and controlling the process through a SCADA system needs to have fresh measurements more frequently than with less dynamic processes. In those applications (e.g., electric power transmission), it is common to see multiple communication circuits with little or no *multi-dropping* (sharing) of those communication circuits across multiple RTUs. In less dynamic processes (e.g., water/wastewater transportation), it is not uncommon for all RTUs to be polled on a single, shared radio channel, resulting in much longer times between field data updates.

The presentation of information to a human operator is a fundamental feature of SCADA systems, and in the 1960s, this could be accomplished in several ways. The high-resolution video, projection, and flat-panel display technologies of today were not available to the system designers of the 1960s. In fact, little commercially available display technology existed. Therefore, SCADA vendors were once again required to develop their own HMIs.

A common approach for information presentation was to use a *map board* (also called a *mimic panel*), a wall-sized drawing of the process with indicator lights and numeric meter-style readouts mounted on the wall display at appropriate positions representing physical process areas. These lights and numeric displays were electrically controlled by I/O signals from the host computer and updated based on data received from the RTUs. In many SCADA system control rooms today, you will still find the equivalent of a mimic panel/map board display, but implemented with modern video projection technology.

Information presentation in the 1960s would also have included printed reports, logs, and alarm messages. It might also have included very basic *cathode-ray tube* (CRT) displays with tabular, alpha-numeric information or very primitive and simplistic, monochromatic, semigraphic displays (similar in nature to figs. 1–3 and 1–4, respectively). Such CRT-based displays would probably have used hardware and software developed by the SCADA system vendor. As a general note, these early SCADA systems were programmed in assembly language (with an occasional application written in Fortran), and essentially 100% of the software (and a good bit of the hardware) was proprietary to, and developed by, the vendor, including the operating system software.

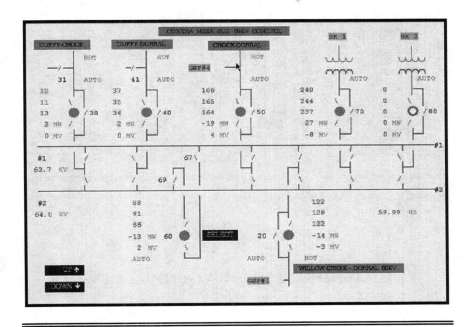

FIG. 1–3. *Example semigraphic operator display*

It should be noted that these examples of early CRT displays are actually more advanced than was generally available in the 1960s. Video display technology was in its infancy and the technology available for commercial applications (as opposed to military applications) was low resolution, monochromatic, character-oriented and fairly expensive. Figures 1–3 and 1–4 are intended to convey the general idea of the style of such displays, but these images actually come from systems of an early 1980s level of technology. Actual images from the 1960s would only survive as photographs, since no digital image capture technology had yet been invented.

STATION POWER CONSUMPTION							
TAGNAME	DESCRIPTION	LOCATION	PULSE	RUNNING TOTAL	LAST TOTAL		DATE FROZEN
BA0932JI	P32 MISCELLANEOUS	PCU-23-PCP-31		0.0	0.0	RESET	02/25/99 13:04:20.
CA0241JI	MCC P41 KWH	PCU-23-PCP-41		0.0	0.0	RESET	
CA0251JI	MCC P51 KWH	PCU-23-PCP-41		0.0	0.0	RESET	
CA1991JI	SUBSTATION U91	PCU-23-PCP-91		0.0	0.0	RESET	
DD0261JI	SUBSTATION U-61	PCU-64-PCP-64		0.0	0.0	RESET	
EA0281JI	SUBSTATION U-81,P-81	PCU-81-PCP-81		0.0	0.0	RESET	02/25/99 15:16:41.
EA0282JI	SUBSTATION U-81,P-82	PCU-81-PCP-81		0.0	0.0	RESET	02/25/99 15:16:37.
EA0283JI	SUBSTATION U-81,P-82	PCU-81-PCP-81		0.0	0.0	RESET	02/25/99 15:16:36.
EA0284JI	SUBSTATION U-81,P-82	PCU-81-PCP-81		0.0	0.0	RESET	02/25/99 15:16:34.
EA0285JI	SUBSTATION U-81,P-82	PCU-81-PCP-81		0.0	0.0	RESET	02/25/99 15:16:33.
EA0291JI	SUBSTATION U-91	PCU-81-PCP-81		0.0	0.0	RESET	02/25/99 15:16:31.
FA0911JI	SUBSTATION U111,P111	PCU-81-PCP-11		0.0	0.0	RESET	
FA0912JI	SUBSTATION U111,P112	PCU-81-PCP-11		0.0	0.0	RESET	
FA0913JI	SUBSTATION U112,M111	PCU-81-PCP-11		0.0	0.0	RESET	
FA0914JI	SUBSTATION U113,M111	PCU-81-PCP-11		0.0	0.0	RESET	
GB0901JI	SUBSTATION U-101	PCU-103-PCP-1		0.0	0.0	RESET	
JA0221JI	SUBSTATION U21	PCU-23-PCP-23	PULSES	71232.0	19604.0	RESET	02/25/99 13:05:10.
JA0222JI	SUBSTATION U22	PCU-23-PCP-23		178330.0	54432.0	RESET	02/25/99 13:05:06.
JA0224JI	LINE 1 MPL 224	PCU-23-PCP-23		284332.0	69548.0	RESET	02/25/99 13:05:04.
JA0225JI	LINE 2 MPL 225	PCU-23-PCP-23		425568.0	118412.0	RESET	02/25/99 13:05:01.
JA0231JI	SUBSTATION U31, P31	PCU-23-PCP-23		260848.0	48522.0	RESET	02/25/99 13:04:58.
JA0232JI	SUBSTATION U31, P32	PCU-23-PCP-23	PULSES	220604.0	41822.0	RESET	02/25/99 13:04:56.
JA0501JI	JOY COMPRESSOR-1 KWH	PCU-23-PCP-23		0.0	0.0	RESET	
JA0502JI	JOY COMPRESSOR-2 KWH	PCU-23-PCP-23		0.0	0.0	RESET	
JA0503JI	JOY COMPRESSOR-3 KWH	PCU-23-PCP-23		0.0	0.0	RESET	
JA0921JI	SUBSTATION U23, P21	PCU-23-PCP-23		80966.0	15348.0	RESET	02/25/99 13:04:43.
JA0922JI	SUBSTATION U23, P22	PCU-23-PCP-23		30988.0	3128.0	RESET	02/25/99 13:04:40.
JA0923JI	SUBSTATION U23, P23	PCU-23-PCP-23	PULSES	136466.0	31326.0	RESET	02/25/99 13:04:46.
JA0924JI	SUBSTATION U23, P24	PCU-23-PCP-23	PULSES	31480.0	8606.0	RESET	02/25/99 13:04:49.

FIG. 1–4. *Example tabular operator displays*

Minicomputers and Microprocessors

The introduction of mainframe computers into telemetry systems, to create the SCADA system, was a significant technological advance, because custom application programs could then be developed to make use of the real-time process data—for trending, performing reasonability/alarm checking, and generating additional information by making calculations, as well as for presenting the data to the operator in a variety of formats. The biggest drawback was that mainframe computers were very expensive and not very reliable (so you needed a redundant set). Thus, SCADA systems were restricted to applications that could justify the high implementation costs involved.

The next two major advances in SCADA systems technology were the introduction first of the (relatively) low-cost, 16-bit *"minicomputer"* and then of eight-bit microprocessors, in the 1970s. The minicomputer was a much more cost-effective computing platform as compared to the mainframe computers of the time. They were also much simpler devices and were easier to cobble together into a redundant configuration. By using minicomputers as the host computers, SCADA system vendors were able to drastically reduce the cost of a system. Thus, many more applications could be financially justified.

It was also common to see hybrid systems—in which redundant minicomputers performed the real-time polling of the RTUs and provided the operator display and remote control functions and a nonredundant mainframe computer was used to run nonessential advanced applications and models. As with mainframe computers, the software that ran the minicomputer-based SCADA systems was generally written in assembly language and was usually 100% proprietary to the system vendor. Eventually minicomputers evolved into "super" (32-bit) minicomputers, and computer vendors started providing general-purpose operating systems that were suitable for real-time applications and operating system interoperability standards (e.g., Portable Operating System Interface [POSIX] and X-Windows) were developed.

In parallel with this activity, the personal computer came into being and ultimately evolved into the powerful devices we have today, with commercially available operating systems, networks, relational databases, peripherals, and much more. The eight-bit microprocessor revolutionized the design of RTUs in the 1980s, because RTUs based on microprocessor technology could be (re)programmed to add to or expand their functions, perform much more sophisticated functions, and even provide local, closed-loop control.

Occasionally pre-microprocessor RTUs have been referred to as *dumb* remotes, and those with microprocessors have been called *smart* remotes. That delineation has become blurred, as the computing power of RTUs has kept pace with overall microprocessor technology. A modern RTU could be considered brilliant in comparison to the earliest eight-bit microprocessor models.

One major difference between smart and dumb RTUs was in the sophistication of communications protocols they could support. To perform remote control functions with a dumb RTU, SCADA systems often employed what is called a *select-check-operate* message sequence. Messages sent between the host computer and the RTUs were subject to interference and distortion from any number of environmental or communications system sources. Protocol messages are, in actual form, just a string of binary numbers represented by 1s and 0s. If a message were electrically distorted (i.e., if one or more bits were changed), that could mean that a command that was supposed to operate device X would appear to the RTU as a command to operate device Y.

The error-checking and -detection capabilities of pre-microprocessor RTUs was very limited and not always reliable. To prevent a communications error from causing an improper or dangerous control action, early RTU protocols often required a strict sequence of multiple messages (called a *check-before-operate* or select-check-operate sequence) in order to effect a control output. In this case, the human operator was an integral part of the message error-checking process. In a select-check-operate protocol, several messages and responses are exchanged in a defined sequence:

1. The operator sends a "select control output *n*" message to the specific RTU.

2. The RTU returns a "control output *n* is selected" message and starts a countdown by a *dead-man timer* in the RTU.

3. The operator sends a "prepare to perform operation *x* on selected output" message to the RTU.

4. The RTU returns an "operation *x* is to be performed" message.

5. The operator sends a "perform the operation" message to the RTU.

6. The RTU performs operation *x* on control output *n* and returns an "operation successful" message to the operator (and also cancels the dead-man timer).

At any point in the sequence, if the operator doesn't like what the RTU says (e.g., if it responds that it has selected output *o*, rather than *n* as requested, or if a different RTU responds), the operator can send a "cancel" message—or just let the dead-man timer expire, which will cause the RTU to automatically cancel the activity. The human operator provided message verification and error checking through this process.

With the introduction of microprocessor-based RTUs, it became possible to implement protocols that incorporated comprehensive message error-checking and -correction schemes, thus eliminating the need for operator intervention to validate messages. (However, in the electric utility industry, it is still common to require that the operator verify control actions in this manner.) Having reliable protocols is even more important when supervisory control commands are to be issued automatically by application programs running in the host computer; operator interaction would not be practical in those instances. With microprocessor-based RTUs, a whole range of additional capabilities were introduced, but a very significant one was having the ability to *download* parameters, program logic, and calculations into the RTU, via the communications (polling) channel. This capability enabled remote modifications of the RTU's functionality, although it required implementing a more sophisticated RTU protocol that included message types for performing such downloading or parameter-modification functions.

Central Architectures

Starting in the 1960s and continuing into the early 1980s, the vast majority of SCADA systems used a central architecture in which a single powerful central computer was responsible for managing and performing all of the functions, including RTU polling, data processing, display generation, report generation, data archiving, and running application programs. Because of the questionable reliability of computers, these centralized architecture systems invariably employed a second, identical (*redundant*) computer, and the two computers maintained some form of dialog to keep the redundant computer synchronized and updated (fig. 1–5).

In a redundant computer configuration, one computer would be designated as the *primary* unit and the other as the *backup* unit. The primary unit would perform all of the SCADA functions and then transfer updated

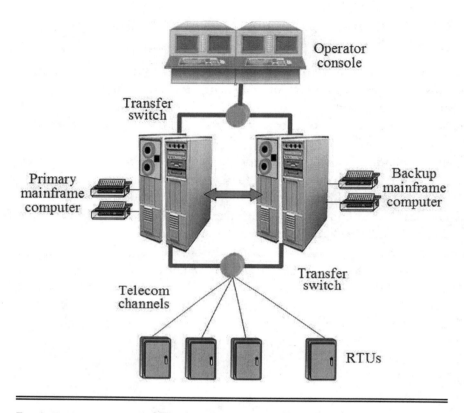

FIG. 1–5. *Centralized, redundant SCADA system architecture*

information to the backup computer, so that on any failure of the primary unit, the backup unit could take over and continue operations. The goal of a redundant design is to render a computer failure as transparent as possible to system users (with no loss of data, no loss of control capacity, no missed alarms, no loss of application programs, etc.).

Making redundancy work successfully was the biggest challenge to most SCADA system vendors. Early schemes that involved high-speed copying of memory areas from the primary to the backup computer (via *direct memory access* [DMA]) would instantly corrupt the backup if the primary became corrupted. Redundancy schemes were often complicated because of the need to transfer communication circuits, key peripherals, and operator console hardware from the primary to the backup computer. These early systems often used electromechanical transfer switches to implement such peripheral transfers. In other instances, the design of shared equipment, such as operator video displays, would incorporate a *dual-ported* capability, so that either computer could interact with those devices.

For the triggering of an automatic transfer to the backup computer, some means was needed to automatically determine that the primary was inoperative. Most systems included a special hardware device/circuit called a *watchdog timer*—a circuit that would generate a trigger signal, when a countdown by its hardware timer reached zero, unless that timer was constantly reset by commands from the computer. Both the primary and backup computers would incorporate a watchdog circuit, and each would have an application that was run periodically to reset their respective timers. If either computer stalled or had a hardware failure, or if its programming went into an *infinite loop*, the watchdog would count down to zero and generate an electrical signal that would cause the transfer of peripherals and notify the alternate computer to take over operations. At least, that is what was supposed to happen. In reality, such redundancy schemes often failed to operate or mis-operated (e.g., triggered a transfer when the primary computer had not actually failed).

Many redundancy designs were implemented, but few worked as advertised. One measure of the quality of a redundancy scheme was the time lag between the data in the primary system and the backup. Some vendors claimed that the backup would lag the primary by seconds; others updated the backup only every few minutes. Another differentiation in redundancy designs was their classification as fully automatic, bump-less, or hot-standby schemes, as compared to offering a warm-backup or cold-backup scheme. The last two of these schemes are less than perfect and possibly even require some level of manual intervention.

In a centralized SCADA system architecture, a single computer is doing all of the work of polling RTUs, processing and alarming the incoming data, generating and updating operational displays and reports, performing calculations, and running application programs. Through all of this, that single primary computer still had to allocate central processing unit (CPU) resources and time to update the backup computer with the newest data. Invariably, the number of RTUs, I/O points, calculations, and other functions grew beyond the initially implemented design capacity, and the redundancy scheme would be taxed and degraded. With a centralized design, the only way to add capacity to the system was to replace the computers with newer, more powerful models. This is one of the primary reasons why a popular replacement design eventually supplanted centralized architecture.

Distributed Architectures

Starting in the 1980s and up to the present, the majority of SCADA systems followed the trend of computer technology and erected a distributed architecture in which multiple computers were networked together and specific functions were assigned to particular computers. The introduction of local area networking (LAN) technologies (particularly Ethernet) made this possible and practical.

One of the most common architectural strategies was to separate out the RTU polling process, placing this function in dedicated *front-end* computers (fig. 1–6). This strategy also simplified the problem of computer redundancy, because front-end computers could be stripped down to their basics—RAM, serial ports, and LAN controllers—making primary-backup updating much less complicated. As a given front-end computer received data from RTU polling, it could send data-update messages to all other computers on the LAN, thus keeping them synchronized.

Another distributed-architecture strategy was to use a separate, dedicated computer to run large, complex, processor-intensive applications. This computer might not be made redundant, because a temporary loss of those applications would not affect the operator's basic ability to control and monitor the process.

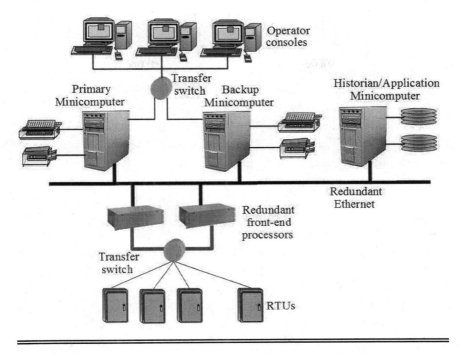

FIG. 1–6. *Distributed SCADA system architecture*

As historical archiving of data gained importance, yet another distributed strategy arose, in which a specific computer was assigned the responsibility for long-term data-archiving/trending functions. This computer would need much more online storage than the rest, as well as removable media storage devices for long-term off-line archiving of historical data.

A distributed architecture was the next logical step from a centralized design, because it increased overall computing power by spreading the various SCADA functions into additional computers dedicated to performing those specific functions. It also improved overall system reliability by making it possible to lose only certain SCADA functions, as a result of a fault or malfunction in one of the computers, rather than losing the total system. This ability to suffer a partial functional loss is usually described as *graceful degradation*.

Client/Server Designs

In the 1990s, with the advent of powerful 64-bit microprocessors and personal computers—as well as Transmission Control Protocol/Internet Protocol (TCP/IP) networking technology, high-speed Ethernet, and commercial real-time operating systems—the design of SCADA systems took another evolutionary step. In effect, SCADA systems began to look very much like the corporate information technology (IT) systems of the time. These new systems were designed to be *scalable* and *fault tolerant*, and the software that performed the SCADA-specific functions was redesigned and rewritten for distribution across multiple computer *servers*. Software that had been monolithic in prior generations (e.g., operator console display software) was broken into interacting components that could be run in the same computer or in different ones, with cross-LAN communications. The need for peripheral transfer switching and complex redundancy schemes was replaced with smarter software. *Clients* (e.g., any program that generates operational display updates) could seek out their respective servers (e.g., an RTU polling program) across the LAN to get the required data. If for some reason the server became unavailable, these clients could automatically switch to an alternative server if one was available. If more computing capability was required, additional servers could be connected to the high-speed network, and more copies of the client/server software could be loaded and run (fig. 1–7).

SCADA was becoming a special set of applications that could be run on any conventional, commercial computing platform. In fact, there are several commercially available SCADA software packages (e.g., the FIX and Wonderware) that can be purchased as packaged software and loaded onto conventional personal computers (PCs) and servers, as a do-it-yourself SCADA system. One of the major developments that came out of the migration toward the client/server design was a set of standards that define a mechanism for exchanging data between clients and servers developed by different vendors. The Object Linking and Embedding (OLE) for Process Control (OPC) standards were codeveloped by a group of vendors and end users and currently form the basis for a large number of commercially available SCADA software products.

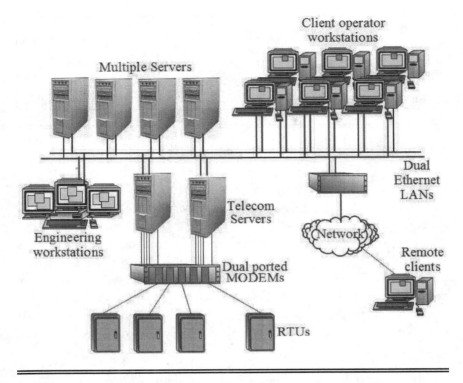

FIG. 1–7. *Client/server SCADA system architecture*

Technological Convergence

Because SCADA systems are based on computer technology, their designs have evolved in step with advances in computer technology. This also means that as computer technology has been expanded—to include, for example, LANs and wide area networks (WANs), workstations, high-resolution video displays, standard operating systems, TCP/IP networking, Ethernet, and massive storage capacity—the designers of SCADA systems have incorporated these technological appurtenances into their system architectures. In comparison with the SCADA systems of the 1960s, those produced today have undergone a huge decrease in the percentage of proprietary hardware (excluding RTUs) and software (including operating systems, HMIs, and network software) used in creating these systems (see table 1–1).

	1960s	1970s	1980s	1990s	Today
Proprietary hardware	60%	50%	30%	10%	2%
Proprietary software	100%	90%	75%	50%	30%

TABLE 1–1. *Trends in the evolution of system architecture*

There have been significant commercial benefits to this trend: SCADA systems cost much less to construct today (regardless of how much a vendor may charge you to purchase one); they are interoperable across vendors and with other types of computer systems; it is easier to find technical personnel with relevant programming and operating system skills; and there are many more off-the-shelf applications available from third-party suppliers. That is the good news. The bad news is that all of this has made the SCADA systems of today far more susceptible to malware, hackers, and cyber attack.

Today most SCADA systems built use multiprocessor servers based on Intel or Intel-compatible microprocessors. (A few suppliers continued to use Digital Equipment Alpha computers until the late 1990s, but that ended in a series of acquisitions.) Modern SCADA systems use a distributed client/server design, with all computers connected via (redundant) high-speed Ethernet switches and TCP/IP networking and running either a Microsoft or a Unix/Linux operating system; use a standard, commercial relational database (e.g., Oracle, SyBase, or the OSI-PI) as data historian; provide the human-machine (operator) interface on standard PCs or workstations; create operator displays via X-windows, Web server, or Microsoft graphical presentation technologies; and may support the OPC standard and use it for interprogram data exchanges. The point is that this is the same technology taught in every college and university and used for office automation, on every desktop, and in most homes.

Moreover, this is the technology that is well known to the hackers of the world. A SCADA system from the 1960s and even the 1970s and 1980s would probably be safe from a cyber attack, because of the proprietary operating systems, communications protocols, and operator display technology. However, they would also be incapable of providing the interoperability, connectivity, and compatibility of current systems. We can't go back to obsolete technologies; thus, we have to make design changes to modern SCADA systems, so that they are secure from hackers and cyber terrorists.

Generalized Software Architecture

The technology underlying SCADA systems has evolved in lockstep with corresponding advances in digital electronics, communications, and computing. The architectural designs of SCADA systems have been changed to take advantage of these new technologies. Regardless of the hardware architecture and technology employed, SCADA systems still perform a basic set of functions:

- They communicate with field-based outstations for retrieval of up-to-date process information.

- They maintain a constantly updated set of this information in a database.

- They provide an interface that enables human operators to examine and display this information.

- They provide some mechanism for a human operator to effect a process change by sending a control command back to the outstations.

It would be a pretty poor SCADA system, however, that didn't provide at least a few additional functions, such as

- Automatic comparison of field measurements against user-defined alarm limits and against their prior values.

- Automatic annunciation and logging on detection of alarms and events.

- Long-term recording of the value/status history of selected field inputs.

- The generation of user-defined reports and logs that incorporate available measurements, calculations, and historical/recorded data.

- The calculation of new values based on user-defined equations that incorporate available historical and real-time measurements.

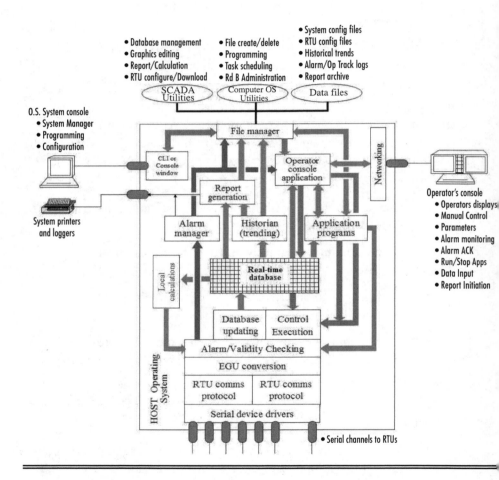

FIG. 1–8. *Generalized information flow within a generic SCADA system*

All modern SCADA systems support the features and functions listed previously, and most support a whole lot more, including industry-specific applications that customize the SCADA system for the unique requirements of individual market segments. Figure 1–8 provides a simplified information flow diagram for the basic functions and features of a generic SCADA system. The actual implementations will depend on the specific architectural and technology choices made by the individual SCADA system vendors.

Remote Terminal Units

Basic Features and Functions

As previously mentioned, the purpose of a SCADA system is the remote sensing and control of geographically dispersed processes. To achieve this aim, a SCADA system incorporates multiple RTUs, physically placed in the field at key measurement and control locations. The RTU began as a hardwired, fixed-function electronic device that could respond to simple commands received as serially transmitted numeric codes. Early RTUs were used for remote telemetry purposes, even before SCADA systems were created, through the integration of a central computer.

RTUs were connected, through serial communication channels, to *master terminal units* (MTUs), electronic devices that provided an interface for a human being, so that data from the RTUs could be displayed and control outputs of the RTUs could be manipulated. An MTU generally consisted of an alphanumeric readout or display and a keypad for entering parameters and commands (fig. 2–1). An operator could enter an RTU ID and an input number and press a poll key. The MTU would send a serial numeric code (message) to the RTU(s), receive the response from the RTU (in the form of a coded numeric message), and display the value of the requested input point on its readout. RTU control outputs could be manipulated in a similar fashion. More sophisticated MTUs supported multiple numeric readouts and continuous, automatic polling. Like their corresponding RTUs, the MTUs were electronic devices with hardwired functions and features, rather than programmable computer-based devices. When computers were introduced to replace the electronic-MTUs (and programmed to replicate the communication protocol messages) the term MTU was often thereafter applied to the computer. You will still hear SCADA central computers called the "host," the "central unit," or occasionally even the "MTU."

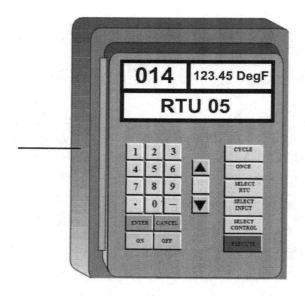

FIG. 2–1. *Typical MTU console*

When the first SCADA systems were developed, the obvious strategy was to replace the MTU with a computer, programming that computer to send and receive the same simple numeric messages that had previously been generated and processed by the MTU. The set of messages to and responses from the RTUs constitute a communications protocol. Because the early RTUs and MTUs were electronic, but not based on any form of programmable computer technology, they had to be designed with electronic circuits that could generate and interpret these simple numeric message codes. As might be expected, this kept the number and complexity of such messages to a minimum. The only functions supported by early RTUs were reading and transmitting the current value of analog and status inputs and generating analog and contact outputs in response to a properly formatted control message. Somewhat surprisingly, given the pace at which other technologies have changed since the 1960s, the types of input and output signals supported by RTUs, until very recently, were limited to the same type of analog, status, and pulse signals as would have been found in pre-SCADA MTU-based systems.

Analog inputs

An analog input signal is generally a voltage or current that varies, over a defined value range, in direct proportion to a physical process measurement. It is very common in most industrial processes to use a 4–20-milliamp signal to represent physical measurements such as pressure, flow, and temperature. Other industries, such as the electric utilities, use signal ranges like −1 to +1 milliamp or 0 to 1 volts or −10 to +10 volts. In addition, there are special sensory devices, like thermocouples and Resistive Temperature Device or Detector (RTDs), that work in nonlinear, millivolt (1/1000th of a volt)–level signals, that vary with the temperature of the device, and require special handling and processing.

Inside an RTU, a special circuit called an analog-to-digital (A2D) converter produces a binary number that corresponds to the voltage level read. Early RTUs generally had 8-bit A2D circuits, which means that they could represent an input voltage range as a binary value from 000 to 127. In current RTU technology, 16-bit A2D circuits have become common. The number of bits defines the resolution accuracy available for the reading of inputs. More bits means more resolution—although in some cases that resolution is wasted because the field device producing the measured signal is not very precise.

Because A2D circuits are expensive, the tendency among RTU manufacturers was to build RTUs with only one; this circuit was then shared by *multiplexing* analog inputs, one at a time, with additional circuitry. Multiplexing took time to operate (because early on it was done using electromechanical *reed relays*); thus, if there were a large number of analog inputs, the scan time for reading all of them for their latest value could extend to several seconds or even tens of seconds. If the process was highly dynamic, this might not be acceptable; therefore, some RTU manufacturers designed RTUs that could be expanded with multiple A2D circuits. With the advent of microprocessor-based (smart) RTUs, it became possible to configure the RTU to scan selected analog inputs more frequently (possibly eliminating the need for additional A2D circuits) and to expand protocols to provide means for fetching critical analog inputs more frequently than noncritical ones.

The successful reading of analog inputs requires that the input be free from noise or electrical distortions. Current-loop (4–20 milliamp) signals are generally immune to typical electrical noise sources, which is one reason for the popularity of this signal standard. Voltage signals, especially very-low-level voltage signals such as generated by thermocouples, are far more susceptible to noise and distortion (in particular, the ubiquitous 60- or 50-Hertz alternating current [AC] electrical noise); thus, the analog input circuitry design of an RTU had to deal with this noise. Many RTU manufacturers elected not to support RTDs and thermocouples as inputs, instead requiring that the user convert these into a conventional milliamp signal external to the RTU. Other vendors implemented hardware filtering (or with smart RTUs, software filtering), to reduce or eliminate signal distortion. A software scheme commonly used to this date is to sample an analog input value twice and average the two samples. These two samples had to be taken exactly 8.333 milliseconds apart (or 10 milliseconds for 50 Hz noise), thus placing the two samples 180° apart on the AC sine wave (i.e., so that the AC noise cancelled itself out). RTUs today still use this scheme for noise reduction.

Analog outputs

An analog output signal is generally used to manipulate and adjust the operating point of such process equipment as modulated valves and variable-speed motors and drives. The process and pipeline industries make extensive use of this type of output, whereas the electric utility industry almost never uses them.

Status inputs

A status or contact input is a two-state input generally received as either an actual contact/switch closure or a voltage/no-voltage signal. These inputs provide a simple means for indicating the present status of a two-state system: open/closed, on/off, running/stopped. All industrial segments make extensive use of status inputs. In many RTUs (and in all of the dumb ones), status inputs are scanned whenever their current values are requested by the host computer.

In some instances, status inputs are used to *time-stamp* critical events or to differentiate the timing between events. In those cases, it may be necessary for the RTU to continuously scan all of the status inputs, looking for changes. This capability was not possible before the development of microprocessor-based RTUs. In the electric utility market, it is now commonly required that an RTU scan all status inputs every millisecond and that the RTU keep a record of all changes (time-stamped to a one-millisecond accuracy) between polls by the host computer. This means that the RTU must have an accurate time source and memory in which to record input change events. This capability is generally called *sequence of events* (SOE) recording.

Another issue with status inputs is that the process equipment that produce these contact inputs can be mechanically bulky and subject to vibration and sensor-alignment problems. All of this can mean that a contact signal might not be as clean as the flip of a switch. Often, an RTU actually records that a status input flip-flopped a few times when transitioning from one state to the other. This is called *contact bounce* and has to be handled by the RTU. In dumb RTUs, a simple resistor-capacitor (RC) filter circuit was placed across the input, to filter out the bounce. (An RC filter circuit smooths out impulse noise and causes voltage jumps to turn into exponential rises/decays. Only a persistent jump will make it through the filter—and only after it persists for a given amount of time [the time constant of the RC circuit].) In modern RTUs, which might be performing one-millisecond SOE monitoring on such inputs, *debouncing* is done with software logic, since the use of an RC filter would actually cause a time delay before sensing the input change and thus would result in inaccurate time tagging for SOE purposes. In such logic, the first transition time is recorded, even if it is a momentary transition, and is then assigned as the input's SOE time tag if it turns out to be an actual transition and not just noise.

Contact outputs

Contact outputs, or controls, are switch closures generated by the RTU, usually in the form of an electromechanical relay driven on and off by RTU circuitry and logic. Every industrial segment makes use of these types of output. Contact outputs can be broken into two subcategories: latched outputs and momentary outputs. A latched output is one that is turned on or off by the RTU and stays in that state (possibly even if power is removed) until a specific command is given to place it into the opposite state. Momentary outputs are outputs that will be turned on and then back off by the RTU as a single-command operation. The duration of the "on" state may be fixed or variable, depending on the capabilities of the RTU. Dumb RTUs normally had a hardware-set "on" duration that could not be adjusted. Modern RTUs often make the "on" time a user-definable parameter per contact output. The process industries make extensive use of latched outputs (and some momentary ones), whereas the electric utility industry uses momentary outputs almost exclusively.

Since contact outputs are often used to operate equipment that also has a local manual control panel, it is not uncommon (particularly in the electric utility market) to see pairs of outputs assigned to control a given device. For local manual control, many types of industrial and electrical equipment have one button for "on" (or "start") and a separate button for "off" (or "stop"). With some RTUs, momentary contact outputs are grouped into control pairs such that one would be wired to the "on" and the other to the "off" circuitry. The electric utility industry generally utilizes momentary contact outputs in this control-pair manner; in fact, RTUs for that market sometimes include hardware or logic that prevents concurrent control of both outputs in a pair. (You would never press the "on" and "off" buttons at the same time, would you?) When dealing with electric utility SCADA personnel, you will often hear this configuration referred to as *trip-close pairs,* because a very common use of RTUs is the remote control of circuit breakers (which you can either "trip" [open] or "close").

In the process industries, a variable-duration momentary contact output pair may be used to control large motor-operated valves (e.g., in a water transmission system or a pipeline). With such valves, there is typically one contact that will drive the valve in the open direction and a second contact that will drive the valve in the closed direction. If such a valve is to be operated in an adjustable mode, the RTU controlling it will need to generate open/close contact outputs of a duration based on the travel rate of the valve (% per second) and the amount of change in position needed. In these cases, there is control logic in the RTU to compute the necessary contact duration and pass it to the control output software.

Pulse inputs

Pulse inputs are a special class of contact input (although they yield a numeric value like analog inputs) and may be handled by the contact input hardware by use of special software. There are two broad categories of pulse inputs: pulses that are continuously counted (called *accumulators* or *totalizers*) and pulses that are counted over a precise time interval. In both cases, the individual pulses generally represent a specific quantity of something: a barrel of oil, a cubic foot of gas, a kilowatt of power. If we want to totalize these quantities, then we just keep counting pulses and multiply by a scalar that converts pulse count to material quantity; by contrast, if we want to know delivery rates, then we count pulses over a fixed time interval to come up with gallons per minute, cubic feet per hour, and so forth.

In the process industries, pulse signals are often used for both purposes, and pulse rates may be as fast as 1.5 kilohertz (1,500 pulses per second) or even faster with measurement devices like turbine meters. RTUs normally require special pulse-counting hardware for these types of signals. In the electric utility industry, pulses are often used to totalize power delivery, and pulses are generated by electromechanical power meters at a very slow rate (slower than one pulse per second). With dumb RTUs, this still required special hardware; however, with smart RTUs, no special hardware is required, since the pulsing is slow enough to be sensed by the status input hardware. Many smart RTUs allow individual contact inputs to be designated as status inputs or accumulator inputs under software control.

Pulse outputs

Pulse outputs are a special class of momentary contact output and are typically handled by the contact output hardware and special software. Pulse outputs are a modification of the variable-duration momentary contact output; in place of a contact that is held in the "on" position for a specified amount of time, the output is toggled between "on" and "off" a specified number of times (fig. 2–2). As with variable-duration contact outputs, this is usually implemented in smart RTUs as a software function and doesn't require any special contact output hardware. Pulse outputs were mainly used in the process industries, and are rarely used anymore.

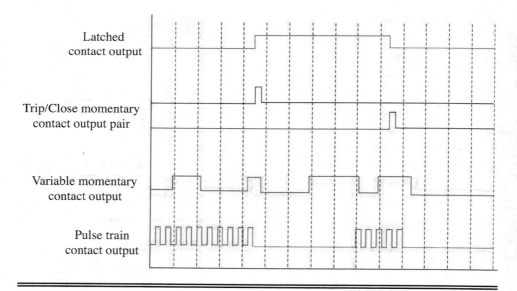

Fig. 2–2. *RTU contact output (control) types*

Smart RTU Technology

RTUs underwent a fundamental change with the introduction of microprocessor-based units. Prior to that evolutionary step, adding any features and functions to an RTU involved a massive hardware redesign and changes to the protocol messages. No real effort was ever made to do much more with dumb RTUs than just expand the maximum quantity of input/output (I/O) and the types of I/O supported by those RTUs. However, with a microprocessor running the RTU, changes were mainly a function of software modifications, including protocol enhancements. The early smart RTUs used eight-bit microprocessors like the Intel 8080 and 8085. These RTUs were limited in memory capacity (4–16 kilobytes was typical) and processing power; still, they were capable of supporting functions that were not possible with dumb RTU technology, such as simple calculations (fig. 2–3). As microprocessor technology advanced and CPUs became faster and were expanded to include math coprocessors and more memory, it became possible to add more features and functions to the RTUs.

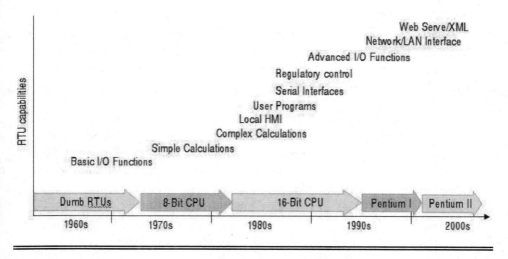

FIG. 2–3. *Evolution of smart RTU technology and capabilities*

RTU feature evolution was not the same across all industry sectors using SCADA technology. SCADA system vendors tended to maintain a primary presence in one key segment (pipelines, electric power, transportation, etc.) and focused product developments, including RTU developments, on the needs of that market segment. Many SCADA system vendors that attempted to cross over into other market segments to expand their business base discovered that their systems and RTUs lacked features and capabilities that had become standard in these other market segments.

Probably the most advanced RTUs, from a feature and function perspective, are those used in the oil and gas pipeline market. RTUs in the pipeline industry were used to perform local regulatory and sequential control functions as early as the mid-1980s. These RTUs could download user-defined control schemes and logic over the polling communication channel and could perform advanced calculations, such as the American Gas Association (AGA) volumetric computations (AGA-3, -5, and -7 and NX-19). They also had to support serial communications with other smart instrumentation to get the data to perform some of those calculations. These RTUs, once downloaded with the appropriate logic, would function as independent, autonomous local controllers, able to perform their assigned functions without any operator intervention, even if communications to the host were lost. As memory capacity expanded, some of these RTUs incorporated the ability to buffer data in the event of extended communication outages and then to upload this information to the host when communications were restored.

All of these capabilities required extensive modifications to the RTU communications protocols. Even as vendors moved rapidly to match the capabilities of their competitors, protocol versions were released at an even faster rate—sometimes every few months. If the revisions merely added functions, without changing any preexisting functions, then it was generally possible to mix RTUs with different protocol versions on the same communication channel. However, occasionally a protocol enhancement would modify the protocol sufficiently that such mixing was not viable, and SCADA system owners would have to send technicians to the field, to make *firmware* changes to all of the existing RTUs or at least to those on a shared communication circuit. Keeping track of protocol versions and compatibilities was a major headache for SCADA system owners and vendors.

Over time it became typical for SCADA vendors to have a wide range of RTUs with differing features and functions (and prices), and a set of different protocols that would be used, based on the particular RTU being supplied. Although there have been successful cases of multiple RTU serial protocols coexisting on the same communication channel, this is not recommended. It is all too possible for messages and data sent using one protocol to be accidentally interpreted as a valid message by the other protocol.

Serial ports

RTUs normally come with at least one serial port, through which the SCADA host communicates with the RTU. This serial port is typically dedicated to supporting the protocol messages, either by hardwired logic or program logic. With the introduction of microprocessor-based RTUs, it also became typical to have a second serial port, dedicated to local interrogation of the RTU for diagnostic and configuration purposes (often referred to as the *console port*). The second serial port was usually managed by a special program in the RTU called a *command line interpreter* (CLI), as in Microsoft DOS. The CLI understood simple text commands and provided a service technician with a way to examine and modify internal settings and parameters and to run whatever diagnostic routines were available. A typical use of this console port would be to tell the RTU how to configure the host polling port (in terms of baud rate and number of stop bits, etc.) and what its ID was; the console port also allowed for manual reading and controlling of the RTU's I/O.

In some industrial applications, it was occasionally necessary for two separate organizations, with their own SCADA systems, to use the same field measurements. Initially, this meant placing two separate RTUs at the same location and wiring the same inputs to both units. This worked well enough for inputs, but if both organizations needed to control the same field equipment, double wiring presented a problem. The solution eventually developed was to use multi-ported RTUs.

Additional serial ports were added to RTUs, and separate protocol drivers were assigned to each port. Each SCADA system could interrogate the RTU (possibly using different protocols) on their port, and either could issue control commands to the RTU. A mechanism for coordination of who was or was not to issue controls was needed, and most systems with multiple ports had a scheme in which a parameter or flag in the RTU was used to identify the SCADA system that currently had control rights. The protocol software in the RTU had to be modified to examine these flags when receiving a control command message, to determine whether to accept and execute the command. RTUs with multiple host connections are most common in the electric utility market. Dual (two) connections are the most common, but there have been situations with as many as five separate hosts connected to a single, shared RTU.

In the common vernacular of SCADA systems, the RTU and host computer are said to be in a *master and slave* protocol arrangement. The master in this style of protocol is the computer that initiates all communications, and the slave responds to messages from the master. These two terms have decreased in popularity owing to their historical connotations, but it is still important to understand the concept. Today we might refer to this type of communication scheme as a poll-response architecture.

For polling and communications to work, one device must follow the master sequence of the protocol definition, and the other must follow the slave sequence. Normally, the polling ports on the RTU will be configured to support the slave portion of the specific protocol. However, in many applications it has been impractical to provide direct communication channels to every RTU, and in those cases, selected RTUs have been used as a submaster or *concentrator*.

It is not unusual to have a large, higher-capacity RTU act as both slave and master, on separate communication ports. This concentrator RTU might have one port connected to a radio transceiver and be running a master protocol on that port, in order to poll several smaller RTUs in the general vicinity (fig. 2–4); its other port would run the slave protocol, to respond to host polling. In this sort of architecture, the concentrator RTU typically combines all of the inputs received from its slave RTUs into its own input table and presents all of this aggregated information to the host as a single, *virtual RTU*. For control outputs, the concentrator RTU identifies commands that are actually intended for control points in its slave RTUs and initiates the equivalent output control message sequence to the respective slave RTU. With a concentrator RTU arrangement you also have the option of using different protocols on each of the ports, so that the concentrator is also acting as a protocol translator or converter. In truth, it is really functioning like a small SCADA master because polling of its own slave RTUs is normally done asynchronously to the polling for the data from those other RTUs by the central SCADA system. (The concentrator RTU polls its slaves and retains a local copy of their most recent data, which is what it uses to answer the central SCADA system's requests for such data.) Only with out-going control commands, that must pass through the concentrator RTU, is there usually some form of coordination.

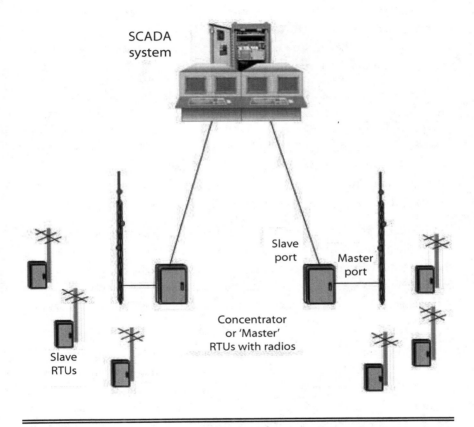

Fig. 2–4. *RTU hierarchy using master and slave protocol combination*

In recent years, especially in the electric utility market, it has become commonplace for RTUs to support a large number (16–32) of serial ports (while the amount of physical I/O has decreased). Many of the measurements and status points that would normally be wired to RTU analog and status inputs are being wired into other microprocessor-based devices, and the value of these inputs can be obtained by serial communications with those other devices. The electric utility industry has coined the term *intelligent electronic device* (IED) for such microprocessor-based equipment. *Substation automation,* or *substation data concentration,* is the process of using an RTU with a large number of serial ports (and possibly no physical I/O at all) to collect all of the data from the IEDs in a substation, so that it can be sent to a SCADA system over a single communication circuit. Most RTUs manufactured today support multiple serial ports, and they can be configured as either a master or a slave port, using any number of available serial protocols.

Intercommunication is a problem in some cases, because of the complex types of data in the IEDs. RTUs were initially designed to support two basic data types: numeric values and binary values. Initially, the numeric values were integer only, although today many RTUs can support floating-point or long integer values. Similarly, binary values were originally single-bit only; today multi-bit versions are supported (to represent devices with multiple states: e.g., a valve could be open, closed, or traveling).

Modern RTUs also support date/time information and quality tags that indicate the validity of the data to which they are attached. However, there are many other types of data, as well as data structures that combine multiple values and different data types. Most RTU protocols do not support advanced or sophisticated data types and therefore are useless for extracting all but simple data from IEDs.

A common IED in the electric utility industry is a protective digital relay, the device that tells circuit breakers to open when bad things are happening to the power line. Inside a digital relay, there can be dozens of measured and calculated numeric values and status bits. These relays also do SOE recording, power totalization over time intervals, and high-speed recording and capture of the AC voltage and current waveforms on all three phases. Getting this complex data by use of a conventional serial RTU protocol is at best very messy and is at worst impossible. Other types of protocols have been developed for this purpose (e.g., the utility communications architecture [UCA2.0]), and the newest RTUs support such protocols and complex data types.

Local display

Since RTUs contain a lot of real-time process information, it is occasionally useful for a service technician or process engineer in the field to have the RTU provide a display of its information. This might be so that instruments can be calibrated or because no other display is provided for the data in question. Once RTUs became smart, it was possible to provide a range of electronic displays that could be driven and updated under software control. Today an RTU might have an Ethernet port (or *Bluetooth* wireless capability) and could offer up dynamic Web pages on your laptop PC. However, in the early days of smart RTUs, such technology did not exist, so any display capability had to be built into the RTU hardware itself. An RTU might have a simple number/function keypad on its front panel and a multiline liquid crystal display (LCD) screen (fig. 2–5). The user could punch in an input number and see it displayed on the panel, or if no keypad was provided, the LCD might be set to cycle through all inputs on a continuous basis. If output control was needed, then a keypad of some sort would be necessary. Importantly, the analog inputs and status inputs could be displayed only in an unconverted form (e.g., as *raw counts* or percentage of range), unless there was sufficient configuration data to allow a conversion calculation.

When an RTU reads an analog input, the A2D converter generates a binary number proportional to the range of the input value. Thus, if the input signal is 4–20 milliamps and the A2D converter is an eight-bit version, then at 12 milliamps (50% of the input range), the binary number from the converter should read "064" (i.e., half of the 000 to 127 conversion range). In this case, the RTU could present either the raw counts of "064" or the percentage of range this represents: namely, 50%. No additional data are needed in order to provide/compute these two display values. However, the input in question is actually a temperature, and the 4–20 milliamp signal range has been set for 150–350°F. What will be displayed for this input reading, at the host computer, will be a value of 250°F, which is the *engineering unit* value for the input. To compute this from the raw counts, the host has additional information about the engineering unit range; to supply engineering unit displays at the RTU, the RTU also needs a copy of that additional information. A similar situation occurs for status inputs. In the RTU, these will be seen as a 0 or 1 raw value, but in the host

FIG. 2–5. *Typical RTU multiline LCD and keypad*

computer, we know (because of additional data) that a 0 means the pump is stopped and that a 1 means that the pump is running (and that is how the input would be displayed to the operator at the host computer).

With early smart RTUs, there was insufficient memory to hold tables of engineering unit conversion factors, and the protocols were inherited from dumb RTUs, which sent only raw counts and binary values. In the electric utility market, it remains common for RTUs to send all of their analog and status inputs as raw counts and for all engineering unit conversions to be done at the host level. Many of the protocols still in use in that segment support only raw counts.

In the pipeline and water/wastewater industries, performance of calculations—and even sequential and regulatory control—is more common at the RTU level. Many of the calculations used are based on thermodynamics or physics and require that the equation elements be in defined engineering units: pounds per square inch, degrees Fahrenheit, cubic feet per minute, and so forth. Thus, it may be necessary to perform at least some engineering unit conversions within the RTU itself. In some RTUs, this is accomplished by user-written calculations or program logic in which the conversion factors were built into the logic or calculations. In other RTUs, the vendors have allowed the engineering unit conversion tables to be downloaded into the RTUs and have modified their communications protocols to support floating-point numbers.

An additional extension was the downloading of the alarm limit value tables, so that the engineering unit values could be checked against these limits. This required even more memory in the RTU and appropriate protocol extensions. RTUs that supported this full range of input processing were capable of providing local information displays that were much like those provided at the host (if equipped with the necessary display hardware). There were some instances of such RTUs having printers attached to them, so that they could print out alarm logs and reports.

Downloaded logic and parameters

The first smart RTUs were preprogrammed at the factory, and all of their functions were set into the firmware forever (to emulate the dumb RTUs they were replacing). But why have a computer and not make use of the added capabilities it offers? In the evolution of smart RTUs, there have been three levels of remote configuration, each being successively more complex to implement but more flexible in application:

1. Preprogrammed functions with remotely adjustable parameters and flags

2. Downloadable library of user-selected and connected function blocks

3. User-written program download and execution

Most vendors provided one or more of these capabilities. The more advanced capabilities often incorporated the lesser functions.

It didn't take long for SCADA vendors to start adding simple function blocks and calculations that could be enabled and (re)parameterized via the communications port. The logic and programming to perform the functions was still factory installed, but the user could adjust *supervisory points* (binary and analog values stored in the software of the RTU) via the RTU protocol (fig. 2–6). Just as the RTUs supported real analog and binary I/O points, the smart RTUs added this new type of point, whose only purpose was to allow the host/operator to manipulate RTU functions by sending down supervisory point control commands. The idea of supervisory (software) points was eventually expanded to include both incoming points (to receive data and parameters from the host) and outgoing points (so that RTU logic could send values to the host computer). Some obvious uses for supervisory points include parameter setting in simple logic and equations and changing details like meter factors in simple totalization calculations, the timing or duration of momentary contact outputs, and calibration

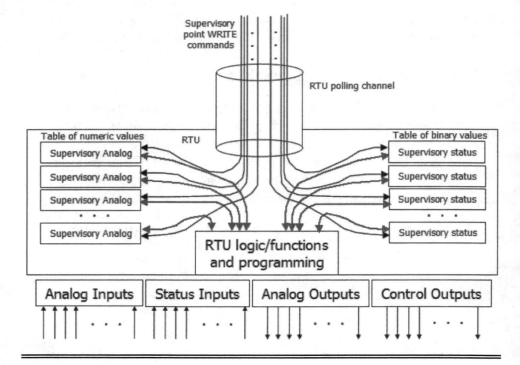

FIG. 2–6. *RTU protocol with adjustable supervisory points*

scaling values. Using supervisory points eliminated the need to go to the field and change RTU firmware in order to make simple adjustments. Support for supervisory points required very minor enhancements to an RTU protocol. These points looked very much like conventional I/O except that they had no physical hardware associations.

In addition to supervisory points, many SCADA vendors provided simple mechanisms, in the form of host-level configuration tools, for defining simple calculations and logic that could then be downloaded to the RTU for execution. Figure 2–7 shows two examples of simple calculations defined via a host utility. The text shown could be entered into a file via a text editor and then compiled (by another vendor-supplied application) into a data block that would subsequently be downloaded to the RTU, where a prewritten program would know how to interpret the data block and perform the defined calculations.

```
:& Calculation temperature correction
: $1 = I001 * I002
: $2 = 3.1415 * I005
: $3 = $1 * $2
: $4 = $3 / I004
: $5 = SQRT[$4]
: SI001 = $5 * 0.473


:& Interlock Boolean logic
: #1 = S001 AND S002
: #2 = S003 AND S004
: #3 = S005 NOT S006
: #4 = #1 OR #2
: #5 = #3 OR #4
: SS001 = NOT #5
```

FIG. 2–7. *Example host definition of downloaded calculation functions*

In the examples shown in figure 2–7, the "$*number*" and "#*number*" designations respectively are for numeric and binary temporary storage registers (in the RTU software) where intermediate values can be stored; the "I*number*" and "S*number*" designations respectively indicate physical analog and status input values are to be used in the calculation; and "SS*number*" and "SI*number*" designations respectively indicate that results are to be placed into supervisory status and analog points (where they can be fetched via RTU polling, just like real inputs). SCADA systems generally have a utility that permits the user to define any number of computations (using real inputs and the results of other calculations) at the host level. However, in the pipeline and water/wastewater industries, there are many instances where some level of calculation capability is needed at the RTU level.

The addition of downloaded calculations and logic required further enhancements to protocols, so that there were message types for sending (and receiving) these data blocks and confirming successful delivery. If the calculations or logic incorporated supervisory points, this permitted additional flexibility, as such points could have their values manipulated through other RTU message types, as discussed previously in this section. Until very recently these sorts of capabilities involved vendor-developed proprietary host-based utility programs that would input and process such logic and mathematical calculations, and convert them into data (or actual program code) that could then be downloaded to the specified RTU, either locally or over the polling circuit using protocol extensions devised for such purposes. Within the RTUs would be software to deal with the data or install and execute the programming. Today there are some widely adopted standards that have evolved for accomplishing the same results.

Regulatory and sequence control

In the pipeline and water/wastewater industries, the RTUs installed in the field were often located at physical locations around the process where there was a need for some level of local regulatory control and sequence logic. Basic SCADA systems are *supervisory* control systems, meaning that the decisions to take a control action are made at the host level and then dispatched to the RTU to execute. This is fine as long as the communications bandwidth is sufficient and reliable. If gas pressure needs to be controlled at a delivery point and the target pressure needs to be adjustable based on conditions, then control adjustments to the pressure-regulating valve may need to be made every second or faster. With the low-baud-rate serial communication schemes used by most SCADA systems (not to mention channel sharing across multiple RTUs), it is typically not possible to read the gas pressure, send it to the host, make a control adjustment calculation in the host, and send a control output command to the RTU all within a second. In the past, in order to provide local regulation for such applications it was typical to have some form of instrumentation and control panel at the site, to perform the regulatory control, and the RTU would merely interface this panel via analog, pulse, and contact I/O points (fig. 2–8).

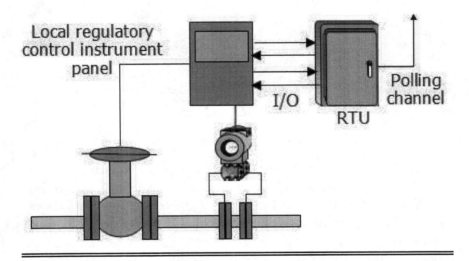

FIG. 2–8. *Supervisory control of local regulatory control panels*

In the 1980s, microprocessor-based RTUs had become reasonably powerful, and at the same time, a revolution was taking place in the process control industry. Traditional analog instrumentation and control panels were being replaced with computer-based technology. Specifically, the *distributed control system* (DCS) had been introduced and, for reasons both financial and technical, was attaining wide acceptance as a replacement for conventional instruments and controls. DCS consists of distributed process controllers, all tied to a high-speed (for the 1980s) LAN, or data highway, and operator consoles. The distributed process controllers were microprocessor based and had a full complement of I/O. Architecturally, a DCS very much resembles a SCADA system, aside from the use of LAN communications instead of WAN communications (fig. 2–9).

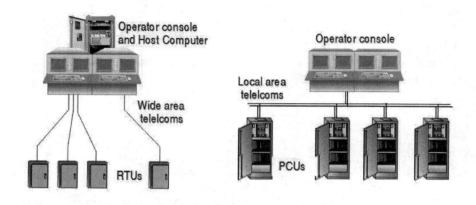

FIG. 2–9. *Basic SCADA system and DCS architectures*

There are many fundamental differences between these two types of systems, an important one being that distributed process controllers were intended to perform local regulatory and sequential control from the outset. The microprocessor technology and I/O technology of a process controller is not incredibly different from that of an RTU, although process controllers usually came in fully redundant or one-for-N fault-tolerant designs.

It didn't take SCADA vendors long to realize that they could add value to their RTUs by incorporating some of the control functions used in the process control industry. Computer-based process control systems had been around since the 1970s, although they were in centralized architectures. A set of algorithms had been developed by control system vendors to mimic the actions of the analog controllers replaced by computer technology. The basis for most regulatory control functions was provided by algorithms such as the proportional-integral-derivative (PID) controller, the lead-lag algorithm, the ratio-bias controller, and the on-off ("bang-bang") controller. These were all numerical algorithms that could be either used individually or combined mathematically to process analog inputs and generate analog outputs, performing the analogous functions of the older analog panel instruments. SCADA system vendors, at least those serving the pipeline and water/wastewater industries, started offering these algorithms in their RTUs. That eliminated the need for the local panel instruments, where customers were willing to accept an RTU as a process controller.

RTUs have enjoyed a reputation for reliability. They are expected, after installation, to operate flawlessly 24/7 over the next 10 years. The fact of the matter is that most RTUs have done just that, or even more. (There are electric utilities still using RTUs manufactured in the 1980s.)

By contrast, many DCS vendors found that making a process controller fully redundant was just as difficult as the SCADA system vendors had found making their host computers redundant. Many DCS redundancy schemes failed to live up to their promise (just like the SCADA systems), and there were examples of process controller redundancy being disabled or removed by customers, to improve process controller reliability. At that point, a process controller and an RTU are very nearly the same device. Today many pipeline and water/wastewater SCADA systems still rely on the local regulatory control capabilities of their RTUs.

In addition to regulatory control (which generally involves analog inputs and outputs), many local control problems needed the capability of sequence and state-driven control, which is based on Boolean logic. Actually, a hybrid of regulatory control, altered and manipulated by Boolean logic, tends to serve best for sophisticated control. Many SCADA system vendors expanded their RTU features and functions to support both capabilities. The mechanisms used for this differed by vendor. Not all vendors could support top-down configuration (developed in the host and downloaded to the RTU), and not all vendors took a block approach. Several vendors developed their own special process control programming language (often a BASIC-like language), which included PID as a library function. Users developed sophisticated controls by writing programs in these languages and then loading these programs into the RTUs, possibly through the console port, prior to field installation.

Low-power operation

Another major difference between RTUs and process controllers is that process controllers are installed in plant and manufacturing facilities where power is generally available. In many instances, RTUs have to be remotely located at field sites that have no electrical power or telecommunications infrastructure. In those cases, the RTUs have to be capable of running off *solar power* (or other low-power sources, e.g., *thermoelectric generators*). An entire class of RTUs has been developed through the years to operate at very low power levels, using schemes like powering off nearly everything until a polling message is received or powering up only for short time intervals on a scheduled, periodic basis. Many of the power-saving schemes employed in laptop PCs today were pioneered by low-power RTU designs in the 1980s and 1990s.

Low-powered RTU technology developments are primarily focused on the pipeline, transportation, and water industry segments. This is generally because most electric utility industry RTUs are near a source of electric power; don't forget, however, that when power goes out, that may be when an RTU is critical, and it will need to operate without the electric power that it was monitoring. There is a difference between very-low-power RTUs, which are capable of continuous operation from low-power sources, and conventional RTUs equipped with a *battery backup* facility. A battery-backed conventional RTU is expected to run off a normal electric power source (the primary source), but it also incorporates a battery-based power supply that is maintained in a fully charged condition by the primary power source. A conventional RTU may require many watts of electrical power in order to function. On power loss, the RTU reverts to the battery-based power supply, either to ride through a short-duration outage in the primary power source or to take actions to shut down or bring the process to a safe/stable state. Battery-based power supplies support only a limited amount of operational time before the batteries are drained. With low-power RTUs, the power requirement of the device is generally reduced, through various means, to a sub-watt level.

Solar panels (which generate low-power direct current [DC] from sunlight) are a commonly used low-power source for low-powered RTUs because of the general availability of sunshine, at least during part of each day, everywhere in the world. (Along a gas pipeline, thermoelectric generators can be used, owing to the availability of gas as a fuel source.) A solar-panel power supply *also* has a battery-based backup component, to supply power during periods of darkness. This battery is recharged every day, from the power produced by the solar panels (which must also power the RTU), to make up for the power used during the hours of darkness.

Accumulator freeze

As previously mentioned, a common use of pulse inputs is to count them over time to determine material or energy quantities that have flowed past a particular measuring point. In pipelines (and electric power applications), this is an important task, because what goes *in*, should come back *out* elsewhere (adjusted for parameters like pressure and temperature). Pipelines generally count pulses as material (gas or liquid) moves past a measurement point. All inflows and outflows are metered in this manner. Thus, if we can capture the information about what is currently passing in, out, and through the various measurement points in the pipeline, we can, at the same instance in time, figure out if there is a problem. If such measurements are not taken at the same time, then by the time that all accumulators have been collected, something more will have moved past the measurement point(s), and we won't be able to balance the inputs and the outputs. A big problem would be if we seemed to be losing or gaining material—indicating a leak and a miracle, respectively. Neither situation would be good.

The vast majority of RTU protocol messages are destined for a particular RTU, as designated by the RTU ID contained in the message. However, a few messages need to be directed to all RTUs simultaneously. Such messages are called *broadcast messages* in protocol terminology. One common function of RTUs and their protocols is the ability to send out an *accumulator freeze* broadcast message. The purpose of such a message is to get all RTUs to take snapshots of their accumulators, at the same instance in time, and hold them for collection by the host computer. This becomes more complicated when there are multiple polling channels, as a mechanism is needed to stop all polling and then, once all polling channels are idle, to send out this freeze message on all of them at the same time. This is how it was accomplished with dumb RTUs (as well as on the first smart RTUs).

With smart RTUs, there was no reason not to allow each RTU to have a local *clock*. A clock is just a counter that, if properly designed, counts at an exact rate, so that time changes can be related to the count change. Early clock circuits were balky and temperature sensitive and could drift off by a significant amount if not reset frequently. One broadcast message type supported by most RTUs was a time broadcast that could be used to (re)set the local clock of all of the RTUs. Most SCADA systems broadcast the time from the host on a periodic basis, to keep RTU clocks in reasonable synchronization with the host clock. This was an effective scheme when a time skew of many milliseconds was acceptable, either between the host and a given RTU or between numerous RTUs themselves.

Schemes that timed the message transit time from host to RTU were employed for improved accuracy. The *telephone company algorithm* ("At the tone the time will be XX:XX:XX exactly") was used by many vendors to make the broadcast as short and quick as possible. (Send this message first and then a very short message as the tone.) Time lags in communication circuits and in the message retransmission across all communication circuits introduced such skews. It was difficult, but possible, to obtain time synchronization, among all of the RTUs and the host computer, as accurate as ±10 milliseconds. For most applications, this was good enough. For the electric utility industry, though, it was insufficient. Electric utilities had achieved 1-millisecond SOE time-tagging accuracy *within* each substation, using the local RTU's clock. However, because of the problem with cross-RTU time synchronization, there was no way to correlate SOE data among substations, as the time tags couldn't be trusted to be on exactly the same time basis owing to time skew between the substation RTUs.

Global Positioning System time receivers

It has already been mentioned that in some instances, the status inputs of an RTU will be used to time events or to show the SOE. The local time tagging of a contact input state change merely means saving a record of what bits changed, to which state, at any given millisecond in time. To do this, an RTU must examine all of its status inputs every millisecond and determine whether any have changed from their value at the prior millisecond. When changes are found, a record is made, showing the time (to the millisecond) and the inputs that have changed.

Even though RTUs have for years had sufficient computing power to provide a one-milisecond time scan of all status inputs, a problem remained in that the local time of every RTU could not be easily synchronized to the exact same millisecond. The only solution was to use a highly accurate time source that could be made available to all RTUs. For many years, the U.S. government has operated a radio station called WWV, whose purpose is like that of the time service of the telephone company. WWV broadcasts the exact time on an ongoing basis. Special receivers were available to listen to the WWV transmission and produce a time signal that could be fed into an RTU. If all RTUs were so equipped, then they would all keep the same time, to a high level of precision. However, such receivers were expensive, and proper reception might entail erecting a tower and mounting a large antenna. Because of this, few utilities elected to avail themselves of this technology.

Then, in the mid-1990s, the U.S. government placed the Global Positioning System (GPS) satellite network into orbit, and suddenly we had a low-cost, high-precision time source, available as long as you could see the sky. GPS technology has made it possible to have RTUs anywhere in the world all be time synchronized to one-millisecond (or better) accuracy. Furthermore, the host can use this technology too, so that the clocks in a SCADA system keep the exact time.

This brings up another idiosyncrasy of SCADA systems. Because they cover large geographic areas (e.g., with a pipeline that spans a good portion of the United States), it is quite probable that the local time where one RTU is situated may be in a different time zone than another RTU and even the host. Rather than keeping local time, most SCADA systems elect either to keep time based on where the operators (and host) are located or to use Greenwich mean time (GMT) for the system time. This second choice may be taken to deal with another time-related problem: the daylight savings time adjustments made each autumn and spring.

Daylight savings time

Computer systems often store data chronologically (by date/time). The date/time information is stored in data tables. This causes a problem when, in the autumn and the spring, the time suddenly changes by an hour. This time-shift issue has plagued SCADA systems since they started collecting and archiving data. Imagine that you are recording a temperature and suddenly time jumps ahead one hour. It will appear that you had no data for an hour because the time stamp on the measurement recorded just prior to the change and the sample taken just after the time change will have time stamps an hour apart, even though they were taken within moments of each other. The opposite is even worse: if you have already stored an hour's worth of data time tagged as happening in hour X and suddenly it is hour X again, what do you do with the data you already recorded? To avoid such problems, many SCADA vendors use GMT in their systems (at least for time tagging of data) and never make those spring and autumn time adjustments.

Transducer-less AC inputs

The electric utility industry has a few RTU features and functions that are unique to that particular industry segment. High-resolution (one-millisecond) SOE recording has already been discussed. However, one of the other most important differences is that whereas to all other industries AC 50/60-Hertz electric power is a source of noise to be filtered out, to the electrical industry that is what they want to measure.

Until the mid-1990s, RTUs used in the electric utility industry had to employ external devices called *transducers* to convert AC voltage, current, power, and other attributes into a DC voltage or current value that could be read by a conventional A2D converter. In the 1990s, the digital signal processor (DSP) was invented, making it economically possible to take high-speed samples of the actual AC waveform and then apply calculations, like the fast Fourier transform (FFT) or the discrete Fourier transform (DFT), to extract frequency-domain information. This also provided a way to compute real and reactive values—and determine spectral component energy levels—for the electrical signals being measured.

Today transducer-less RTUs are common in the electric utility industry. For the most part, few electric utilities are interested in having RTUs perform calculations or local control. RTUs in that industry have had few feature or functional enhancements (other than being forced to upgrade to newer microprocessor technology when older parts became unavailable). Nevertheless, over the past few years, the electric utilities have suddenly been looking at multi–serial-port RTUs as data concentrators for collecting (simple) IED data in a single device. (This trend will be discussed in more detail in a later chapter.)

Top-Down and Bottom-Up Configuration

When SCADA systems were initially introduced, the companies offering them also designed and manufactured their own RTU equipment, including designing and implementing their own serial protocols. In some instances, these companies were previously manufacturers of the non–computer-based telemetry systems that predated SCADA. In other instances, new companies were formed as others were acquired.

In the first 10 to 20 years of SCADA systems, most RTUs were purchased from a SCADA vendor. There were advantages to this arrangement. The SCADA vendors generally provided reasonably good tools (utility programs) for configuring the system. With dumb RTUs, this amounted primarily to defining the number of RTUs on each polling channel and the I/O compliment of each. However, as smart RTUs replaced the dumb ones and as these RTUs were expanded with advanced capabilities, the configuration tools had to support these added functions. With RTUs that could execute user-defined calculations and logic, there had to be utility programs for defining these and for sending them down the communication link to the RTU.

Where RTUs were expanded to support user-written programs, the system had to support program development tools, as well as the utilities for sending new program logic to the RTU. Certainly, there were SCADA system vendors that did not support remote downloading, although they did offer these advanced functions in their RTUs. In those instances, the vendors generally provided software tools that could be used to load these calculations, logic, and programming into the RTU, prior to its being deployed and commissioned in the field, through a separate configuration port (possibly through the console port). Remember that portable and laptop PCs (and even desktop PCs) did not exist until the late 1980s. Thus, these software utilities were run on the SCADA system mainframe/minicomputer.

Although initially all RTUs were supplied by the respective SCADA vendors, as part of an overall system, SCADA vendors were not always able to maintain a successful and profitable business (many went out of business), and therefore in the 1980s several third-party companies entered the field as RTU suppliers. There is a long list of names of former SCADA vendors that no longer exist, and most left behind customers with running systems and an installed based of thereafter unsupported RTUs. The owners of these systems had spent a great deal of time and money getting them installed and operational and training personnel in the use and maintenance of the system, making them disinclined to just throw the system away and find another vendor (who could just as well go out of business in the future). This situation opened up a business opportunity for the manufacture of third-party replacement or expansion RTUs that could be sold to the owners of these orphaned SCADA systems.

By the late 1980s, there were several suppliers that had entered the market and manufactured such RTUs. One of the challenges with utilizing a third-party RTU was that, even though the basic RTU protocol functions (e.g., reading inputs and controlling outputs) used by a SCADA vendor could be emulated or reproduced easily enough, there were advanced functions (for accepting downloaded calculations, logic, and programming) that could not be replicated. If you tried to use the SCADA system's configuration tools to send configuration files to these third-party RTUs, those files would typically be rejected. One reason for this was that the data and instructions generated by the SCADA system's tools would have been specifically structured and formatted for the type of CPU and programming logic used in the SCADA system vendors' RTUs. Another was that even though the RTU vendors might have basic protocol specifications, they did not have the knowledge of the proprietary structure and content of the data files or program logic generated by the SCADA vendor's utility programs. They might be able to receive such a download (there were protocol messages for that) but they had no way to emulate the advanced functions programmed into the original SCADA vendor's RTUs.

Complexity and cost made creating a viable emulation of the advanced functions and utilizing the host-created configuration files both technically daunting and financially questionable. Third-party suppliers were generally able to offer only basic I/O polling and control functions. Since these RTU manufacturers could not or would not create the logic needed to deal with the advanced functions and those relevant protocol commands and data files, they had to provide some other way to configure their RTUs. Most used the RTUs' console ports and implemented command and configuration functions that could be used to set up the RTU by connecting a dumb terminal to that port.

Because of the inability to mimic the advanced functions supported by the downloadable RTUs from the original SCADA system vendors, the manufacturers of third-party RTUs had their greatest success in the electric utility market, where little or no use was made of such capabilities. Eventually (in the 1990s), RTUs became powerful enough to support *interpreted* languages (computer hardware independent) and standards, such as the IEC61131-3 control logic standard that had emerged and gained wide support. Those factors, together with the emergence of standard protocols and *application program interfaces* (APIs), have created the current environment in which it is possible to mix and match SCADA software, PLCs, RTUs, and commercial application software to create a customized SCADA system.

The Emergence of PLCs

The biggest problem for many owners of SCADA systems was that vendors tended to appear and disappear, leaving them with an orphaned system and no ready source for more RTUs, software enhancements, and support. This happened a lot in the water/wastewater industry because of its traditionally low bidder procurement practices—that is, selecting the lowest bidder and not the best-qualified supplier. (This has changed somewhat in recent years owing to the long list of never-completed or obsolete-when-delivered SCADA projects in that industry segment.)

At the same time that SCADA suppliers and third-party RTU manufacturers were disappearing from the scene, in the factory automation sector, manufacturers of PLCs were making considerable inroads by constantly enhancing the features of their products, improving the reliability of their products, and even reducing the cost of their products at the same time. PLCs had success in crossing over from the discrete manufacturing sector into the process control sector when they finally added analog I/O (initial PLC offerings had I/O suitable for machine control: discrete I/O, stepping motor controllers, etc.) and augmented their relay ladder-logic programming languages with function blocks that performed the regulatory control functions previously discussed in this chapter.

PLC manufacturers opened up their communication networks and invited third-party vendors to make complementary products. This attitude led to such developments as the Modbus protocol (introduced originally by AEG/Modicon) as a de facto serial protocol standard and numerous PC-based software products for interacting with and programming these PLCs. The water/wastewater industries have two sides: water and sewage *treatment plants,* which are geographically constrained to a given facility and prone to using DCS or PLC automation technology, and *distribution or collection systems,* which are geographically distributed and often employ SCADA automation technology. Because of highly competitive pricing and relative ease of use, PLC equipment suppliers had a lot of success in getting their technology incorporated into water/wastewater processing and treatment plants. This eventually let to its use as RTU equipment in SCADA systems for these industries.

Today just about every specification written and issued for the competitive public procurement of SCADA systems for that industry segment will specify PLCs, from one of the major manufacturers, for the RTU equipment to be included with the system. It is just as likely that they will require the Modbus protocol for the communications between the

SCADA system and these field-based PLCs. PLCs today have extensive capacity for sequential controls, interlock/safety logic, regulatory control, and general calculations. Most provide programming tools that allow both local reconfiguration and remote reconfiguration via the Modbus protocol.

Initially, PLC manufacturers developed their own tools and techniques for programming the logic to be performed by PLCs. Relay ladder logic (RLL) was popular because it mimicked the electrical wiring diagrams used by plant electricians for designing the hardwired relay logic that predated PLCs. In the 1990s, the IEC61131-3 standards were developed, and today just about every PLC vendor and third-party software vendor complies with this standard. The standard defines a set of configuration/programming schemes that can be used to define the logic in a PLC (and today, even a fair number of RTU products). It includes not only RLL but also *sequential-function charts* (SFCs), structured English, function block chains, and other control logic and computational definition tools. Many DCS vendors now also offer IEC61131-3–compliant programming tools for the configuration of process controllers. Many of the field sites where a water/wastewater RTU (now PLC) would be placed are locations where local regulatory control, interlock logic, and sequence logic were required. PLCs offer all of these capabilities. Most PLCs can also be easily equipped with a variety of off the shelf local operator panels if required because of the number of such devices that have Modbus protocol support.

Legacy Protocols

The SCADA industry has produced a huge number of serial protocols, both bit and character oriented, over the years. Their names or designations remind us of former SCADA system vendors: WESDAC, SGM, Tano-3, CDC Type- I, Tejas V, S3, L&G 8979, and Harris 5000, among numerous others. In effect, all such protocols do the same basic operations: send input values to a host computer and generate control outputs when commanded to do so by a host computer (fig. 2–10). Of course, beyond these basics, the different protocols tended to divide into classes or categories, based on the more advanced features and functions supported.

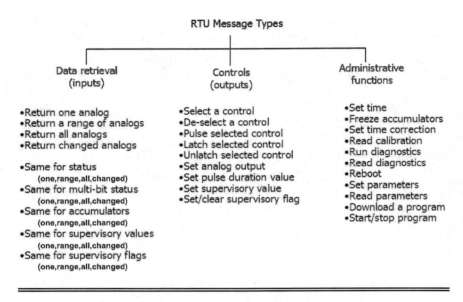

FIG. 2–10. *Categories of typical RTU protocol message types*

One very critical point about all such serial protocols (those intended to operate on slow speed serial channels with minimal overhead and limited, well-defined functionality) is that they were never conceived or designed with any of the sorts of protections (e.g., encryption and authentication) that we now use for networking protocols. This is due in part to the tremendous overhead imposed by such protective measures, the computing power required for such functions and the very low data rates generally used for RTU polling. But it is also true that no one ever thought that SCADA systems and RTU communications would need to be protected. We know better today.

Most RTU serial protocols were designed for efficient performance over slow-speed communication circuits. In the early days of RTUs (dumb ones), the modem technology available offered a mere 110- or 300-baud rate. Shortly thereafter, the rates went up to 1,200 baud. That is what a lot of SCADA systems still use today, even though modem technology has jumped well past those speeds. Many early RTUs had modem circuitry built into the RTU circuitry, so upgrading to a faster modem is not possible unless the RTU is replaced. If multiple such RTUs exist on a polling circuit, you must replace them all to upgrade the channel bit rate. (Although it has been tried, and there have been limited exceptions, normally you can't mix different protocols and/or data rates on the same communications channel.) Many of the older RTUs have very limited computing power and can't actually support high data rates, and some old SCADA systems have front-end processors that don't have the computing power or the serial port clock circuitry to handle higher data rates.

Many improvements have been implemented to make RTU protocols as efficient as possible, so as to reduce polling-response times or so that more RTUs can share a common channel without extending the overall polling time cycle. Early (dumb) RTUs generally did a full report of the current readings for all inputs (or possibly all analog or all status inputs) every time they were polled. In many cases, these inputs had not changed since the previous polling request (especially the status inputs). Taking time to send the same values again was wasteful. With smart RTUs, it was possible to use the logic in the RTU to keep track of prior and current values for all inputs and to identify those that had changed. More advanced protocols support *report-by-exception* polling, whereby the host doesn't ask for a report of values, but rather asks for a report of changed values since the prior poll request. A host could still ask for a full poll every so often (often called an integrity poll), to ensure that nothing has been missed.

The problem with polled exception reporting is that when all data aren't reported, additional information must be collected to identify which values are being reported as changed. There is a threshold above which this added information makes it better to do a full report rather an exception report. (E.g., if all but one point has changed, the added data to identify all of the other values would be more bytes of data than reporting the one value that didn't change.)

A more recent advance is the development of *unsolicited report by exception*. In this scheme, the host computer does no polling (except an occasional integrity poll) and leaves it to the RTUs to send messages when values change. This scheme is best for processes where values change slowly and where you never see a lot of the measured parameters changing in lots of places at once (in other words, in the water/wastewater industry).

One problem with unsolicited report by exception is that you can't tell the difference between an RTU that has nothing to report and an RTU that has failed. To differentiate between these possibilities, these schemes usually require either that the RTU send an occasional "I'm still alive" message or that the host still polls every RTU occasionally.

Another problem with unsolicited exception reporting is *collision recovery*, which is when multiple RTUs decide to report their changes at the same time. This type of reporting is popular in applications in which a lot of RTUs have to share a single, low-speed channel (e.g., a radio channel). If multiple RTUs start transmitting at the same time, the host will just hear garbled noise. A mechanism is needed to ensure that collisions either don't occur or are detected and a process is followed to retransmit the data from the colliding RTUs. A commonly used mechanism is having smart radios that use *out-of-band signaling* to coordinate with each other to ensure that only one RTU initiates transmission at any given instance in time.

The primary mission of a communications protocol is to successfully and accurately deliver a message from one computer/device to another. Doing it efficiently and doing it securely are secondary issues. We have already discussed the incorporation, in most RTU serial protocols, of some means for identifying which RTU a message is for/from, in order to permit multi-dropping of RTUs on a common channel. All RTU protocols include some scheme that makes it possible for the message receiver to verify that the message arrived uncorrupted (by including something extra [a *check code*] with the message).

The robustness of these schemes was greatly improved with the introduction of the cyclic redundancy check (CRC) code calculation in the 1980s. Prior to that time, a checksum and/or longitudinal redundancy check (LRC) was used for this purpose but proved to be untrustworthy (hence the use of select-check-operate control sequences). Unfortunately, beyond these features, all legacy serial protocols fall flat.

An RTU or host computer cannot actually determine who is sending a message. If a message arrives on the communication channel with the proper formatting and a valid check code, the RTU and/or host will accept the message as legitimate and process it accordingly. (More will be made of this in later chapters.) There are simpleminded protections: if the host sent a polling message to RTU X and got a reply from RTU Y, then it would probably discard the reply and repoll RTU X. But with off-the-shelf *protocol test set* software, it is incredibly easy to masquerade as a host or RTU and create valid-looking message traffic. There have been well-documented instances in which RTUs were commandeered by attackers using commercial radio communications equipment, a portable PC, and test set software.

Protocol Standards

Because of the number of incompatible, though essentially similar, serial protocols, there has been a push, from the SCADA system customer base, for a standard protocol that provides an all-encompassing set of features and functions, to replace all of the older proprietary protocols. The hope is to provide for compatibility and interoperability between and among vendors and products. Some popular proprietary serial protocols, like Modbus and Bristol Standard Asynchronous/Synchronous Protocol (BSAP), have become de facto standards because of their publication, ease of implementation, and widespread adoption. Others, like DNP3.0, were brought into the public domain and turned over to committee for oversight.

With the rapid evolution of communications technology over the past two decades—particularly the development of LANs and WANs—other protocols suitable for use across networks have emerged. Protocols like IEC870-5-101 and -103, IEC61850, Inter–Control Center Communications Protocol; also called TASE.2 or UCA1.0 (ICCP), and UCA2.0 were defined by committee, to run over LANs and/or WANs, and were then published and promoted by standards organizations. (Note that these protocols did not initially incorporate sufficient [or any] security features, but all are currently being reviewed with that objective in mind.)

Network versus serial protocols

A fundamental division separates currently existing protocols: there are protocols that are stand alone and only require a voice-grade communication circuit; and there are those that expect a functioning digital network (LAN or WAN) of some type, composed of a communications circuit and an underlying basic networking protocol to provide *transport services*. When we discuss modern, digital communications protocols, we are generally referring to a class of protocols that have been broken down into functional layers, each of which provides services for the layers above and employ services from the layers below, all the way down to the *drivers* that deal with the actual communications hardware. Such protocols often expect an underlying network to deal with intermediate transport of messages. As an example, in a substation, if there are IEDs that are remotely accessible via the IP version of DNP protocol, these IEDs probably use Ethernet (with its SDLC protocol) as the connection mechanism to the communications interface device in the substation (e.g., a FRAD or Router) and the interface device delivers messages to the wide area digital network (e.g., frame relay or a private IP network) which delivers them to another Ethernet LAN where they get routed to an engineer's desktop PC. Neither the IEDs nor the engineer's PC need to know about the underlying networking. They speak IP-DNP protocol and then the magic happens. With legacy SCADA protocols, we have a single software module that does all of the work and expects nothing between host and RTU except a reliable voice-grade communication circuit (fig. 2–11).

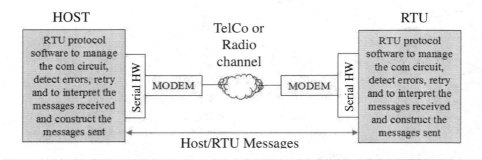

FIG. 2–11. *Simple RTU serial protocol architecture*

Some digital communications protocols can be used across the same voice-grade communication circuits that were used by traditional serial RTU protocols. For example, in a TCP/IP network, the lowest functional layer of the protocol, the one that deals with the hardware connection out of the given computer/RTU, can be the point-to-point protocol (PPP). When you dial up over a telephone connection to your Internet service provider (ISP), your PC is probably utilizing PPP to move bits over the telephone line (using a modem as the electrical interface to the phone system). The problem is that there are layers above PPP that want to send their own messages to the other computer to manage the functions for which they are responsible (and consume bandwidth and time in this process). In addition, PPP carries a lot of overhead in its base message structure, to deal with more sophisticated communication issues not relevant to RTU polling, so a simple analog input value report message will require many more total bits than with a conventional serial RTU protocol (fig. 2–12).

For these and other reasons (e.g., memory and computing power consumed by network protocol software), it was not generally viable, prior to the mid-1990s, to consider either using digital networking protocols over the slow, low-bandwidth communication circuits that were utilized by SCADA systems or running these protocols in older, 16-bit RTUs. Today there are 32- and 64-bit processor based RTUs with tremendous computing power, running commercial operating systems, and supporting communication speeds, that even over voice-grade circuits, are much higher owing to modem technology advances. Better still, telecommunication providers can supply *digital circuits*, rather than voice-grade communication circuits, and these offer the much higher bandwidth capacity needed for real-time networking.

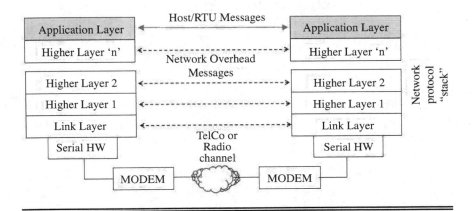

FIG. 2–12. *Network-based serial protocol architecture*

Encapsulated protocols

With the availability of LAN and WAN technology, two well-accepted and widely adopted serial protocols (DNP3.0 and Modbus) needed a face-lift to make them available for use over such digital networks. Both protocols were rereleased, in the early 2000s, in an Internet Protocol (IP) version suitable for use over any network that was IP based. (IP networking is discussed in a later chapter.) The most popular usage of these two protocol variations has been on high-speed Ethernet LANs. In fact, they are often referred to as Ethernet Modbus or Ethernet DNP. Transmission Control Protocol (TCP; part of the IP suite) is commonly used to transport and deliver messages (data) over LANs and WANs. TCP doesn't really care what the data is; it is just responsible for delivering the data without errors. In this case, the data being delivered are the actual bytes that would have been sent over a serial communication channel, when the normal versions of these protocols are employed. Rather than sending these bytes over a wire, they are delivered as the data portion of TCP/IP messages. The process of sending one type of message as data within another type of message is generally called *encapsulation*. We have already discussed how both TCP and UDP messages are carried over the Internet by IP packets. That is another example of protocol encapsulation.

IP-Ready RTUs and Protocols

In the 2000s, the computing power of RTUs has made a great leap forward, with the availability of lower-power-consumption (higher-temperature-range) versions of the popular Intel Pentium processors (and compatibles). At the same time, several full-featured commercial operating systems, with real-time extensions, became available to run on these computing platforms. As a result, high-performance IP-ready RTUs were introduced that can support both legacy and standard serial protocols, as well as having the LAN/WAN interface and computing capability to deal with the more sophisticated, network-based protocols. These RTUs come with integral Ethernet and TCP/IP support and offer a platform on which a wide range of applications can be deployed. These new RTUs will be of interest to industries that are converting from traditional, analog serial communications and replacing them with some form of digital networking.

One of the interesting features of this new generation of RTUs is that because they extend IP networking to the field, they offer the possibility of employing the same network security technologies on these communication links as are used to secure other corporate networks. Another interesting capability of these RTUs (if supported by the vendor and an appropriate IP-based protocol) is the ability to have *peer-to-peer* communications directly between and among RTUs, independent of the host computer(s). With traditional serial protocols, the RTUs could communicate only with the host computer, so any inter-RTU data exchanges require host cooperation and support. One last aspect of these RTUs worth mentioning is their ability to support multi-session communications (which comes for free with a good TCP/IP implementation.) When a SCADA operator has replicated control centers, or just a fully redundant system design, most IP-ready RTUs can simultaneously process and respond to polling messages from multiple sources. This eliminates the need for one host (in a redundant pair) to poll all RTUs and send updates to the backup unit, or for messy communication switching between a primary and alternate operating site.

Currently the list of IP-compatible RTU protocols is fairly short: DNP3.0, ICCP, UCA2.0, and Modbus. There is really no reason to restrict oneself to SCADA protocols, as there are many fine and well-proven computer protocols that can be used for data transport. Certain limited SCADA applications use File Transfer Protocol (FTP) as a mechanism for data exchange between RTUs and the SCADA host. In other applications, *extensible markup language* (XML)–based Web pages have been used for those data exchanges, transported by Hypertext Transfer Protocols (HTTP and HTTPS). There are also implementations of the IP version of DNP3.0 that have been deployed with virtual private network (VPN)–based security (which adds encryption, session keys, and authentication functions).

If an RTU (and the host with which it is communicating) can support an IP-based protocol, the SCADA system owner has a wide range of commercial communication service providers and technologies available. (This will be discussed further in the next section.) This even includes utilizing the Internet itself as a communications system. A major electric industry entity has already successfully demonstrated using the Internet as a means for real-time data collection from a large number of IP-ready RTUs located throughout a major Western state.

Another interesting aspect of TCP/IP networking is the ability to share a single communication channel across multiple applications. As will be discussed in a subsequent chapter, there are SCADA applications in which multiple host computers need to access a common RTU. With conventional serial communications, this requires individual communication circuits from each host to the RTU site and an RTU with a sufficient number of serial ports. If digital (TCP/IP) networking is used, the RTU can concurrently handle communications transactions from all host computers, via its single connection into the digital network (much the same way that a Web site can service numerous browsers concurrently).

Some of the more advanced IP-ready RTUs today are able to support a local Web server function so that the RTU can offer a range of Web pages to anyone with a laptop PC, a Web browser, and an Ethernet cable (fig. 2–13). Such Web page services may be used for data transfer purposes (e.g., using XML pages, as previously mentioned) or for human interaction with the RTU. Some vendors offer their bottom-up configuration functions via integral Web pages offered by the RTU. Others also provide diagnostics and real-time I/O value displays through these Web pages. Some vendors even offer tools that allow customers to create, or at least customize, their own Web pages. It is not surprising that most of the IP-ready RTUs on the market today are running a Microsoft Windows or Unix/Linux operating system variation and taking advantage of open source web server applications like Apache, much like the commercial Web sites on the Internet.

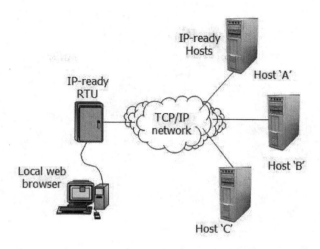

FIG. 2–13. *IP-Ready RTU providing web displays via the LAN and exchanging data via the WAN*

3

Telecommunications Technologies

Voice-Grade (Analog) Telephony

When SCADA systems emerged in the 1960s, there were only two choices for long-distance communications: the telephone system (or telephone system technology) built and operated by the Bell Telephone Company ("Ma Bell"); and private, licensed radio. (Telex and telegraph existed, but are not worth consideration. Television provides only a *simplex* channel and requires large bandwidth.) Both of these technologies (radio and telephone) were designed for the long-distance, bidirectional transmission of voice/sound (although it was possible and common to send *Morse code* over a radio channel). Most of the communications technologies we take for granted today—satellites, cell phones, and the Internet, among others— did not exist or were inappropriate for SCADA usage (although the first satellite-based telephone links, between Europe and the United States, were established in the 1960s). Thus, in designing SCADA systems—and in particular the mechanisms for transporting messages between the field-based RTUs and the SCADA host—an approach compatible with these two available technologies was required. If you ask the question, what is the basic business of the telephone company? the fundamental answer is: to move a reasonable facsimile of the human voice from point A to point B in real time. The telephone company figured out that this takes approximately 64 kilobits of data per second (in the digital world), and that particular number forms the basis for most telephone company bandwidth metrics. (You will see a circuit with this bandwidth called a DS0 or one voice-grade channel. Other higher-bandwidth channels—e.g., T1/T3—are rated in terms of how many DS0s they support. As an example, a 1.536 Mbps T1 circuit can be decomposed into 24 DS0 voice-grade channels.)

The same function (delivering voice from one point to another) is essentially true for radio communications (unless you are a Ham (amateur radio operator) and like sending Morse code). SCADA systems don't need to carry on a conversation between the SCADA host and the RTUs; they need to exchange binary numbers that represent data and commands. In the 1960s, there were fledgling remote computer communications systems in place. Computer time-sharing systems existed, and modems were used to convert electrical, binary-digit (0 and 1) signals into sounds that could traverse a telephone or radio channel. Even today, with modems capable of 56 kilobits per second, the actual data encoding is in the form of sound. The squealing sound that you hear when you dial, through the telephone system, into your ISP is the sound of a modem sending 0s and 1s (although with modern modems, it is a bit more complicated than simple sound).

Telephone technology

The (analog) telephone system of the 1960s did not add value. (Today that is not the case. You can have call forwarding, voice mail, caller ID, etc., as part of your service.) The telephone company provided a reasonably reliable, somewhat noisy, low-bandwidth (voice-grade) channel over which you were welcome to send electronic signals in the frequency range of the average human voice. You could generate those signals with the telephone handset they provided (and by speaking) or with some other electronic device, such as a modem. Establishing a connection (dialing), maintaining a connection, selecting a signaling mechanism and symbol set, detecting and correcting errors, managing and pacing the data flow, and terminating the connection were all considered to be the responsibility of those who wanted to use the telephone system. (In a later section dealing with network-based IP protocols, these functions will be similar to those provided by IP.) For most consumers, the establishment of a call began with dialing a telephone number and waiting for someone to answer. The process of dialing takes a surprising amount of time, and this was even more time consuming back when pulse dialing was still used. For a SCADA system to have to dial a telephone number to reach an RTU (and then do it again and again) would thus be inefficient.

For best efficiency, a SCADA system needs a permanent telephone connection to its various RTUs. The telephone company accommodated SCADA system owners by providing private *leased lines*. These were telephone circuit connections that had the same appearance and functioned as if a number had been dialed and answered, but the circuit was locked such that it never disconnected or broke any of the intervening connections. Actually, with older electromechanical telephone switching equipment, this was implemented by going to the various switches and placing actual clips on the connections so that they were mechanically latched. That is not to say that the telephone company was providing a *metallic circuit* between the SCADA host and the RTU; the leased line was a voice-grade circuit with amplifiers and coupling transformers along the way to boost the signal, not just a set of wires.

These leased circuits—and the telephone system in general—were *analog* in the 1960s (and well into the 1970s). This means that you could connect a telephone modem (or even a handset) to the telephone line at any point along the leased circuit and eavesdrop on the SCADA-RTU messages going back and forth (or even inject some false messages).

Today many SCADA systems still depend on leased lines provided by the local telephone company, although the underlying technology of the telephone is no longer analog. Starting in the 1970s and accelerating in the 1980 and 1990s, the telephone system was converted from analog to digital. Only the *local loop*, from the nearest telephone switching center to your home, is analog anymore. Everywhere in between is digital. For a SCADA system that uses analog, leased telephone circuits for RTU communications, the local loop at both ends of each circuit is a potential security vulnerability. With readily available equipment it would be possible to record, replay, or simulate valid-appearing message traffic at either of the two end points.

A typical office will have its own private branch exchange (PBX) that deals with analog telephones but makes a digital connection (via one or more T1/T3s) into the public telephone system. For SCADA systems that still use analog leased telephone lines, this often means that the telephone system is digital up to the panel in the telecommunications room of the facility where the SCADA host is located and analog from there up to the room where the SCADA system front end and modems are physically placed. In the field, this means that the circuit is digital to the nearest switching center and analog to the field RTU site.

For electric utility substations, many telephone companies have a policy of running an analog telephone line to the *demarcation point* outside the substation facility (usually a well-marked and obvious box) and making it the responsibility of the utility to bring the line into the substation and to the RTU. This means that the analog (and easily tapped) leased telephone circuit exists only at each end of the line (but often in unprotected areas).

The telephone system provides a *full-duplex* communication channel: sound can be sent in both directions at the same time—unlike *half-duplex* channels, as provided by a walkie-talkie or an intercom, and *simplex* channels such as television, which only sends information in one direction. In most simple, serial SCADA protocols, that capability is not utilized. The vast majority of serial protocols work totally on a half-duplex basis: a message goes out from the SCADA host to the RTUs, and the appropriate RTU formulates a response and sends it back. This isn't an efficient use of the full-duplex nature of the telephone system, and modern computer networking protocols usually support data flowing in both directions at once. One reason that SCADA serial protocols don't utilize this full-duplex capability is that a protocol needs to be far more sophisticated to manage two independent, concurrent data streams. The other reason is that most such protocols, when they were developed, needed to work over the other major available communications technology, radio, which tends to be a half-duplex channel. In fact, radio can be used only in a full-duplex mode with point-to-point applications and not with point-to-multipoint applications. (For full-duplex operation, you must transmit on one frequency while receiving on a different frequency. This works well between two parties, but is useless among a larger group.)

Analog (leased) telephone circuits are still commonly used, but most SCADA owners are finding that they are either paying a premium for or are unable to obtain additional analog circuits and that their telecommunication provider(s) is pushing them to transition onto digital circuits. The telephone companies don't want to maintain analog circuits (which are really digital up to the end points), but a large portion of installed RTUs and SCADA hosts are incapable of connecting to a digital network. Some very old RTUs still in use even have built-in analog modems (usually a Bell 202 series), which in transitioning to digital networks usually makes RTU replacement a requirement. If there are multiple RTUs on a given leased telephone line, you can't change communications protocols or the data transmission rates on that circuit unless you can simultaneously change it for all of the RTUs. Although analog telephone lines restrict data transmission rates to low speeds (generally under 34 kilobits per second [kbps]), they have been sufficient for basic SCADA applications, because traditional SCADA systems and RTU protocols were designed for even lower transmission rates (1.2–9.6 kbps).

Licensed radio

Radio communications technology from the 1960s fall into two categories: point-to-point, high-bandwidth microwave transmission, and point-to-multipoint ultrahigh-frequency (UHF) and very-high-frequency (VHF) radio transmission. The telephone company pioneered the use of microwave transmissions to carry a great number of *multiplexed* communication channels over long distances. You still see microwave repeater towers in the countryside in some parts of the United States. For some vital applications that use SCADA technology, the owners/operators had to make a decision about relying on third parties (e.g., the telephone company) for critical SCADA communications.

In many instances, electric utilities and water companies, whose service areas were covered by a local telephone company, elected to construct and maintain their own communications infrastructure, rather than being dependent on a third party. Water utilities have often chosen to implement a UHF or VHF radio–based SCADA communications system, with one or more master radios used to send/receive messages to RTUs operating on the same frequency. To cover more area or to speed up polling times, multiple master radios, operating on different frequency channels, could be used, each with its own set of RTUs with radios set to their particular master radio's frequency (fig. 3–1).

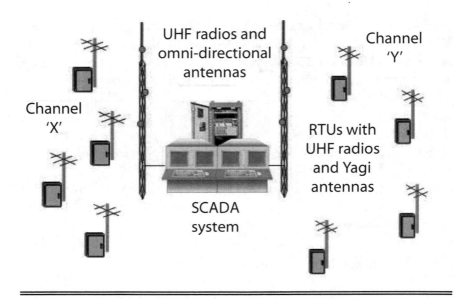

FIG. 3–1. *SCADA host with multiple master radios on separate frequencies*

A general problem faced by people trying to use licensed radio is the congestion on the available frequency slots, particularly in urban areas. It isn't always possible to find an available frequency slot. The Federal Communications Commission maintains a geographic directory of frequency assignments, so that overlap and interference can be avoided (a handy source for someone who wants to know the frequency you use to control your RTUs).

Just as RTUs became intelligent with the infusion of microprocessor technology into their designs, radio equipment also became smarter. Originally, radios were just a transmitter and receiver that were controlled by the SCADA host or RTU, just like a person controls a walkie-talkie. A modem circuit was used to convert the binary digits into sounds, and the RTUs and SCADA hosts had program logic to deal with keying the radio (switching from receive to transmit mode) and providing time delays between the end of a receiving a message and starting the transmission of a reply. It was also necessary for every RTU to listen to (and interpret) every host message, so that it could check the RTU ID in each message and find out if it was the recipient of that message.

With the integration of microprocessors into radios, the radios could use a small portion of their bandwidth to send messages to each other (a process called *out-of-band signaling*), and they (the radios) could make decisions and identify messages that the RTU actually needed to hear. Radio systems became a bit more flexible with the introduction of the multiple address system (MAS) and trunked radio systems. The connection between the radio and the computer became a serial (RS-232/C) connection (i.e., computer to computer), and the radios could identify that messages were being directed to them (the radios had a unique ID); thus, RTUs received and had to process only those messages sent specifically to them by the host. The bottom line, however, is that conventional radio is used when a SCADA system owner wants a privately operated and maintained telecommunications system.

Broadcast radio propagates outward from the transmitter in a circular pattern, like ripples in a pond when you toss in a rock. The circular radius may extend as far as 20 miles, based on terrain. That allows a large geographic area to be covered by the signal, and it can be sufficient to blanket a large urban area. Notably, conventional radio technology provides a low-bandwidth (voice-grade) channel and offers no intrinsic security features. Also, broadcast radio has line-of-sight limitations unless *repeaters* are employed to extend the range by retransmitting (boosting) the signal and to bypass such physical barriers as hills and tall buildings.

Communications backup

Although utilities might elect to construct, operate, and maintain their own private radio communications systems, they could also use the telephone system as a backup in case of radio failures. It was not uncommon, once multi-ported RTUs became available, to have critical RTUs configured with an auto-answer modem and dial-up telephone line, as a backup to the primary radio polling channel. If the SCADA host could not reach a critical RTU via the radio system, it could dial a telephone number and reconnect to the RTU via the public telephone system, to poll the RTU or to send a control command. If there were multiple critical RTUs and none could be reached via radio, the SCADA host could cycle through the set of RTUs by dialing them consecutively, polling and then hanging up and dialing the next in sequence. This wasn't very fast, but was much better than having no communications at all. The opposite strategy has also been frequently used: use leased telephone lines as the primary polling and communication mechanism, and fall back to radio to reach the critical RTUs if the telephone system goes down.

Private telephone systems

Although it could be very convenient to call the telephone company and ask them to supply a leased telephone line from point A to point B, there was a problem if those two points were not in the main service area of the local telephone company. For processes covering great distances and located away from civilization, often the only practical choice was to construct a private telecommunications system. In those instances, the typical approach was to use the same technology and equipment that the telephone company used, constructing a microwave repeater station backbone along the pipeline or electric power transmission line *right-of-way* and using telephone multiplexing equipment to create a voice-grade telephone system. Such systems would have the capacity for a large number of voice-grade channels, and a relatively small number of those channels would be allocated to the SCADA host polling functions, with the rest used to provide telephone service to the remote sites (fig. 3–2). In essence, the SCADA system owner would purchase telephone equipment to build their own communications infrastructure in the same way the telephone company would have, had they been willing.

As telephone technology evolved to include satellite links and fiber-optic cables, the organizations that elected to construct their own telecommunications infrastructure tended to migrate to those technologies. Many owners/operators of SCADA systems (particularly electric utilities and pipeline companies) ended up creating large and highly competent telecommunications support organizations to maintain and extend their private telecommunications systems. Unfortunately, as technology shifted to digital networks in the mid-1990s, few such corporations expended the funding or effort required to upgrade the skill sets of these internal telecommunications organizations. It is all too common today to find

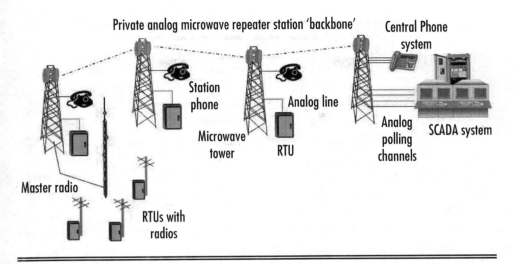

FIG. 3–2. *Typical microwave–based private telephone system*

telecommunications groups that only understand voice communications technology but are responsible for providing data telecommunications services between and among computer systems, including SCADA systems and field-based RTUs.

Private telecommunications systems continued to evolve as the telephone companies and Bell Labs (and its successors) introduced new technologies like fiber optics and synchronous optical networking (SONET). By adopting these technologies, many SCADA system owners both reduced their initial costs of their private telecommunications infrastructure and ended up with excess capacity that they could sell or lease to the telephone companies or regional/local municipalities. Electric utilities were stringing fiber-optic cable on their transmission lines, and pipeline companies were burying fiber-optic cables alongside their pipelines. In fact, many utilities entered the telecommunications market by selling or leasing their excess communication bandwidth. In a couple of surprising instances, electric utilities formed separate business units to market this excess bandwidth and ended up not retaining enough capacity for their own SCADA system. Go figure.

Commercial Voice/Data Carriers

In the 1960s, organizations that preferred not to construct, operate, and maintain private telecommunications infrastructure had few alternatives if Ma Bell couldn't meet their needs. But their choices started to expand in the late 1970s, and today they are quite numerous. In the 1970s, there was a major adoption of computer technology in the commercial and retail world. Point-of-sale terminals and smart cash registers replaced prior technology. Stores linked their branches with headquarters for faster inventory and accounting updates. Systems like the old American Airlines SABRE (Semi-Automatic Business Environment Research) airline reservation system were expanding their coverage. All of this meant a growing need for computer communications. The telephone company offered a poor set of overpriced options to a company that had numerous branches full of dumb terminals that needed to send occasional data bursts back to the home office. You could lease a high-bandwidth, high-priced T1 circuit to each operating branch and have it hardly utilized (based on average bandwidth usage)—and then do that for every branch. Commercial data carriers came into existence to compete for these dollars.

X.25 packet switching networks

To better address the market need to move lots of small data bursts from lots of places to a few central locations without spending a fortune on communication circuits, independent commercial data carriers devised a new technology. These commercial data carriers were companies that placed computers around the United States in major cities and then leased those expensive T1 and T3 circuits from the telephone company. They would drop a packet assembler/disassembler (PAD) at a company's various facilities and headquarters (and the facilities of other similar organizations in the vicinity), and that company would pay them for the messages they sent, not for any fixed amount of bandwidth. By getting a sufficient customer base in an area, they could keep the leased T1s full, yet charge customers for just the fraction of bandwidth that each actually utilized.

These message packet delivery systems were based on a standard called X.25. (Although they still exist today, most X.25 packet switching systems have been supplanted by a new technology, frame relay.) Thus, if you needed digital messages (not voice) delivered from one place to another, you could turn to X.25 packet switching services for your communication needs. Aside from supporting wired connectivity, X.25 turned out to be a reasonable technology for use with satellite communications. Most X.25 packet switching communication suppliers could provide a low-cost ground station, anywhere in the United States, linked to their network (fig. 3–3). The X.25 protocol is serial, relatively low speed, asynchronous, and simple enough to even be implemented in the front-end processors of many SCADA host computers. At the RTU level, the network is essentially transparent. The PAD does all the hard work and handles the actual X.25 protocol. Several pipeline companies, with very remote field sites (i.e., pump stations), found this satellite connectivity ideal for their situation.

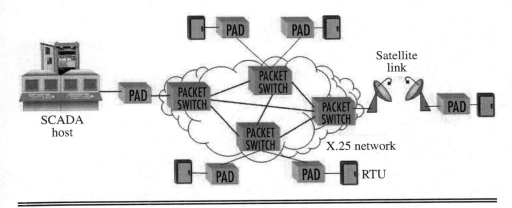

FIG. 3–3. *Use of packet switching networks for SCADA communications*

In the 1980 and 1990s, the telephone companies transitioned from the analog world to the digital world. This means that instead of sending an actual voice signal from one point to another, they *digitized* (using an A2D converter circuit) the voice as close to the source as possible (converting it into a stream of eight-bit binary numbers at the rate of 8,000 of these numbers per second [if you do the math, this adds up to 64 kilobits per second]). These numbers could then be treated just like any other type of data—transmitted from one computer to another, stored, copied, and so forth. When they arrived at their destination, the numbers were reconverted into an analog signal via a *digital-to-analog* converter circuit. If you want to hear that process in action, just pick up your cell phone and make a call (unless you have a very old cell phone).

The digital telephone company

Today the digital telephone on your office desk performs the digitization (and reconversion to analog) of your voice; thereafter, your voice exists only as a stream of binary numbers, until reconstituted by the telephone of the person you are calling. (Home telephones still remain mostly analog, although with a digital subscriber line [DSL] circuit, the digitization happens in the DSL modem supplied by the telephone company.) Since the underlying systems of the telephone company are now just moving binary numbers around, why limit that to numbers that represent voice? Why not move numbers that represent data files, text documents, and spreadsheets—in other words, generic data? In fact, today you hear the telephone companies talking about voice and data services. That is because it is really all the same to them, just moving binary numbers from point A to point B.

It actually takes extra circuitry and fuss for the telephone company to create the effect of an analog circuit for companies that need them for their SCADA systems. The telephone company would much rather provide digital circuits, and they can offer several types. Remember that the telephone company deals with *connection-oriented* communications services. This means that you need to know in advance all of the locations where you want communication connections, and you can't change these on the fly, once the connections are established. (You can always go back to the telephone company and march through the paperwork and process to have new circuits added and things changed.) Since SCADA host computers and RTUs tend to stay put once installed, this is usually not a problem for SCADA applications (fig. 3–4). Remember that the majority of telephone company data transport technology is predicated on setting up and maintaining semipermanent, point-to-point connections and not on providing dynamic connection networking as has been implemented on the Internet.

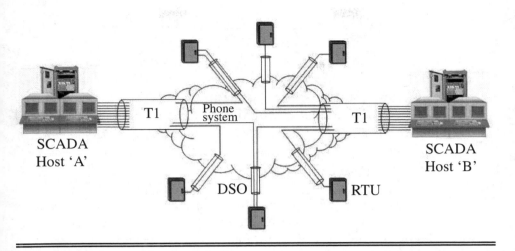

FIG. 3–4. *Connection-oriented telephone circuits*

T1/T3 circuits

The basic unit of communication bandwidth, when dealing with the telephone company, is DS0 (64 kilobits/second), which is the bandwidth needed to digitize and transmit the human voice. Your telephone company can supply communication circuits with much higher bandwidth capacity, especially using fiber-optic SONET technologies, but their multiplexing (combining) and de-multiplexing (separating) technologies are always based on multiples of a DS0. On the one hand, if you are dealing with analog data transmission and have a DS0, this means you use a modem to encode the binary numbers as sound and then get up to 38.8 kbps over the circuit, if you have a low-noise circuit and use a top-of-the-line modem and the wind is at your back. (With regard to 56 kbps modems, it is important to understand that this performance level involves pre-transmission message compression in the modem, which yields results only when sending big messages—e.g., files—and not short SCADA polling messages.) On the other hand, if you use digital encoding and transmission over the same phone wires, you actually get nearly all of the 64 kbps, almost double the best analog data transmission rate.

If a SCADA host requires a large number of individual voice-grade (analog) communication circuits in order to connect with all of its RTUs, the actual circuit that comes to the SCADA facility is probably one or more T1 or T3 circuits. At the SCADA facility, or at the nearby telephone switching center, the telephone company will install multiplexing equipment (channel banks) that decompose the T1s or T3s into individual DS0s, which will then be put through converter cards that make them into analog circuits, suitable for interfacing with the SCADA system front-end computer's modems.

By contrast, if the SCADA system is of a more modern design and able to connect with and communicate across digital networks, the T1s would probably terminate directly into a router, which would then provide a high-speed Ethernet connection to the SCADA system. In the field, with IP-ready RTUs, the telephone company DS0s would again connect directly to a low-end router that would offer an Ethernet connection to the RTU (fig. 3–5). In effect, the telephone circuits are creating a path between separate LANs, so that these Ethernet networks can exchange data. The telephone system is *not* providing any networking services, just point-to-point connections between routers. Figure 3–5 shows an architectural theme that will be repeated frequently when we discuss IP networking (and taking IP out to the field sites) regardless of the type of wide area network used to connect the various sites.

Integrated service digital network

At the very end of the 1980s, when the telephone systems were still using mainly analog lines for home and small office services and PCs were becoming a standard fixture in most offices, the telephone company introduced a higher-speed digital connectivity option that eliminated analog modems and offered up to 128 kbps data transmission rates. The integrated service digital network (ISDN) was the first digital offering by the telephone company. Today this technology has been totally eclipsed by other telephone company offerings. It was never really adopted for use in SCADA systems, but was frequently used for linking information technology (IT) systems with branch offices. The Internet did not exist as we know it today and so this was a technology for private networking

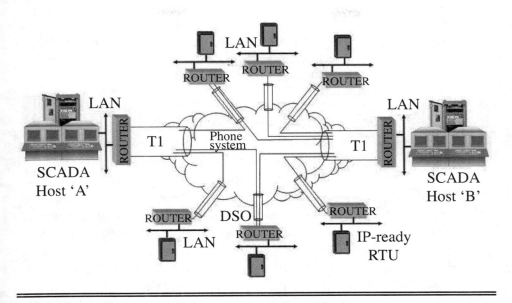

FIG. 3–5. *Using telephone circuits to bridge LANs*

through the telephone system. Today, a DSL line, which actually connects a customer onto the Internet, would be the technology of choice for equivalent purposes (as long as your firewall, virus scan, and spam blocking software were kept up to date). But this is also why most SCADA system operators would avoid using DSL technology.

Frame relay

The technology that the telephone company prefers to offer to those who want data services today (without being put onto the Internet) is frame relay, which in architecture resembles an X.25 packet switching network but offering much higher performance at a slight reduction in reliability. The X.25 packet switching system was designed to link a large number of geographically dispersed dumb terminals with remote mainframe computers. These dumb terminals could not execute programs because they had no computer components. They were much like the early dumb RTUs; they could send short binary messages in response to users hitting keys on the keyboard. Thus, the PAD had to collect messages from a large number of these terminals, form them into an X.25 message, and send them over the network to the destination. The PAD retained a copy of this message until delivery had been confirmed or sent it again if delivery failed.

Today we have no dumb devices. The RTUs (and sales terminals) are computer based and able to perform many of the functions performed by a PAD. This means that the delivery security and routing features built into the X.25 networks could be discarded in favor of better performance. As telephone companies push SCADA system owners away from conventional analog leased lines, the technology they are offering as an alternative is usually frame relay. A frame-relay system is basically connection oriented: you designate points where equipment will be connected into the frame network and the bandwidth you want for each connection, and then the frame network is configured to set up these *permanent virtual circuits* (PVCs). Today frame-relay technology has advanced to a point where a lot more flexibility is possible, but it is not a totally dynamic networking technology, as is TCP/IP. Frame relay is intended as a computer-to-computer networking technology and has its own protocols.

For SCADA systems that need to replace their analog leased telephone lines, frame relay doesn't totally solve the problem. However, there are vendors of devices called FRADs (frame-relay access devices), which provide similar functions as PADs did for X.25 networks. A FRAD is essentially a router with frame-relay protocol support and one or more serial ports that can be bound to corresponding serial ports on other FRADs elsewhere on the frame-relay network. A SCADA system can use a group of FRADs interfaced to the SCADA system's front-end processors, to provide the equivalent of the telephone lines it used previously, and a FRAD at each RTU location, to complete the virtual circuits (fig. 3–6). The effect is as if actual dedicated serial circuits were run from the ports on the SCADA system to the RTUs (which is why this ability of frame relay is referred to as a PVC). More advanced FRAD product offerings even support VPN technologies for communications security. The connection to the FRAD is generally a serial (RS-232/C) circuit; therefore, with older RTUs that have built-in analog modems, this unfortunately presents an interfacing problem. We will return to frame-relay technology later in this chapter, when we discuss the alternative digital networking technologies available for SCADA systems.

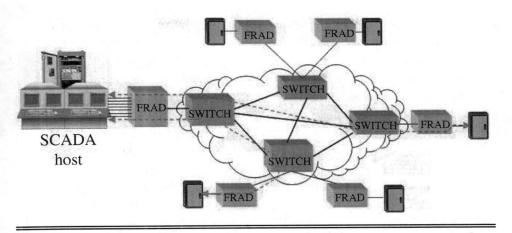

FIG. 3–6. *Frame relay and FRADs used for replacement of SCADA analog leased lines*

DSL technologies

Your local telephone company can probably also offer you some form of DSL circuit, but this is not a general purpose circuit. This is a special circuit that offers you high-speed connectivity directly onto the Internet. There have been successful experiments in California involving moving real-time data from a large population of geographically dispersed field sites to SCADA host computers over the Internet. In this instance each remote used a DSL circuit for its Internet connection and VPN software, in all of the RTUs and the SCADA masters, was used to provide security. However, most SCADA system owners would probably shy away from considering the Internet as a secure telecommunications technology, particularly with all of the publicity concerning viruses, hackers, and attacks on computer systems.

Options for Wireless Communications

Conventional licensed VHF analog radio (and its lack of security) has already been discussed. An alternative to that technology is unlicensed, spread-spectrum radio. Spread-spectrum radio gets its name because it transmits data on a range of frequencies (channels), rather than on a single frequency. Unlike licensed radio, where the user typically gets exclusive use of a specific frequency in their geographic area, all spread-spectrum radio equipment shares a common range of frequencies (channels) regardless of proximity to other spread-spectrum radio systems. This is possible because of the use of *frequency hopping*, a technique that causes the transmitted information to be spread out over a large number of channels and the radios jump from channel to channel following a mutually agreed upon pseudo random sequence (fig. 3–7). (There is a second type of spread-spectrum radio called direct-sequence spread spectrum, which adds synthetic noise (called a chipping code) to the transmitted data so that it seems like random noise, rather than an actual data-carrying signal.) Both types of spread spectrum technology make it more difficult (but not impossible) for an eavesdropper to listen to communications traffic.

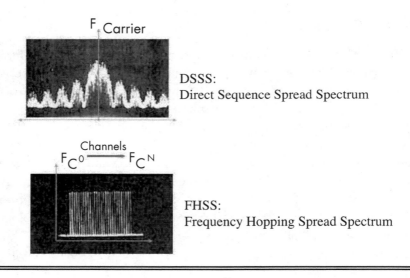

FIG. 3–7. *Spectral energy (frequency) distribution of spread-spectrum radio*

Although initially commercially envisioned as a local area wireless technology (it is used in cell phones, wireless Ethernet, and Bluetooth-enabled devices), some spread-spectrum radio equipment on the market today is higher powered, with transmission ranges comparable to conventional radio (10–20 miles, line of site). Also, since unlicensed spread-spectrum radio is relegated to two VHF bands (900 megahertz and 2.4 gigahertz), it can support much higher data rates (144 kbps typically) than does conventional radio. Spread-spectrum radio has been used by the military for years, owing to its much greater security: it is much harder to intercept and to jam than conventional radio.

Almost all new SCADA system installations based on radio communications utilize spread-spectrum radio, unless the owners already have an investment in (i.e., an installed base of) conventional radio equipment. However, just using spread spectrum radio is not, in and of itself, sufficient for communications security. It is possible to intercept spread-spectrum messages, particularly if they are repeated on a regular basis (as are SCADA polling messages), given the right equipment and patience.

WiFi and WiMAX

One particular category of spread-spectrum radio that has been standardized and commercialized is IEEE 802.11 wireless Ethernet, or WiFi. Although initially designed for LANs or personal area networks (PANs), a version with much higher power and greater range called 802.16, or WiMAX, is now becoming commercially available. WiMAX is essentially wireless Ethernet over a large area (creating a municipal area network [MAN]) and is intended to provide high-bandwidth data rates (244 million bits per second [Mbps]) over municipal areas. WiMAX is Ethernet-ish and thus is intended for computers that have digital networking capabilities. It includes advanced encryption capabilities and supports point-to-multipoint communications. A modern IP-ready SCADA system, with IP-ready RTUs, would be able to use this type of communications infrastructure for real-time polling and supervisory control and still have lots of bandwidth left for deployment of other applications and systems.

Currently, building and maintaining a WiMAX system would be the responsibility of the SCADA system owner, just like any other radio communications system. However, in the future, municipalities may construct WiMAX systems to offer Internet connectivity to inhabitants and visitors and for their own municipal networking needs. SCADA system owners operating within the WiMAX service area will probably be able to utilize these systems for their communications (although security and reliability may dictate having a backup strategy). The downside of this technology is that anyone in the service area who has appropriate commercial hardware and software will also be able to use this wireless MAN and could attempt to attack the SCADA host or RTUs.

Cellular

The local telephone company offers several wired communications options, as discussed earlier. However, they also offer wireless communications options. The various digital cellular telephone systems installed in major municipal areas of the United States can be used for data communications, as well as for voice communications. As mentioned previously, a modern cell phone actually sends and receives data that represent digitized speech (using spread-spectrum technology). The cellular system is a wireless mechanism for putting data onto the wired telephone system, where it can be transported in a conventional manner (possibly to another service area where it leaves the wired telephone system and gets onto another cellular system).

For SCADA systems installed in a municipal area, such as water/ wastewater, electric power, or gas distribution, the cellular telephone system offers a flexible means for establishing field communications. RTUs can be equipped with commercially available cellular modems that can be dialed just like any conventional telephone number by a SCADA host. It is also possible to have the equivalent of leased connectivity (nondialed, continuously connected) via the cellular system (fig 3–8), in which case a wireless connection is maintained continuously; the cost for this type of service is based on traffic (messages sent/received), and the telephone company routes this traffic back to the SCADA system via conventional wired (or wireless) means.

Most cellular service providers charge by the message; thus, this technology best suits RTUs that employ a report-by-exception protocol design. For newer, network-ready RTUs, there are digital modems and

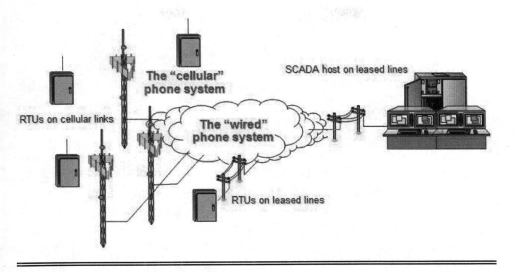

FIG. 3–8. *Cellular data communications architecture*

PCMCIA cards that can provide IP networking connectivity throughout the cellular system. These must be differentiated from the plug-in PCMCIA cards that provide laptop PCs with Internet connectivity. The plug-in cards are a wireless, cellular version of a DSL circuit; they are there just to connect your laptop PC to the Internet (via a telephone company server), not to offer cellular-to-cellular or cellular-to-wired telephone connectivity. These would be used in a modern RTU only if it was intended to utilize the Internet as the basic means for communications. One of the challenges with using cellular communications is that there are several incompatible cellular technologies used by the competing cellular service providers. A CDMA enabled cellular modem (or cell phone) won't work on a system that uses GSM technology and neither will it work on a GPRS based network (three of the incompatible cellular technologies used today). Regardless of the technology you use, the folks that invented digital cellular recognized the need for confidentiality in voice communications and thus imbedded a reasonable level of link-layer encryption in the basic design of all cellular technologies.

Digital Networking Technologies

Over the past few years, most SCADA system vendors have expanded their system capabilities to allow for communications between the host and RTUs via digital networking. This is partially because of the migration, by conventional telecommunications service suppliers, toward digital communications in place of analog communications. It is also because of the proliferation of available digital networking technologies and the widespread adoption of IP networking and the Internet. One of the qualities of most digital networking technologies is the ability both to support multiple, concurrent communication sessions (conversations) over a single physical communication link and to provide a flat communication architecture. In other words, any computer can communicate directly with any other computer, if this is needed (as when smart RTUs exchange data directly with each other or with multiple hosts). These are both useful capabilities for SCADA systems and are not generally available with conventional analog technologies.

There are many digital networking technologies available to a SCADA system owner, depending on the desire to use commercial suppliers or to construct a proprietary network. By network-ready SCADA systems and RTUs, we normally mean those that support IP networking with one of the currently available IP SCADA protocols: IP-Modbus, IP-DNP3.0, ICCP, or UCA2.0.

Frame relay

We have already discussed frame relay as an analog line replacement technology available from the telephone company. But frame relay is, moreover, a digital networking technology. Frame-relay data communication services are available from most of the telephone companies in the United States and almost anywhere there is telephone service. Frame relay is a digital networking technology intended to provide point-to-point data transport between computer systems or other networks. The telephone company can provide several levels of bandwidth at the various connection points.

As previously mentioned, FRADs can be used to make a frame-relay system look (virtually) like a bunch of conventional serial communication circuits to an older SCADA system and RTUs. However, for network-ready (IP-capable) SCADA systems and RTUs, a frame-relay network is just one of the communications technologies available for establishing communications between the SCADA host and all of the field sites.

A digital network based on frame relay would employ a router at each connection point that would deal with frame-relay protocol and DLCI-to-IP-address mapping. (A DLCI [data link connection interface] is the unique house address of a connection to a frame-relay network. An IP address is the same thing for an IP network.) The frame-relay network merely delivers IP messages from one DLCI to another (fig. 3–9). Each RTU, with its local Ethernet connection to the router is a separate IP network (with one member), and it has its own DLCI address on the frame network. The frame-relay network and the routers are transparent to the SCADA host and RTUs. As far as they know, they are speaking a common IP protocol, and somehow the messages flow back and forth. That is a basic attribute of network protocols: they assume that the underlying network handles all the magic of transport and reliable delivery. It's kind of like when we make a conventional telephone call; all the things done by the telephone company are transparent (invisible) to us. This is a good time to bring up another concept of digital networking that needs to be understood. When a SCADA systems uses conventional analog phone lines to poll its

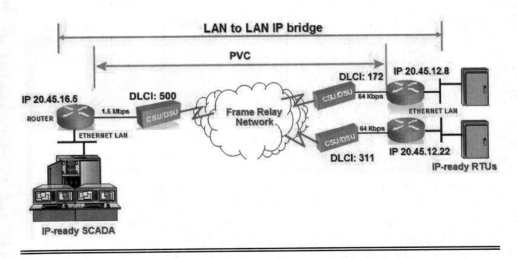

Fig. 3–9. *Frame-relay DLCI-to-IP-address mapping in routers*

RTUs, each RTU gets a fixed amount of bandwidth (like 1200 bps), but the SCADA master has the sum of the bandwidth on all of the separate polling channels. When going digital, there is only one network connection to the SCADA system, and it has to support concurrent communications with all of the RTUs. Thus with a frame relay network, each RTU might get a 64Kbps DS0 circuit, but the SCADA master will need something that aggregates to a bandwidth level sufficient to handle polling all of the RTUs at once. This means it would be typical for the SCADA system to have a T1 or even T3 interface into the frame relay network.

Fiber-distributed data interface

Another networking technology that is available to SCADA system owners is the fiber-distributed data interface (FDDI). This technology uses a counter-rotating fiber-optic ring, running at 100 Mbps, to move data from one point on the ring to other points on the ring. This networking technology was popular with small to medium-sized municipalities that wanted to create a fault-tolerant private voice/data network to link all of their offices and facilities. If the municipality operated its own gas, electric, or water utilities, then this same network could be used to provide voice-grade connections for linking the SCADA host to its RTUs. Today that same type of network could provide digital connectivity between the same points.

FDDI, like most other networking technologies, moves messages from one local network to another local network. FDDI easily interfaces to Ethernet LANs and transports IP messages between these LANs. Because of its counterrotating ring design, FDDI has the useful ability to self-heal if the ring is severed (which is always a distinct possibility). Messages arriving in a repeater station on one ring could be sent back out the other ring if the repeater detects a link failure downstream (fig. 3–10). One of the issues with a shared network is the possibility that noncritical traffic will slow down the important messages (like when you are in a hurry and all those other people are clogging up the highway and slowing you down). FDDI networks are reasonably *deterministic,* which means that the time to deliver a message through such a network is always within a predetermined time span. The same can't be said for the getting onto and off of the FDDI network, through the Ethernet LANs.

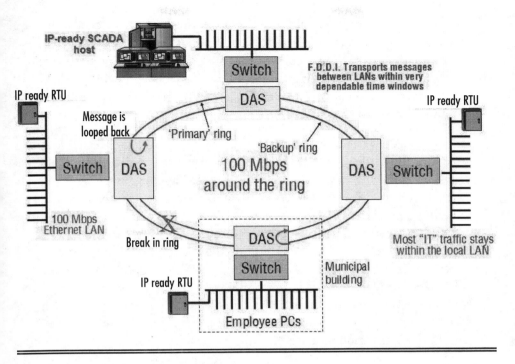

FIG. 3–10. *FDDI counter-rotating ring design*

Asynchronous transfer mode

Actually, the use of FDDI networking was just catching on, in the early 1990s, when another networking technology came onto the scene. Asynchronous transfer mode (ATM) equipment was invented by the telephone companies as their backbone technology for building and expanding the telephone system. ATM networks operate at very high data rates enabled by the underlying fiber-optic–based communications technology. Data rates of many gigabits per second (Gbps) are possible, and an ATM network can have a very flexible topology, including a self-healing ring like FDDI.

Originally, ATM equipment was quite costly, particularly the top-quality (single-mode) fiber-optic cable used to make the physical communication connections between locations. In the intervening years, however, prices have fallen on this technology. In addition, the bandwidth capacity of ATM goes well beyond that required for a SCADA system, so organizations that installed systems using this technology were able to underwrite costs by selling or leasing their excess bandwidth. ATM networks can be small (e.g., a campus or small municipality) or huge, because of their scalable architecture.

Just as ATM technology eclipsed the FDDI networking technology about the time when it started to gain market traction, SONET has eclipsed ATM, particularly for large-scale applications. SONET technology was a further development by the telephone companies. The underlying networks that form the basis for the Internet are ATM and SONET networks, as are the networks used by the telephone companies to transport voice. (In fact, they are often the very same networks.) Some electric utilities and pipeline operating companies have adopted fiber-optic ATM or SONET technologies for building or upgrading their long-haul communications infrastructures. Laying a fiber-optic cable in the trench with the pipeline, or stringing it along the transmission line conductors, has become a common practice.

TCP/IP Networking

The IP suite of protocols (including TCP) was developed as part of the U.S. government's desire to link together the computer systems and facilities of various government agencies, the military, research laboratories, and universities. The original project that evolved into the Internet we know today was run by the Defense Department's Advanced Research Projects Agency (DARPA) and remained a private, government-owned network for many years. In the late 1980s, the Internet was *privatized* by the government, and the rest is history. Because the Internet was originally private and run by the Defense Department, the design omitted a critical factor: there were no security or confidentiality features included in the design. This was corrected in the past few years with the introduction of IP version 6 (IPv6), although not every computer or device connected to the Internet supports IPv6.

Just about every country in the world is linked to the Internet and provides Internet connectivity to their citizens. The Internet is unique in that it employs connection-less communications. This means that there is no need, in advance, to establish communication paths between computers that need to exchange messages. In fact, such predefined paths would be an impossible burden given the size of the Internet today.

The Internet uses an addressing scheme, rather than specific connections, and all properly addressed messages tossed onto the Internet will generally be delivered to the intended recipient. In this way, the Internet is somewhat like the U.S. Postal Service. You don't need to know the physical location of, or means for getting to, a destination address. The post office takes care of all of that for you, as long as you provide a valid address. (It is often useful to use the postal service as a model for explaining how IP networking works.)

The technologies developed for and used on the Internet are not restricted to the Internet. Anyone can buy the components and software to build an IP network. In most corporations, the company-wide network will be an IP-based network. When you buy a PC or laptop computer today, regardless of the operating system you prefer, that computer will invariably come preconfigured with support for IP networking. All of the vendor proprietary networks developed over the years—like Digital Equipment Corporation's DECnet and IBM's Systems Network Architecture (SNA), among others—have been almost completely eliminated by IP technology.

IP also stands for inter-networking protocol, with its purpose being to allow separate, autonomous local networks to be interconnected. Within an IP WAN, there may be numerous LANs that employ different LAN technologies. Just as IP has driven out almost all other WAN contenders, Ethernet has just about eliminated all other LAN technologies. In most private IP networks today, you will find Ethernet LANs with clusters of computers, peripherals, and PCs, and these LANs will be interconnected using routers and long-distance communication technologies (e.g., frame relay or leased digital telephone circuits).

In many cases, the long-distance communications technology will be the Internet itself (fig. 3–11). Any company that wants to transact business today is essentially forced to connect to the Internet, if only to host a Web site and provide e-mail support. If critical control systems (e.g., SCADA systems) are connected via IP networking to the business and IT systems that have Internet connectivity, then these critical control systems are theoretically accessible over the Internet. That is the strength and the weakness of IP-based networking. Remember that any systems connected to a system that is connected to the Internet is also connected to the Intranet.

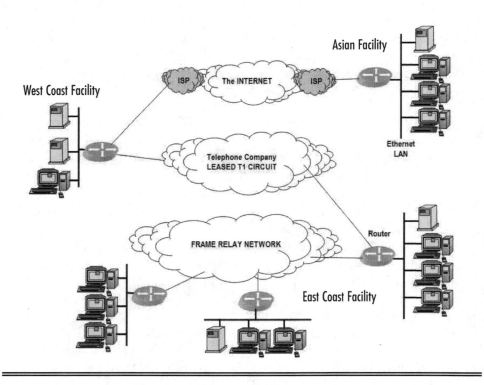

FIG. 3–11. *Typical corporate IP network architecture*

Every modern PC comes with Ethernet hardware and TCP/IP networking software. You merely have to plug into a network switch port and launch your Web browser to be on the Internet (admittedly, there are a couple of other steps, but it is no big deal requiring computer expertise). The good and bad thing about all of this (from a cybersecurity standpoint) is that the hardware and the software for IP networking (and Ethernet LANs) are readily available in commercial off-the-shelf (COTS) hardware and software. The means for connecting to and utilizing IP networks are available to anyone. Unfortunately, the Internet itself is home to innumerable Web sites that offer software and tips on hacking, creating viruses and worms, and launching attacks on computer systems. All of these *hacker tools* work just as well on a private IP network as they do over the Internet. (In fact, your IT folks probably use the same tools to test your cyber defenses that hackers use to attack them.)

Because SCADA systems are beginning to use IP networks for RTU communications and because these systems are often connected with, or are placed onto, corporate IP networks and exchange data with other systems (using IP networking and possibly doing so over commercial networks), it is important to understand some basic concepts and terminology associated with IP networking. In a later chapter, we will discuss various vulnerabilities associated with IP networking and typical types of attacks used to penetrate computer systems. To begin, let us just establish basic terminology.

The fundamental communications protocol used to move all messages through the Internet (or any private IP network) is called, not surprisingly, the Internet Protocol (IP). IP delivers messages from one host (computer) to another host, allowing intermediate computers to assist in moving the message to the destination. (In the case of LANs, IP moves messages between autonomous LANs and expects the local network to deal with local delivery.) In reality, however, it is typically necessary to deliver messages between *programs* running on different computers.

For the design of IP to account for specific programs (also called *processes*) and not just computers, two front-end protocols were layered onto IP: TCP (Transport Control Protocol) and UDP (User Datagram Protocol). Application programs can request either TCP interconnectivity or UDP interconnectivity. TCP provides a more reliable connection, hides packetizing activities, and deals with all sorts of guaranteed-delivery issues. UDP is a bare-bones delivery scheme that puts the burden of guaranteed delivery on the two programs that are communicating. The quality of the connection between communicating programs and the need for rapid delivery are factors that could push the choice one way or the other. If applications are communicating among computers on a common LAN then either might be fine, and UDP could boost performance. But for communications that traverse the Internet, it is far more common to use TCP. Since an application developer might not know in advance how communications will occur, a safe bet would be to elect TCP (and many developers do just that). For this reason it has become commonplace to think of the two protocols: TCP and IP to be consolidated, and thus the prevalence of calling it TCP/IP. TCP and UDP messages are carried as data (the *message payload*) in IP messages across the Internet or local network. (If it is across a LAN, then the IP packets themselves are carried as data in the link layer protocol of the LAN [such as SDLC with Ethernet.])

One feature that these two protocols add is the idea of *ports*. Computers on an IP network have (IP) addresses, but there can be many different programs concurrently running on a computer and attempting communication with other programs running on other computers. Ports were added to distinguish these programs from one another. (Just like a street address can include a specific person's name so that the letter gets to the right person at the address, an IP address gets more specific with the addition of a port number, so that messages get to the right program.) There are over 65,000 possible port numbers as they are represented by a 16-bit integer (0 to $2^{16}-1$). Unlike IP addresses, we have not run out of those numbers. For common applications that are found on most computers, a standardized set of so-called well known port numbers have been assigned (only about 2,000 of them so far). Returning to the postal service metaphor for the moment, it was mentioned that a port address is like specifying the specific person at an address. A well known port number is equivalent to using an addressee such as "Accounting Department" or "Human Resources", in place of a specific person's name. Since most companies have such departments, you can get your mail delivered, even if you don't know a specific name. Using a well known port number is how you get connected to a computer's email server, Web server and the like. Unfortunately, because they are well known, hackers can attack these ports and exploit known vulnerabilities in these system-level applications.

IP addresses (until IPv6) were just a 32-bit binary number. (That number is usually written as four decimal numbers separated by periods: e.g., 128.156.12.33.) The people who initially cooked up the Internet couldn't envision there ever being more than $2^{32} - 1$ computers connected on a single network worldwide. They were wrong. We ran out of unique IP addresses a few years ago, and there have been temporary work-arounds employed to keep things going. In IPv6 the address is a 128-binary bit number (and that should last us a while). Currently, both types of addresses are still used (because, even though IPv6 has a lot of advantages, it will be a long time before all IPv4-based systems and equipment connected to the Internet are replaced or upgraded). When an IP message (also called a *packet*) arrives at a computer, the message has the IP address/port number of both the destination and the sender. (This is like the return address on a letter, the original purpose of which was so that you could send a return message using that address information.) Today that sender information might also be used to decide if the message should be accepted or discarded (that is called packet filtering and it is a low-level firewall function that is easily defeated). Unfortunately, it is all too easy to falsify that information in an IP message.

For most people, the mysteries of IP addresses and ports remain hidden, and the only Internet address they are aware of is the uniform resource locator (URL). A URL is the string that you type into a Web browser or e-mail system to specify a person or Web site on the Internet (or within a private IP network). Most people won't recall an IP address and port number but can remember something like tim.shaw@ourcompany. org. That text string is more human friendly than a group of numbers, but as previously mentioned, sending something over an IP network requires an actual IP address. For that reason, there is a special message protocol that can be used to look up an IP address when given a URL. On the Internet (and in private IP networks), there are computers whose function is like telephone company directory/yellow-pages services.

If you send a message containing a URL to a domain name server (using DNS protocol), it will look up the domain name (the "ourcompany. com" part of the text string) and send back to you the IP address. Most computers retain a local copy of this information (called a DNS *cache*) so that you don't have to ask for it again (like writing down the telephone number you get from the directory assistance, folks). Next time you use that URL, the computer will just refer to its local copy. One way hackers attack computers is by overwriting the DNS cache so that your computer gets the wrong IP address. (Imagine someone changing the telephone numbers in your directory, so you call them when you think you are calling your bank or broker.) When we speak of IP, we are really discussing a huge and growing suite of protocols layered onto IP or existing down within the layers of IP itself (fig. 3–12).

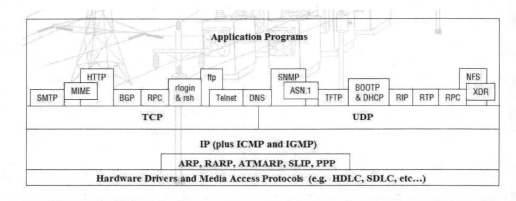

FIG. 3–12. *Some of the basic protocols in the IP suite*

IP was initially intended as a protocol and mechanism for moving messages between local, autonomous (proprietary) networks. As mentioned earlier, Ethernet won the LAN war. Today the vast majority of LANs are Ethernet based, and IP messaging can be used among the computers on an Ethernet LAN, as well as between such LANs. Every computer on an Ethernet LAN needs to have a special, unique address for that LAN (called its media access control [MAC] address). This is because Ethernet was developed independently of IP and has its own separate standards. To be connected to a basic Ethernet LAN, a computer is equipped with a circuit card called a NIC [Network Interface Card]. That NIC has a built-in 48-bit number (the MAC address) assigned by the card manufacturer at the factory. As with IP addresses MAC addresses were supposed to be unique (we ran out of those also). When a computer wants to send a message it is put into a suitable format in accordance with the SDLC standard, and includes the MAC address of the sending computer and the destination computer. NIC cards inspect messages (the destination MAC address in the message header) to see if they are the intended recipient. If computers on an Ethernet LAN want to use IP networking, the IP packets are carried over the LAN as data inside the SDLC messages. In order for computers on an Ethernet LAN to send IP messages to each other, there needs to be a way to convert a MAC address to an IP address. Fortunately, there is a protocol called Address Resolution Protocol (ARP) that can be used to look up an IP/MAC address pair. These address pairs are then kept in a local (ARP) cache inside your computer, so they can be reused when needed. As you might have already guessed, another way hackers attack systems is by overwriting the contents of the ARP cache and substituting a bad MAC address, so that your messages go to the wrong computer (just like the DNS cache example described earlier).

A continuous stream of new protocols have been layered onto IP: instant messaging, voice over IP, and Web radio are just a few examples, and there are many more. Each of these new protocols typically claims one or more of the unassigned port numbers available with TCP and UDP. This also creates potential security problems. Hackers can hide their attacks within these protocols or stage attacks by sending messages to a port that has not been properly protected. Some protocols (such as OPC, which will be discussed later) just pick unclaimed ports at random, which makes it hard to set up a packet filtering function in a firewall, since you don't know in advance what ports it will claim..

Along with new protocols, various security features have been added, to correct the lack thereof in the original IP design. In IPv6, full message encryption and end-to-end *authentication* (usually called IP$_{SEC}$) were added, but enabling these capabilities is optional. Authentication and cybersecurity technology will be discussed in detail in subsequent chapters.

IP networking involves a multilayered network architecture, with a great number of specialized protocols that perform the background functions that make all of this stuff work. Just like a successful Broadway play requires a huge support staff working in the background, IP networking depends on a large number of background functions and out-of-band messaging.

IP suite of protocols

Sending IP messages from one program/computer to another comprises a number of steps that must be taken in the right order and conformational checks that must be made at the right points along the way. Some indication must be given as to which way (preferably the best way) to send message packets when multiple choices are available. It is important to know that messages make it to the destination. All of this is made possible by the exchange of special messages, using numerous protocols defined for these special purposes. Hackers have developed a number of ways of faking such messages and creating invalid messages that can be used to probe, damage, or invade systems that have inadequate protective measures. The vulnerabilities of TCP/IP networks and the Internet will be discussed in greater detail in later chapters. For now, let us focus on major highlights and significant technologies.

Secure Socket Layer

Because the Internet was designed with no inherent security/confidentiality mechanisms, creative vendors had to devise ways to accessorize TCP/IP networking to make it suitable for major applications such as the use of Web server/browser technology (the basis for the World Wide Web) in electronic commerce. People would not be willing to conduct financial or other sensitive transactions via Web sites unless a means was provided to ensure the confidentiality of the transaction and of the financial information necessary to complete such a transaction.

Netscape devised a means for adding customer-to-Web-site security by utilizing *digital-certificate*-based authentication and *session-key* message encryption. This mechanism was called the *Secure Socket Layer* (SSL). This was not part of the TCP/IP system design, but rather something added in front of the formal TCP/IP mechanisms. A Web site and browser that supported SSL would perform a series of security set-up operations *prior* to the conventional HTTP Web page delivery, and all further transactions with this Web site would be subjected to security mechanisms at both ends of the connection, as well as message encryption. SSL became a de facto standard because it worked, solved a major problem, and didn't upset the underlying TCP/IP networking mechanisms.

VPN

Another mechanism that was devised to layer security onto IP networking is the VPN. This technology is similar in nature to SSL in that it incorporates a set of authentication and validation functions layered on top of IP and includes message encryption and digital certificates. The major difference is that SSL was specifically designed for secure Web-browsing activities, whereas VPN technology protects all forms of IP application messaging.

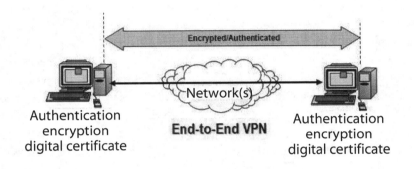

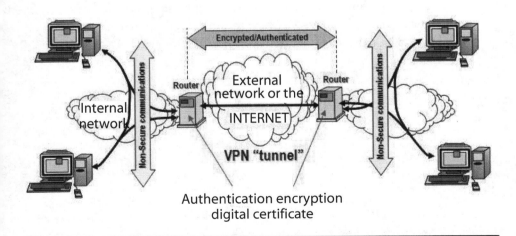

Fig. 3–13. *VPN tunnel versus VPN client/server design*

There are two basic forms of VPN—the VPN tunnel and end-to-end VPN—although a very common hybrid combines these two approaches. Where there are two or more sites with numerous computers that need to exchange message traffic between and among the sites, a VPN tunnel can be created by setting up VPN functions (authentication, encryption, digital certificate validation, etc.) in the routers that interconnect the sites. Communications among the computers on the local networks are not protected, but if any of the communications traffic flows outward through the local router to an external network, that traffic is protected until it reaches the opposite router at the distant LAN. In effect a safe tunnel through the external networks is created by the routers. Setting up a tunnel like this is transparent to the existing computers and applications: they don't need any modifications to take advantage of the tunnel. With end-to-end VPN, every computer fully implements all of the necessary protective functions so that all traffic is protected. (If every computer in question supports IPv6, and makes full use of the IP_{SEC} features defined in IPv6, then you have created an end-to-end VPN.) This is more complicated than setting up a tunnel, and it may not be necessary as long as you can trust the security of your LANs. A common hybrid of these two approaches is to use a VPN server to allow remote PC users to connect to a LAN, through remote access (dial-up telephone or via the Internet). Each remote PC implements VPN client software, and there is essentially a private, individual tunnel between each remote user and the VPN server. But, once the traffic from any such PC passes through the VPN gateway and is placed onto the LAN, it is no longer secure.

The Internet

Although today it is uncommon to see the actual Internet used as a communications system for real-time supervisory and control applications, there have been successful demonstrations of this capability. As SCADA host computers and RTUs with IP support become available, it is likely that the argument will be made, if purely for financial reasons, that the Internet should be considered. Thus, some knowledge of the Internet (as opposed to IP networking) is essential. As with IP networking technology, the Internet is too complex a subject to cover in any detail within this book (or in 10 books, really). So we will limit our discussion in this chapter to architectural, reliability, and performance considerations; security issues related to IP networking and the Internet will be discussed in a later chapter.

Backbone (including MBONE)

The Internet itself is composed of a number of backbone computer networks interconnected by very-high-speed communication links. Within the United States, this network is operated by a number of the regional telecommunication and telephone carriers. These computers provide the routing and message-forwarding mechanisms that carry IP messages from one autonomous computer network to another. (The Internet itself routes messages from network to network, using the individual network gateways as the points of connection. An autonomous network could consist of one computer, but usually they are more like your own company network, which will have only one actual connection to the Internet [via your ISP].) There is a lot of communication bandwidth built into the backbone, as well as a lot of fault tolerance. (It was initially intended to survive a nuclear attack.) Direct interconnection to the backbone is restricted and is almost never available to a commercial user. Most direct backbone connections have been to governmental organizations and facilities, major research laboratories, and major universities with governmental research programs (and to the Internet networks set up and run in other countries).

The initial design of the Internet did not address issues of real-time message delivery. But today people want to stream audio and video across the Internet and use it for point-to-multipoint video conferencing. In the past couple of years, the Internet Engineering Task Force (IETF), the folks who maintain and improve the Internet, added some real-time protocol extensions to the IP suite of protocols and created a virtual real-time multicast capability called the multicast/multimedia backbone or *MBONE*. This is not a separate network with separate backbone computers and network connections, but rather a functional enhancement that runs over the existing Internet infrastructure.

Internet service providers

Surrounding the backbone are Internet service providers (ISPs) that do have direct, high-bandwidth backbone connections and that sell full-time, moderate-bandwidth connectivity. Most of these are the same regional carriers that run and maintain the backbone systems. ISPs who sell dial-up, occasional-use, low-bandwidth connectivity often get their actual Internet connection through one of these other ISPs. The type of connection you make to the Internet and the type of ISP through which connect have a lot to do with your connection reliability and responsiveness. The more layers between you and the backbone, the lower the reliability, availability, and responsiveness. Your ISP creates a local autonomous network (which includes your computer) and handles the gateway function of connecting to the actual Internet backbone and routing messages to and from your computer. In most cases your ISP also loans you a temporary, reusable IP address for your computer.

IPv4 and IPv6

For many years, IP has remained at a stable level—up to and including the fourth major release of the IP standard(s)—called, as you would expect, IPv4. In the late 1990s, when lack of IP addresses and the growing concern over the security and responsiveness of the Internet became major topics for discussion at the IETF, a new design was proposed and eventually led to the current release, IPv6. This latest version introduced a lot of improvements aimed at addressing the shortcomings of the prior version. As was already discussed, IPv6 introduced a much larger IP address and added the optional facility for built-in communications security (IP_{SEC}), among other enhancements.

Possibly just as important was the addition of performance guarantees for special quality of service (QoS) requests. Streaming real-time data over the Internet had been a problem holding back developments like voice (telephony) over IP (VoIP), video conferencing, streaming audio (Internet radio stations), and other applications. IPv6 added mechanisms for designating categories of message traffic that needed priority handling (quality of service and real-time service), so that end-to-end message delivery times can be kept under a minimally acceptable threshold. This would be an important consideration for any supervisory real-time monitoring and control application deployed across the Internet. SCADA system users need to know that if they click on a display to send a control to the field, that the control will be delivered to the remote within a guaranteed, acceptable time limit. Networks that can make such a guarantee are said to be highly deterministic. Until IPv6, the Internet (and IP networks in general) could not promise deterministic performance. If loading got heavy, response and delivery time could and would degrade.

As will be discussed in the next section, some forms of supervisory control models (e.g., pipeline leak detection) require a full data update, from all remotes, within a narrow time span in order to function properly. Within an IPv6 environment, this could be guaranteed, across any connection points on the Internet. Note that in a private IP network, where traffic could be controlled and limited, acceptably reliable message delivery times can be achieved, even with IPv4. However, on the Internet, you have no such ability to manage the traffic loading from moment to moment. This is why IPv6 enhancements for QoS are important. Nevertheless, remember the warning made earlier in the chapter: although the basic Internet backbone is now running IPv6, much of the equipment surrounding the Internet (in private corporate networks, ISPs, universities, etc.) are still running IPv4 and thus cannot take advantage of the enhancements introduced by IPv6. Only in 2004 did Microsoft upgrade the TCP/IP networking of their Windows operating systems to support IPv6 and its corresponding enhancements.

4

Supervisory Control Applications

The software that runs on a SCADA system (host), plus the data and configuration information it needs to perform its functions, is essentially the target of attack when we are discussing cybersecurity. Although it makes for great special effects at the movies, it is not actually possible to cause a computer to explode, spray a shower of electrical sparks, or burst into flames by sending it secret commands. It is, however, possible to shut down or disable a computer, or destroy valuable information stored on the computer, by sending the right commands.

The software that composes a SCADA system can be described in terms of layers. The first layer is the software that owns the computer and its resources and makes them available to application programs. That is the operating system layer. The next layer is the basic SCADA system functions—including RTU polling and communications, basic display generation, alarming and reporting, and other fundamental SCADA capabilities. The top layer consists of the advanced supervisory application programs that make use of the collected information to perform more advanced calculations and potentially send control commands back down to the RTUs in the field. Figure 4–1 shows this simple layering model.

Operating System Utilities

In the early days of SCADA system development, there were many vendors of computer hardware, each with their own proprietary designs.

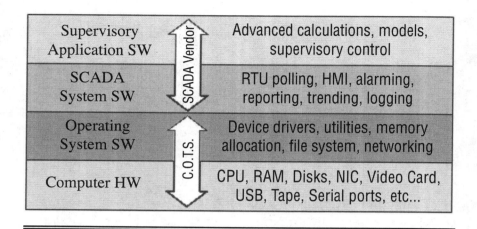

Fig. 4–1. *Software layers comprising a typical SCADA system host*

Most did not supply an operating system, as we know it today, with their computer equipment. A SCADA manufacturer would receive a set of program development and debugging tools (text editor, assembler, compiler, and simple debugger) and possibly a simple set of utility programs (file utility, diagnostic routines, copy program, etc.). All of the software needed to perform SCADA functions and to control and manage the computer hardware was up to the SCADA supplier to develop from scratch. In the 1980s, this changed as computer manufacturers began to provide at least rudimentary operating systems—and then more advanced, multi-user operating systems—along with their hardware. From the 1970s up to the present, the overall amount of software supplied by a SCADA vendor has probably increased, based on the growing list of advanced applications most vendors offer (fig. 4–2). However, in that same time frame, the percentage of basic software, including the functions performed by a modern operating system, has dropped to a minimal level. Also, because of the migration toward a standardized platform, many more third-party applications are available.

Today nearly every SCADA system sold runs on an Intel Pentium series–based (or compatible) computer platform, with either a Microsoft Windows or a Unix/Linux operating system. There are a few VAX/VMS–

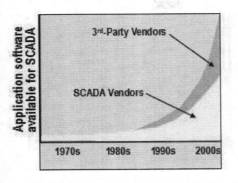 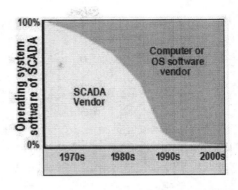

FIG. 4–2. *Evolution of SCADA software with commercial software*

and Sun/Solaris–based systems still being produced, but they are rapidly falling to the wayside. This consolidation of technologies and platforms has a beneficial side: very good application portability; availability of third-party vendor, "best of breed" layered applications; readily available technological resources for software support; lower cost of ownership; and a good migration path for long-term system hardware support. All of these provide good, financially sound business reasons to explain why this consolidation has occurred. Unfortunately many of these positives become negatives when considering the cyber vulnerability of SCADA systems. The problem is that there is a wealth of information publicly available about these operating systems and hardware platforms, including information about how to damage them, invade them, or cause them to malfunction. Hackers trade tidbits and techniques on their Web sites and sponsor contests to see who can break the latest protective measures introduced by companies like Cisco, Microsoft, and IBM. So you can assume that anyone desiring to attack your SCADA systems will have no difficulty obtaining expertise in at least the standardized operating system and its components, which form the underpinnings of the SCADA system.

Included within every commercial operating system are utility programs that are used to manage, administer, and configure the operating system and its components. (These should not be confused with the SCADA-specific system utilities, which are covered later in this section.)

Access to these utilities is a major objective of hackers. In most operating system configurations, these utilities may be restricted to only personnel with administrative rights, because of their complexity and the ability to wreak havoc if misused. Hackers have developed evil versions of many of these common utilities and would like nothing more that to substitute their versions for the real one. In the Unix/Linux world, this is possible because the source code for all such utilities is publicly available. For the Microsoft world, there are tools to decompile the machine code distributed by Microsoft (as well as occasional pirated copies of source code illegally released by insiders).

A major reason that hackers would want to plant a replacement utility on your system is that many of the utility programs run at the highest access level in the system and thus bypass all of the access-control protections. Aside from having hackers invade your systems by replacing real utilities with bogus copies containing *back doors,* just having an ill-intentioned employee gain unauthorized access to these utilities is also a security consideration. These utilities provide ways to peruse and even modify confidential information, to change the access rights of valid users and grant access rights to invalid users. Worse yet, some of these utilities can be used to destroy all of the critical information in a computer system and to disable the system itself. In most SCADA systems, the use of these system utilities should be totally restricted to the smallest possible number of qualified personnel.

The day-to-day operations of a SCADA system rarely require the use of these utilities. In fact, one way to identify tampering with a SCADA system is to monitor the access to these utilities by checking the system logs. When a SCADA system is fully operational and not undergoing a software or hardware update or an expansion, these utilities have little purpose in normal operations. For routine system administration purposes, some of these utilities may be needed. The same is true if system-level or application programming is taking place. Otherwise these utilities would not typically be used. (The one possible exception is the text editor, which may be used for routine operational functions, as long as it runs at the access/priority level of the operational staff member.) Table 4–1 describes typical system utilities, their function, and the personnel who would normally need access to such utilities.

Utility	Description/Misuse	Valid Access By
User account management	Allows adding, deleting and modifying user accounts and user access privileges. User can create new accounts and grant administrative rights to a user.	System administrator
Command line interpreter	Like the DOS tool in Windows. Provides command access to other system utilities and functions, generally at the "root" (system administrator) level.	System administrator System programmer
File/storage manager	Permits listing of files, creation of files and directories, copy and movement of files, deletion of files, modification of file protection settings, transfer or copy of file to removable media	System administrator System programmer
Task scheduler	Controls the time at which various programs are run and the frequency. Scheduling can be revised, postponed or cancelled. New tasks can be added to the queue. If event triggering supported then trigger causes can be modified or disabled	System administrator System programmer
Task manager	Displays running, blocked and paused tasks, allows priority changes, reallocation of CPU, blocking of tasks, elevation of task's access rights	System administrator
Network utilities (ftp, telnet, ping, etc.)	Used to transfer files between computers, gain remote access to the command line interpreter and to diagnose networking problems. Could be used to probe for vulnerabilities, to replace files, to 'map' a remote network and to misuse remote utilities	System administrator System programmer Network administrator
Network management utilities	Assign IP addresses and computer names, work group and domain names, network sharing of resources, peripherals and files, remote access rights, firewall administration, router administration, enable/disable ports and services	System administrator Network administrator
Peripheral configuration utilities	Setup parameters for various peripherals, define naming conventions, assign backup peripherals, enable and disable peripherals, modify their operation	System administrator
Relational database management	Create accounts and access rights to databases and tables, maintain tables, delete or empty tables, modify table structures, add/delete table entries	System administrator Database administrator System programmer
Printer management	Assign printers to given applications, groups, establish buffering and backup assignments, enable and disable printing	System administrator
Backup management	Defines where, when and what to copy to backup media, maintains audit trail of backups, controls mode of backup (full/incremental) and backup verification, controls number of backup versions and deletion of old backups	System administrator
Text editor	Examine file contents, creation of new BATCH files, editing of files, modify system setting files, modify configuration tables, modify BATCH scripts	System administrator System programmer Network administrator Database administrator

TABLE 4-1. *Standard operating system administrative utilities*

Because operating systems have differences, the utility programs are described in a generic manner, nonspecific to any particular operating system. Also, system tools used for program development and maintenance have been separated. These tools and utilities are addressed later in this section. SCADA system vendors generally have to rely on the security features built into the commercial hardware and operating systems they use as the basis for their systems. They may add additional layers of access control (for the SCADA portions of the system). However, they generally rely on commercial security solutions for their basic operating system and networking security.

In a later section, cybersecurity technologies, including *intrusion-detection systems* (IDSs), will be discussed in detail. Essentially, an IDS is like a burglar alarm for a computer and/or computer network. One way to monitor for intrusions (or irregular use of the system utilities) is by learning the typical ways that various system software is used: by whom, with what frequency, for how long, using how much memory and CPU time, on what days, and so forth. When setting up an IDS, it is important that the access to standard operating system utilities be monitored. A more difficult problem arises when a bogus copy of a utility is substituted for the real one. There are ways to attach a *digital signature* to a program so that you can verify its authenticity and absence of modifications, but most operating systems don't support this capability (yet). Another way to detect such tampering is by noting that such a utility is suddenly doing things it never did previously (e.g., sending outgoing IP messages to another computer). An IDS can spot such activity and alert the system administrator, who can reinstall the proper software from vendor-supplied backup media.

SCADA System Utilities

Just as a basic operating system will come with a set of standard utilities, a basic SCADA system will include specialized utilities necessary for SCADA system configuration, maintenance, modification, and expansion (not for normal operational use). These are utilities specific to the SCADA system vendor and particular SCADA software package(s). While a generic hacker will probably not have familiarity with these utilities (or with SCADA systems), a terrorist (or a disaffected ex-employee) who intends to target a specific SCADA system can be assumed to have access to the necessary documentation and even vendor training or personnel with practical experience with this specific model of SCADA system. Keeping track of who uses what SCADA system utilities is more difficult, as the various utilities may be required on a regular basis or when problems arise. It is often more difficult to establish a normal usage pattern for these utilities. However, as with the operating system utilities, not everyone needs access to these utilities, and their use should be restricted.

Most SCADA systems include an additional level of operational access control that is incremental to and separate from that provided by the computer operating system. Access to SCADA system utilities and configuration tools may—or may not—require this additional level of authorization. Some less sophisticated SCADA systems merely rely on the computer operating system passwords and access controls to restrict access to SCADA utilities. This is a less preferable scheme, because people who may need access to operating system functions often have no reason to utilize SCADA utilities and tools (or adequate training) and vice versa.

It is commonplace for the majority of SCADA system vendors to further restrict access to SCADA utilities by either job function or with specific user access authority. Thus, a senior system operator (Fred) may be granted access to use the graphical display editor, whereas an operator trainee (Joe) would be refused access. Fred's SCADA system login and password would define his access to SCADA utilities and functions, separate from any operating system access he may have. In fact, Fred may have *no* operating system access rights and yet have full SCADA system access rights.

One of the most critical of the SCADA utilities is the user account management utility, which is used to grant access rights to the SCADA system operational and support personnel (fig. 4–3). In most SCADA systems, this utility provides a means for determining the specific set of resources available to a given user and the limits on how those resources can be used. In that aspect, this utility is much like the account management software of the operating system, except that it specifically deals in SCADA system resources. The assignment of access rights in a large percentage of SCADA systems is along job category lines. A senior operator, for example, will have more access rights than an operator trainee. Often the main purpose for such security is oriented more toward prevention of human errors than protection against a cyber assault.

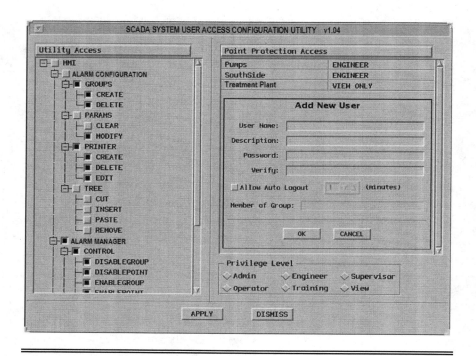

FIG. 4–3. *SCADA system user account management utility*

Table 4–2 lists standard SCADA system utilities, their function, and typical access frequency during normal operations. As mentioned before, each SCADA system vendor will have its own utilities, which may be slightly different in name, organization, and function from those given in table 4–2; but a good representation of the basic SCADA utilities found in most, if not all, SCADA systems is provided.

The SCADA functions of a system normally provide for a wide range of operational configuration flexibility, since a given vendor's SCADA product needs to be able to accommodate a wide range of application and industry variations. Many of the SCADA utilities exist for the purpose of setting up customer-specific and application-specific configuration tables that direct the actions of the generic SCADA software modules (fig. 4–4). For example, the number of polling channels, the number of RTUs per channel, baud rate per channel, and protocol to be used on each channel are all customer-specific configuration parameters that would need to be defined in order for the SCADA system to perform its RTU polling duties.

Utility Type	Description/Use	Usage Frequency
User account management	Allows the creation of a new user, changing access rights, deleting users	Infrequent, only when personnel changes are made
Configuration	Modification of physical and or logical configuration of system, adding or removing RTUs, polling channels, operator consoles	Frequently during initial system commissioning and then again when system expansions or changes are made. Otherwise not used.
Database	Edit, delete, expand, the database definitions, space allocations, supported types, logical groupings, access levels	Constantly during initial system commissioning and then again when system expansions or changes are made. Otherwise not used.
RTU downloading	Initiate download of parameters, configuration, initial programming, database information, local calculations, new firmware, local control logic	During initial RTU installation and commissioning and again if RTUs are repaired or replaced. Otherwise not used.
RTU polling	Assign RTU polling priority, add or remove from polling, force a poll, inhibit polling, change polling parameters	During initial RTU installation and commissioning and again if RTUs are repaired or replaced. Otherwise not used.
RTU diagnostics	Run tests on RTU, control outputs, read inputs, force tests of RTU HW and communications, read inputs and control outputs	During initial RTU installation and commissioning and again if RTUs are repaired or replaced. Otherwise not used.
HMI configuration	Setup the semi-automatic and automatic displays, assign displays to groups, set up navigation, assign access requirements	Frequently during initial system commissioning and then again when system expansions or changes are made. Otherwise not used.
HMI custom display editor	Build and modify custom graphics, assign controls, set links to other functions, set up program triggers	Frequently during initial system commissioning and then again when system expansions or changes are made. Otherwise not frequently used.
Operator access management	Define and modify the specific levels of access (run/read/modify) assigned for each user category, utilities allowed, fields and controls allowed for user access, modification	Infrequent. Mainly used for initial system setup and commissioning. Rarely used thereafter.
Operator log	Manual log book for recording of operational information and for passing important messages and notices between operational shifts. Messages can be entered, listed, printed, removed, messages can be directed to job categories, specific personnel, and can have pre-defined topics for sorting purposes. Messages automatically time tagged and operator tagged on entry	Used constantly during normal operations
Alarm management	Defining and modifying alarm levels and thresholds, defining alarm annunciation options, enable/disable alarming on points and groups, creation of alarm groups, enable or disable alarm notification, assign printers to alarm levels and groups	Frequently during initial system commissioning and then again when system expansions or changes are made. Otherwise not used.
Trending management	Assigns values to be collected, removes values from collection, edit archive files,	Frequently during initial system commissioning and then again when

TABLE 4–2. *Standard SCADA configuration maintenance and management utilities*

	purge archive files, change collection intervals, set storage durations	system expansions or changes are made. Some functions may be used on a regular basis for system administration purposes
Reporting package	Configure report formats and content, define calculations, define values to be reported, define report triggering events and time triggers, remove reports from list	Frequently during initial system commissioning and then again when system expansions or changes are made. Otherwise not frequently used.
Computations and calculations	Define, modify and delete calculated values, adjust calculation parameters, assign re-calculation intervals	Frequently during initial system commissioning and then again when system expansions or changes are made. Otherwise not used.
Logging	Assign alarms and events to logging, remove from logging, print logs, purge logs, assign printing and archive directory to logs, define log retention intervals, define operator and other user actions to be logged, define other activities to be logged, remove activities from logging	Frequently during initial system commissioning and then again when system expansions or changes are made. Some functions may be used on a regular basis for system administration purposes
Data exchange	Setup values and status and controls to be exchanged, assign placement and scaling of values in exchange messages, add or remove points, controls and functions offered to the exchange partner	Frequently during initial inter-system link commissioning and testing and then again when system expansions or changes are made. Otherwise not used.
Redundancy synchronization	Establish the trigger events for fail over to backup, establish schedule for data update of backup computer, enable or disable fail over function, enable or disable data synchronization functions	Used during the initial commissioning and testing of the system. Not normally used thereafter.

TABLE 4–2 (CONT.).

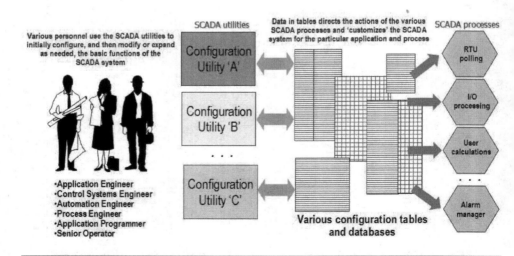

FIG. 4–4. *SCADA configuration utilities*

Configuration activities go well beyond merely setting up the polling channels. It is necessary to describe each and every input and output that the SCADA system is to process for every one of the RTUs. The description for each I/O signal (point) includes assigning a *tag name* to the signal, defining what type of signal it is, providing all of the processing and alarm-checking information necessary to manipulate the point, defining the frequency at which the point is to be processed, the actions to take if the point's value exceeds acceptable limits, and many other items.

The process of filling in all of the necessary tables with detailed configuration data used to direct the collection and processing of RTU I/O is sometimes called *building the tag/point database*. In addition to the actual physical inputs from the field, SCADA systems also generally compute a large number of other values using the inputs from the field-based RTUs, manually entered parameters and even archived data. These may be simple or complex numeric calculations or even logical (Boolean) calculations that produce a true/false result. In many SCADA systems, the point definition database creation utility may also be used to define these pseudo-points whose values are derived by user-defined calculations (fig. 4–5). If not the calculations themselves, the point definition creation utility may at least be used to assign alarm checks and display parameters to these pseudo points. The point (or *tag*) database contains information that will be used to direct the host computer's collection and processing of the RTU inputs, and in the case of smart RTUs, some of this information may be downloaded into the RTUs themselves. If any of the logic or calculations needs to be performed in the RTU, then these definitions would need to be sent to the respective RTUs. If an RTU needed to have engineering unit values for local calculations, control or display purposes, then engineering unit (EGU) conversion factors, and possibly even alarm limits, would need to be downloaded into the respective RTUs. And finally, if the RTUs are to perform control and sequence logic, this will need to be defined and loaded into the respective RTUs. All of this information definition and data entry takes a lot of time and energy and is a large portion of the overall manpower invested in system implementation.

Intentional or accidental corruption of the SCADA system's configuration tables can cause a partial or total loss of a SCADA system's operability. Undetected corruption of or modification to configuration

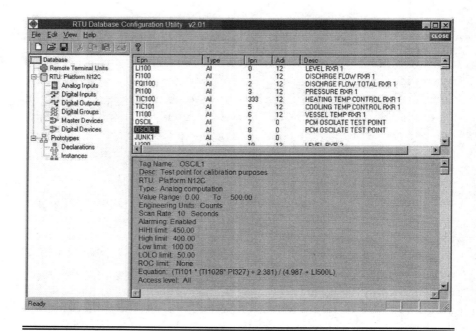

FIG. 4–5. *Database point and calculated point creation utility*

tables can cause bad data to be presented to operational personnel and supervisory application programs. Most SCADA systems have some ability to check their databases for corruption and errors. In some cases this can be done online (while the system is operating), possibly even on a continuous basis. In other cases an off-line diagnostic check may be required. Incorrect (accidental) configuration information has been known to cause mis-operation of equipment and even equipment damage. One of the most important tests performed on a SCADA system, prior to its being put into production, is a point-by-point verification of each input and output definition, preferable spanning from the actual RTU I/O all the way to the HMI displays.

Many SCADA systems maintain a tracking/audit log of modifications made to the various databases (*if* modifications were made using vendor-supplied SCADA system utilities). Some SCADA systems make use of commercial relational database packages to hold their configuration information. In those cases it could be possible to examine and modify table entries without using the SCADA system utilities, thus circumventing the modification-tracking process. Remember that these modification-tracking processes were established to aid in correcting human errors, not for the specific purpose of system cybersecurity.

Full configuration of a SCADA system involves much more than just building the point database. SCADA systems have to present information to human operators, and although most systems support some level of automatically created displays, most SCADA system operational personnel work from customized, graphical displays that have to be created using an editor utility. SCADA systems have included graphical editors for creating custom displays since the 1970s, although the graphical quality and sophistication have obviously improved since. The graphical display editor (fig. 4–6) allows the development of customer-specific displays that can be

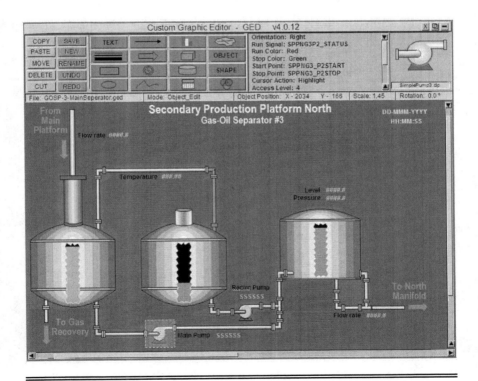

FIG. 4–6. *Graphical display editor*

built without any need for programming. Custom graphical displays can incorporate actual images, schematic representations, a variety of drawing elements, and even audio and video clips. Such displays generally present a set of user-selected inputs and outputs, with color coding and animation to indicate potential problems, in addition to the use of graphical elements to convey the process/plant operating conditions.

These same displays usually provide control access to physical outputs via a select-and-command sequence built into the graphical display. In addition to direct controls, the displays may offer access to user adjustable parameters and even to alarming functions. One of the security issues relative to SCADA systems is the level at which access controls are enforced. In some systems, operator access control is enforced within the HMI package. Each graphical display makes checks based on the user currently logged in to an operator's console and based on logic in the HMI package. This means that if someone could access and modify the graphical editor, it would be possible to create a graphic that did not make such checks and then to run that graphical display to gain inappropriate control access. Most SCADA systems place access control information directly into the point database and embed access verification in the underlying database level. This prevents evil graphical displays (and application programs) from bypassing access control mechanisms. In many systems the access to all I/O (and the point database) is managed by a central access library that makes authority checks on the rights of the calling application, regardless of it being a graphical display or an optimization routine. Such an access library can also make safety checks (e.g., Is the requested control point tagged?) and reasonability checks (e.g., Invalid to send an analog value to a contact input!) So that access controls cannot be bypassed, it is essential that such a centralized mechanism be in place and itself protected from tampering. Obviously the tables (access control lists, tag lists, user ID lists, etc.) that such a library uses also need to be protected from tampering. Insuring this integrity is a basic cyber security concern.

There are many more SCADA system utilities, as can be seen from table 4–2, but we are not going to explore and discuss them all. The important issue in regard to SCADA system cybersecurity is to control access to these utilities, track their usage, and employ whatever protective measures are available to restrict their usage to suitably trained and appropriately authorized personnel. From a SCADA systems security design standpoint, enforcing access controls and security policies (for users and application programs) and insuring configuration integrity, are primary objectives.

Program Development Tools

Separate from operating system utility programs and SCADA system utility programs are the system and application programming tools included with most SCADA systems. These are generally a combination of programming tools provided by the operating system vendor (compilers, editors, debuggers, etc.) plus additional extensions added by the SCADA system vendor. A system may provide general-purpose programming tools, as well as specialized application-oriented programming languages that are unique to a given SCADA system product. For the most part, developing and running user-defined application programs is a tricky business that requires knowledge of both the operating system and the SCADA system. It is important to ensure that customer-developed applications don't interfere with the essential functions of the SCADA system. In theory a badly written program, when allowed to run at a very high priority level, could usurp most or all of the processing power of the CPU and the main memory of the computer, thus effectively shutting down the SCADA system. One reason that most SCADA system owners maintain a separate development system (versus the production system) is so that application programs (as well as configuration changes, operating system patches, and even SCADA software updates) can be tested in a noncritical environment. Some SCADA system owners actually remove the program development tools and utilities from their production systems so that it is impossible to develop application software on those systems. Unfortunately, most pre-production testing of application programs is done by the same programmer that also wrote the program. This opens up the real possibility of having a timebomb or Trojan function embedded within the application code. With the outsourcing of software development to foreign contractors, the possibility of having this happen is even greater. Only recently have strides been made in the technology of automatically checking program logic for hidden logic, and most software will never be subjected to such tests (what SCADA system operator has access to such technology?) A procedural strategy to prevent the introduction of malicious applications into production systems is to have a different programmer review the program source code, compile, build and then verify or test program operation. Breaking up an activity so that multiple people are needed to perform it to completion is called *separation of duties* and is a common practice in financial institutions and the intelligence community

Most SCADA vendors have attempted to provide a wide range of configurable utilities that address the vast majority of functions required by their customers, to eliminate or at least minimize the need for custom application programming. This is partially a defensive move, as badly written applications can degrade (or block) the operation of the basic SCADA system. When there is no choice but to address a unique need with custom-developed application software, most SCADA vendors prefer to perform this programming work (and be paid to do so) because of their expertise and knowledge of the inner workings of the SCADA software. Although the migration to standardized operating system platforms has made it possible for third-party vendors to supply certain types of application software, most SCADA vendors don't like to have software supplied by others running on their systems. (Some vendors will test and validate third-party applications and provide a list of these approved packages.)

The emergence of standardized APIs, such as OPC, has made it easy for third-party suppliers to produce software that integrates well with various SCADA products. When custom applications must be developed, most SCADA system vendors provide specialized *software libraries* that can be incorporated alongside the user-developed programming and that provide a range of pretested functions that connect the application programs to the SCADA system (fig. 4–7). Some of these functions may also (if used) ensure that user-developed application programs don't violate access controls or usurp system resources. Of course this assumes that the author of such application software actually wants to write a safe and properly controlled application. In most SCADA systems, the special library functions extend the base set of functions that a programming language such as C/C++ would include (e.g., file reading/writing, math functions, peripheral device read/write, and date/time functions). These special library functions provide controlled access (and even logging of such access) to various SCADA system components and information. A well-designed SCADA system incorporates security mechanisms that cannot be bypassed so that the only way for an application program to have access to system resources and facilities is by calling upon the vendor-supplied library. This should be true for both customer developed and vendor-personnel developed applications. Obviously the system needs a means for verifying the integrity and authenticity of this library. But this is true for all of the SCADA system utilities and databases.

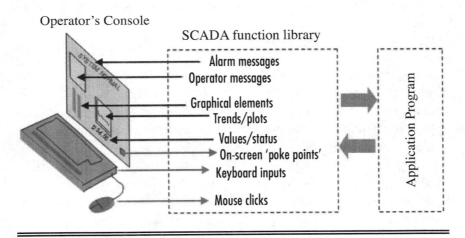

FIG. 4–7. *Application program interacting with HMI via SCADA library functions*

Some vendors even supply pretested application program templates that, if used as the basis for custom-written applications, ensure that these applications are well behaved, clean up prior to exiting, don't leak memory, and run at a suitably low level of priority (relative to critical SCADA system functions). This assumes that the authors of all application programs will follow the rules and use these templates. It has generally been assumed, by SCADA vendors and their customers, that all application programs will be developed and then thoroughly tested prior to being deployed, and thus there is no need to make run-time checks on what those application programs are doing. Making run-time checks on applications does add a performance penalty, and to a degree, that is what an intrusion detection system is for. It watches to see if applications start doing weird and atypical things. (Intrusion detection technology will be discussed in a later chapter.) In order to prevent the running of malicious (or just really badly written) applications, a SCADA system essentially needs to eliminate general-purpose programming tools and replace them with vendor-specific versions that force programmers to adhere to predefined rules and guidelines. One reason that vendors supply special application-oriented languages is that these give the vendor control over what a programmer can, and cannot, do.

Application programs normally have unrestricted access to all components of the SCADA system. Some of the SCADA system components that could typically be made available to an application programmer, via such a library, are listed in table 4–3. As should be obvious, application programs normally have a great deal of access to vital system tables and databases. An evil application program could seriously damage and disrupt the operation of a SCADA system. The process of application program development, testing and deployment needs to be made as secure as possible with adequate checks and verifications made at key points. The installation of new applications onto a production SCADA system ought to be viewed as a rare and dangerous event during which security procedures need to be followed. Access to operating system level services and objects (like files) is a separate issue, but application programs ought to be restricted from having direct (non-verified) access to these capabilities. Some SCADA vendors replace standard C/C++ header files and libraries with special versions that inject access verification checks where appropriate.

Scripting languages are another way for SCADA vendors to provide user customization while maintaining control of the system resources and integrity. A scripting language is normally a high-level programming language that is specifically tailored to perform supervisory control functions and includes advanced language features that access system functions in a controlled manner. Such languages are called high level because they tend to be functional (what to do) rather than procedural (how to do it) as are low level languages. A scripting language doesn't normally generate actual computer program code. It is translated into data that are processed by a

SCADA component/Data	Functions
Alarm manager	Read current alarm log entries, append entry to alarm log, read and modify alarm limits on points and enable/disable alarming on points and groups
Real-time database	Read the current value/status of any input or computed point value. Read, change any parameters or settings in the database tables
Configuration file/table access	Read, modify, delete configuration table entries
Log read/write	Read log entries, append to logs, delete logs, delete entries
HMI interaction	Establish trigger events and data inputs from operational displays, write data to display objects and regions, send messages to operator consoles, adjust the values of displayed data, manipulate graphical objects. Cause pop up windows to appear, redirect console to alternate display page(s)
Historical data access	Read historical data, append to historical data file
Supervisory control	Send control commands out to RTUs to manipulate analog, pulse and contact outputs. Modify values of supervisory points. Run/stop local control logic in RTUs
Parameter changing	Read and modify parameters including calculation constants, timers, counters, durations, change settings such as on/off scan, on/off poll

TABLE 4–3. *Typical SCADA application programming library functions*

vendor-supplied *interpreter* program allowing the vendor to strictly control both what such a script can (and cannot) do and the resources allocated for (and priority of) script execution. Scripts are often used to perform a long sequence of checks and/or to manage long and involved supervisory control procedures that would normally be done manually and interactively via an operator's console.

Scripts are often linked to poke points on operational displays, so that they can be initiated by operators through a simple mouse click. They may also be linked to and triggered by alarm conditions and even the system clock and calendar function. (Run this script to refill that tank every week day at 2:00 AM.) The scripting language restricts the user from getting access to anything other than what the scripting language provides. The vendor's script execution software (the interpreter) ensures that scripts can't run too often or run forever or usurp excessive amounts of memory and CPU time. Nevertheless, most SCADA system supervisory scripting languages are designed for automatic supervisory control, and thus scripts can reach out to the RTUs and manipulate outputs, making them a danger, if not properly validated. (Scripts with unintentional errors have caused enough problems, imagine what an intentionally malicious one could do!)

Thus the development, testing, and installation of supervisory control scripts, onto production SCADA systems, needs to be treated with the same care and cautions as suggested for user-developed application programs. The following example of a supervisory control script demonstrates some of the capabilities of such languages, particularly the ability to effect automatic, supervisory control of field equipment:

```
** Script to bring pump station 81N to maximum
   pumping state

** Begin by starting all three pumps

ENABLE COMMAND LOGGING

** Set bypass valves for re-circulate mode

COMMAND VLV3N2C4 TO CLOSE

COMMAND VLV3N11D TO OPEN

WAIT FOR ALL COMMANDS TO COMPLETE OR FAIL IN 120
   SECONDS

IF NOT FAILED

   COMMAND PUMP3N1 TO RUN

   WAIT TILL PI3N1D EXCEEDS 22.0 PSIG

   COMMAND PUMP3N2 TO RUN

   WAIT TILL PI3N1D EXCEEDS 45.0 PSIG

   COMMAND PUMP3N3 TO RUN

** All pumps running, now end re-circulation mode

   COMMAND VLV3N2F TO OPEN

   WAIT FOR 60 SECONDS

   COMMAND VLV3N11D TO CLOSE
```

```
WAIT FOR ALL COMMANDS TO COMPLETE

NOTIFY OPERATOR "Pump Station 3N running at
full capacity"

EXIT

** If both bypass valves did not operate properly

IF FAILED

     NOTIFY OPERATOR "Command timeout on Pump
     Station 81N"

     END COMMAND LOGGING

     EXIT
```

A malicious supervisory script (or application) could send out commands to operate process equipment in a manner that causes equipment damage, disrupts operations and even creates a hazard to health or life. Some SCADA system owners require that supervisory control applications and scripts be developed with added steps that call for human confirmation of all control and parameter change functions. In such a scheme the program/script would reach a point where control was called for and pop up a message asking the operator for permission. In some cases the operator is given 'x' seconds to either approve or abort the action, or else the program/script defaults to 'approved' and implements the action. This is fine for applications that run infrequently, but if an operator has to constantly hit the approved button, it becomes automatic and reflexive and the operator doesn't even look to see what is about to happen. Also, inclusion of operator permission checking is not enforced by technical means, making its inclusion something left to the programmer to incorporate. One way to enhance SCADA security would be to have operator permission checking embedded in the scripting language (and access library), for any controls or parameters designated (during system configuration) as critical. Thus the system would enforce such an authorization check, regardless of a programmer including it in his program logic.

Standardized APIs

When SCADA system vendors started consolidating their products onto standard operating system and hardware platforms in the 1990s, this opened up the possibility of having application software developed by third-party vendors—in the same way that anyone can develop software for a Microsoft Windows/Intel (Wintel) platform. All SCADA systems have to deal with the collection and movement of both real-time and historical data, including moving these data (bidirectionally) between applications and the places where the SCADA system maintains this data. To manage this activity and make program design more uniform, most SCADA systems include some form of API, offering a well-defined means for application programmers to request and exchange real-time and historical data.

Originally vendors devised their own proprietary APIs, since no one else was going to supply software to run on their systems! In the 1990s a lot of work went into defining standards for APIs on the commercial/business side of computing, and the standards that resulted eventually found their way into the SCADA systems because of their adoption by the operating system vendors. Although there was often a goal of nonpartisanship when defining standards, they all eventually fell into either the Unix/Linux camp or the Microsoft camp. Today you will find SCADA systems that incorporate one or more of the following popular APIs.

OPC

OPC is a data-exchange standard that came out of the process control world as a result of work done to interface PC-based graphical display packages (e.g., the FIX and Wonderware) with PLCs and other smart devices. In the beginning, these devices mainly used slow-speed, serial communications to exchange data, often with the well-known Modbus protocol. This protocol was ill designed for handling the more complex types of data that were commonly available in such devices and originally did not support an Ethernet LAN version. OPC defined a more sophisticated set of client/server interface mechanisms so that complex data (data with time and quality tags, sequence of events, etc.) could be exchanged among applications running on the same (or different) computer and so that multiclient/multiserver equipment configurations could be built on top of a high-speed Ethernet LAN (fig. 4–8).

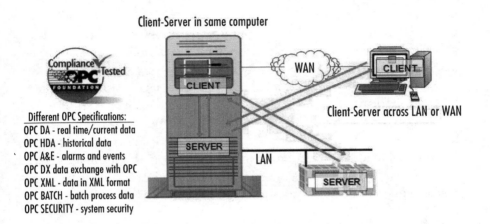

FIG. 4–8. *OPC client/server types and configuration alternatives*

Today several commercially available SCADA systems are built from hardware and software components from multiple manufacturers, with intercomponent data exchanges (often over LANs and even WANs) done via OPC. Importantly—and typical of pre-9/11 product and standards development—OPC had no intrinsic security features (although at present it is being extended to support some) and has several well-known security vulnerabilities. OPC is an API for a Microsoft Windows operating system environment, as it makes use of the Microsoft OLE and Distributed Common Object Model (DCOM) features. (OPC vulnerabilities will be discussed in more detail in a later section of the book.) Recently, work has begun on making a platform independent variation of OPC that uses XML (eXtensible Markup Language) for data exchange. Of course there is a huge installed base of OPC-based systems that do not incorporate any of the new features or security extensions.

Standard Query Language

The Standard Query Language (SQL) is not an API per se, but in many SCADA systems, the mechanism for exchanging data with other systems, or between sophisticated application programs, is to pass it through tables in a relational database server (fig. 4–9). (Some types of applications, like pipeline models, involve so much data and configuration information, that the application uses relational tables for its own storage. GIS applications normally use relational database tables to hold their data as well.) This scheme is facilitated through the availability of a platform-independent database query language (i.e., SQL) and the migration of popular SQL-compliant relational database packages onto Wintel and Linux/Unix platforms. SQL implementations vary in their level of error checking and validity checking, but in general it can be assumed that current levels of security are insufficient and that there are vulnerabilities that can be exploited to attack a relational database or the applications that interact with and through such databases. SQL-compliant relational database are available in both the Microsoft world and the Unix/Linux world.

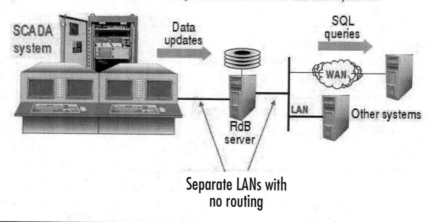

FIG. 4–9. *Using a SQL-compliant relational database server to exchange SCADA data*

Common Object Request Broker Architecture

The Unix world was a much more diverse place in the late 1980s and 1990s, as many different computer hardware manufacturers accepted that their own proprietary operating systems were waning in popularity and that a Unix implementation might be a good marketing move. Digital, IBM, and Hewlett-Packard (among others) came out with their own versions of Unix. Although these systems did share a Unix heritage, they were nevertheless incompatible hardware platforms. One of the holy grails of the computing world has been to allow cross-platform, distributed computing, without regard for the make or model of the computers involved. We seem to be reaching that point today, but only because all of the computers will actually be the same (Intel or equivalent).

One effort that came out of work toward that end was the Common Object Request Broker Architecture (CORBA). This was a set of cross-platform services and communication mechanisms, as well as an API, that allowed programs running on one computer to request services (look up a value in a database, perform a statistical calculation, etc.) from another computer, without having to deal with the incompatibility issues. Larger, multi-computer SCADA systems, based on Unix variants, have employed CORBA for their data exchange mechanisms. CORBA also lacked security mechanisms, although committee efforts are underway to address this shortcoming. Originally, CORBA was to be ported to all computing platforms, even Microsoft Windows variants, but Microsoft decided to devise their own, proprietary scheme (with some justification).

A particular implementation of cross-application/computer data exchanges using the CORBA approach is being used in the electric power industry. A group of utilities have cooperated in creating the Utility Information Bus (UIB), which is a specific implementation of CORBA with a layer of customization to address the particular types of data found in the various computer systems (including SCADA) used by electric utilities. UIB is a class of middleware that offers publish-and-subscribe mechanisms for sending data only as it changes, from the place where the data is maintained to all applications that need to know when that data changes.

DCOM

Not to be outdone, as CORBA was being promoted in the Unix world, Microsoft fought back with its own version: the Common Object Model, which was for a single computer on which applications needed to communicate; this was followed by DCOM, which worked across networks. Once again DCOM, as with all of the other APIs, did not include inherent security mechanisms. Microsoft, to its credit, has been adding them as quickly as vulnerabilities are uncovered and reported. As was mentioned above, the OPC standard was built upon the DCOM services offered by Microsoft and so the vulnerabilities in DCOM correspond directly to vulnerabilities in OPC.

ICCP

Ever since the early days of SCADA, the electric power industry has needed to exchange information between local SCADA systems and regional/district control centers. In an effort to standardize these data exchanges, the industry devised ICCP (also called TASE.2 and UCA1.0) to provide a mechanism for automatic data exchanges. Initially ICCP was designed to run as an application layer on top of an OSI/ISO seven-layer protocol stack, but in the past 10 years, with the success of TCP/IP, almost all implementations now use that protocol (IP) as the underlying network stack. ICCP has been extended to support a basic level of authentication (association of control system elements [ACSE]), although this is optional and not always implemented. Because it is normally carried by an underlying IP network, it is possible to use conventional security mechanisms (VPN, link encryption, etc.) to secure an ICCP connection.

UCA2.0

In the past 8–10 years, work has gone forward within the electric and water utility industries to define an all-encompassing data and communications architecture that can connect any data source to any user of that data. Although progress in fully defining and promoting this standard has not been without problems, it has started making inroads with some utilities and product manufacturers. Various manufacturers of protective relays and substation equipment now offer UCA2.0 communications, and there have been numerous demonstrations of the various components of this rather broad standard. Within a facility, UCA2.0 utilizes high-speed (100 Mbps, switched) Ethernet LAN technology. Between facilities and to upper-level supervisory systems, the standard provides for transport over IP networks and even low-bandwidth serial connections. UCA2.0 also suffers from a lack of security mechanisms and is vulnerable to attacks on the underlying communications transport mechanisms. But like ICCP, if it is transported across an IP network, conventional security mechanisms can be applied.

Although most of these popular APIs have no intrinsic security mechanisms (as opposed to error detection, correction, and prevention mechanisms), if they are used in distributed system architectures that communicate across a LAN/WAN, it is often possible to tunnel them with VPN technology (for a discussion of VPN technology, see chap. 3). This does not eliminate the security vulnerabilities present with applications that are co-residing on the same computer and using one of these data-exchange mechanisms. All such mechanisms accomplish is to prevent inter-application message traffic to be tampered with or falsified as it traverses the intervening IP network.

Operator Interface

Access-Control Mechanisms

Once a SCADA system is installed, commissioned, and placed into continuous operation, it is primarily the system operators who interact with the system and use the system to monitor and control the target process and field equipment. Other personnel still have to maintain and administer the SCADA system and perform routine housekeeping and support functions, but it is the operational staff who predominately access the system on a constant basis.

When you enter the control room of a SCADA system, depending on the industry and the age of the system, you are frequently faced with rows of equipment consoles filled with color CRT displays. You may also see wall-sized informational displays based on projection video technology or mosaic-tile panel board technology. You may even find instrument panels with chart/pen recorders, indicator lamps, and manual, push-button controls. Figure 5–1 shows a simple control room design that includes two separate consoles filled with CRT displays; a multi-window projection video wall, onto which live data from any of the CRT screens can be directed; and a master clock. The two consoles allow two operational groups (or two operators) to deal with different problems simultaneously (and provide equipment redundancy). For logging and reporting purposes (and so that hard copy printouts of screen images can be made), the operating consoles each include a set of printer/loggers. Of course there are also small SCADA systems that consist of a desktop PC, a printer, and a master radio, all sitting on a desk in the corner. Pipeline and electric transmission utilities tend to have the big, fancy control rooms.

Small water utilities and rural electric cooperatives (RECs) tend to have the desktop SCADA systems.

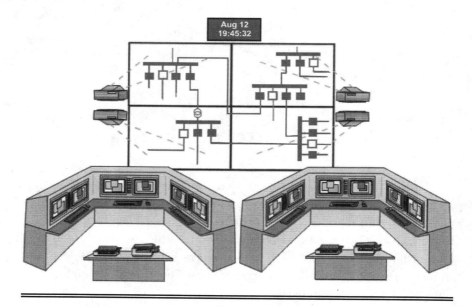

FIG. 5–1. *Example SCADA system control room console design*

The purpose of all this equipment is to give operational personnel a real-time view of the state of the process they are monitoring and to provide them with a means for initiating control actions, as necessary. Obviously, we don't want unauthorized (or untrained) personnel making use of the system and controlling field equipment. So that only authorized personnel have access to the system (aside from physical isolation and protection of the equipment), all SCADA systems include some type of access-control mechanism. In the vast majority of cases, this is an ID/password scheme, whereby either each user or each category of user is issued a unique ID/password pair that enables (and disables) the functions and features authorized for this user or category of user. The problem with such protective measures is that people don't change or protect their passwords, they log in to system consoles and never log out, and they even let other people use their passwords; in addition, most vendors build in secret passwords (known to only every current and former employee of that vendor plus anyone who has ever gone to them for formal classroom training) that they can use when customers get locked out of their own systems. Password protection is better employed for reducing human errors and providing an audit trail of activity than it is for cyber-protective purposes. Also, in most computer systems today, the operating system–level passwords are protected by stored in an encrypted form. In some SCADA systems, which have a separate password scheme for system operator login, those IDs and passwords are stored in an ordinary database table or a text file, making them easy prey for someone with computer skills.

ID/password schemes are used for the purpose of *authentication*—in other words, proving that a person actually is who they claim to be. ID/password schemes are far too easily foiled, and thus you can't rely on them to ensure that a person using the ID/password of Fred Smith *could be only* Fred and no one else. The basic problem of computer-based authentication is that a computer can only judge by the data provided, it can't see you or recognize your voice (yet). Recently, some SCADA system vendors have started offering *strong authentication* technology, in the form of multifactor identification schemes, or even using biometric technology. Strong authentication technology will be discussed in detail in the next section. Suffice it to say that strong authentication schemes are aimed at ensuring that Fred must be Fred, in order for him to gain access to the system, and that no one else can successfully pretend to be Fred. Authentication schemes have taken on a much greater importance with the ability of SCADA systems to support remote users and operators. A stranger wandering into a SCADA control room would probably be stopped and questioned, because others would not recognize an intruder. But a stranger coming into the SCADA system electronically, via some remote networking technology or via telephone access has to be recognized by the authentication software of the SCADA system. If the only mechanism for personnel recognition and access control is an ID/password scheme, then the SCADA system is far too vulnerable. One way to make remote access more secure is to use VPN technology, not just because this protects the message traffic between the SCADA system and the remote user, but because most VPN technologies require additional authentication in the form of a *dongle* or a *challenge-response* scheme. This, in effect, when combined with the user ID/password login, provides multi-factor (strong) authentication.

Standard System Displays

All SCADA systems collect real-time and historical information and then provide operational personnel with a wide range of modes in which this information can be displayed and accessed. With most SCADA systems, there are process-related (operational) displays and system-related (diagnostic) displays. We have already discussed the wide range of operating system and SCADA system utility programs that are used to initially configure the SCADA system to perform the necessary tasks. The displays and presentation modes discussed in this section have been created using those utility programs or automatically created using the data provided during the configuration process.

Diagnostic displays

From time to time, it will be necessary to be able to examine the operational performance of the SCADA system and verify that it is functioning properly or to make adjustments or modifications as needed. All SCADA systems provide a set of system diagnostic displays that allow operational and maintenance personnel to check and adjust various aspects of SCADA system operation. A very common SCADA diagnostic display would be an RTU polling channel status display—showing the current polling status of the individual RTUs and the communications robustness of the various polling channels, as well as diagnostic error counters and indicators. Such a display will also often provide a means for altering polling assignments and polling priorities, placing a polling channel in and out of service, and placing RTUs on and off polling. Figure 5–2 gives an example of such an RTU polling and communications diagnostic and configuration display. Obviously access to, and manipulation of the controls and settings in such diagnostic displays, needs to be controlled through suitable authorization mechanisms. An untrained, or malicious, user could disable polling on critical remotes.

Another typical diagnostic display supplied with most SCADA systems is a system operational status display that shows the gross operational status of the equipment and peripherals that form the system's hardware basis. With some systems this is an automatically generated tabular display,

| | RTU POLLING LIST – CHANNEL ASSIGNMENTS SC-01 | | | | | | | | | | | | | | | NEXT | PRIOR |

RTU Drop	CHANNEL 0 1200 baud PG&E				CHANNEL 1 1200 baud PG&E				CHANNEL 2 2400 baud DNP3.0				CHANNEL 3 1200 baud CDC-T1			
	ACT	PRI	ERR	RTY	ACT	PRI	ERR	RTY	ACT	PRI	ERR	RTY	ACT	PRI	ERR	RTY
00	X	1	0023	0058	X	1	0001	0008	X	1	0016	0009	X	1	0013	0008
01	X	1	0003	0003	X	1	0003	0003	X	1	0003	0003	X	1	0003	0003
02	X	1	0000	0004	X	1	0000	0004	X	1	0000	0004	X	1	0000	0004
03	X	2	0001	0001	X	2	0000	0000	X	2	0001	0001	X	2	0001	0001
04	X	2	0237	0079	X	2	0005	0003	X	2	0007	0009				
05	X	1	0000	0004	X	1	0000	0004	X	1	0000	0004				
06	□	0	0000	0000	X	1	0000	0000	X	3	0000	0000				
07					X	2	0001	0001	X	1	0000	0004				
08					X	2	0004	0002	X	2	0001	0001				
09					X	1	0000	0004	X	2	0002	0001				
10					□	0	0000	0000	X	1	0000	0004				
11									X	1	0000	0001				
12																
13																
14																
15																

FIG. 5–2. *Typical RTU polling and communications diagnostic display*

and with others a (manually created) graphical pictorial representation is provided, with color encoding and equipment status legends (see fig. 5–3). As with the RTU polling and communication channel diagnostic display, the purpose of this diagnostic display is to offer a straightforward means for operational personnel to identify and isolate system problems.

Since the vast majority of SCADA systems are built with some level of redundancy, these displays can also provide operational personnel with assurances that the backup equipment is actually functioning—and even with a means for manually initiating an operational transfer to the backup equipment. It is common practice to perform software updates to redundant SCADA systems by first loading the new software (after sufficient testing on a nonproduction system) into the backup equipment and then initiating a transfer to this equipment, which then enables the loading of the new software into the former primary equipment. This strategy also allows a return to the old software and equipment, in case the transfer to the new software and equipment is unsuccessful for any reason. As with all such system-level displays access to, and manipulation of the controls and settings in such diagnostic displays, needs to be controlled through suitable authorization mechanisms.

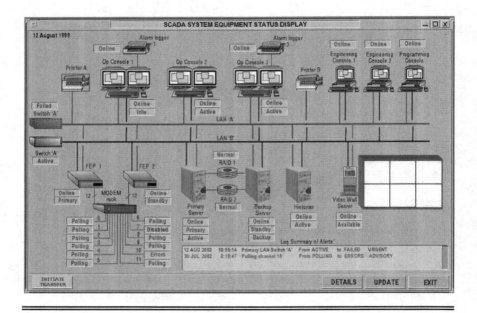

FIG. 5–3. *SCADA system operational status display*

All SCADA systems incorporate other types of standard (automatically created) displays, as well as displays that require a limited amount of configuration effort. A good example of another standard display that is usually automatically created would be an RTU current value display. Such a display provides a tabular list of the current I/O values for any selected RTU and possibly additional RTU diagnostic information. An operator can usually select an RTU (from an automatically generated list or via an on-screen poke point in some other display) and get an immediate RTU value status display. In some systems, the operator can demand an immediate *integrity scan* of the selected RTU, thus guaranteeing that the data values are current. Figure 5–4 shows what a typical RTU summary display might look like.

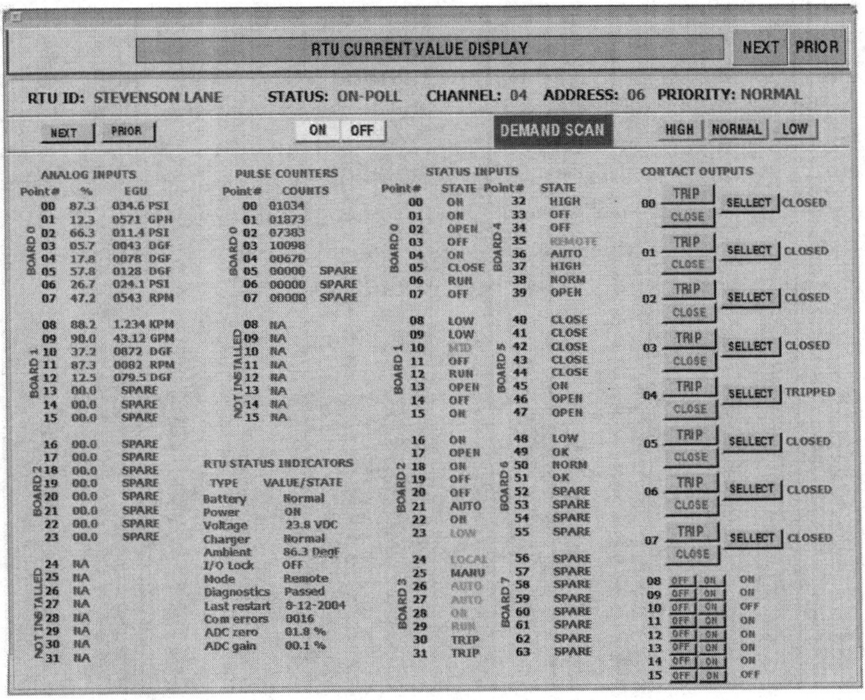

FIG. 5–4. *RTU current value display*

Other types of automatically generated standard displays include alarm summaries and equipment tagging lists, as well as displays that list available historic trend pages, custom graphical displays, and log/report pages. Semiautomatically generated displays (requiring a minimal amount of configuration) include point group displays (tabular, bar graph, etc.), where a user must merely define the points/tags to be in each group and possibly a group descriptive heading. These automatically generated and semiautomatically generated displays often compose the largest percentage of the overall display pages available to system users. Since SCADA systems supplanted older telemetry technology in which numeric values were often presented as a voltage signal into an actual panel meter, it was (and still is) common to simulate the same type of informational display on CRT screens. Figure 5–5 shows a meterlike point group display. SCADA vendors have explored a multitude of presentational formats for offering information to operational personnel; meters, bar graphs, slider controls, line plots and textual presentation formats are normally available with any SCADA system. A Japanese vendor once explored a novel means for indicating the alarm/severity level of a measurement by means of using happy face icons where the facial presentation went from happy to very upset as the alarm and severity level of a condition increased. This idea never caught on with SCADA system owners, but has been adopted by instant message users (the so-called emoticon.)

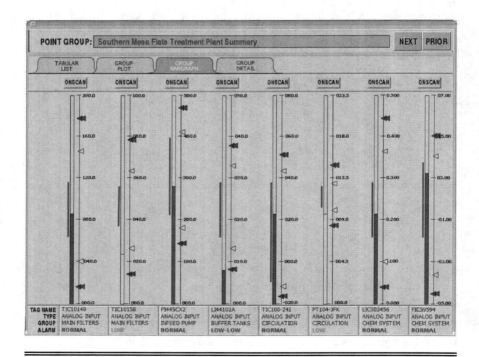

FIG. 5–5. *Point group display (bar graph mode)*

Two other important types of (semi)automatically generated displays are historical trending displays and alarm summary/information displays. These displays are sufficiently important to justify a lengthier discussion, which follows later in this chapter.

Site/Industry–Specific Displays

Most modern SCADA systems (since the 1990s) have used semigraphical and now fully graphical custom-developed displays as the primary way of presenting information to the system operators. These displays typically require a good deal of time and effort to design, create, edit, and test. Creation of these displays uses a special (vendor-specific) graphical editor utility (one of the SCADA system utilities discussed in chap. 4) that offers the ability to assemble graphical elements, dynamic data elements, control elements, and other components into a user-defined display. Depending on the industry and application, these user-defined display pages may be in the form of process-flow diagrams, map displays, or plant layout displays.

The ease of creation and editing will vary greatly between products from different vendors, but all graphical editors since about 1990 have supported drag and drop of graphical elements from a menu or table. The drawing capabilities found in a PC package like Microsoft PowerPoint™ or Corel Draw™ are similar to those found today in most current SCADA system graphics packages. Most customized graphical editor packages for SCADA systems allow importation of standard graphic images in a standard file format such as JPEG or TIFF. These images may be used as *wallpaper* on which other dynamic and static drawing elements can be placed. Since graphical displays are used to present SCADA system information, the graphical editor has to include the ability to select data points and present them, in some form, on the display page. Numeric data may be presented as a textual numeric value, a bar graph, a meter display, a pie chart, or a trend plot or even used to alter the physical placement and/or color of other graphical elements. Status information can also be presented as textual descriptions, multistate objects, or color changes or even used to make other graphical elements appear or disappear from the display. The most popular Microsoft Windows based SCADA packages include custom graphic editors that support Visual Basic (VB) scripts being attached to specified graphical elements and controls. VB scripts can be used to add animation, user interactivity, input validity checking, and display flexibility to custom graphic displays. Because VB scripts can potentially interact with system settings, controls, and resources, they need to be treated much like a supervisory control program and validated prior to being placed into a production system. The VB scripts built into a user graphic display potentially open up another security vulnerability that could be exploited.

Since graphic displays are often required in order to enable operator supervisory control actions, the graphical editor must offer mechanisms for selecting control points and issuing valid control commands. The graphical editor must also tie in with the operator access control mechanisms to ensure that control actions can be performed by suitably authorized operational personnel only.

In most if not all SCADA systems today, there are really two parts to user-defined graphical displays. The first part is the graphic editor, which provides for graphic design, editing, and modification. This editor actually builds a data file that tells the second part what to draw, much like an HTML file tells a Web browser how to draw a Web page. The second part is the graphical display execution package, which actually draws and updates the displays and interacts with the user. This display execution package may perform the access-control checks when a user requests a display or attempts to initiate a supervisory control action or alter a protected system or operational parameter. Because access checking is done in the vendor-supplied graphic execution program (which treats the graphic merely as data), there is no way for a graphic to bypass these checks.

In some older SCADA systems, the graphical editor actually creates an executable program (the graphic display is compiled as the final step in creation). In this case, the graphics program needs to have automatically embedded program logic that makes calls to the SCADA system access library to verify access rights and restrict supervisory control privileges, just like any other supervisory control application. This second type of graphical editor is a potential cybersecurity vulnerability if it doesn't enforce access control checking, because it would be possible to write supervisory applications that call the same function library as the user defined graphics, thus bypassing security checking. To automatically embed access-checking logic calls, the vendor would probably include a library of special program logic with each graphics program, automatically making this logic part of each graphic. Another way to bypass access controls with this type of graphical editor would be to replace the library with null program logic that performs no such checking. This would disable access-control checking for all operational graphical displays. Note that making these two modifications would require access to, and proprietary knowledge of, the SCADA system vendor's programming and logic and/or significant programming skills. But if, as has already been demonstrated, people are motivated to release Microsoft's source code to the hacker community, there is no reason to believe that another vendor's source code is beyond access.

Graphical displays

As was already mentioned, most modern SCADA systems make extensive use of graphical data presentation technologies. Graphical data presentation—particularly when there is a physical, geographic, or process-flow relationship—tends to be the clearest and least ambiguous way to deliver information to operational personnel. User-defined graphic displays begin as a blank page onto which a user decides what to place and where and how the display will interact (if at all) with the user.

There are many ways to present individual data elements graphically. A custom graphical display provides a means for organizing and presenting a lot of data in a way that an operator can immediately comprehend. Since most applications that utilize SCADA technology are geographically dispersed, a common graphical display strategy is to offer data arranged in a geographically aligned manner. Figure 5–6 shows an example of a geographic display, using an actual map as the wallpaper so that SCADA data can be directly related to the physical locations where it is collected.

The pipeline, transportation, and water/wastewater industries tend to make extensive use of geographic displays and the electric utility industry

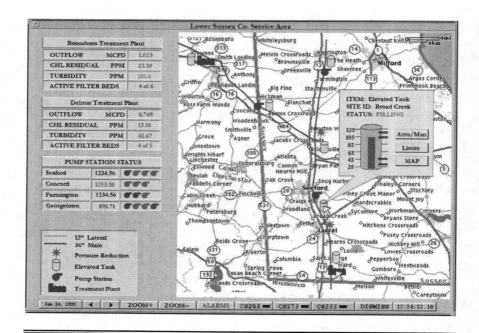

FIG. 5–6. *Geographic layout operational display*

as well, to a lesser degree. Often such displays are part of a hierarchy of displays that permit a broad, all-encompassing informational view with *drill-down* capability that takes operational personnel to whatever level of detail is required. For example, an entire pipeline could be displayed on such a display, and using poke points, an operator could rapidly zoom in to a specific pump station and a specific control point or loop in that pump station.

Another commonly employed graphical presentation design is the process-flow diagram, which provides a simplified physical interconnection drawing. Initially these diagrams tended to be stick figure drawings. But today, with libraries of graphical images and the ability to import actual photographs of equipment, such process-flow diagrams are far more realistic and interesting. Process-flow diagrams tend to be used to display specific equipment sets or facilities within the overall process being monitored by the SCADA system. An operator might watch a high-level *overview* display that is geographic in nature and then *zoom in* to a more detailed process-flow graphic that shows the specifics of the selected substation, pipeline pump station, or water-pumping/storage facility. Figure 5–7 shows a simple example of a multi-window process graphical display that is designed to represent the physical process and equipment for superior operator clarity and comprehension. This figure could represent the lowest level of display drill-down for an operator watching over a large oil/gas offshore production field. Going from a field-wide overview display, to the platform specific display shown in Figure 5–7, might only require one or two mouse clicks. Thus an operator can rapidly go to a display level that affords the desired level of information detail. This is essential with SCADA systems that have lots of display pages.

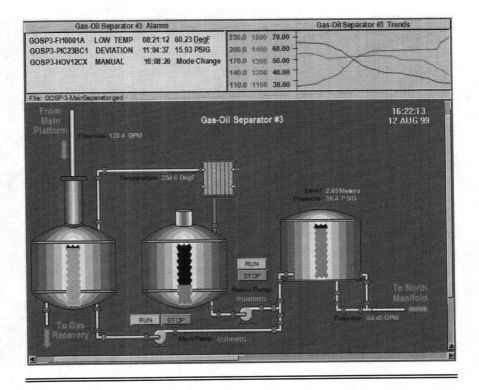

FIG. 5–7. *Process-flow operational graphical display*

Display hierarchy

In most SCADA systems, there will be hundreds to thousands of display pages available to the operational personnel. Even the best operator can't remember and mentally organize that many pages, let alone the naming scheme used to uniquely identify each. For this reason all SCADA systems provide some method for quickly and efficiently locating and navigating between these pages.

One commonly used approach is to build displays into a hierarchy, or tree structure, so that any page can be found by starting at the top of the hierarchy (the bottom of the tree) and following linkages down or up to the desired page. Such a hierarchy will often begin at a home page that is brought up as a result of the user's login. This home page will incorporate links to logically adjacent or logically dependent display pages.

Today everyone is familiar with interpage navigating on the World Wide Web using hyperlinks. A SCADA system will have a similar set of interdisplay linkages. Some SCADA systems now offer their displays in the form of Web pages, thus allowing Web browser and hyperlink technology to be employed. Other systems with non–Web-based operational interfaces employ similar navigational schemes. Navigation may be accomplished by using poke points on displays that transfer to other displays, pull-down menus of available pages, or for geographically associated pages, a north/south/east/west navigation control (see fig. 5–8) that calls up the display page that corresponds to the geographically adjacent area. One use for this type of navigational control would be to follow a pipeline or a power line across a series of map pages to the desired location. In most SCADA systems part of the task of setting up the display pages is establishing the navigational links between and among the various pages. With automatically generated displays (such as diagnostic displays and status displays) the SCADA system will usually automatically create a directory of all such pages. But graphical pages, with associations to specific (semi)automatically generated pages, usually require some user input to define these navigational linkages.

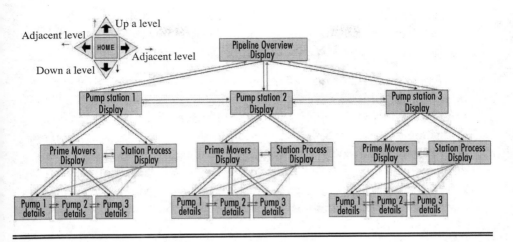

FIG. 5–8. *Display hierarchy and interdisplay navigation*

Pan and zoom

In the electric utility industry, a display navigation convention has become a standard. This is the use of displays that can be *panned* and *zoomed*. The electric utility industry was an early adopter of geographic information systems (GIS) and advanced display technology. All of the SCADA vendors serving that industry (at least for Energy Management Systems [EMS]) offer graphical display editors with the ability to define huge, highly detailed graphic displays that encompass a large geographic area and incorporate utility, geographic, topological, and physical infrastructure information. These graphical displays often require huge relational databases to hold all of the data associated with the display.

The graphical display presentation software is responsible for scaling and windowing the selected display view and creating an actual display image. A user can elect to enlarge or shrink the area displayed on their workstation, much like selecting a map with more or less detail. This is called zooming and establishes the magnification used for data presentation. Any display element that is too small at a given level of zoom is discarded and is not placed on the display. Zooming in to higher magnification will result in the reappearance of some formerly discarded display elements, although the area encompassed by the display window (the viewable area) will have shrunk correspondingly.

At a given level of magnification, only part of the entire display may be presented, and the rest is outside the display area. This is like looking through a window. You can only see the portion of the world framed in the window. Panning is the act of moving the window so that different portions of the overall display become visible, while some previously displayed areas are lost (like looking at the world through a different window). Figure 5–9 shows a map-based GIS display with compass-point navigation, adjustable zoom level, and user-selectable layers.

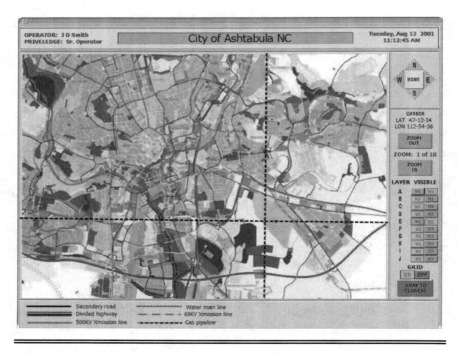

Fig. 5–9. *GIS example display*

Decluttering

Many electric and water utilities are multiservice utilities and have power, water, and even natural gas and cable television offerings. For this reason, it is often important and useful for them to incorporate all sorts of information, important to each of the service offerings, into their GIS displays. Thus, a view of a particular geographic area might be a composite of information about the physical facilities for all of these utilities, as well as pertinent geographic and infrastructure information, such as the location of roadways and waterways. This much information can make for a very busy (cluttered) display and can distract the system operator from the critical points of interest. Thus, SCADA systems with GIS display capabilities usually offer the ability to add and remove categories of information. An operator interested in the electric power system might elect to remove the information about the water and sewer mains and the natural gas pipelines, thus simplifying (decluttering) the display considerably. At a later time, someone from construction or engineering might want to see a composite of all of this information, for the purpose of laying out the path for a new electrical feeder. There is also an aspect of decluttering in the zoom feature, as objects will be removed from the display once they shrink below a specified size, as the zoom level decreases (the view becomes more distant).

Layering

The normal way to achieve decluttering is to allow the grouping of related information (e.g., all electrical infrastructure) into imaginary layers, with the ability to individually add or remove layers to display the desired view. The idea is similar to taking several clear plastic sheets, drawing separate information on each, and then laying them on top of each other to form a complete display. By removal of individual sheets (layers), the display can be simplified or specialized. In some instances the act of removing display objects that get too small for practical display, due to the level of zoom, is also called decluttering.

Display navigation

GIS-based graphical displays are, by their nature and design, geographically based. Thus, navigation around the display is also in terms of geographic positioning. Most GIS displays offer some form of compass-point scheme with north/south/east/west selection icons (panning). There are also usually control icons for zoom manipulation and additional controls for layering and decluttering. In addition, it is typical to be able to click on objects and locations within the display and call up additional detailed information about those items or to cause a transfer to a different display that is specific to the selected item or location. With the advent of GPS technology, many water, gas, and electric utilities have begun storing GPS coordinates in their geographic/asset databases, so that an alarm received from a given location provides the display system with GPS coordinates and the display can automatically pan to the source of the alarm. Anyone that uses online map generation services (like www.mapquest.com™) or portable map/navigation technologies (such as an automobile navigation system), is familiar with the concept.

Alarms and indicators

Since SCADA systems tend to deal with large volumes of constantly changing data (2,000–70,000 tags, depending on the application), it would be infeasible, and far too time consuming, for a human operator to constantly cycle through all of the data looking for problems. Therefore, it is important that the SCADA system provide at least basic validity and alarm checking on all of the data. Detecting alarm and abnormal conditions—and bringing these to the attention of the operators—is a primary function of SCADA systems. Part of the configuration work required in order to commission a SCADA system involves defining the alarm thresholds to be used for each point. Some systems allow for a default set of alarm limits, and most also have built-in checks for invalid inputs. (E.g., if an analog input is to be a 4–20-milliampere signal, then readings much outside of that range would indicate a potentially invalid and probably useless input signal.) Figure 5–10 shows how as a signal value traverses its expected (or possible) value range, it goes in and out of differing levels of alarm severity and indication. In most SCADA systems, unless some form of

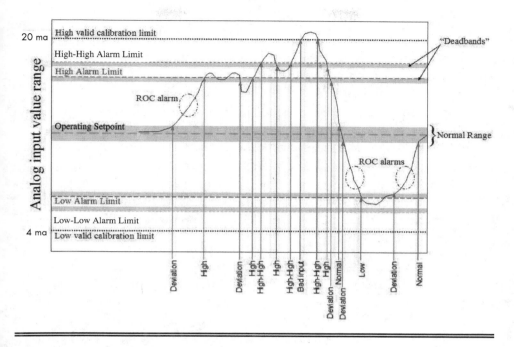

FIG. 5–10. *Alarm limit checking on a typical analog input point*

alarm inhibiting or disabling has been placed on an input, having its value transition across a pre-defined alarm or validity limit will cause some form of alarm indication and recording. This usually results in some form of visual indication on all displays containing that input, and a corresponding entry being made in a chronological log of all alarm events. Having the inputs value return to a valid (normal) value is also usually accompanied by changes in the visual presentation and by another log entry.

When most SCADA systems are initially powered up and initialized, because they have no prior data, they need to request an integrity poll of all of their RTUs, so that a complete set of real time data is developed. This process is usually time consuming and generates a lot of spurious alarms unless the system has a means for suppressing them. Once this process is complete, most systems are generally stable and just continue the polling and alarm checking process. But during the initial start up process, many

SCADA systems are essentially unusable, and the operators blinded. If communications are lost to an RTU, many systems will mark all of the associated points in the real time database in some manner that indicates that the data contained in that database, for those points, may not be trustworthy. (Some systems have an off-line flag, some use a "questionable" flag, and some mark the data as "old.") In a less sophisticated system this may also cause a flurry of alarms on all of the RTU's points. When the RTU is restored to communications, the flags have to be removed, the RTU is commanded to perform an integrity poll, and again, there can be a flurry of alarms, depending on how things changed during the communication outage. Managing the way a SCADA system deals with alarms, and its impact on the operators, is an important consideration (and potential vulnerability.)

Analog inputs are generally given a validity check (to determine if the input can be trusted), followed by one or more sets of upper- and lower-allowable-value range checks (often called high- and low-level checks) and possibly a rate-of-change check and an expected value (set point) deviation check. Most inputs to a SCADA system are assigned a set of fixed alarm limits, but some alarm limit checking may be based on the operational state of the process being monitored and may employ some form of mathematical model that is used to dynamically set and adjust the alarm limit values. The violation of alarm and validity limits is of differing levels of importance, based on the measurement in question. Since operators usually rely on alarm checking to alert them to potential problems, it is important that alarming functions be operating properly and that limits be properly set. If alarming functions were disabled, or limits changed to extreme values, dangerous conditions could go unnoticed by the operational personnel, resulting in damage, outages, and even threats to health and safety.

Another aspect of system configuration is the assignment of these alarm limits and of a severity level to each of the potential alarm conditions for each input. Unless properly configured, a SCADA system can generate a lot of nuisance alarms or fail to alarm critical conditions. When a system generates a lot of alarms the operational staff tend to become insensitive to these alarms and either ignore them, or disable the alarming functions, neither being a safe operational situation.

Contact and status inputs have similar alarm-checking provisions. Contact inputs can be checked for their current state (on/off) and for unexpected changes of state. Contact input status changes may be considered as either alarms or events, depending on the circumstances. If the operator sends a command to start a pump, and receives a confirmation of the pump's status changing to RUN, then that status (contact input) change is not an alarm, but rather an event. On the other hand, if no such command was sent and the pump status were to change to RUN, that would be an alarm condition (un-commanded change of state). Operational personnel typically ignore events (which may not even be annunciated in any manner by the system.) As with analog inputs, it is important that the alarm checking be properly performed on contact inputs as well. For some applications, in which precise (one-millisecond accuracy or more) time tagging is used on contact inputs, the determination, from a group of contacts which may be in different physical locations, of the first contact in the group that changed determines the alarm severity and type (called a *first out* alarm). In most SCADA systems, user-defined computed values (numeric and Boolean) are checked for alarm conditions each time they are recomputed, in much the same manner as physical inputs. When an input (or computed value) goes out of its normal operating range and into an alarm condition, the operational personnel need to be alerted, with the method used dependent on the severity of the alarm condition detected. Proper alarm checking on computed values can be as critical as that performed on physical inputs.

To ensure that alarms are actually noticed by operational personnel, most systems incorporate the concept of positive acknowledgment of alarms. When a point enters an alarm state, it is, by default, unacknowledged until an operator takes an action to acknowledge the alarm. This unacknowledged condition may be specifically indicated with a color or blinking condition on any display where the point is presented. Most SCADA systems differentiate between acknowledged (definitely seen by the operational personnel) and unacknowledged (ambiguous as to having been seen by the operational personnel) alarms. They may even be placed into different display pages to differentiate them even further. Figure 5–11 shows a typical alarm summary window with a few active, serious alarms, as well as the highlighted alarm, which has returned to normal without being acknowledged by the operator. (The active alarms would be in red, and the unacknowledged one would be blinking in green.) Such displays usually present alarms in either chronological order or sorted by severity, and the display window alarm list will grow and shrink as alarms enter and exit. Many systems provide scrolling lists to accommodate large numbers of alarms. Many systems use blinking to indicate unacknowledged alarms, and this persists even if the point returns to a normal value, until acknowledged by an operator.

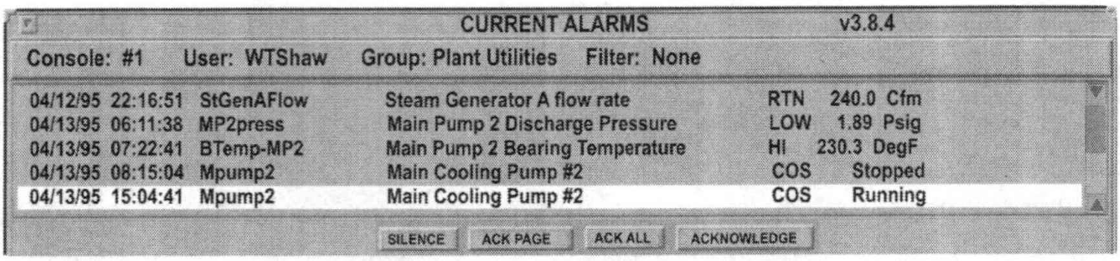

CURRENT ALARMS			v3.8.4
Console: #1 User: WTShaw	Group: Plant Utilities Filter: None		
04/12/95 22:16:51 StGenAFlow	Steam Generator A flow rate	RTN	240.0 Cfm
04/13/95 06:11:38 MP2press	Main Pump 2 Discharge Pressure	LOW	1.89 Psig
04/13/95 07:22:41 BTemp-MP2	Main Pump 2 Bearing Temperature	HI	230.3 DegF
04/13/95 08:15:04 Mpump2	Main Cooling Pump #2	COS	Stopped
04/13/95 15:04:41 Mpump2	Main Cooling Pump #2	COS	Running
	SILENCE ACK PAGE ACK ALL ACKNOWLEDGE		

FIG. 5–11. *Typical current-alarm summary display window*

Alarm filtering

In the event of certain types of operational or process-upset conditions, there may be a flood of alarms from the field, and this can distract operational personnel. This could be caused by an actual problem or by such activities as shutting down a process area or turning off an RTU. In a large SCADA system that supervises an extensive geographically distributed process, different operational personnel might be responsible for a subset of the overall process. In those cases, it is important that a given operator not be distracted by alarms and notifications related to a subset for which he or she has no responsibility. (For example, if Joe is responsible for the northern district, he doesn't want to be distracted by alarms coming in from the southern district, which is the supervisory responsibility of Bob.)

SCADA systems have incorporated mechanisms for reducing and focusing the information presented to operational personnel. Alarm filtering is one such mechanism. With most systems, the operational personnel will have the ability to designate the logical or physical process areas from which they do, or do not, wish to receive alarms. They may also be able to define categories or severity levels of alarms that they wish to be excluded from their displays. When a field site is disrupted by on-site work, it is desirable to prevent spurious alarms from being generated at the SCADA system every time an on-site worker turns the power to a piece of equipment or an RTU on or off. It is usually possible for a SCADA operator to select predefined filter options from a list or to define customized filter options.

Of course, it is important that operational personnel be aware that alarms are being filtered and that filters require some periodic reapplication so they aren't forgotten and left in effect by accident. A possible cybersecurity vulnerability of SCADA systems would be having the alarm-monitoring/presentation software modified to filter out all alarms, since in many cases, operational personnel depend primarily on alarms to direct their attention to problem areas. An equally dangerous alternative would be causing the alarm-detection software to flood the operator and operational displays with false alarms. The overall issue of display alteration or information manipulation is a general cybersecurity concern since operational displays provide the primary mechanism through which operational personnel identify and correct emerging process problems.

Alarm annunciation

When new alarm conditions are detected, it is incumbent on the SCADA system to bring these to the attention of operational personnel. One of the primary means for accomplishing this is to place the new alarm information into the active/current-alarm summary list and display. Another commonly employed mechanism is to generate some form of audible signal that will attract the attention of operational personnel. This may be a set of unique sounds played through the speakers of the operational workstation(s) or an alarm signal generated by an external Klaxon or bell. To stop this audible signal, the operational personnel would normally be required to acknowledge the new alarms and possibly operate a separate control to silence the annunciation.

For particularly serious alarm conditions, some SCADA systems might also extend the range of personnel to be notified (outside the immediate control room), by using mechanisms such as personal pagers, cell phone text messaging, and e-mail to send automated alarm messages to relevant senior technical, management, and supervisory personnel. The danger in utilizing e-mail (and some forms of cell phone) notification is that there must be some form of IP connectivity—from the SCADA system to a corporate intranet and mail server, and maybe through that server to the Internet itself, depending on the recipients—to make e-mail delivery possible. As we will discuss in a later chapter, in IP networking, having other IP-based systems between you and the Internet doesn't mean you are protected from attacks coming from the Internet. Similarly, in order to make use of pager systems, and some forms of cell phone text messaging, it is typical for a SCADA system to need a permanently connected telephone circuit so that it can call the pager service and send a message. This also opens up a potential vulnerability for cyber attackers to exploit.

Alarm history file

At any given point in time, there will typically be some subset of the entire set of inputs and calculated values that are currently *in alarm* (outside their normal, acceptable operating range). This list will vary over time, as inputs return to a normal (nonalarm) condition and others enter an alarm condition. An alarm summary display (fig. 5–11) will usually be provided, to list the signals currently in an alarm state. (Most systems will purge from this list points that return to normal, unless they have not been acknowledged by the operational staff.)

It is also useful to keep track of all the alarm comings and goings, as well as the actions of operational personnel. Most SCADA systems have some form of historical logging function, whereby alarm transitions, events, alarm acknowledgments, operator actions, and system messages are placed into chronologically ordered tables so that this data can be reviewed and (data) mined, to look for situations that indicate a process problem, an operational problem, a training problem or a system problem. A specific and useful log maintained by most SCADA systems is an operator action (or tracking) log wherein a record is kept of the parameter adjustments, alarm acknowledgements, control commands, and other actions taken by each operator. This log is especially helpful when keeping track of different operational shifts, evaluating the performance of operator trainees and keeping an audit trail of remote personnel with operator control authority. An intrusion detection system would definitely need to make use of this log in order to learn what is normal for each operator and to identify unusual and abnormal operator actions. Preserving this log from destruction and alteration is an important cyber security consideration. SCADA systems usually provide a means for displaying, sorting, filtering, and printing these tables. Deletion or alteration of such tables should require a higher level of access and different (administrator level) tools.

The term *log* is usually used to describe the printed results of such operations. Most SCADA systems provide a range of predefined logs and even some level of configurability in formatting the resulting printed documents. In earlier ages of SCADA technology, a system might come configured with several printers, each dedicated to a particular class of log—with boxes of form-feed, fanfold paper providing a continuous, printed, chronological audit trail of alarms, events, operational actions, and system messages. Storing this information in relational database tables, rather that printing it onto reams and reams of paper, has undoubtedly saved a great number of trees and made the information much easier to sort, organize, search, and utilize. Nevertheless, some SCADA system owners still prefer the use of printed logs, because they can be harder to manipulate and falsify (or delete—but not destroy) than data stored in a computer file or relational database table.

Alarm-state visual indication

In every SCADA system, color and blinking are generally used in the operational displays to indicate current alarm status. If a measurement is present on an operational display and is within its normal operating range, the system may be configured to display the value of that measurement in green (although this varies a bit by industry). Red, yellow, and other colors are often used to indicate parameters that have entered an alarm, or questionable, condition or which are disabled. In earlier SCADA systems, for which color-enabled video display hardware would not have been readily available (in the 1970s), alarm conditions were indicated by using reverse video and by adding code letters adjacent to the displayed value.

Today, in addition to color and blinking, special icons or symbols may be appended to a displayed value to indicate specific conditions. As an example, if an input point has been taken off scan, or is having its value manually set by the operator, then those conditions will typically be indicated as well. Every display in which a given parameter or point is presented should incorporate the same set of color/symbol/letter codes for that parameter or point. Since many conditions can be present concurrently, it is not unusual to see combinations of color, icons, and code letters being employed. Figure 5–12 shows examples of point-presentation variations.

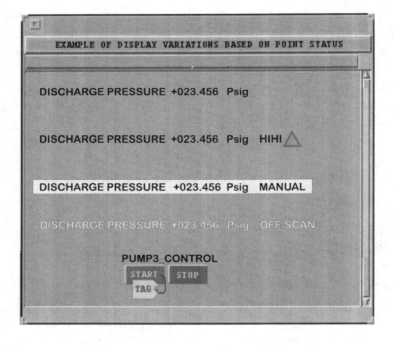

FIG. 5–12. *SCADA systems use symbols or code letters to indicate measurement conditions.*

For control output points, it is common to show a tagged indicator next to the control signal on all displays where that control is presented and available for control action initiation. *Tagging* is the process of disabling a control-output-form supervisory control for the purpose of equipment and/or personnel safety. The term derives from the practice of placing actual physical, paper tags onto control handles on equipment, so that people would see the tags and avoid operating or activating the equipment. In theory, tagged control outputs cannot be operated through the SCADA system until all user-assigned tags are removed. Tagging is common in the electric utility industry and has become more common in other industries over the past decade, as SCADA vendors introduced their technologies into other market segments.

Enforcement of tagging can be implemented at various levels on a SCADA system's software. The most robust implementations use information written directly into the configuration database of the RTU that contains a tagged control point, so that checking for a tagged condition happens right at the level on which actual manipulation of those physical outputs takes place. SCADA systems usually allow multiple tags to be assigned to any control point, by different personnel, and *all* such tags must be removed to restore supervisory control of any given control output. SCADA systems that implement tag enforcement at the host level (which is the most commonly used design) or the operator permission–checking level are potentially vulnerable to tag bypassing. An attacker is not prevented from sending control commands to the RTU and having them acted upon, because the RTU is unaware of tagging. Likewise, an application program could send such commands, because tags are only checked on manually initiated (through the HMI) control actions. Figure 5–13 shows tagging activity being initiated, via the operator's display, on a circuit breaker in a substation. The ability to violate tagging opens up the distinct possibility of causing damage, serious injury, or even death to on-site personnel. (Unfortunately a very newsworthy and frightening event.) Most experienced organizations don't fully trust the SCADA system and require manual disabling of controls in the field, possibly by switching off control loop power at the RTU.

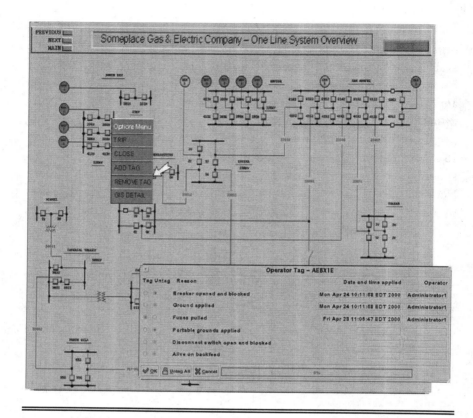

Fig. 5–13. *Control-point tagging display*

Historical Trending

SCADA systems collect a constant stream of updating real-time data from the RTUs in the field and update (overwrite) their real-time database with these new values. However, just as important as knowing the current value of a measurement is knowing the past value changes (history) of many of those same measurements. Knowing that a tank level is currently at 15.56 feet doesn't provide the same understanding of what is happening as being able to see that this level has dropped (or risen) to that point over the past few minutes. All SCADA systems incorporate some level of historical data recording, whereby the operational personnel have the capability of reviewing the past history of a selected set of key measurements (or calculated values) for some predefined time span extending into the past. Prior to SCADA systems, one of the primary mechanisms for monitoring a remote measurement was to use that measurement value to move a pen up and down across a strip or disk of moving paper. Figure 5–14 shows a typical electromechanical, multichannel, strip-chart recorder from the 1980s. The historical trending functions and displays of most SCADA systems essentially mimic the actions of those obsolete (but still used) electromechanical devices.

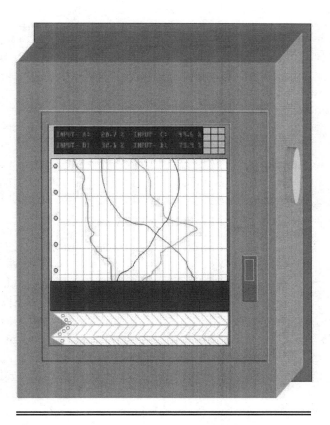

FIG. 5–14. *Mechanical strip-chart pen recorder*

Strip-chart and circular-chart recorders were invented for pre-computer data recording purposes and have remained a staple of the process-monitoring and control industry up to the present day. The historical trending and display functions of a SCADA system are an electronic reproduction of that older technology. Today historical trending packages are available from third-party vendors, particularly for systems based on the Microsoft Windows operating system and the OPC data-interchange standard. In prior decades, SCADA system vendors generally had to develop their own proprietary versions. A major aid in doing this came in the mid-1990s with the evolution of commercial relational database packages that had adequate performance capabilities, and the massive increase in the storage capacity of disk drives.

Historical trending involves four aspects: initial configuration of the data collection and display functions; actual collection of the specified data values; storage and management of the collected data; and finally, the presentation of the recorded data to operational personnel. Computers have dramatically increased in computing power and storage capacity over the past few decades. In spite of those advances, computers still have practical and physical limitations. It is often not physically possible or practical to attempt to collect and continuously store every measurement, status input, and computed value within the SCADA system. No matter how powerful your computer, you can bring it to a halt by placing upon it too great a processing and data manipulation burden.

Similarly, it is not possible to equip a computer with an infinite amount of mass storage. For those reasons, all SCADA system historical trending packages require the user to pick a subset of the available database points. These selected points will be the only measurements assigned to historical trending. Likewise, SCADA systems limit the user in the amount of such data that can be physically accommodated by available online storage. All field measurements are not equal in their importance or in the rate at which they can change. A bearing temperature could be very important and might change rapidly. The water level in a lake might also be important, but is unlikely to change very rapidly under any reasonable conditions. Therefore, a user may wish to store samples of these different measurements at a different periodicity.

Historical trending packages often manage the storage and collection process by offering prespecified *trend groups*. For example, a trending package might allow data to be written to historical storage, from the real-time database, at a 1-, 5-, 15-, or 30-minute collection rate (i.e., one sample stored to the trend files every 1, 5, 15, or 30 minutes). Obviously, over any fixed time period, the data collected once per minute will be of a much greater quantity (60 times as much) than that collected once per hour, if the number of trended parameters is the same for each collection rate. Such a trending package might place maximum limits on the number of parameters that could be assigned to each collection rate, thus predefining the maximum amount of disk space that could be used by the historical trending function. (For group 1 [data collection every 1 minute], up to 200 points may be assigned; for group 2 [data collection every 5 minutes], up to 1,000 points may be assigned; and for group 3 [data collection every 15 minutes], up to 3,000 points can be assigned.)

Once the predefined maximum amount of data has been collected, there is, in theory, no further storage space available, so either historical trending has to cease or additional room must be made available. In many systems, the storage that is pre-allocated is treated as if it were logically structured into a *circular buffer*: when the end of the buffer is reached, the subsequent data are stored at the beginning of the buffer, overwriting the oldest previously recorded data values. Using storage in this manner prevents the filling of all available storage space (and shutting down of the system), while ensuring that there is a specified amount of prior history available for any given measurement assigned to historical data collection.

Another way in which trending packages save space is by reducing data quantities through statistical data manipulation (e.g., taking all of the data samples for a 15 minute interval and reducing them to just the average, maximum, and minimum values for that time span). Figure 5–15 shows a variety of data archiving, storage, and reduction methods, for long-term historical recording purposes. The purpose of collecting and archiving data is to provide a historical perspective on the actions of critical measurements and values. Historical trending applications provide a limited look back in time for the values being archived.

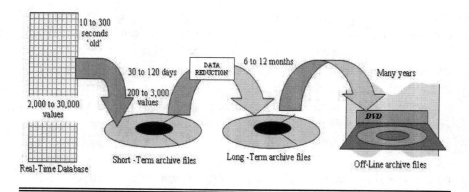

FIG. 5–15. *Data storage hierarchy for historical trending*

It may be important to have 1-minute data samples on a given point *x* for the most recent 24 hours. Beyond that time span, it may not be as critical to collect data that often, so sampling and collection of *x* values could be reduced to once per hour. One can achieve this by placing point *x* into both a 1-minute collection group and a 60-minute collection group. This approach leads to the problem of storing more data than is necessary (although when storage is plentiful, this may not matter).

When sampling is extended over a long time interval (an hour, a day, or a week, etc.), there is always the potential problem of missing something important during the intervening time between sample captures. Some SCADA systems address this problem by computing, for example, the hourly value (rather than fetching the current value at the hour demarcation), using the minute data collected in the prior hour. This approach facilitates deriving a more representative value, rather than merely saving the instantaneous reading at each hourly point. The average/mean, maximum value, or minimum value (or all of them) can be computed from the prior hour's data and used as the hourly recorded value(s).

Many SCADA systems offer an alternative to merely overwriting (and losing) the oldest historical data as additional data is stored. In these systems, prior to overwriting (and losing) the oldest data values, those values are copied onto some form of removable storage media, such as a magnetic tape cartridge, a compact disc (CD), or these days, a digital versatile disc (DVD) (fig. 5–16). The data preserved in this manner are no longer immediately available for display on the SCADA system, but if needed at some point in time, the data can be copied (temporarily) onto the system disk, or the removable media 'mounted' in the appropriate removable media drive, and made available for display. Data that are not immediately available but must be brought back into a system via some manual intervention (and possibly a data transfer process) are usually called *off-line* storage. Data that reside on the hard drive(s) and can be immediately accessed by application programs are usually called *online* storage. Removable, directly readable media, such as CD and DVD, have blurred this distinction a bit. The data contained on them is not immediately available, but there is no requirement to copy the data onto a hard drive in order to access this data. In some industries it is of regulatory and legal value to maintain historical data records with no limit on the time span being preserved. Using off-line storage as a permanent means for data archiving addresses this need, without placing undue demands on the production system (or exposing this data to cyber tampering or destruction). In some cases the historical trend data may be of financial importance (e.g., used for documenting that contract pressures or flow rates were maintained or for deliver totalizing computations) and therefore its loss or alteration could have a potential financial impact.

Historical trending displays

Once historical data are collected by a SCADA system, they are available to the operational personnel, usually in the form of trend (time plot) displays. A trend display usually provides some description of the data being presented, as well as some form of scale or grid to determine the values being plotted. Data are presented in the form of an X-Y plot of values (on the Y axis) against time (on the X axis). Most historical trending packages allow multiple signals to be co-plotted on the same display grid for comparison purposes. Most historical trending packages allow the user to rescale the X and Y axes to obtain the desired resolution and data clarity. Most also permit the scrolling of data forward and backward in time, within the constraints of the available data. (No, you can't scroll into the future to see what is going to happen.) Figure 5–16 shows a multi-pane,

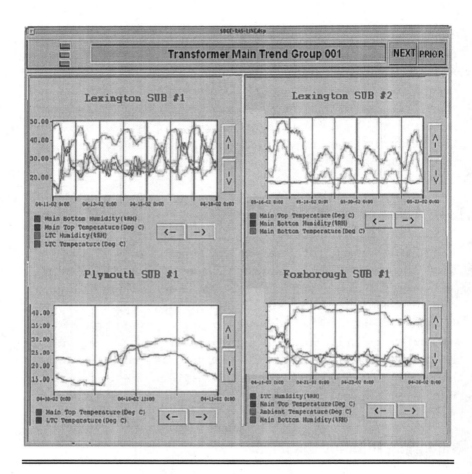

FIG. 5–16. *Typical historical trending display*

multi-trace historical trending display of various measurements associated with transformer performance.

There are a wide range of more advanced functions that can be found in various historical trending packages, and it is not the goal of this book to enumerate all of these features. A historical trending package deals with fixed data, recorded at some time in the past, possibly up to the present moment. For that reason, such trend displays generally are static. (Once the requested data has been presented, the display has no reason to change or update.) Most packages also allow for some form of *quality code* to be

attached to the stored data. This is used to indicate an\
the validity or integrity of the stored data values. For
values were from physical inputs that were being man
code might be used to indicate this state. If no data w
time interval, the display may leave a corresponding gap ... ... p....
The specific features, formats and functions will depend upon the SCADA
system vendor, unless they use a third-party commercial historian package.

Real-time trending

There are also occasions when it is useful to continuously monitor a
measurement (or several measurements) over a period of time—watching
what the values have been, as well as the current value(s). Such trending
can be supplied either as an extension of the historical trending package
or as a separate capability. The term *real time* has to be interpreted in light
of the processes being monitored and the communication capabilities of
the SCADA system. Because of the generally slow-speed communications
between the SCADA host and the field-based RTUs in some industries,
fetching new data values is usually what limits the ability to provide real-
time trending. In the water/wastewater industry, a real-time trend may
update only every few minutes, whereas in the electric utility industry,
trend updates may be possible every few seconds—simply because of the
differences in the communication architectures and technology.

An important consideration when configuring a real-time trending
package is to avoid attempting to collect and store data at a rate that is
faster than the actual values are being updated by polling of the RTUs.
The process of updating the real-time database is typically asynchronous
of (disconnected from) the process of writing database values to historical
files. An RTU could scan and update a particular measurement every 10
seconds and be polled for that value every 30 seconds (so the data could
be up to 30 seconds old in the real time database of the SCADA system),
and yet the operator has it on a trending display that updates at a 10
second rate. An operator might be fooled into thinking that a process or
particular measurement was stable because a real-time trend plot of values
was holding steady. However, in reality, communications to the particular
RTU might have been lost. In most SCADA systems the historical and
real-time trending packages normally fetch their data from the real time

database that is refreshed by polling RTUs. So it is important that the status of data in the real time database be included and updated, and not just the value.

As with any operational display, it is important to somehow alert a system user that the data being viewed could possibly be invalid or questionable or is just not available. In SCADA control rooms, real-time trending displays, just like alarm summary displays, are a critical component of the overall operational data presentation. Many SCADA system operational personnel were originally trained with older panel instrumentation (a wall filled with chart recorders and indicator lights) and telemetry and prefer trending displays, based on their training.

In many Microsoft Windows based systems, OPC is used to link many trending packages to their data sources. Thus, a third-party commercial historian/trending package might receive data updates from one or more sources, over a LAN and/or WAN connection. Other third-party historian packages employ Modbus-over-IP or other IP-based communications to receive their data updates. A potential cybersecurity vulnerability in SCADA systems that use this type of historian package is an attack that disrupts such communications or that sends falsified data to the historian. In some instances, the historian is a separate computer, in which case it could also be subject to a direct cyber attack, much as any other computer that is part of the overall SCADA system. Of course the actual impact of such an attack may merely be at the irritating nuisance level.

Logs and Reports

Aside from the use of SCADA systems to provide real-time monitoring and supervisory control, a major objective for most systems is to utilize the collected data to automatically generate (printed) reports and/or logs— for corporate purposes, regulators, and government agencies and other organizations that require regular reporting. In the water/wastewater market, it is not uncommon for daily, weekly, quarterly, and annual reports to be required by the appropriate regulatory agencies. All businesses need regular reporting on operating costs, inventory, actual production, asset productivity, and asset utilization. Since a SCADA system collects and processes data from many sources, it is a logical place to generate the reports that require these data.

It is a good idea to differentiate between logs and reports. Logs are a chronological accumulation of associated information, sorted by category—generated by the occurrence of conditions that are defined as abnormal or worthy of recording. They are, in effect, an audit trail of monitored conditions. If, in a given time interval (e.g., a day or a week), no occurrences of monitored conditions are detected, then there is nothing in the log. Reports, by contrast, are a predefined set of data and computations based on those data, that are to be put into a predefined format (and probably printed) either on a scheduled basis or on an event-triggered basis. When a report is generated, it should not be blank unless problems prevented the collection of the specified data. An empty log may be a good thing; an empty report (one with no data) is not. Figure 5–17 shows a demand log for a given operating area (the user-selected filter criteria) listing control events recorded over a user-specified time interval.

Calculated values

Although most reports involve collecting and presenting a predefined set of data, most useful reports also require that some level of calculations be performed on the data. An hourly list of water quantities delivered to custody points will typically include a total for each custody point and a total across all delivery points for the day. Addition is a simple mathematical function, but some mechanism is needed to perform the calculation. In some older SCADA systems, all such calculations needed to be created using a separate user defined calculated point facility. Any computed values needed for report generation had to be defined in the form of computations that generated pseudo-analog or binary database points, and these could then be referenced in any subsequent reports (which added significantly to the overall size of the point database of the system). Today most reporting packages have integral calculation capabilities, much like those found in popular spreadsheet programs.

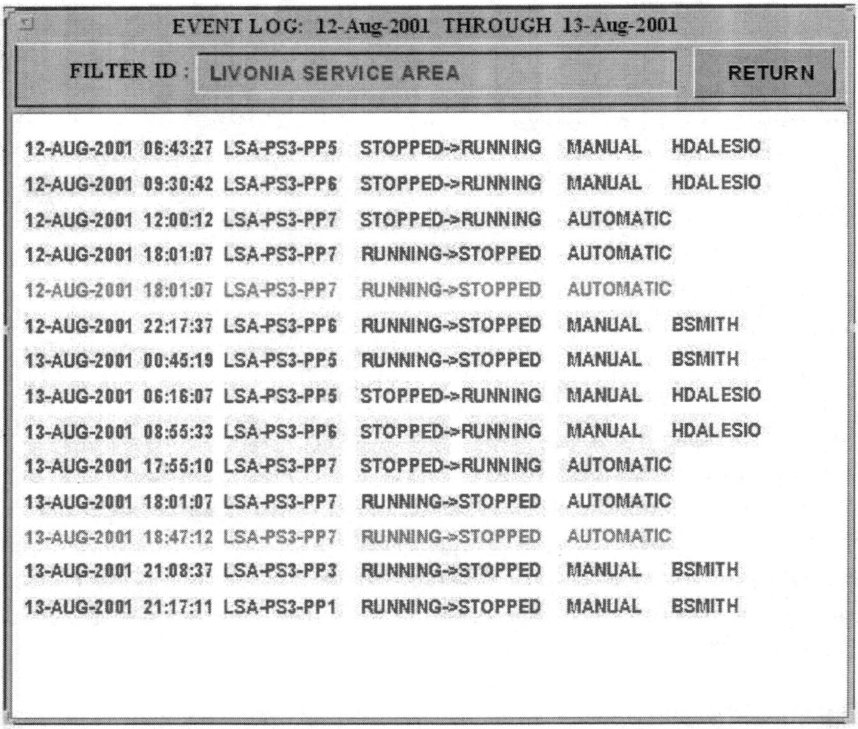

EVENT LOG: 12-Aug-2001 THROUGH 13-Aug-2001				
FILTER ID : LIVONIA SERVICE AREA				RETURN
12-AUG-2001 06:43:27	LSA-PS3-PP5	STOPPED->RUNNING	MANUAL	HDALESIO
12-AUG-2001 09:30:42	LSA-PS3-PP6	STOPPED->RUNNING	MANUAL	HDALESIO
12-AUG-2001 12:00:12	LSA-PS3-PP7	STOPPED->RUNNING	AUTOMATIC	
12-AUG-2001 18:01:07	LSA-PS3-PP7	RUNNING->STOPPED	AUTOMATIC	
12-AUG-2001 18:01:07	LSA-PS3-PP7	RUNNING->STOPPED	AUTOMATIC	
12-AUG-2001 22:17:37	LSA-PS3-PP6	RUNNING->STOPPED	MANUAL	BSMITH
13-AUG-2001 00:45:19	LSA-PS3-PP5	RUNNING->STOPPED	MANUAL	BSMITH
13-AUG-2001 06:16:07	LSA-PS3-PP5	STOPPED->RUNNING	MANUAL	HDALESIO
13-AUG-2001 08:55:33	LSA-PS3-PP6	STOPPED->RUNNING	MANUAL	HDALESIO
13-AUG-2001 17:55:10	LSA-PS3-PP7	STOPPED->RUNNING	AUTOMATIC	
13-AUG-2001 18:01:07	LSA-PS3-PP7	RUNNING->STOPPED	AUTOMATIC	
13-AUG-2001 18:47:12	LSA-PS3-PP7	RUNNING->STOPPED	AUTOMATIC	
13-AUG-2001 21:08:37	LSA-PS3-PP3	RUNNING->STOPPED	MANUAL	BSMITH
13-AUG-2001 21:17:11	LSA-PS3-PP1	RUNNING->STOPPED	MANUAL	BSMITH

FIG. 5–17. *A typical SCADA system event log*

Statistical calculations

Frequently, the mathematical processing of data involves statistical calculations, such as computing the mean, the median, or the standard deviation for a set of values. This set of values may actually be the historical set of values for a single measurement, over some selected time interval (e.g., the prior day or week). In these cases, the reporting package needs to be able to interact with the historical trending package to fetch the necessary data points. Again, in some systems, this can be handled in the reporting package, but in others, such computations need to be performed with separate capabilities and made available to the reporting package. If very complex calculations are required in order to generate a value for a report—particularly a calculation that involves multi-pass algorithmic logic—then once again, this may be done in separate software and a value made available to the report package.

Spreadsheet report generators

With the migration of SCADA systems to the Microsoft Windows and Linux operating system platforms, it has become possible to make use of commercial spreadsheet software packages for report generation. These packages all have several forms of data import mechanism and allow vendor-written add-ins that can be used to connect them to SCADA system data sources (or by collecting and placing such data into a file where the spreadsheet can use its import capability). The computational and output-formatting capabilities of such packages are prodigious and very flexible. Almost any reasonable report can be defined using the capabilities of such packages. Most current SCADA systems make use of (*integrate*) these commercial spreadsheet packages. Figure 5–18 shows a daily water production report (taken partway through the day) giving hourly breakdowns of volumes and water-quality information. Most commercial relational database packages support an ODBC (Open Database Connectivity) interface as do most commercial spreadsheet packages. SCADA systems that maintain all of their data, even the real time data, in relational database tables, make it easy to select and fetch the desired data into a report spreadsheet. A final requirement for reporting is to have a means for triggering reports at pre-specified times and dates. Most SCADA systems have a means for specifying these, even in non-specific forms such as last day of the month, second Tuesday of each month, last day of the year, etc.

Reports as data-exchange mechanism

Reports are obviously designed primarily for presenting information to human beings in a format that makes the data understandable. However, reporting packages, particularly spreadsheet-based reporting packages, have also been used to produce data that are intended as input for other programs and applications. It is very easy to create a report the textual output of which will be in the form of a series of numeric and status values,

SOMEWHERE WATER SYSTEM
DAILY RAW WATER QUALITY SUMMARY
DATE: 08/12/2001

HRS	PARTICLES TOTAL / ML CALCPP1PCTOTAL	TURBIDITY NTU RAWWRNTU	PH VALUE RAWWRPHO	DO MG/L RAWWRDOO	TEMP C RAWWTRMP	CONDUCT US/CM RAWWRCND
01:00	1395	0.24	8.12	9.34	14.10	844.38
02:00	1396	0.24	8.12	9.28	14.10	844.38
03:00	1380	0.24	8.12	9.25	14.10	844.38
04:00	1356	0.24	8.12	9.37	14.10	844.38
05:00	1317	0.23	8.12	9.50	14.10	844.38
06:00	1295	0.23	8.12	9.50	14.10	844.38
07:00	1295	0.23	8.12	9.45	14.10	844.39
08:00	1295	0.22	8.12	9.31	14.10	844.38
09:00	0	0.00	0.00	0.00	0.00	0.00
10:00	0	0.00	0.00	0.00	0.00	0.00
11:00	0	0.00	0.00	0.00	0.00	0.00
12:00	0	0.00	0.00	0.00	0.00	0.00
13:00	0	0.00	0.00	0.00	0.00	0.00
14:00	0	0.00	0.00	0.00	0.00	0.00
15:00	0	0.00	0.00	0.00	0.00	0.00
16:00	0	0.00	0.00	0.00	0.00	0.00
17:00	0	0.00	0.00	0.00	0.00	0.00
18:00	0	0.00	0.00	0.00	0.00	0.00
19:00	0	0.00	0.00	0.00	0.00	0.00
20:00	0	0.00	0.00	0.00	0.00	0.00
21:00	0	0.00	0.00	0.00	0.00	0.00
22:00	0	0.00	0.00	0.00	0.00	0.00
23:00	0	0.00	0.00	0.00	0.00	0.00
00:00	0	0.00	0.00	0.00	0.00	0.00
AVG	446	0.08	2.71	3.12	4.70	261.46
MAX	1396	0.24	8.12	9.50	14.10	844.38
MIN	0	0.00	0.00	0.00	0.00	0.00

FIG. 5–18. *Example of a spreadsheet report for a water utility*

represented as ASCII strings and separated in the output stream by either a comma or a space. This is, of course, the definition of a comma-separated value (CSV) or file, which is commonly used as a mechanisms for moving data between spreadsheet packages.

A major challenge, for many years, was establishing reliable, automatic, and flexible (reconfigurable) data exchanges between SCADA systems and other systems that needed access to some subset of the SCADA system's data. Complex and messy data-exchange protocols, such as ICCP (also called TASE.2 and UCA1.0) were developed to address this requirement. But these protocols were often expensive and cumbersome to implement. Some SCADA system vendors and customers found that they could use their spreadsheet reporting packages to collect the required data and produce a CSV file, which could automatically be sent to another computer using such readily available IP networking applications as FTP. Developing applications that could parse and utilize such files as their data inputs was normally considered a simple programming task. The problem with such as scheme was that any change required reprogramming.

Today another type of ASCII text file is beginning to be used for intersystem data exchange: the XML data file. Although it takes a bit of work initially, it is possible to use most spreadsheet reporting packages to create XML data files as well. This data-exchange technology will be discussed in greater detail later in the book. Figure 5–19 shows an example of an XML Web page that might be generated either by an IP-ready RTU or through a properly designed and cleverly configured spreadsheet reporting package. It was previously mentioned that a recent extension of the OPC standard is also based on using XML files for data exchange.

The XML file can be displayed in a standard Web browser (as seen in Figure 5–19), although that is not the actual goal. The XML document contains both information and descriptive *tags* (delineated by matching pairs of angle brackets) that help clarify the information; in this example, the RTU is providing its own identification and the time and date corresponding to the data. It then provides two analog and two status values, along with their descriptions, engineering units, and alarm status. If just the data were provided, the file might look like a string of numbers. The descriptive tags, although somewhat wasteful of space and transmission bandwidth, make it clear to a viewer (or an application program) what the data mean and to what each value corresponds. XML files are sometimes called self descriptive data files since they contain actual data values, plus lots of descriptive information that aids in identifying and interpreting that data.

```xml
<?xml version="1.0" ?>
- <RTUupdate>
    <RTUid>LowerWestStreet</RTUid>
    <UpdateTime>08:45:32</UpdateTime>
    <UpdateDate>12-Aug-2001</UpdateDate>
  - <AnalogPoint>
      <PointName>PhaseAvoltage</PointName>
      <PointValue>14.234</PointValue>
      <PointUnits>KV</PointUnits>
      <PointStatus>Normal</PointStatus>
    </AnalogPoint>
  - <AnalogPoint>
      <PointName>PhaseAcurrent</PointName>
      <PointValue>123.41</PointValue>
      <PointUnits>Amps</PointUnits>
      <PointStatus>HighAlarm</PointStatus>
    </AnalogPoint>
  - <StatusPoint>
      <PointName>F34BreakerStatus</PointName>
      <PointValue>Tripped</PointValue>
      <PointStatus>Fault</PointStatus>
    </StatusPoint>
  - <StatusPoint>
      <PointName>F34RecloserStatus</PointName>
      <PointValue>Disabled</PointValue>
      <PointStatus>Fault</PointStatus>
    </StatusPoint>
  </RTUupdate>
```

FIG. 5–19. *Example of an XML data file*

6

Conventional Information Technology Security

SCADA systems have migrated to commercial hardware and operating system platforms and incorporate many well-known, commercially available components (e.g., relational databases and Web browsers and servers). In effect, a SCADA system today is architecturally identical to any other IT system except for the specialized application programs that make it a SCADA system (versus, e.g., an accounting system) and the need for 100% availability. Thus, it is not surprising that many, if not most, of the techniques and technologies employed in securing IT systems have direct applicability to modern SCADA systems. That is not to say that all of them are applicable. Certain procedural approaches that are considered normal in the IT world would be unacceptable in the SCADA world.

Many organizations that use SCADA systems also have formal IT support departments. Surprisingly, though, there has been a continuous lack of trust and cooperation between system users and support personnel. There are historical reasons for this situation. Large and complex SCADA systems can be difficult to configure, commission, and put into operation, and once these systems are operational, most SCADA system users are loath to allow any changes, unless made specifically to correct a known and intolerable bug. The methodologies of an IT group may not match well with this mentality. Classically, IT groups immediately deploy and install all patches and new software releases, to keep all systems up to date. They also like to mandate *baselines* and standards that may not be in keeping with the equipment supplied by a SCADA system vendor. For these and many other reasons, interdepartmental clashes result, much to the detriment of the overall organization.

Today, with SCADA systems utilizing much of the same technology that is employed in IT systems—and needing to be interconnected with other corporate and external systems via LAN, WAN, and Internet technology—it is important that IT and the operations group (the typical users of the SCADA systems) cooperate in making SCADA systems secure from cyber threats. To foster such cooperation, SCADA system personnel should understand the basics of cybersecurity as practiced by most IT organizations (and IT personnel should be encouraged to listen to the issues posed by the SCADA personnel).

Availability, Integrity, and Confidentiality

When IT security personnel discuss cybersecurity, they are generally addressing the need to provide mechanisms (a mix of technology, architectural choices, company policies, and operational procedures) that ensure availability, integrity, and confidentiality. *Availability* means ensuring the proper operational state for a business to operate—that is, the state of the computing assets, applications, networks, and data, whenever they are needed. In the case of SCADA, this includes the computing components and peripherals that constitute the system. Still, the concept goes further than that. It also means addressing essential communications (e.g., to the RTUs and any system that needs to provide data to or exchange data with the SCADA system) and essential data required by the SCADA system—such as relational database files that hold historical data for reports and system configuration files for the basic functioning of the SCADA system. For a SCADA system that needs 100% availability, this includes issues like the need for a redundant design of the system and its communications, the choice of having alternative (backup) facilities, establishing (and following) proper system backup procedures, and even requirements like the installation of an uninterruptible power supply (UPS) to ensure power availability.

Integrity means ensuring that information displayed by and stored in the system is accurate, up-to-date, of known quality, and confirmed to have come from the correct sources and been processed in the correct manner (in other words, that you can trust the data). The concept also extends to preventing unauthorized modification of data or configuration information. It also means ensuring that the system itself (hardware or software) is not changed without going through the necessary validity testing and recertification processes. SCADA systems usually include some level of data validity checking and quality flagging at the point where field data are processed and placed into the real-time database table. Few, if any, systems make checks beyond that point because the data are refreshed continually with new data from the RTUs. Some systems include mechanisms for validating their configuration tables (e.g., a CRC code or some form of data check code), but few perform such checks on a regular basis. Most make such a check only immediately after reloading or modifying the configuration information or if an application crashes due to bad data. Thus unauthorized and deliberate modifications to these tables could easily go undetected. The prevention of unauthorized system modifications is usually relegated to user ID/password access controls. Simple password schemes provide only weak protection against a determined cyber attacker.

Confidentiality is the concept of ensuring that information, both stored in a computer system and transmitted over communication links to other computer systems, is kept from being available to unauthorized personnel or applications. One of the key ways in which information can be made unavailable to the unauthorized is to store it (or transmit it) in an encrypted version (ciphertext), so that only someone with the proper knowledge (e.g., a secret decryption key) can decrypt the ciphertext and recover the original data. Encryption and decryption technologies will be discussed later in this section.

Importantly, until recent years (certainly not prior to the events of 9/11), SCADA system vendors did not entertain any thoughts of incorporating cybersecurity mechanisms in their system designs and software. Even today most SCADA system vendors are able to offer only whatever protections have come from the IT world and from the operating system and computer platform vendors. Work is under way in several committees, industry organizations, and professional societies to define recommended cybersecurity enhancements for future SCADA system products. However, it will take a couple of years for any of this work actually to yield basic product changes. For now, the goals of availability, integrity, and confidentiality will have to be sought using available IT (and security) technologies, good architectural designs, operational best practices, and carefully crafted procedures.

Remote Access

Everyone is concerned about hackers or terrorists gaining access to their critical control systems and wreaking havoc. Hackers and terrorists are not magical creatures. They use the same technology as everyone else; they just put it to bad use, rather than good. (The term *cracker* is sometimes used to differentiate those who use hacking skills for evil; ethical hackers, using the same skills for good, are sometimes referred to as *white-hat hackers*.)

There are really only two ways to make a cyber attack on a computer system: you need physical access to the system; or you need electronic access to the system. If you have physical access to a SCADA system, you probably wouldn't be restricted to making a cyber attack, although that might be your preference, depending on your objectives and desire not to get caught. If you had no physical access, then you would need electronic access to launch an attack. In general, by electronic access, a telecommunication link via LAN (possibly wireless), WAN, or telephone technology is meant. Hackers or terrorists who cannot physically gain access to your SCADA system(s) need to establish a communication link of some type to do their dirty work. A slightly less clear issue is the possibility of using removable media as a way to communicate with your SCADA system (or is that gaining physical access, since someone, although not necessarily the attacker, has to bring it to, and introduce it into, the system?)

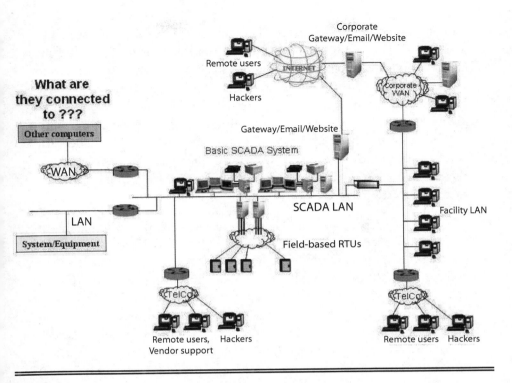

FIG. 6–1. *Telecommunication interconnections to a SCADA system*

Communication connections can come from many sources—and from unexpected directions (fig. 6–1)—with a highly interconnected SCADA system. Prior to the widespread establishment of the Internet, that communication link would mainly have been via telephone dial-up. Most SCADA systems used to have auto-answer modems and dedicated telephone lines that enabled the system vendor to dial in to the system, for troubleshooting and diagnosis of problems and installation of updates and patches to software. Some SCADA system users employed these same capabilities to enable remote access by their operational personnel and added more modems and telephone lines for that purpose. IT support groups within the corporation might also make occasional modem connections, to enable remote monitoring and support. If pager based notification was a feature of a SCADA system, there might be a modem and phone line allocated for that function. It was (and to some degree still

183

is) not unusual to find several modems and telephone lines connected to a large SCADA system, most left in place but no longer used. Modems can be connected directly to computers, to PCs on your network, and to routers on your network. There are a number of technologies that have been used to secure modem connections, such as *dial-back modems*. These are modems that on receiving an incoming call, expect to be given a code number and then hang up and dial a predefined telephone number that corresponds to the entered code. Call-forwarding technologies have made this protection somewhat obsolete, as the outgoing call can be redirected to a hacker's telephone number.

One key aspect of SCADA cybersecurity is the elimination of unnecessary communication paths into the SCADA system and the placement of protective measures on those that remain. A good starting point is to find and remove all such modems and telephone lines. (Check your telephone bill to see what telephone numbers you are purchasing, and then call any you don't recognize. If a modem answers, find it and disconnect it immediately.) Hackers developed programs called *daemon dialers* or *war dialers* many years ago, and such programs are readily available on the Internet at *hacker Web sites*. A war dialer program is given a fractional telephone number (e.g., the area code and first two digits of a phone number) and then dials all possible telephone number combinations, one at a time, recording what it finds. The program serves to look for modems, and when it finds one, depending on the program's sophistication, it may send a few test messages to see what response is generated by the computer it has located. The response may tell the program what operating system software is running on the computer it has just reached. Later, at leisure, the hacker will review the information recorded by the war dialer program to decide if any of the computers should be further probed using other *hacker tools*. Your IT department can also employ such a tool to search for abandoned or unregistered modems within your own facility. (They can locate forgotten FAX machines as well!)

Today, with the prevalence of the Internet and the universal adoption of TCP/IP networking, telephone-based war dialing has been replaced by its IP equivalent: IP address *sweeping* (or *ping sweep*). With IP networking, every computer on a network is given a unique IP address (like a street address), and a message containing a particular address will, when sent onto that network, will delivered to the computer with that address, if one exists. The postal system is a useful model for TCP/IP networking. People you don't know elsewhere in the world can send mail to your house, just by having your address. In fact, they don't need to know you or that this is your address; they just need to write down an address that looks valid, and if it happens to be yours, you get the letter. Valid IP addresses are much easier to guess than valid postal addresses (although there is probably a 100 Main Street in every downtown). Using an IP address scanner, a hacker can automatically send messages to a vast number of IP addresses to see if any computer actually responds. If one does, then more advanced hacker tools—like network mappers, port scanners, and TCP finger printers—can be used to probe for vulnerabilities. Commercially available (and hacker Web site) tools exist for this purpose. A program called *nmap* (for wired networks, *AirSnort* for wireless networks) will search for and identify host computers, gateways, and network devices. It will also identify available ports and services. A package called *nessus* can then perform a test of known vulnerabilities and identify all that apply. (Your IT folks should be using these, or similar tools, to test your cyber security.)

If a SCADA system is connected to any other system(s) via LAN or WAN technology, then the possibility exists that a hacker or terrorist could gain remote access to your SCADA system through those interconnections. Understanding how they accomplish this and what you can do to stop them is the main topic of the remainder of this chapter.

TCP/IP Suite

In the 1970s and 1980s, most computer vendors had developed their own proprietary operating systems and networking technology. This was fine as long as you purchased computers only from a single vendor. Unfortunately, that was not always possible or desirable, so the problem of *interoperability* (or the lack thereof) came to the forefront. It was always necessary to cobble together custom programs that could provide limited, hard-coded and minimal data exchanges, when attempting to link computers from different vendors. Computers from different vendors had hardware architectural differences (e.g., the number of bits in a word and the bit orientation) and operating system differences (e.g., file structures, data representations, and command syntax).

During this same time period, a project was started within the Department of Defense Advanced Research Projects Agency (ARPA) to create a robust networking mechanism that would actually provide interoperability between and among all of the computer systems used by various government agencies, research laboratories, and defense contractors. The result of this project was called ARPANET (or DARPANET) and eventually evolved into the Internet we now know and love. The underpinnings of the Internet include a protocol suite of software (and the definition of a *virtual architecture*) that enables computers with different operating systems, file structures, data representations, and command-line interpreters to interoperate. Within this software suite is IP, which is the protocol that actually carries all messages across the Internet. This is the protocol that utilizes the unique IP address assigned to every computer directly attached to the Internet.

In addition, there are other protocols, like TCP, that improve the reliability of message transmission and allow messages to be directed to specific applications (or standard system services like e-mail) running on the destination computer. Because so many application programs actually make use of TCP, it has become typical to refer to TCP/IP, rather than just IP. In all, there are dozens of protocols that are used to maintain, coordinate, and supervise the operation of the Internet. One of the important aspects of the Internet is that these underlying protocols are published standards that are freely available to anyone who wants to implement IP networking.

At about the same time that the Department of Defense was developing TCP/IP, there was ongoing work on an inter-networking standard called International Standards Organization—Open Systems Interconnect (OSI). But the emergence and overwhelming acceptance of the IP suite as a standard has pretty much killed off OSI and all of the vendor-proprietary networking standards. (This is not to imply that the OSI reference model was abandoned entirely. It is still used as a model against which other networking architectures—e.g., IP—are compared.) Figure 6–2 compares the layers defined in the OSI model and in TCP/IP. Initially, some vendors proceeded to write program code for implementation of the OSI model. However, no actual software implementation of the OSI model (if any remain) would be in any position today to compete with the complete dominance of IP-based networking.

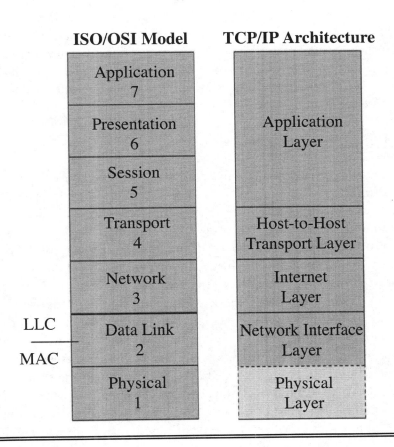

FIG. 6–2. *The OSI seven-layer model and IP equivalent-function layers*

Today almost all intercomputer networking, regardless of LAN or WAN, is done with IP networking technology. A corporate WAN and/or LAN will employ IP networking technology, regardless of being connected to the Internet. In fact, such a stand-alone network may be called an *extranet*. If it is connected to the Internet, then the corporate network may be called an *intranet*. The IP suite of protocols is provided with all of the popular operating systems and is built into most of the networking components (e.g., routers and gateways). So when we speak about a hacker attempting to gain remote access to a SCADA system, via LAN or WAN networks, we mean that the hacker is using the mechanisms of the IP suite to connect with your SCADA system. Since IP, as well as all other technical aspects of the Internet, is fully in the public domain, hackers have a vast amount of information to assist them in devising their attack methodologies. Still, an even greater number of white-hat (good) hackers and IT security professionals can use this same information to devise protections against threats by evil hackers.

IP addresses and gateways

As previously mentioned, all computers directly connected to the Internet must have a unique IP address. But for most of us, our personal and office computers are not directly connected to the Internet; we sit on a corporate LAN or WAN, or connect via an ISP. Only one computer on the corporate LAN/WAN may actually have an Internet connection. The remainder must access the Internet by passing messages through this *gateway* computer. There are at least two good reasons for this architecture. The first reason is that most of the message traffic on the LAN/WAN is for destinations within the LAN/WAN, so there is no reason to pass them onto the Internet. The second reason is that the world was actually running out of unique IP addresses, because of the unforeseen growth and spread of the Internet (rectified by IPv6). By hiding the computers on a LAN/WAN behind a gateway, we have the opportunity to reuse IP addresses. This is similar to the way that every town has an address like 100 Main Street, yet mail gets correctly delivered because the address also includes the name of the town (and a unique zip code). The computers inside the network all use special, reusable IP addresses that can never be sent across the Internet. These computers all send their messages to the gateway computer, which puts them onto the Internet, using its own IP address (which is a real IP address). It was mentioned earlier that an IP address is like a street address. To be more accurate, an IP address has two parts: a network address and a host address. To use our postal department analogy, this is like the city/state portion of the postal address and the specific street address portion. You need both for a complete address (both on the Internet and with the postal service). Within an office building you have room/floor addresses (which will be repeated over and over in other buildings) which can be like the reusable IP addresses that are used internal to a local network, but which won't work over the Internet.

The process of re-addressing messages on their way in from and out to the Internet is called *network address translation* (NAT). The gateway computer performs this re-addressing for all of the other computers on the private network (fig. 6–3). Hackers like to attack your gateway and mess with its NAT table, but IT professionals know how to protect against such attacks. If hackers can't get through the gateway, then they can't get to the other computers on the network.

NAT - Network Address Translation

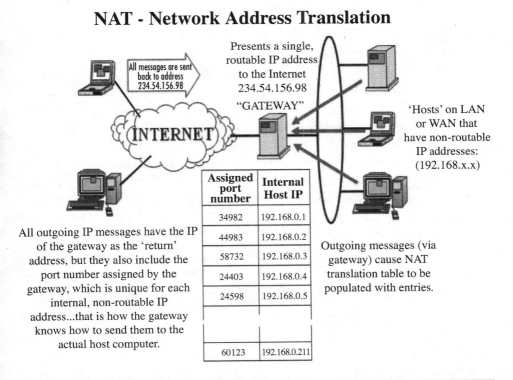

Presents a single, routable IP address to the Internet
234.54.156.98
"GATEWAY"

All messages are sent back to address 234.54.156.98

INTERNET

'Hosts' on LAN or WAN that have non-routable IP addresses: (192.168.x.x)

All outgoing IP messages have the IP of the gateway as the 'return' address, but they also include the port number assigned by the gateway, which is unique for each internal, non-routable IP address...that is how the gateway knows how to send them to the actual host computer.

Outgoing messages (via gateway) cause NAT translation table to be populated with entries.

Assigned port number	Internal Host IP
34982	192.168.0.1
44983	192.168.0.2
58732	192.168.0.3
24403	192.168.0.4
24598	192.168.0.5
60123	192.168.0.211

FIG. **6–3.** *NAT in a gateway computer*

Firewalls

In most cases, in which a computer or a network (WAN/LAN) of computers is connected to the Internet or even to another network, the need exists for a gateway-type computer to deal with addressing issues. The computer used in most cases is a special-purpose computer called a *router*. This name describes its function: its job is to figure out how to route and deliver messages. While the Internet was being developed, the designers used the term *gateway* to describe computer functions dealing with addressing issues. The notion was that these routing functions would be assigned to one of the general-purpose computers on the network—that is, to the computer with a physical communication link to the Internet. Equipment manufacturers began building lower-cost, special-purpose computers programmed specifically to perform these functions and gave them the name router.

Today when we speak of a gateway, we are more likely speaking in particular about a router that is performing NAT functions (as well as other functions). Since *all* IP messages must travel through the gateway/router before reaching the other computers on any given network, the gateway/router is the logical place to try to detect and block the entry of messages that are intended to harm any of the computers on the network. Routers with additional logic for the checking and blocking of IP messages are usually given the generic name of *firewall*. Initially firewalls performed very simplistic checks, based purely on the address information contained within an IP message (a *packet* or *datagram*). All IP messages contain the IP address of the computer that is sending the message (the return address) and the IP address of the computer to which the message is to be delivered. Further, if TCP (or UDP) messages are used, there will be source and destination port numbers, as well as the IP addresses (fig. 6–4).

This limited addressing information is insufficient today to identify message traffic that is harmful, both because malicious software can be hidden inside the message transported in the TCP/IP packets and because it is all too easy to fake address information. (The term *IP spoofing* is used to describe methods for creating messages with fake address information.) Hackers have become ever more clever in their methods for getting through

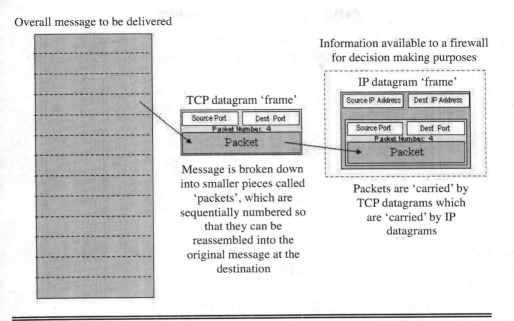

FIG. 6–4. *IP and TCP (or UDP) datagram header information for firewall inspection*

firewalls, which is why no one depends solely on firewalls for complete protection of essential computer systems. Nevertheless, a good firewall at each interconnection point is still the best starting point for establishing an electronic security perimeter.

Cyber attacks against a computer system can come in many forms, depending on the objectives of the attacker. The attack approaches will differ if the attacker is trying to obtain information stored in a computer system or make use of the computing resources of a computer system, as opposed to trying to shut the system down or kill its networking capabilities. With a SCADA system, it must be assumed that a serious terrorist attack would be intended to cause newsworthy damage, through the use of the system. As Lenin said, "The purpose of terrorism is to terrorize." Disabling a computer system may require merely identifying what version of the operating system is running on the target computer—and therefore, what known vulnerabilities are available to be exploited. Readily available hacker tools can accomplish this automatically. Breaking through the protection mechanisms of an operating system and gaining privileged access to its utilities and resources constitutes a far more complex process, requiring much higher skill and knowledge levels. Regardless of the intent of a cyber attack, the process involves sending a variety of specially crafted IP messages to the target computer.

Classes of attack messages

The classes of messages sent to a computer as part of an overall cyber attack can generally be categorized into four broad types, based on the intentions:

- Messages sent to probe and explore a computer/network

- Messages sent to overload a computer or network

- Massages sent to deliver malware (viruses, worms, Trojans, etc.) into a computer

- Messages sent to exploit specific operating system or application program vulnerabilities

Probing and exploring

The TCP/IP suite includes a set of protocols whose purpose is the management and coordination of the computers on the Internet and traffic moving through the Internet. In particular, the Internet Control Message Protocol (ICMP) is used by computers to advise each other of situations when interconnecting communication links are overloaded and when messages in transit are discarded as undeliverable. Hackers have found creative ways to use these messages to gain information about the network and computers hiding behind the gateway. Every IP packet has a *time to live* (TTL) counter, which is decrementally adjusted as the packet passes through successive computers. If it reaches a value of zero, the computer with the packet would delete it and send a message to that effect back to the originating computer. By sending a properly crafted sequence of packets, starting with a TTL of one and with each successive packet adjusting incrementally by one, it is possible to discover a lot about what lies behind a gateway/firewall. Today most firewalls give you the option of discarding and ignoring a range of message variations known to be used for such network probing.

Another type of probing consists of sending malformed or incorrectly sequenced messages or messages to specific TCP and UDP port numbers, to see how (or if) the system responds. It is often possible to identify a great deal about the software version of an operating system, the level and extensiveness of its security patches, and the robustness of its security mechanisms by using such techniques. With this knowledge, a hacker can reference online lists of known vulnerabilities and attack methods, posted on hacker Web sites. There are readily available hacker (and security testing) tools that automate this process and generate a complete summary of available vulnerabilities. Your own IT group can use such a tool to identify vulnerabilities in your SCADA system computers.

Overloading

Computers do not have infinite memory, file storage, or computing capacity. It is possible to place an excessive and persistent load on a computer such that one or more of those critical resources is consumed. At that point, the computer system will either have to reboot or grind to a halt, ceasing performance of its required functions. An old cyber attack called *SYN flooding* exploited the failure of the IP implementation in most operating systems to keep track of how many connection requests were made from a given remote computer or of how long it had been waiting for that initiating computer to complete the connection negotiation. A hacker tool would send a continuous stream of IP connection requests (never fully completed), causing the target computer to fill its memory with storage buffers (one per connection request) until all memory was used and the computer operating system crashed. Today all proper IP software implementations (and *stateful inspection* firewalls) can identify this type of attack and stop it before it endangers the computer system.

A more difficult but similar attack is the *denial of service* (DoS) attack. This is where a computer (or its network connection to the Internet) is overloaded by having a large number of computers simultaneously send perfectly valid service requests (e.g., requesting a Web page) but at such a rate and quantity that all of the targeted computer's resources are usurped, thereby making the computer unavailable to valid users. Such an attack requires the participation of a large number of computers in cooperation, but hacker groups have successfully established huge collections of *zombie computers* (also called bot networks), spread all around the Internet, that they can use to launch DoS attacks. Modern firewalls can be configured with anomaly-detection technology to prevent the flood of messages from reaching any of the computers behind the firewall. (This would not necessarily prevent the DoS attack from tying up the firewall computer and making the Internet connection unavailable to the remaining computers.) DoS attacks have been launched mainly against Web sites (e-commerce and online gaming in particular), but any exposed, unprotected computer system could be vulnerable to such an attack.

Malware delivery

The term *malware* (malicious software) is used to describe a range of programs that are specifically designed to violate one or more of the three tenets of cybersecurity (confidentiality, integrity, and availability). The most common forms of malware are *viruses, worms,* and *Trojans.* A virus and a worm are both self-replicating programs that spread copies of themselves. Viruses spread by attaching themselves to frequently used programs; worms spread by sending their copies over network connections. A special variation of these two types of malware is one that replicates endlessly and shuts down a computer by consuming all of its resources; this may also be called a *bacteria.* A virus or a worm might also have a payload, which is a special set of instructions that are triggered by defined conditions. Payloads are often used to cause damage by deleting files, corrupting data, altering application programs, or just displaying messages.

Trojans are an especially sophisticated and dangerous form of malware, because they reside in your computer and secretly perform activities that violate the confidentiality and integrity tenets. Trojans get their name form the original Trojan horse—which appeared to be a boon but harbored something with malicious intent. Many Trojans are disguised as useful shareware programs that provide desirable functions and features. Inside those same programs, however, is program logic, waiting for the right trigger (such as a time or date or a special user-input code) or performing other secret tasks in the background. Once activated Trojans may do any number of tasks: log user keystrokes to capture passwords, monitor LAN/WAN traffic to read e-mail, provide remote access that bypasses the system authentication process, and so forth. Some people get the idea that if they have a firewall that blocks outgoing traffic, other than acceptable messaging such as email and web page requests, that such Trojans are defeated, since they might collect data, but they can't send it back to the hacker. This is not the case since hackers have found interesting ways to tunnel (encapsulate) one type of message traffic inside another. A Trojan in your computer can be designed to send a web request (using http protocol messages) to the hacker's computer, where a corresponding program responds with a false Web page that is actually commands to direct the action of the Trojan. The outgoing Web page request normally contains supposed data (the URL of the page being requested, plus a lot of header stuff supplied by the browser). These can be used to deliver the collected data. To a firewall the transactions look like normal Web browsing, but the http protocol is actually being used to carry communications between the implanted Trojan and the hacker's monitoring program. Such *covert channels* are commonly used by hackers to get through firewalls.

It is important not to allow malware into your systems; once it enters, it spreads and is difficult to eliminate. Modern firewalls maintain a list of all discovered versions of malware and search through incoming message traffic for signs of such malware. Firewalls that perform these checks are called *deep inspection* firewalls. Hackers are clever and have found ways to break up malware and embed it in multiple messages. But firewall builders have countered by looking for code fragments or using heuristic algorithms. Therefore, it is very important to keep your firewall software up to date with the latest malware information.

Web browsing, e-mail, and instant messaging. One very insidious mechanism used to deliver malware to computers is by embedding such malware in the data stream sent from a Web site. The majority of Trojans introduced into computer systems each year have come from Web browsing on sites that either accidentally or intentionally include such malware along with the Web content they deliver to your browser.

The second major source of malware is as attachments to unsolicited e-mail (*spam*) or embedded in e-mail headers (which your browser processes but which isn't normally part of the visually presented Web display information). Web technology has expanded to include *scripting languages* that permit a Web site to send programs (also called *mobile code*) to your PC or Web browser, where they are subsequently executed. This makes it possible to have interactive, dynamic Web pages. Unfortunately, such active content (ActiveX controls, VBscript, and JavaScript) can also be used as malware or to deliver malware.

In a similar manner, all of the new instant messaging (IM) technologies have the potential for transporting malware. Virus scanners need to watch IM traffic, as well as conventional e-mail traffic. In our modern business environment, it is not realistic to forgo e-mail and Web browsing, even though they can be subverted. For these reasons, it is not uncommon for a company to keep PCs on a separate network (or at least a separate, virtual LAN [VLAN]), to prevent infected PCs from contaminating the SCADA system. Having virus-scanning software in every PC, as well as in the e-mail server and the firewall, is currently the best defense against these malware delivery mechanisms. Again, keeping scanning software up to date is critical. This is not as easily done in facilities where critical PCs reside on a SCADA LAN behind a firewall. Agents (programs that run and reside in your PC and communicate with the vendor's support server via the Internet) fetch and install updates only when they can get access through your firewall (which for the sake of security you want to block anything that you haven't specifically authorized).

Many SCADA systems now utilize conventional PCs (with Microsoft Windows operating systems) as their operator and engineering consoles. In an effort to reduce costs or for the sake of convenience, organizations occasionally allow these same PCs to be used for non-SCADA functions— as an office PC in addition to a SCADA console. This may involve providing the PC with a separate LAN connection (a practice called *dual homing*) so that it physically connects to the SCADA LAN and the corporate/facility LAN, or it may involve providing VLAN access to both VLANs. This is actually a dangerous practice in that the PC can act as an IP bridge to permit message traffic to cross over from one LAN to the other (fig. 6–5). In addition, if malware enters the PC as a result of Web browsing, IM, or e-mail usage, it can then find its way onto the SCADA LAN and the other computers on that LAN. When the connections are obvious, because they are hardwired, it is easier to identify PCs that may be bridging two LANs. Unfortunately today many laptop PCs come with built in wireless Ethernet (Wifi, also branded as Centrino™ by Intel) and/ or Bluetooth, which also act as a second (wireless) LAN interface and can enable the same contagion problems. (More on the issue of wireless technology and security later in the chapter.)

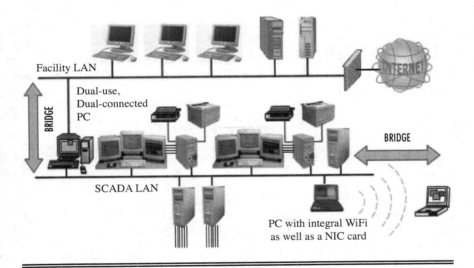

FIG. 6–5. *Dual–use PC–bridging LANs*

Another protective mechanism (and security policy) used by many companies is to have the firewall and e-mail server keep a list of forbidden Web sites (a list of URLs) and a list of spam sites (e-mail addresses). Attempts to browse a forbidden Web site will be rejected by the firewall, as will incoming e-mail from spammers. This particular protective mechanism, although intended as an aid to users, always seems to be a source of contention between the IT group and employees, who find that legitimate Web sites and e-mail are being blocked.

Hybrid delivery mechanisms. Up to this point, we have been discussing the delivery of malware to a SCADA system by means of remote electronic access, ignoring delivery by direct physical access (which will be discussed later). However, the possibility exists that a delivery mechanism could be employed that relies on a form of access, electronic as well as physical—*but not by the attacker.*

Today many laptop computers, handheld personal digital assistants (PDAs), and cell phones have built-in wireless networking capability in the form of *WiFi* and/or *Bluetooth*. These wireless communications technologies allow such devices to interoperate and exchange data with other similarly equipped devices. There are documented instances of this wireless technology being used to introduce malware into such portable devices, which then infect other computers when they are physically connected or brought into proximity. This problem is discussed in greater detail later in this chapter.

Exploitation. Through an experimental process of trial and error and through collaboration with others, hackers routinely discover that certain programs, either operating system utilities or common application programs, have been designed without sufficient error-checking and error-handling logic. Most useful programs accept incoming data (input), perform some operation on those data, and then generate and present the resulting output. The input to a program can consist of many types of data—numeric, text, Boolean, and/or date/time, among others. For most types of input, there will be a valid range of acceptable input (e.g., time can't be a negative number, and telephone numbers shouldn't contain letters of the alphabet). If programs don't do a sufficient level of input validation, the program may perform in an unexpected manner that opens unauthorized access when presented with invalid input data. Hacker Web sites are filled with lists of such known vulnerabilities and directions for exploiting them.

The data input to a program has to be placed into memory so that it can be used by the program. Most programmers allocate space inside their programs (in *buffers*) to hold the input or make use of a dynamic operating system buffer called a *stack*. If input is in excess of the expected amount and no checks are made for this condition, then the incoming data can overwrite portions of the program itself. Exploiting such *buffer overflow* vulnerabilities allows a hacker to modify a program's logic by replacing the real program code with their own program code. This is especially dangerous when the program being exploited is a key system utility that runs at a high level of access. Modifying such a program provides a hacker with a means of obtaining administrative-level access, through which all of the conventional operating system protective mechanisms (e.g., file access controls) can be bypassed or disabled. Hacker Web sites are filled with information about various programs and operating system utilities known to be vulnerable to various types of attacks. The ultimate defense is to rewrite the offending program so that it makes checks on all of its input data sources for range validity, quantity, data type, etc. A large number of "security related patches" issued by vendors are exactly that: program updates that fix these mistakes and eliminate yet another vulnerability. It is also important to remember that just because a vendor comes out with a patch doesn't mean that every copy of the vulnerable program will be immediately be replaced. Hackers count on the fact that lots of computers may never get these changes installed.

Firewalls can't protect against all such attacks, because in many cases, only the targeted programs (or their authors) can determine if input being received and processed is improper. However, a special category of firewall, called an application *proxy,* can be used to examine the messages and data sent to a specific set of well-known, standardized system utilities, such as Web servers and e-mail servers. An application proxy is a firewall that knows the protocol details used by specific applications and can watch messages to ensure that they are syntactically correct, are in the right sequence, and contain valid data where data is required. Because they have to be specifically designed to know all of the intimate details of each protocol they monitor, application proxy firewalls tend to support only well-used and popular IP protocols, and there is a performance penalty because of the added layer of message checking. (Imagine having someone who reads all your messages prior to giving them to you, and before passing them on to the people with whom you correspond.)

When the point of attack is a Web server, there are other exploitation mechanisms available to hackers. A commonly used one is *SQL injection.* SQL is a standardized transactional language that is used to interact with relational database packages that support and conform to the SQL standard. Many Web sites, particularly e-commerce (like an online catalog store), require large relational databases containing information that is selectively presented through the Web site. The Web site software interacts with the relational database by sending SQL commands. If a Web site has not been designed with adequate input checking, hackers can embed SQL commands in input fields submitted to the Web site, and these commands will be acted on by the relational database. Such attacks are mounted mainly to steal (and possibly to delete or alter) information stored in such databases. (Large-scale identity theft has occurred through this mechanism.) SCADA systems are not e-commerce Web sites and don't usually contain personnel and accounting data, so why would this sort of attack be of concern to a SCADA system owner? Today using Web server/browser technology as a way of offering data to users has become quite popular, for a number of reasons (standards being a central one). Some SCADA vendors now offer remote access (and even local access) to operational displays via Web pages. Some such systems may incorporate Web displays that have to query a relational database in order to get the data to create the Web page. If user input is part of this process (such as selecting a time/data span or picking a category of data) then there is the possibility of having SQL injection used by a malicious insider to cause the loss of such data. In the SQL language a simple command "DROP database_name" can cause the immediate deletion of all of your data.

Wireless LANs

One of the challenges in protecting LANs (and the computers attached to them) is the ready availability of standardized, commercially available, inexpensive, wireless networking technology in the form of WiFi (also called wireless fidelity or IEEE 802.11x) and all of its variations (11.a, 11.b, and 11.g). With hardwired LANs (generally Ethernet), you have physical cables, switches, and hubs that establish the connectivity of a computer into that local area network (fig. 6–6). This makes it somewhat easier to monitor and control who has access to the LAN (although with physical access to the systems and network equipment, anyone could, in theory, make a connection).

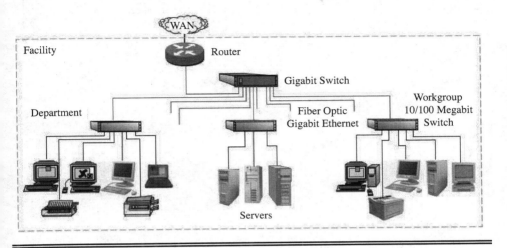

FIG. 6–6. *Typical Ethernet LAN components and architecture*

Today it is possible to extend an Ethernet LAN by adding *wireless access points* (APs) anywhere on the LAN (fig. 6–7). These APs provide a short-range connectivity zone in which suitably equipped computers (typically laptop PCs and handheld devices) can wirelessly link with the AP and have their message traffic routed onto the hardwired LAN. APs (also called hot spots when deployed for public access) are very convenient for portable devices that don't have a permanent mounting location. Unfortunately they are also one of the easiest ways for an attacker to gain access to your systems and bypass your firewalls. Anyone who gets close enough for a radio signal to be received and transmitted could obtain a network connection onto your LAN.

Although the various WiFi standards are designed to provide limited geographic range for wireless users, it has been demonstrated that with a suitable antenna (made from a famous tubular potato chip container), WiFi communications may be eavesdropped on from a surprising distance (up to many miles). There is even a game, called *war driving*, in which

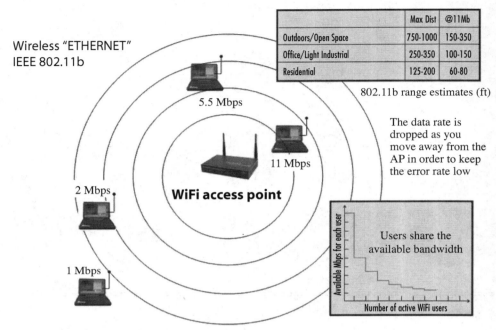

The actual bandwidth/data rate you get varies with distance and number of stations

FIG. 6–7. *WiFi APs*

portable PCs with WiFi cards are driven around a city, in an effort to locate the greatest number of WiFi APs. There are Web sites that list the results and hacker software that can break through the basic protective encryption that was initially built into the WiFi standard. (Wired Equivalent Privacy [WEP] is a 40-bit encryption scheme that has proven all too easy for hackers to break.) A readily available software package called AirSnort can accomplish this after just a few minutes of monitoring the encrypted message traffic.

There *are* mechanisms available to protect your WiFi APs. The old original WEP scheme has been updated/replaced by new encryption standards: WiFi Protected Access (WPA) and WPA-2, which use 128- and 152-bit encryption keys, respectively. (You may, however, need to update the firmware of your APs to get this protection.) It is possible to explicitly specify the Ethernet media access control (MAC) addresses (WiFi cards have a unique MAC address just like normal Ethernet NICs) of devices allowed to utilize the AP(s); the *service set identifier* (SSID) beacon, a regularly broadcasted message announcing to all listeners that an AP is available, can be disabled; and the support, in your APs, of Dynamic Host Configuration Protocol (DHCP) (the protocol that gives visiting computers a temporary IP address they can use on the network) can be disabled. All of these actions make it harder (but not impossible) for an attacker to establish a wireless connection to your LAN.

Rogue APs

All of these mechanisms, if properly applied and maintained, offer pretty good protection for your APs. The problem comes when employees install WiFi equipment for their convenience and fail to implement or maintain the necessary security measures. These unauthorized (*rogue*) APs can be a major security hole and can jeopardize your entire network. A very important cybersecurity policy is to make it known that no employee or contractor may attach a WiFi device to any network or computer. All APs (if permitted at all) should be installed by the IT group, after ensuring that suitable protective measures have been implemented and verified.

Hackers have found a surprising number of ways to abuse WiFi technology. One cute trick is to set up an AP physically adjacent to a valid one (perhaps in an office across the hall) and have it masquerade as the valid AP by setting its SSID to match. A hacker can then wait for a person to attempt to login to the network/server via this *evil-twin* AP and capture the authentication messages, or at least the employee's user ID and password.

Another danger is the commonality of portable PCs with both WiFi and conventional, wired Ethernet LAN capability (e.g., Intel's Centrino technology). When brought into the office and docked, these PCs will generally have a wired LAN connection through their docking station and yet still have an active WiFi capability. Once the PC has been authenticated on the wired LAN, a hacker could connect with the WiFi port and be bridged onto the LAN, having the access rights of the PC's owner (fig. 6–8). This is the wireless equivalent of being dual homed onto two LANs.

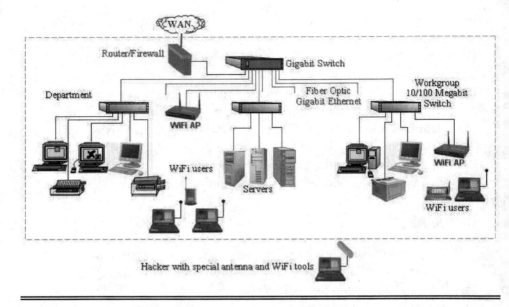

FIG. 6–8. *Using WiFi APs to bypass firewall protections and access a LAN*

Administration and supervision of wireless LAN (WLAN) technology is complex, but there are technologies available to assist with this challenge. With the appropriate software, specifically positioned APs can actually be used as monitoring devices whose function is to listen for WiFi traffic and identify rogue APs, those without appropriate protective measures enabled and evil-twin APs.

Bluetooth and WiFi ad hoc networks

As mentioned previously, an increasing number of portable and handheld computer devices (PDAs, cell phones, Laptop PCs, etc.) come equipped with wireless networking hardware and software preinstalled. Both Bluetooth and WiFi support an operating mode called *ad hoc,* which means that they can spontaneously establish a communication link with one or more nearby computer devices that have a similar capability. (For WiFi that means using the same SSID and being locked to the same channel.) WiFi cards can also be set to infrastructure mode, meaning they will only connect to a LAN via the user-selected AP, and not make a direct connection with other nearby WiFi equipped devices. The danger with ad hoc mode is that a hacker can use this mode to establish a surreptitious connection to your device and use that connection to implant malware or to extract information. There have been widely publicized instances of celebrities having this happen with their PDAs or cell phones. In the case of Bluetooth enabled devices, the terms *Bluesnarf* and *Bluejack* have been coined to describe two ways of exploiting the vulnerability of such devices. There is even a Bluejack Web site. If a worm or a virus is placed in your laptop through an ad hoc connection, the next time you connect to an AP internal to your network (or make a hardwired Ethernet LAN connection), that implanted malware can find its way out onto the LAN and into other computers.

Authentication and Validation

When a person wishes to access the facilities and resources of a computer system today—regardless whether that person is physically adjacent to that computer system or physically remote—the procedure typically involves going through an authentication process of some sort. In most cases, this merely means entering a valid user ID and the corresponding password. If the system accepts these two items as valid, then the person is granted the access rights corresponding to that particular ID/password, as assigned by the system administrator. Sophisticated operating systems support some form of access control list (ACL) that defines the access rights and limits for each user. Most users of a system will be restricted to running the applications they are allowed to use and working on their own files. Accessing protected applications and system utilities or altering/ deleting files belonging to others is not normally allowed to any user unless that user has administrative rights (the term administrator is commonly used in the Microsoft Windows world—Somewhat like being the root or superuser in the Unix world).

The operational users of SCADA systems often have to deal with a unique user-authentication process. That is because they are not conventional users from the standpoint of a computer operating system. SCADA system operators actually interact with a suite of applications (the SCADA software) running on the computer system (in particular, the operator console and alarming functions).

There are four categories of personnel who need access to the SCADA system:

- Operational personnel

- Engineering personnel

- Application programming personnel

- System administration personnel

A fact of life in some organizations is that staffing limitations force individuals to wear several hats and assume duties that fall across multiple categories. Sometimes a single individual wears all of the hats. That is a potential security risk. An organization has to make a business risk assessment and decide if the risk is worth the cost savings. (Risk assessment and business justifications are addressed later in the book.)

The first category (operators) consists of the people who sit in front of the operator display consoles—watching graphic displays, alarm summary lists, and historical trending displays—to supervise and control the process being monitored by the SCADA system. These personnel typically do not have a computer or even an engineering background, but rather are specially trained to understand the process being monitored and controlled—specifically, to use the SCADA system displays and interfaces to manage and adjust that process. Because these people have direct supervisory control over field equipment (e.g., circuit breakers, pumps, valves, and motors), there is often a subcategorization of access restrictions related to the training level and experience of the individual operational personnel (e.g., senior operator, operator, operator trainee).

The second category of personnel (engineering) often make use of the data collected by the SCADA system for reports, calculations, modeling, and process optimization. These personnel usually have the responsibility for making configuration changes to the SCADA system (adding RTUs, database points, calculations, reports, etc.) as required. They usually have reasonable familiarity with the operational aspects of the system (often having been responsible for creating the displays that form the operator interface), although they do not necessarily possess the hands-on experience of the senior operational staff. The engineering staff usually have the most experience in the overall use of the SCADA system configuration utilities, communications systems, and computer hardware in general. To accomplish their work, these personnel must usually be given access to the full range of system configuration tools and the actual files that define the system functions and configuration. In this category would be the application/automation engineers, the telecommunications support staff, and even the hardware technicians that setup, install, and commission the RTUs.

The third category of personnel (programmers) may not be separate from the second, although in large organizations that is more likely. These personnel have specific programming expertise and have had to learn both the SCADA system–particular mechanisms for program development, testing, and integration, as well as the operating system utilities for the computing platform on which the SCADA system is built. To develop suitable application programs, these personnel must also understand the details of the system configuration (e.g., point tag naming schemes) and the process-related requirements (e.g., open a recirculation valve prior to starting the pump). This knowledge usually comes from interactions with the operational and engineering personnel. To perform their jobs, these personnel often need to be given access to the basic operating system utilities and functions, including the right to delete, alter, and replace the program files of the SCADA system.

The fourth and final category (administrative) is for the personnel assigned to perform the regular, routine, highly necessary system housekeeping functions—such as administering user IDs and passwords, making system backups, installing vendor-supplied software updates and patches, purging old files and old data from the system (possibly after transferring these data to removable media), and reviewing system logs for indications of developing problems. In smaller organizations, these functions may again be assigned to one of the engineering or programming personnel, in addition to their other duties. System administrators must be given access to system backup media, allowed to replace critical system files and software, given the ability to create and modify user accounts, and even granted authority to shut the system down and reboot/restart the system.

It should be apparent that each category of personnel warrants a different level of access and authority and that proper training and care are critical for those positions that include access to system functions that have the potential to disrupt or disable the system if misused. In most SCADA systems, the particular ID assigned to a user will define the access rights of that user—and as we have seen, some users must be granted very high levels of access.

Since a computer is just a machine, it has no direct way to confirm that the person sitting at workstation 3, who just logged in with the ID and password of the senior system administrator, is actually that person. To confirm this as true prior to granting full senior-operator access privileges, the computer must make the person provide some proof. If it were a human guard, the computer would ask for a photographic ID. As a computer, the type of proof must be something possible through programmatic means. The usual mechanism is to have the person provide a secret known only to the person and the computer. That is what a password is supposed to be—a shared secret. Unfortunately, most people use very simple, easily guessed passwords. Worse, many SCADA systems come with a set of default passwords, and the customers either never change them or change them once and never again. Worse still, many SCADA system vendors used to install a secret factory ID/password pair (granting full, unrestricted access) known to all of their current (and former) employees—and it is usually unchangeable by the customers.

It is unfortunately not uncommon to see operator consoles on a SCADA system on which a senior operator has logged in once upon a time and has remained logged in ever since, leaving senior-operator access privileges available to anyone who can physically or logically access that console. It is also not uncommon to see IDs and passwords posted in obvious places (frequently on Post-it™ notes stuck to the CRT display) or the adoption of a single ID/password that everyone knows. If no remote access to systems were possible and if all (current and former) employees could be absolutely trusted, then authentication considerations might not be an issue. In that case, the major reason for such IDs and passwords would be to prevent or reduce the number of human errors. Unfortunately, these days we really do need to ensure that only those with proper authority gain access to critical automation and control systems, particularly if they are remote users making an electronic connection. Fortunately in the situations just described, the problems can be addressed through training, education, and the establishment of appropriate policies and well crafted procedures, Actually it is surprising how much progress can be made toward reducing vulnerabilities and the consequences of an attack, by these same measures, without the need for technical solutions.

Strong authentication

In order for a computer/SCADA system to utilize its ability to restrict access rights, there needs to be a much better mechanism for giving the computer incontrovertible proof that a person attempting to log in is in fact the person assigned with that particular ID. In IT circles, the idea of a better proof mechanism is called *strong authentication*. Authentication can be done using a range of factors—such as shared secrets, like a password, or physical devices, like an electronic ID card. The best security comes from requiring multiple sources of proof (also called multifactor authentication).

In computer security terms, proof is often categorized as either something you know, something you have, or some physical metric of your person that is unique and (hopefully) impossible to counterfeit. Later in the book we discuss physical security and access control, but one of the technologies for access control is a personalized ID card that can be read by a computer, such as a magnetic-strip key card (or a noncontact radio frequency ID [RFID] smart card), and some SCADA vendors now offer the use of those same technologies as a proof component to the computer system login process (fig. 6–9). Recently emerging as another form of non-forgeable proof of identity are the low(er)-cost biometric devices that have come onto the market. Biometric scanners can use fingerprints, hand geometry measurements, retinal patterns, speech recognition, and other individualized metrics to make a unique identification. Of course, none of these technologies is perfect or foolproof. Currently such devices generate a certain percentage of *false positives* (incorrectly confirming a person's identity) and *false negatives* (incorrectly rejecting a person's identity) both of which can be a problem when applied to SCADA system user login. It would be unacceptable to most SCADA organizations to have a user locked out of the system due to a false negative response by a biometric scanner. (The same is probably true for incorrectly entering a password some number of times.) If the sensitivity of a biometric devices is altered to eliminate false negatives, it typically means many more false positives, which are also a risk. Using biometrics where time isn't critical, and where a manual inspection can be made in the case of a false negative, (such as physical access control) is acceptable. As the sole means for user authentication to a SCADA system, it isn't quite so certain.

Things you know:

Passwords
Pass phrases
Personal information
Domain expertise/knowledge
Secrets

Things you have:

Biometric measures:

Smart cards, RFID devices, password tokens, dongles and magnetic strip cards

Retinal, finger print hand geometry scanners plus voice, typing-sequence and signature recognition

FIG. 6–9. *Strong authentication options and technologies*

There are now fingerprint scanners built into laptop PCs to provide biometric authentication that the person attempting to use the laptop is the valid user. A range of low-cost biometric scanners can now be interfaced, as peripherals, to almost any computer. By the combination of multiple factors (something you have: a key card; something you know:

a password; and something you are: your fingerprint), it is possible to make it virtually impossible for an attacker to successfully forge their way through the authentication process. Of course, we have all seen spy movies where some evil mastermind steals the hand or eyeball of some poor sap to get past biometric safeguards. We will discount that as a low-probability threat, even though it makes for good cinema. Since being improperly granted access at high levels of authority poses a severe security threat to a SCADA system, it is important to consider implementing multifactor authentication. Biometrics can certainly be one of the factors, but there may need to be a best two out of three vote in that case.

Password strategies

At a minimum, if your SCADA system vendor cannot accommodate other authentication technologies, password schemes can be greatly improved by insisting on the use of more complex passwords and by changing them on a routine basis. The drawback is that people can't remember complex passwords like "Ax881cGldY77" and inevitably write them down in some convenient spot, thus making them subject to discovery or exposure. One approach people have used is to make up passwords that correspond to something that people *can* remember. A good strategy is to take a song—or some poem or something you memorized (and which is now unforgettable)—and use it to create a password. If you were a Boy Scout, you could use the first letters of the motto ("tlhfckoctbcr" = trustworthy, loyal, helpful, friendly, courteous, kind, obedient, cheerful, thrifty, brave, clean, reverent). Or if you like the Beatles, you could use the first letters from some lyrics you remember. Where possible, alternate between capital and lowercase letters, and perhaps add a number in there somewhere.

Hackers attack password systems by using programs that keep trying passwords until one is found. Such password-crackers may use a *brute force* approach (try the letter *a*, then *b*, then *c*, and keep switching and expanding until every letter combination up to zzzz…zzzzzz has been tried.) Better still (from a hacker's viewpoint) are *dictionary attacks*, where an actual table of possible words provide the password guesses. Hacker sites are filled with available word lists (*dictionaries*), covering dictionaries of the English language and of foreign languages, as well as famous people, sports terms, medical terms, engineering terms, baby names, movie titles, and just about anything else you might use as a password. This is why you are always told not to use actual words (or personal information that could be discovered) for a password.

Another technology that is available for protecting passwords, without the need for people to remember long and complex alphanumeric sequences, is the electronic *token* which is a hand held device that generates a pseudo random number that changes each minute, and which can act as a one time password. With token schemes the users each get their own token password generator and when they want to login they use the currently displayed number as their password. Since it changes each minute, if someone were to get the number, they would have less than a minute to use it, and then it would become invalid. Some recent tokens are USB devices and so the user doesn't have to enter a number, merely plug the token into a handy USB port on their PC. These have mainly been adopted for use in authenticating remote users who are setting up a VPN tunnel to their corporate servers.

Today most computer operating systems place a limit on the number of attempts you can make when trying to log in to the system. Once you have failed that many times, you may be forced to wait for the duration of some timeout interval prior to trying again, or you may have to have a system administrator reauthorize your account. Note, however, that few (if any) SCADA system customers would feel comfortable about the possible liability of having an operator locked out of performing critical control functions just because he was having a bad day and kept making typing errors while trying to log in. That is another reason why authentication via biometrics and/or physical media (i.e., something you have) is preferred; a remote attacker won't have a way to provide this proof (guard your eyeballs and fingers!) and people with poor typing skills won't have login problems. It is worth mentioning again that in many SCADA systems there are totally separate user login mechanisms for people that program, administer, and maintain the system (a login to the operating system) and for operational personnel (SCADA system login). Login attempt restrictions and lockout may be available for operating system logins, but not for SCADA system logins.

Later in this book, possible threat sources and type of attacks are discussed, including attacks by insiders. It is not sufficient to protect against remote attacks staged through electronic access. Strong-authentication mechanisms can be a critical line of defense against an internal attacker trying to gain access beyond his or her authorized level.

Because of the distributed nature of most modern SCADA systems the other problem with passwords is the distinct possibility that they will be sent across a network connection or (in the case of a remote user) a telecommunications link. It doesn't matter how long, messy, and strange your password is if someone with a packet sniffer can catch a copy as it travels over the LAN. In a SCADA system the login authentication of a user may be performed locally, on the computer where the user is working, or be routed to a central location for authentication. If the authentication is done elsewhere it is important that the process involved does not allow your password and ID information to be captured along the way. Different types of authentication servers exist today, many taken from the IT world. Packages like RADIUS, TACACS and others are used for centralized user authentication. The communication mechanisms used to communicate with these packages can be designed with security or without. A protocol called CHAP (Challenge Handshake Authentication Protocol) uses a one-time code, and the user password, to create a scrambled (hash coded) message that can safely traverse a network. Others, like the older PAP (Password Authentication Protocol) send the user ID and password as clear, readable text. If you take the effort to enforce strong passwords, it may be wasted if you don't insure that they are transmitted (and stored) in a secure manner.

Encryption and Ciphers

As mentioned at the beginning of this chapter, two of the objectives for cybersecurity are confidentiality and integrity. SCADA systems probably don't seem like a source of secret information, involving national security, on which people would be clamoring to get their hands. However, in specific industries and applications, the information in a SCADA system might be considered as business confidential, and there could be legal implications or competitive advantages gained if this information were released. In the deregulated electric power industry, a lot of information regarding generating plants is considered to be confidential and competitive in nature, and disclosure of this information could cause market irregularities and lead to legal action. With a free market in electric power, knowing in advance, for example, that a plant was scheduled to be taken out of the market for maintenance, could provide an unscrupulous trader to have an illegal advantage. In the pipeline industry, knowledge about pipeline capacities, current product delivery scheduling, and even facility operational status and other such information could be of value to a competitor, to a person playing in the futures market, and to a terrorist seeking a sensitive place to create an explosion. Although we have focused so far on the threat posed by a terrorist or hacker, it is also worth remembering that another cyber threat could be posed by a competitor (who might pay a hacker to break into your systems) or criminals seeking financial information.

One of the best ways to protect information, both stored in a computer and during transmission between computers, is to make that information useless to people who don't have the right to access that information. Encryption is the (reversible) process of running messages (documents, RTU polling commands, data exchanges, etc.) through a mathematical process that converts them into something incomprehensible and then, at a later point in time, translates them back into the original message.

It is worth stopping for a moment and remembering a basic truth about computers and digital communications: *everything* is represented as binary numbers (0s and 1s). Regardless of whether you are trying to store or transmit a textual document, a graphic image, an e-mail, or a video clip, all of these are stored as a series of binary numbers, inside the computer or when transmitted across a communication channel. That said, encryption can be explained as the performance of a series of mathematical operations on binary numbers to obscure their original values; to get back to the original numbers, these operations are then reversed.

As an overly simplistic example, you could choose to multiply all of the numbers making up a message by some other number, say 27. The person receiving the scrambled message would just have to divide all incoming numbers by 27 to recover the original message. Of course, this means that both of you must know that 27 is the value used to (un)scramble the data. In the world of encryption, that number is called the *encryption key* or simply the *key,* the unscrambled (original) message is called *plaintext,* and the scrambled (encrypted message) is called *ciphertext* (fig. 6–10). Of course, an encryption scheme that just multiplies by a small numeric value would not take long to figure out (*breaking the encryption,* as it is known). In the real world, keys tend to be really big numbers (at least 128-bit values; remember that keys are stored as binary numbers as well), and the encryption schemes (ciphers) involve a lot more than simple multiplication. The basic objective of encryption is to make it take a lot of time and effort to break the encryption, preferably so great that the effort is too costly to the attacker, or so long that the value of the recovered information will have diminished significantly. For example, if it will take a year to break the encryption on a message about a delivery schedule, it isn't worth the bother since the information is obsolete by the time the attacker has it.

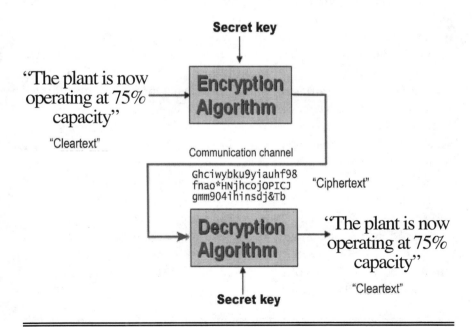

FIG. 6–10. *Using encryption to protect transmitted information*

There are different approaches taken when protecting information stored on a computer, as compared with protecting the confidentiality of messages sent across a communication channel. All information stored on a computer will be in the form of files which are managed and controlled by the file manager services of the operating system. All such file managers have basic protective mechanisms that are intended to keep a user, or application, that isn't authorized to access a file, from doing so. File access controls usually encompass the right to read, copy, alter, delete, and execute. (Execute is for the case that the file contains an executable program.) Any given user typically has all of these rights over their own files. A user will have some classes of system programs for which they are granted execute authority. A given user will *not* normally have any of these rights over the files of another user, unless that user allows those rights. File protection mechanisms (like cheap locks) are mainly intended to keep the honest people honest. Hackers have found numerous ways of bypassing such protective mechanisms.

Information stored in files within a computer can be encrypted (executable programs normally can't be encrypted) at the time of its storage, and that encryption usually doesn't change. (There is no automated mechanism to periodically re-encrypt such files using different keys.) It is assumed that access controls will keep unauthorized people from accessing the information and that the encryption is just additional security (fig. 6–11). Many commonly used office-automation application programs allow users to encrypt their own files, at the time of storage, with some simple user-defined password used as the key. For high-security applications (e.g., those used by various government agencies), it is possible to have a secure file system (part of the operating system) that provides encryption on all files, not leaving this as an option for individual users and applications. Most current operating systems make use of some level of encryption for the storage of sensitive information, such as user IDs and passwords (which need to be kept secret). It would be a hacker's lucky day to uncover a file (in plaintext) that has all of the user ID/password combinations used on a system.

For messages crossing a communication channel (e.g., a wireless Ethernet LAN or the Internet), we usually don't have the access-control protections since the channel itself is potentially insecure and physically

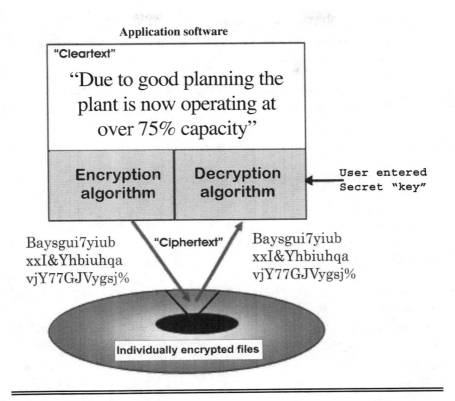

Application software

"Cleartext"

"Due to good planning the plant is now operating at over 75% capacity"

| Encryption algorithm | Decryption algorithm |

User entered Secret "key"

Baysgui7yiub
xxI&Yhbiuhqa
vjY77GJVygsj%

"Ciphertext"

Baysgui7yiub
xxI&Yhbiuhqa
vjY77GJVygsj%

Individually encrypted files

FIG. 6–11. *Encrypting files for greater security*

accessible; thus, encryption *is* our primary mechanisms for protecting the messages. Someone attempting to break your encryption and read or fake your message traffic has to figure out your key and algorithm. There are a small number of well-known encryption algorithms (also called *ciphers*), so that isn't the problem; guessing your key is the challenge. If we remember that a key is just a binary number, attackers simply have to try numbers, one at a time, till they find the right one. One reason for using a big key (a lot of bits) is that this can mean the possibility of a lot of numbers to try. A 128 bit key represents a huge number of possible key values ($2^{128}-1$) and even with today's computers, and a huge number of them cooperating to find the right number, it could take thousands of years to make enough guesses. On the other hand, the more messages an attacker gets and the more they know about the nature and content of your messages, the better their chances are of figuring out your encryption key. Thus, we need to think about our message traffic with respect to the decryption difficulty engendered by the nature and frequency of the message traffic.

Most message traffic can be divided into three broad classes:

- Repeated, frequently transmitted messages

- Slightly different, infrequently transmitted messages

- One-shot, never-repeated messages

The first type of message is like a SCADA polling message. The same message is sent over and over, and its context (RTU update reporting) is well known. These messages are the easiest to decrypt as you get lots of messages to play with and you generally know what the message contains.

The second type of message is like a SCADA supervisory command message, or like a fixed-format report being exchanged between computer systems. The data values change; however, the general form of the message doesn't vary, and these messages are not retransmitted nearly as frequently as a polling message. These messages are more difficult to decrypt, because they vary a little each time and because it takes longer to gather a big set to play with.

The third type of message is the most difficult to decrypt. This is because there are no other messages to compare it against. In addition, you have no idea of the content, and there is no repetition.

These categorizations are important, since the necessary sophistication of the encryption scheme employed will be different for each of the three categories, depending on how critical it is to prevent an attacker from compromising (i.e., reading or faking) communications. The ability to fake or forge particularly critical types of messages (e.g., supervisory control messages) certainly needs to be prevented in SCADA applications.

Shared secret

Encryption generally involves a shared secret (the key and to a degree even the encryption algorithm), between the sender of the data and the receiver of the data (or the program storing data to disk and the program bringing up that same data for display). It is not always easy to keep secrets, and no secret lasts forever. Encryption schemes (the algorithms used to [un]scramble) are typically *not* kept secret. The shared secret is the key being used, which as already stated, needs to be a big (128 or more bits long) binary number. Since encryption involves a shared secret (the key), there is a need for some secure way to deliver the key(s) to everyone with whom you need to have secured communications. (You could hire an armored car company or a courier to deliver them, but that is slow and expensive and you risk them being bribed to disclose your keys.) If you don't want a key to be used for too long, there needs to be a fast, secure and easy way to distribute new keys. Key distribution is a very serious challenge for encryption schemes since you need to do it occasionally, but risk the key being intercepted every time you send out a new one. We discuss how this is made possible later in this section.

Key size

The size of a key (i.e., how big the number is) is important. Because the key is the only secret, all someone has to do to break the encryption is to guess the right numeric value. If you used a small number (e.g., between 0 and 100), then at most 100 guesses would be needed to find the key. A computer program could make that many guesses in a tiny fraction of a second, testing each guess with a captured message and each of the well-known encryption algorithms. But, if your number is between 0 and 3.4×10^{38}, then even a really fast computer could take a very, very long time to make all the possible guesses. Today the minimal key size is considered to be 128 bits, because of the possibility that a collaboration of an enormous number (millions) of computers, spread across the Internet, could work together to break your encryption. (This actually happened when the U.S. government proposed the original 48-bit data encryption standard or DES.)

Another way to ensure that someone won't break your encryption (i.e., guess your key) is to change it frequently. The problem that this creates, however, is having to tell all of the authorized folks about the new key every time it changes and getting the new keys to all of them in a secure fashion such that the key can't be intercepted. If these operational challenges can be addressed, having regularly (frequently) changing keys would thwart any practical efforts to break your encryption, because the time required to figure out your key would be much longer than the time over which any one key was allowed to be used.

Public-key, or asymmetric-key (two different keys), encryption is a methodology devised to address these issues. Public-key encryption is a scheme whereby you use two specially calculated (mathematically related) keys: one that you *never* reveal to anyone (your *private key*); and another that you can give to anyone who wants a copy (your *public key*). In fact, you can e-mail your public key to someone and not concern yourself if anyone else gets a copy (but you must never allow your private key to be disclosed). If you want to have secure communications with another party, he or she also has to generate two such special keys, and you both send each other your respective public keys. Now, each of you can encrypt your messages using the other party's public key and decrypt arriving messages using your private key. In theory, only your private key can be used to decrypt a message encrypted with your public key and vice versa. A public key can be thought of as being like a key to your front door that can only be used to lock that door. You don't care how many such keys are created or who has one, since they can't be used to break into your home. Only your private key can open your front door, if locked with any public key. So don't let anyone get a copy of that key!

With a public-private key scheme, you have the option of creating a brand new set of keys at the beginning of any communication session, as long as the first messages between the two parties constitute an exchange of the new public keys (which you don't need to keep secret). With a public-key scheme, no key needs to be used for very long (because you can easily create and exchange a new pair anytime); thus, the chances of someone breaking the encryption (and creating faked messages), even with highly repeatable messages, is very low.

If messages being sent are doubly encrypted (using the sender's private key, followed by the receiver's public key), this scheme adds additional security (fig. 6–12). Using this scheme, the receiver knows not only that the message is secure but also that it must have come from the sender (because the sender's public key can decrypt a message encrypted only by the sender's private key—which no one but the sender should know). *Authentication* is the ability to validate the sending party. From this double-encryption scheme, you also get *nonrepudiation*: the sender can't deny sending the message, as no one else has his or her private key. Most modern encryption schemes make use of the two-key (public-key) strategy. Double encryption using both keys assures that confidentially is protected and authentication is provided as to the source of the message. But what about knowing that the message has not been altered or tampered with in any manner? An attacker doesn't need to know your keys or encryption scheme to intercept and modify a message. How can this be detected?

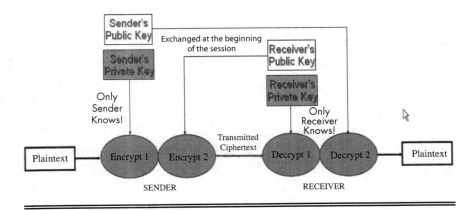

FIG. 6–12. *Dual-key (public-key) encryption/decryption*

Today many of the basic networking devices used to construct networks (e.g., routers) have dual-key encryption (and mutual authentication) as a built-in option that merely has to be configured and enabled. WAN connections between a SCADA system and any other computers can often be made reasonably secure (to external attackers) merely by enabling such protective measures.

Hash code

Although it would seem obvious that an encryption algorithm needs to be reversible to be of any use, there is actually a special category of encryption algorithm called *one-way algorithms*. These algorithms generate a unique number (rather than ciphertext) for a given set of input data—that is, a number that would change if any part of the input data were to be altered. (These are called one-way algorithms or *hash algorithms* because the original input cannot be reproduced given the hash code generated, even knowing the algorithm used. It would be like trying to unscramble an egg.) When data are sent across a communication channel, there is always the possibility that the message could be scrambled by noise, interference, or equipment problems aside from any intentional tampering.

To determine whether messages have arrived unscathed (unaltered), it is common practice to append to the messages a cyclic redundancy check (CRC) code, which is a unique number computed from the initial message. The receiver recomputes this CRC code number from the received message to see if it matches the received CRC code number. If there is no match, then there was a transmission error, and the message arrived altered. (Every RTU communications and computer networking protocol [including IP] uses a similar mechanism.) In the same manner, a data file, a program code file, or any other collection of unchanging numbers stored in a computer can be verified as unaltered if processed by a hash code generator and if the hash codes are recorded someplace secure. At any future time, the data can be run through the hash code algorithm again, and the results can be compared to the prior code; if they match, then presumably the data/program has not been changed.

Hash codes are useful for validating the integrity of data, but can also be used to verify that a system program or utility has not been tampered with or replaced with a malicious version. One way in which an operating system can be made more secure is to require that hash codes be generated for all system program modules and be stored in an encrypted file. Then, as these programs are used, the task scheduler (the part of the operating system that loads and runs programs) would recompute and verify the hash codes prior to loading and executing the program. The downside of this approach is that it would add time delays and degrade system performance. In a SCADA system, where timing responses are far less critical (adding a small fraction of a second prior to running the program usually won't even be noticed), such a strategy could be layered onto the operating system by the SCADA vendor and could be used to validate these particular (and critical) software components. In a similar manner the critical system configuration and setting tables and files could potentially be checked for tampering using a similar scheme. This technique only works for static (unchanging) data/program logic since a new check code value would need to be computed every time the data/programming changed. Unfortunately, the design of many programs and the organization of configuration data often intermix both static and dynamic elements, making it impossible to use such a scheme without a redesign/rewrite effort.

VPNs

VPNs comprise a combination of security technologies that allow a set of computers/users to operate across nonsecure, public, shared networks (e.g., the Internet) but with the security one might expect on a totally private network (unconcerned about outsiders reading their mail, accessing files, etc.). The basic components of a VPN are authentication and encryption. All of the computers that participate in a VPN need a means to prove that they are members of the VPN and to provide encryption for all communications.

With most VPN arrangements, all participating computers are issued a *digital certificate*. This is an electronic document, ideally issued by a third party called a *certificate authority* [CA], that contains unique information allowing validation and authentication to occur. The CA is a company that issues unique, verifiable digital certificates in the International Telecommunication Union (ITU) X.509 standard format (see fig. 6–13) and is available to confirm their issuance to specific parties, when necessary. In effect, they (the CAs) act as a trusted third party that two computers can query in order to prove that the other computer isn't lying about its identity and to validate that its credentials are legitimate. A digital certificate contains encryption keys and digital signatures provided by the third-party CA (see fig. 6–13).

When the CA is on the Internet and the participating computers are as well, the computers can query the CA to validate the proffered credentials, in real time, if any other computer attempts to open communications and claims VPN membership. The two computers exchange credentials and either can query the CA regarding the offered certificate, using public keys for encryption, and the CA tells each whether the other computer's

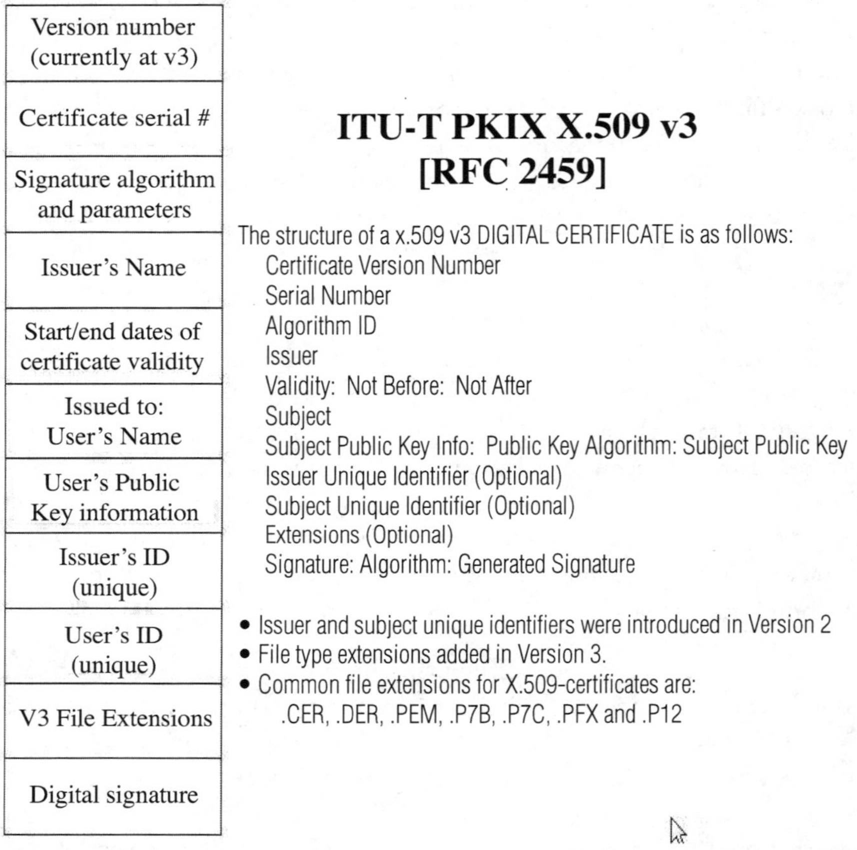

Version number (currently at v3)
Certificate serial #
Signature algorithm and parameters
Issuer's Name
Start/end dates of certificate validity
Issued to: User's Name
User's Public Key information
Issuer's ID (unique)
User's ID (unique)
V3 File Extensions
Digital signature

ITU-T PKIX X.509 v3 [RFC 2459]

The structure of a x.509 v3 DIGITAL CERTIFICATE is as follows:
Certificate Version Number
Serial Number
Algorithm ID
Issuer
Validity: Not Before: Not After
Subject
Subject Public Key Info: Public Key Algorithm: Subject Public Key
Issuer Unique Identifier (Optional)
Subject Unique Identifier (Optional)
Extensions (Optional)
Signature: Algorithm: Generated Signature

- Issuer and subject unique identifiers were introduced in Version 2
- File type extensions added in Version 3.
- Common file extensions for X.509-certificates are:
  .CER, .DER, .PEM, .P7B, .P7C, .PFX and .P12

Fig. 6–13. *X.509 (version 3) digital certificate content and structure*

credentials are legitimate. If so, they can then exchange public keys and start talking. In effect, this process ensures that your computer will refuse to communicate with any other computers unless they can be validated through this process. The term *public–key infrastructure* (PKI) is used to describe this process and relationship structure. This is equivalent to having an FBI agent come to your home and offer his ID as proof, and your calling the local FBI office to verify the authenticity of the person (checking his credentials). It is equally possible to assign a given computer to act as the CA for all other computers on a private network, when Internet connectivity is not available or desirable. If VPN technology were used among all of the computers in a SCADA system, it would be best if this approach (a local, private CA) were used.

The power of computing platforms has increased amazingly over the past decade. Today it is not unreasonable to have RTUs and remote operator/engineering workstations, connected through public networks and even the Internet, as part of a large SCADA system. Using public-key encryption and digital certificate–based authentication with the X.509 standard is not beyond the capabilities of those computing platforms. A major electrical ISO (Independent System Operator) has been deploying RTUs that support IP-based communications (called *remote intelligent gateways*) and a full, digital certificate–based PKI security architecture for several years. This is an excellent way to protect remote communications by using IP networking VPN technology.

Most people are aware of the use of VPN technology to permit remote and/or mobile users to make secure connections to their corporate WAN via public networking (particularly the Internet). This is accomplished by having a VPN client in the remote/mobile PC negotiate with a VPN server, on the corporate WAN, to exchange and authenticate credentials (digital certificates) and to exchange public keys, so that all subsequent communications are encrypted. This strategy protects communications only up to the point of the VPN server. Thereafter, the communications are typically placed onto the corporate LAN/WAN in plaintext and with no further authentication or protection. In practice this is effectively creating a temporary VPN tunnel between the remote PC and the VPN gateway on the corporate network.

A major difference between this type of occasionally connected VPN and a permanent VPN among a defined set of computers (where all have digital certificates and perform routine [re]authentication and where all traffic is encrypted) is the need to occasionally change encryption keys (fig. 6–14). When an occasional connection is made, the keys are created at the time of connection and remain in use until the connection is severed. The encryption keys used for this interval are called *session keys*, because they are created at the start of the connectivity session and discarded when the session ends. With a permanently networked set of computers that are using VPN technology (e.g., the workstations, PCs, and servers that form a SCADA system) as a protective measure, there needs to be a mechanism that initiates an occasional reauthentication and change

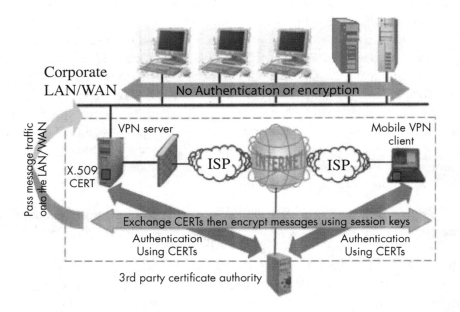

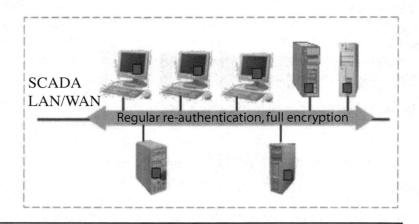

Fig. 6–14. *Occasional VPN connection versus permanent VPN architectures*

of keys. This could be done on a daily basis or even more frequently. With a 128-bit (or greater) key, daily changes of keys would probably suffice. But as has been discussed, the efficacy of a key diminishes with time and the amount of traffic encrypted with that key. With a permanent VPN encryption, keys would become overused if not replaced periodically. Most permanent VPN schemes provide for periodic (e.g., daily) renegotiation and replacement of keys.

Key creation and exchange, as well as certificate authentication mechanisms, are generally transparent to computer users. These capabilities can be built into the basic IP software stack (as of IPv6), can be layered on top of the stack (as with Netscape SSL), or can be added within the logic of specific applications. The terms *transport-layer security* (TLS), *IP security* (IP$_{SEC}$), and *application-layer security* are used to describe these differing alternatives. In any case, the availability of authentication and encryption mechanisms is generally standard in modern operating systems and LANs/WANs, although enabling and configuring these mechanisms usually requires a specific action on the part of the system and network administrators. As of this writing, VPN technology has proven to be immune to traditional network attacks, message sniffing, and message replay attacks. It does not offer specific protections against DoS attack, but that type of attack is thought to be less likely to be used against a SCADA system.

The major use of VPN technology in most organizations is to secure communications between a remote and/or mobile user and a central computer system (fig. 6–15). The dial in telephone lines used in the past by vendors for remote support, were replaced by non-secure Internet connections in the 1990s, and are now being secured through the use of VPN technology. The remote/mobile user may use a dial-up connection or may have some other form of Internet connectivity, and the goal is to provide a secure and authenticated communications session between that user's computer and the central computers. Today the most popular mechanisms for setting up a VPN tunnel use either the Point-to-Point Tunneling Protocol, developed by Microsoft, or the Layer Two Tunneling Protocol (L2TP), developed by Cisco. Both of these are really designed for securing point to point connections. If a complete SCADA system is to be secure—and use authentication and encryption for *all* communications between and among *all* computers that constitute the system—then the most effective approach is to implement IP_{SEC} in the TCP/IP stack of all participating computers and to set up a CA on the network, to provide certificate authentication and revocation services.

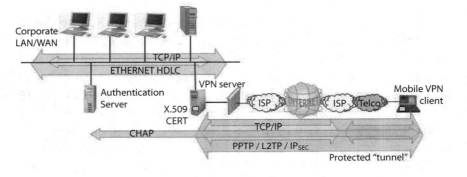

• PPP - Point to Point Protocol (IP layer 1 for serial links)
• PPTP - Point to Point Tunneling Protocol (Microsoft)
• L2TP - Layer 2 Tunneling Protocol (Cisco)
• IP_{SEC} - Embedded authentication and encryption at the IP message level
• CHAP - Challenge Handshake Authentication Protocol (member of PPP suite)

One of these three choices will normally be used to provide securi...

FIG. 6–15. *Logical components of a typical VPN configuration for remote access*

Kerberos

Another means for creating a secure network of computers, and even securing the applications, is to create such a system using a Kerberos secure system architecture. Kerberos (named for the three-headed dog that guarded the entrance to Hades) is an IETF standard and includes a set of protocols, and client/server functions that allow for the tight management of users, applications, and access rights. It was initially developed at MIT and the source code is readily available. In a Kerberos scheme there is authentication required every time a user or application wants to access a service, another application, or system resources. A central ticket granting server performs all of the centralized access management and authentication functions. The problem with Kerberos is that in order to use it, all programs and systems need to be "kerberized" meaning that they have to be modified to make requests to register with and use the authentication and ticket granting service. This means that the technology is not typically available to a SCADA system owner as only the SCADA vendor can make such changes to the operating system and proprietary applications. (And in some SCADA systems, the vendor may use third-party software for which they do not have source code access.)

Intrusion Detection

The very cautious make the assumption that, no matter what you do to keep cyber threats and attackers out of your systems and networks, there are always new techniques and threats that stand the chance of breaking though your protective measures. Based on this assumption, a whole range of product offerings have been created to act like a software burglar alarm that detects the presence of an attacker or of surreptitiously placed malware. These software tools fall under the broad heading of *intrusion-detection* packages. An intrusion detection package consists of software that is placed on every computer that watches the resources and programs, looking for anomalous program behavior (usually called host-based intrusion-detection systems [HIDS]). (Anomalous behavior includes using a lot more memory or computing power than usual or accessing system resources that they never accessed before.) A variation of this is network-based intrusion-detection systems (NIDS) technology, which consists of one or more specialized network appliances (computers) placed on your LAN/WAN that monitor network traffic, again looking for anomalous traffic patterns. (Anomalous traffic includes noticeable increases in message traffic, messages from applications that never sent any before, and messages to new IP addresses, especially any outside the local network.)

Often a combination of NIDS and HIDS (N/HIDS) is employed for the broadest range of intrusion detection (fig. 6–16). If multiple computers are part of an overall system and N/HIDS is used, there will generally be one computer (or an additional workstation) designated to receive information from the software running in each of the other computers (often called *distributed agents*). This computer/workstation will have software to receive and correlate the data from the various agents, looking for simultaneous events and related activities that could indicate an intrusion. Regardless of the technology and architectural approach used, these intrusion-detection systems kick in once your firewall has been breached and someone actually gains access to your systems and networks. (Think in terms of a motion sensor in a room of your home: it can detect the presence of a burglar and call the police, but only after the burglar has actually broken into *and entered* your home.) Vendors of N/HIDS technologies use a range of technologies to detect anomalous behaviors. One product might collect operational statistics and watch for significant deviations from the expected norms. Another might use neural network technology to learn the normal patterns and identify conditions that deviate from normal. In almost all cases, such systems need to study and collect data during all variations of normal operations in order to determine when something appears abnormal. This learning process does not apply to known attacks and malware since those can be recognized by their particular signatures.

The logic that analyzes the data collected from agents and NIDS units and determines that something anomalous is occurring is often called the *analysis engine.* This logic can use one or more of the following techniques:

- Rule-based or model-based detection

- Statistical methods of detection

- Signature-based detection

- Neural network–based detection

There are many technologies used, and every vendor can argue about the benefits of their particular approach. However, remember that all N/HIDS products work on the basis of detecting that something anomalous is going on after it has been going on long enough to prove that it isn't a spurious event—and only after it has generated enough data to trip the alarm thresholds of the N/HIDS package(s). NIDS packages can also work much like a firewall, in that most NIDS packages can rapidly detect activities that take place when a hacker is attempting to probe your systems, using known methods, over a network connection. The important point is the use of known methods. If a hacker is very tricky or has devised a clever way to hide his or her probing (which they do constantly), then an NIDS might take a while to discover the activity or even might fail to recognize it as an attack. Older, signature-based N/HIDS packages, which depend on signatures that may not yet exist, are particularly subject to missing day-zero malware and new forms of attack.

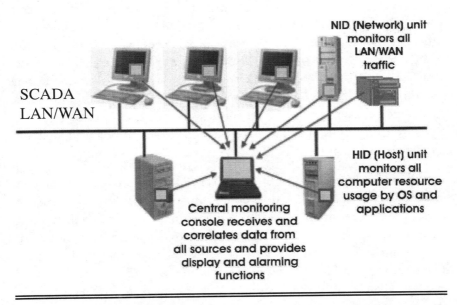

FIG. 6–16. *Intrusion-detection and network intrusion-detection architectures*

Almost all of these technologies require that some level of threshold be exceeded prior to issuing an alarm, to avoid excessive false alarms. On the plus side, though, SCADA systems usually exhibit a very repetitive and well-defined set of operational characteristics, unlike a general-purpose system (with limited control over the applications running and the number of active users). Because of this, anomalies can be spotted rather quickly. N/HIDS technology was devised to catch the hacker who has been regularly entering your system and using your computing power or to catch spyware and Trojans that have been sending your confidential data out across the Internet. It isn't that these are not worthy objectives—of course they are.

Importantly, from a SCADA standpoint, the goal of attackers, especially terrorists, is to get into your system just once and, on that first successful incursion, take the action they hope will achieve their objectives. Truly dedicated terrorists will be aware of N/HIDS technology and will know that they may have only one chance to implement their attack. Hackers who have managed to continuously enter your system/network and who are just playing around in your system to see what can be found will eventually be discovered by an N/HIDS package. Any Trojan or other malware installed during these visits will eventually be found by the N/HIDS (or by conventional malware scanning packages). By contrast, attackers who need only one successful entry to achieve their goal may not be detected by this technology or may not be detected in time to block their actions. Also, if attackers are insiders abusing their access rights and trying to gain unauthorized access, their activity might not even look like anomalous behavior to an N/HIDS package.

One of the problems with most N/HIDS technologies is that they are reactive, meaning that they come into play only after an attack is underway or after malware has been successfully implanted and running on your system. Using N/HIDS technology to discover that a hacker has been using your computing resources and spamming people from your server for the past few minutes or hours is one thing. But that is not good enough when trying to prevent an attack intended to disable or, worse, take control of a critical SCADA system.

Of course, your systems can be subject to a nondirected, nonspecific attack in the form of viruses and other malware introduced through insufficiently protected network connections or via Web-browsing activity by system users on a common network. N/HIDS technologies are good at identifying the presence of such malware. HIDS and NIDS also work continuously and automatically, whereas scanning software has to be run on a periodic basis.

An extension of the N/HIDS product functions that has recently been introduced by vendors is called *intrusion-prevention systems* (IPS). The practical viability of this technology has yet to be proven, but the concept is good: rather than just acting like a burglar alarm and hoping that a system administrator will take some appropriate action, why not let the detection software take immediate action to curb the detected threat? IPS vendors are working on ways to block unauthorized network traffic, shut down malware, and close off access to files and databases to contain any incursion that does occur. The vendors of this technology claim that their agents can almost immediately detect program and user activity that is improper and block them. This technology advance certainly sounds promising, and once sufficiently proven in real-world applications, it should be the logical replacement for conventional N/HIDS products.

Aside from N/HIDS and IPS technologies, for added protection or just for peace of mind, it is also a good idea to monitor all portable computers and PCs that are used for double duty (as both office PCs and workstations on the SCADA system). Virus/Trojan–scanner software is available from a number of vendors, and if kept up to date, this software can usually detect and eliminate a wide range of malware. The major difficulty *is* keeping such software up to date with the latest malware signatures, because most vendors of virus-scanning software expect direct Internet access to your PCs to automatically deliver updates. These packages usually include an agent program, which is automatically installed on your PC and will periodically attempt to contact the vendor's support server, via the Internet, to download updates. Unless certain necessary configuration changes are made, this message traffic will probably be blocked by your firewall and set off alarms in your NIDS package the first time you run the software. Rather than permanently installing such scanner software (and opening your firewall to permit the software-update traffic), an alternative operational approach would be to have your IT group run a malware scan on portable and dual-use PCs on an occasional basis. These PCs can be temporarily removed from the SCADA LAN or moved over to the corporate LAN/WAN during this process, for security purposes.

Many SCADA systems today utilize standard e-mail software and use e-mail as a means for creating operator message logs, for dispersing information to operational staff, and for intershift messaging. E-mail support may be restricted to just the computers and PCs on the SCADA LAN/WAN, or the e-mail capability may be linked to the corporate network and the corporate e-mail server. This would allow communications between SCADA operational staff and other company employees—and possibly even e-mail via the Internet, depending on how the corporate e-mail server is configured.

In the same vein, IM is a readily available communications technology. It does, however, require that a client be installed on your PC, and your messages flow to their destination via the IM server of the service you select (e.g., AOL or Microsoft). IM will not normally work inside a private network, since messages must travel out to the respective server and then back to the designated recipient (unless you stage your own IM server).

IM and e-mail are both useful tools. But both offer the possibility of bringing malware into your systems. Both allow for attachments and for the execution of scripts embedded in the headers and messages. E-mail can typically be set up to be restricted to internal systems only, if that is of sufficient use to the personnel. If external e-mail is needed or if IM is to be supported, then it is critical that your system employ IM and e-mail *scanning and filtering*. E-mail scanning and filtering can be done at the level of your e-mail server, where virus scanning, spam filtering, and content/attachment filtering are easily established. IM filtering and scanning is a more complex issue. IM traffic will pass through your firewall and can also be scanned and filtered at that level. In addition, each PC equipped with an IM client can also have local virus-scanning software (but that brings us back to the issue of keeping such software up to date). It is because of the difficulty in securing these capabilities—while allowing them enough access to be useful—that many SCADA users provide separate PCs and LANs for office-automation functions and keep IM and (corporate) e-mail off the SCADA network.

Architecture

One final word about conventional IT security. In performing security assessments of SCADA systems, it is often discovered that there are multiple interconnections between the SCADA system's network and the corporate/enterprise network, some of them not even recognized as such (like a dual-homed PC that is connected to both). These in turn have the possibility of providing multiple interconnections to the Internet. It is hard enough to keep one access point protected, with the ever-changing cyber threat landscape, let alone several. A good starting point for securing a SCADA system that must be interfaced with a corporate/enterprise network, from external threats, is to insure that there is only one such interface point. Then such architectural schemes as creating a DMZ, using a dual-homed application proxy server, and having dual firewalls, can be applied to secure that interconnection point. SCADA systems unfortunately have the possibility of needing IP connections to other external systems that are not under the control of the SCADA system owner (like a link to a regional EMS or ISO in the electric industry). In theses instances the use of end-to-end authentication and encryption technology would be highly recommended.

SECTION 2:
CYBERSECURITY PRINCIPLES, PROCESSES, AND TECHNOLOGIES

7

Identifying Cybersecurity Vulnerabilities

Threats and Threat Agents

When discussing the possibility of a hacker, a worm, or a terrorist attack on a SCADA system, we are really referring to the probability of such an attack occurring and the consequences were it to be successful. An attacker, regardless of type and motivation, will be looking for the weaknesses in your defenses and will attempt to exploit those weaknesses (vulnerabilities) to carry out an attack. It is important to take reasonable actions to protect your systems, particularly if a successful attack upon them could cause loss of life, injury, or substantial damage, not to mention any additional financial impact. But what is the probability of an attack and the possibility that it could succeed, and who are the potential attackers?

The U.S. government (particularly the National Institute of Standards and Technology [NIST]) has done a lot of work in the post-9/11 environment, classifying and categorizing cyber threats. They use the term *threat agent* to describe the potential source of a threat. Everyone thinks cyber threats are about clandestine cells of anti-U.S. hackers attempting to bring down our government or industry by launching virus attacks across the Internet. In truth, however, the threat agent that knocks down a critical SCADA system could be a tornado, an earthquake, or a member of the cleaning staff who spills a bucket of water (fig. 7–1). When anticipating the possible threat sources, we have to take a broad view. A good starting point for sorting out potential threat agents is to separate them into two basic categories: internal threats and external threats.

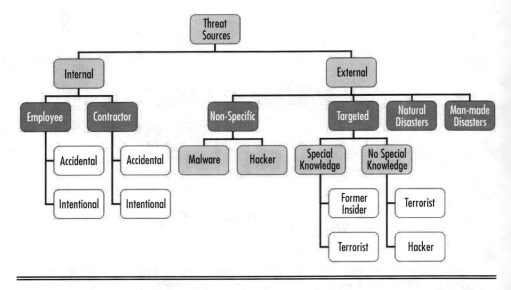

FIG. 7–1. *Taxonomy of potential threat sources to a SCADA system*

Internal threats

Internal threats (threat agents) are people currently working as employees of or as on-site contractors with your organization who therefore have greater physical access rights than someone who doesn't. That certainly means access to a corporate facility, but possibly even includes physical access to the SCADA system equipment or auxiliary subsystems (e.g., UPS/power/telecom/LAN) that support the SCADA system. That person may also have greater access to confidential and critical information (e.g., passwords or IP addresses) and even some level of electronic access rights (e.g., an account on the corporate computer system). An internal threat can be an actual, direct-hire employee or a support contractor, such as someone from among the janitorial staff, maintenance personnel, or even a vendor's technical service personnel.

Internal threat agents can pose intentional threats or unintentional/ accidental threats. Accidents and errors are dangerous because of the physical and electronic access they have. Intentional threats are even more dangerous, because of their specialized access and knowledge. The most acute level of threat would be posed by a high-authority-level, internal threat agent who intentionally wishes to inflict damage—regardless of whether that person is a direct employee or a contractor. As it turns out, disgruntled, existing and former employees can be the most dangerous threat agents.

External threats

In the simplest possible terms, external threats are everything else (that is not an internal threat agent), including natural disasters and man-made disasters (e.g., riot or war). The main difference is that an external threat agent does not have authorized physical access rights to your facility and critical systems and would not (or should not) have access to your confidential and sensitive information.

A critical subcategory of the external threat agent is the *former insider*. This could be an ex-employee who quit just last week and still has confidential information because no one has gotten around to changing the corporate access-control list or deleting his ID and password from the computer systems. A former insider will also know a lot of things that come from having worked in your organization, and such experience can't be taken away as easily as a key to the building. A former contractor (or security consultant) would fall into this category as well.

Even threat agents that have never been insiders can pose a serious threat. It is a mistake to believe that a determined attacker can't obtain an amazing amount of confidential information, if he is willing to spend the time and money. Keep in mind that the same SCADA vendor that supplied your system will sell an equivalent system to anybody with cash, and anyone can sign up and attend their training courses. Many vendors even provide access to their user's manuals and documentation on their Web sites.

A serious attacker can also find out information by locating and bribing or threatening ex-employees of the SCADA vendor and of your own organization. Also, the basic operating systems and LAN/WAN technology of most SCADA systems today are going to be either a Unix variation or a Microsoft offering, both of which are well known and profusely well documented. If a terrorist organization decided to target your systems, they would probably go to great lengths to get someone into your organization, even if just as a member of the janitorial staff. It is amazing to consider that the most secure and restricted spaces in an organization still need to be cleaned and that the cleaning staff often have unlimited and unsupervised access to those spaces.

Targeted attacks

Another broad categorization of threat agents differentiates between those that are targeted and those that are nonspecific. If a hurricane or a flood hits your facilities, it is probably just pure bad luck and not because Mother Nature has specifically targeted you. The same is probably true if a virus or a worm gets into your systems through some unprotected network connection. If a hacker discovers your system by using IP pinging or war dialing/driving, it is probably also just pure bad luck. (Still, shame on you for leaving your systems exposed!) The most serious threat comes from an attacker who is specifically targeting you and your systems. That attacker could be a terrorist or just a disgruntled ex-employee who is a part-time hacker—or even an extremist group that feels it has the right to teach you a lesson for going against their strongly held beliefs (because you're not green enough, left enough, right enough, etc.).

The targeted attack is one that will generally be well planned and executed, and it should be assumed that the attacker will do everything possible to obtain critical confidential information and access to your systems, through whatever means are necessary. This is a good point to introduce another security term and concept: *social engineering*.

Social engineering is the process of obtaining unauthorized confidential information and possibly obtaining unauthorized physical access, through the manipulation of people. Con artists have been using these techniques forever. Social engineering relies on learned behaviors, habits, manners, and basic human nature (good and bad). It also often involves exploiting the nature and culture of organizations.

A prime example of a social engineering strategy for obtaining confidential information about your organization would be dumpster diving. It is amazing what people will toss into the trash, on the assumption that this act alone makes it disappear. (Table 7–1 outlines some well-known social engineering techniques.) This notion isn't limited to paper trash either. Corporate information and secrets have been obtained by pulling the disk drives out of discarded PCs and reading the contents of discarded floppy disks and other removable media. A good procedure for the physical destruction of discarded printed and electronic media— including electronic equipment (computers, PDAs, cell phones, etc.)—is essential to ensure that these materials don't fall into the hands of a threat agent/attacker. A related problem occurs with portable computers and PDAs that are stolen. They can also contain sensitive information that would then be disclosed unless protected in some manner.

- **Dumpster Diving**
- **Buying used PDA and laptop equipment**
- **Calling the help desk (use anger, fear, threat, pity)**
- **Calling after hours to get voice mail information**
- **Piggy back entry to facilities**
- **Pretending to deliver package, pizza, flowers, etc...**
- **Fake ID badge (Visitor)**
- **Phone tag, internal transfer**
- **Asking operator/receptionist to aid in locating a person**
- **Web site information**
- **Acting with authority and conviction/challenge the challenger**
- **Pretending to be a service person, delivery person**
- **Pretending to be from another office/site**
- **Tailgate another vehicle to enter a facility**
- **Call with an "emergency" to get information**

TABLE 7–1. *Social engineering techniques used by attackers*

Social engineering also involves using other tricks to get people to divulge confidential information. Calling around through an organization and using what you learn from one person to leverage your conversation with the next person is another common trick. ("Hi Bob, Joe over in accounting told me to call you when Larry and I saw him at lunch—you know, Larry from tech support? Right, well, Joe said that you could tell me . . . ") Calling a company IT help desk and faking an emergency, to get a new ID/password issued is a commonly used trick (especially if you sound irate and imply that they will take the blame for what will happen if you don't get that new ID right away).

Gaining entrance to unauthorized areas is achieved through a number of tricks. Bringing a pizza or flowers and claiming they are to be delivered to person X up in the control room or computer room can often get an invader into those areas. Timing arrival at a secured door, with hands piled high with stuff, so as to reach the secured door at the same time as a legitimate employee, almost always guarantees that the employee will open and help the invader through the door. Fumbling with a key card or access token (a fake) further increases the success rate of invasion.

Social engineering can also be used to get malware into systems. For instance, a clever hacker once made a CD containing a serious virus, then made a fake music label for the CD and placed it in the jewel case of the real music CD. One morning, he left this CD by the entrance to the facility of the company whose systems he wanted to penetrate. As expected, someone picked up the CD, thought themselves lucky, took the CD to their office and inserted it into their PC, from which a computer virus subsequently spread onto the corporate network.

The best defense against social engineering is an employee education program and well-established policies and procedures that make such tricks unlikely to work. If you can deny targeted attackers the critical information they need in order to be successful, then you can greatly reduce both the probability of an attack, as well as the probability of an attack being successful.

How much is enough? There is no single, simple answer to the question of how much effort and money should be put into building and maintaining cyber defenses. If you are answerable to regulatory agencies that have defined a basic set of requirements (e.g., those established by the North American Electric Reliability Council [NERC]), then you are probably at least obliged to meet these basic requirements. Your legal staff and insurance underwriters will probably also have some thoughts on the subject, depending on the liabilities and exposure a successful attack would bring.

Most critical SCADA systems have been built with a lot of backup and redundancy, even well before the events of 9/11. They are intended to survive a certain amount of damage with either no degradation or at least graceful degradation (they have a *fault-tolerant* design). Nevertheless, they were never designed to withstand an intentional attack. SCADA system designers have always had to deal with the possibility of communication outages and usually build backup or fault-tolerant communications systems. SCADA systems have incorporated redundancy in their architectures since they were introduced.

Supervisory control has never been a substitute for local controls and interlocks. No pipeline control system designer would (should) allow local processes to go critical just because the supervisory system couldn't communicate with the local RTU or PLC. Also, many of the processes typically monitored and controlled by SCADA systems have a lot of inherent stability or capacity (along with local controls and safety systems). In other words, just killing or disabling a SCADA system isn't particularly easy; even if that were to happen, the results might not be catastrophic, or there might well be sufficient time to recover. The biggest threat might be the usurpation and abuse of a SCADA system, and preventing that possibility ought to be where the most effort should be focused. These points need to be considered when making the decision about how much protection is enough.

A classical discussion of risk assessment and mitigation would involve a series of statistical calculations regarding the cost of replacing a critical asset, the cost of losing the use of the asset (and any related costs for damages and liabilities), and the likelihood and frequency of possible threats actually coming to pass. Those sorts of computations and decisions might be relevant when discussing the chances of losing an e-commerce Web server, but they are not as clearly relevant to considerations of SCADA security. This is because losing a SCADA system has impacts beyond just finances or business considerations; rather, it may present a public safety issue. If someone can disrupt the electricity, natural gas, or water supply by attacking a SCADA system, then a typical cost-benefit (financial) analysis may not be appropriate for justifying the investment in the necessary protective countermeasures. (There may be regulatory or legal requirements that would initiate punitive actions against organizations that could not show that they took reasonable and adequate measures to protect their SCADA system.)

Obvious Points of Attack and Vulnerability

To reduce the probability of success of an attack, steps must be taken to eliminate potential points of vulnerability. However, what are the points at which an attacker will concentrate, and what types of attacks can be used? We discuss physical and operational security later (see chaps. 9 and 10). For the moment, we will focus on cyber attacks, rather than physical attacks. The objective of a risk assessment is to identify vulnerabilities that can be exploited by an attacker and to implement countermeasures to either eliminate the vulnerability or reduce the consequences of an attack against that vulnerability (either approach is equally valid). Countermeasures can be technical (e.g., virus scanning software) or procedural (e.g., a policy that disallows wireless devices attached to the SCADA LAN). It is also important that you be realistic in your efforts. It may be outrageously expensive to implement all necessary countermeasures in order to reduce a threat to a zero probability. On the other hand, a small investment might reduce the threat to an acceptable level of probability. Addressing all of these issues is part of a risk assessment process.

Figure 7–2 shows a simplified SCADA system architecture and the typical (and all too obvious) points from which a cyber attack could be perpetrated. These are undoubtedly not the only points of vulnerability, but taking actions to secure these will greatly reduce the likelihood of a successful attack. There are 14 well-understood ways in which an attacker

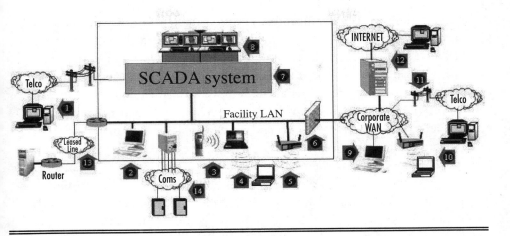

FIG. 7–2. *Typical points of SCADA system vulnerability*

could seek to penetrate your systems. Some of these vulnerabilities assume an inside attacker, others an outside attacker:

1. Any unsecured dial-in telephone line is an obvious point of vulnerability. Use of modem dial-back mechanisms and simple ID/password access controls are not sufficient to secure these points of access. Use of VPN technologies, including strong authentication mechanisms (digital certificates, as well as ID/password mechanisms or even token-based passwords) plus limitations on remote login attempts, is essential if these telephone lines cannot be disconnected. In addition, to protect against an attack by a former insider, there needs to be a policy and procedure to immediately invalidate all digital certificates (a process called *revocation*), system user IDs, and passwords and the electronic access rights of a person who has been terminated, who has voluntarily resigned, retired, or whose contracting services have been discontinued. (This is in addition to the obvious recovery of company owned equipment, software, credentials, keys, etc.). It is also an added deterrent to require that people with access to critical information sign nondisclosure and confidentiality agreements (as part of an employment offer or contracting agreement), which should be reviewed, making clear any ongoing obligations and legal consequences at the time of termination or contract completion.

2. Malware can be introduced into a system and/or network by someone bringing infected removable media into the facility and inserting it into a PC. Use of virus-scanning software in every PC helps to reduce the possibility of infection. However, better still would be to have a policy that discourages bringing unscanned removable media into the facility and a procedure for scanning and cleaning any removable media that must be brought into the facility. NIDS and HIDS packages are also valuable for detecting the presence of malware that manages to slip by other detection mechanisms (e.g., malware brought in intentionally by an inside attacker who obviously ignores the stated policies and procedures). In addition, to protect against an attack by an insider who has electronic access to systems, strong-authentication mechanisms (possibly including biometrics) can be used to prevent an insider from upgrading his or her access rights by stealing another employee's ID/password. This also means that careful consideration needs to be given to the assignment of access rights and to the information and resources permitted under given access rights. HIDS packages (and system log monitoring and scanning programs) can also be used to identify users who are attempting either to elevate their access rights or to use resources or access information that is not permitted to them under their ID/passwords. Another concept of cybersecurity, within the area of operational security (which is discussed in a later section of the book) is *separation of duties*. This is a procedural mechanism to ensure that no single individual, regardless of access rights, has all of the access necessary to cause irreparable damage.

3. A new threat that has emerged in the past couple of years is the possibility of a Bluetooth-enabled device (cell phone, camera, laptop PC, or PDA) being infected with a virus and passing that virus to other devices (e.g., a Bluetooth-enabled laptop PC that also has an Ethernet interface) that can bridge the virus onto the SCADA system LAN. This problem becomes more complex as Bluetooth is embedded in more devices, such as printers and scanners. A virus could be passed to these devices and then find its way into a computer that accesses that device. Again, virus scanning in all laptops would aid in detecting and stopping such a virus, as would a NIDS package. A policy requiring that all such devices be turned off prior to entering an area with sensitive computer equipment (or disallowed in such areas) can also prevent such infections, because of the transmission-range limitation of Bluetooth.

4. Another potential vulnerability is any WiFi-enabled computer that also has an Ethernet connection. An attacker could use the WiFi connection to bridge the SCADA system LAN, potentially obtaining the access rights of the owner of the computer via this connectivity. A policy of disabling WiFi capability while a LAN connection is in use (or disallowing the connection of WiFi equipped devices to the SCADA LAN) can lessen this vulnerability.

5. A rogue or insufficiently protected WiFi AP can be attacked in much the same way, although this would give the successful attacker access to the LAN and additional effort would be needed to break into the systems. A NIDS package would be useful in detecting an attacker's network access, if penetration of an AP was successful. Proper configuration of all APs (disabling DHCP, disabling the broadcast of the SSID, enabling encryption, specifying MACs for authorized users, etc.) is essential. If WiFi usage is extensive, it may be worth considering a WiFi-monitoring package, which acts like a NIDS but uses selected APs to monitor WiFi traffic. Such applications can identify rogue APs, as well as improper security settings. It might also be worth rethinking the use of WiFi; if it can be eliminated, do so and enact a policy that prohibits its usage. Obviously, enforcement of such a policy will require occasional sweeps of the facility, looking for any unauthorized WiFi devices. With WiFi being built into so many devices, it may be more prudent to accept its inevitability and take actions to manage and monitor its usage.

6. All connections between the SCADA system and other LAN/WANs must be adequately protected by firewall technology. An insufficiently configured or technically inadequate firewall can be a point of access for an external attacker. Firewall technology generally advances to keep pace with the latest attack methods employed, and thus, it is critical to keep your firewall up to date with current revisions. Where access can be restricted to a few well known services (e.g., e-mail, Web browsing, ftp) the use of an application proxy server as the firewall enhances the level of security.

7. The most basic vulnerability of a SCADA system is to an insider attack by someone who has physical access to the SCADA system itself. Such an attacker, having first taken steps to damage the restoration media,

could go up to the system console and issue commands to delete critical files and applications on both the primary and the backup systems. A system-level programmer or a system administrator with root (admin) access has essentially unlimited ability to wipe out the software of the operating system, in addition to SCADA-specific programs and data files. This does not even have to happen while that person is present. A high-level batch script (running at the admin/root level) could be placed into the system for execution at a later date/time, and this script could issue the same commands that the attacker would have entered. Such a highly placed insider would undoubtedly be aware of alternative backup systems and operating sites and would probably have the same level of access at those facilities, as well as reasons to visit occasionally. This type of attacker has the highest chance of staging a successful attack; few technical mechanisms would prevent such an attack from happening, since this attacker would, based on his or her authority level, have the ability to disable or manipulate these mechanisms. The best mechanisms to protect against such an attack are mainly procedural, as by enforcing the use of separation of duties.

8. Along a similar line, an insider who had operational access rights on the SCADA system (e.g., a senior operator) could issue commands through the operator's console, causing dangerous or destructive control actions (e.g., tripping circuit breakers, closing valves, and stopping pumps). This would be even more dangerous if that same attacker had remote operational system access (e.g., remote X-terminal emulation or actual operator console software). Few if any SCADA systems offer any mechanism to prevent such operational abuse. It is typically assumed that if this person has been trusted with such access rights, then the person is both properly trained and trustworthy. In the future, SCADA system vendors may offer some mechanism (e.g., a *two-man rule*) that precludes a single individual from issuing critical control commands. Such control actions would require the agreement of a second operator, possibly via a separate password or by biometric authentication. (The military use the two-man rule for operations like launching an intercontinental ballistic missile [ICBM]. Two officers must concur, or the launch can't happen.) In the meantime, one recommendation by NERC is to perform initial and thereafter periodic background checks on all personnel who have such high access levels.

9. Just as malware can be introduced into a PC on the SCADA LAN, the same thing can happen on the corporate LAN/WAN and, if the firewall separating the SCADA LAN from the corporate WAN isn't adequate, the malware can find its way onto the SCADA LAN and into the SCADA system computers. As with item 2, corporate user's access needs to be managed and administered properly so that corporate computers can't be used to access and attack the SCADA system.

10. Just as a WiFi AP can be used by an attacker to break into the SCADA system LAN, the same thing can be done on the corporate LAN/WAN, and this again places the firewall as the remaining defense between the SCADA system and an attacker. All WiFi access points on the corporate/enterprise LAN/WAN need to be suitably protected, and rogue APs, if any, must be identified and removed.

11. In a large and geographically distributed corporation, the likelihood that there are unsecured telephone connections to a corporate WAN is probably greater than the likelihood that such connections to the SCADA system exist. However, these telephone connections into the corporate WAN may pose a threat to the SCADA system and provide a path for an attacker to reach the SCADA system, if the SCADA system is interfaced to the corporate WAN at any point. Those telephone connections also need to be secured using the mechanisms described earlier (see item 1).

12. Corporate Web servers, e-mail servers, and Internet gateways are constantly exposed to attackers coming across the Internet. For these computers to be useful, this is a risk that must be accepted. Most IT departments know how to set up a network demilitarized zone (DMZ), using layers of firewalls and proxy servers to isolate and protect the corporate network while exposing these same servers to the potential attackers. As with any firewall scheme, it is essential to keep this equipment up to date with security patches and the latest virus/worm updates. It is also advisable to have a suitable consultant perform a *penetration test* (commonly referred to as *pen testing*) to validate the configuration and security mechanisms. Computer-security consultants often employ white-hat (ethical) hackers, who attack your systems with your knowledge and permission in an attempt to identify (but not exploit) any vulnerability in your systems.

13. Any point-to-point connections between a SCADA system and another system through a public or private network (possibly a backup SCADA system at an alternative operating site or a regional control center) should employ VPN technology, which can run in the router at each end of the dedicated link. Most routers today can be set up with digital certificates and provide authentication and encryption, including occasional regeneration and re-exchange of the encryption keys.

14. Unfortunately, most SCADA systems use readily available, well-documented legacy, serial communications protocols for interrogating and commanding their field-based RTUs. Just as unfortunate is that a huge proportion of those RTUs are connected by single-frequency licensed radio or leased analog telephone circuits. Although some of the new network-ready RTUs are capable of IP and encryption, the vast majority of the installed RTU base are not, and quite a few of the SCADA hosts would need extensive upgrading to support secure IP. It has already been proven that a person with a radio, a laptop PC, some commercial software, and reasonable physical proximity can take control of RTUs and override the SCADA system. Tapping into a telephone line requires a bit more work, but not much—and in that case, the attacker can cut the SCADA system off entirely and control any RTU on that same telephone line. It may not seem that hijacking an RTU presents much of a threat, but that depends on what that RTU is controlling. If an attacker were to close the right valve, shut off the right pump or trip the right transformer, the effects could propagate and be amplified by the process dynamics. *Bump-in-the-wire* (protocol-transparent) encryption devices, specifically designed for SCADA applications, are becoming available for securing serial communication lines. These seem to work well for asynchronous protocols, but may not work with some of the bit-synchronous protocols still used by the electric power industry. Most such devices expect to be placed between the EIA-232 port of the RTU and the modem of the RTU (unless they incorporate modem circuit and thus replace the model). With older RTUs that have a built-in modem, this won't be a viable solution. As SCADA system owners switch from analog communications to digital communications, other security mechanisms will become available to protect these communications.

Most Frequently Used
Means of Attack

The ways that attackers penetrate a system or network, at these points of vulnerability, are varied. There are known weaknesses (documented on hacker Web sites), however, in many of the various software modules of both Microsoft and Unix/Linux operating systems, and software is available to identify and exploit those weaknesses.

Figure 7–3 lists the most common means used for attacking computer systems as of the end of 2004. Note that this list includes nonspecific, nontargeted mechanisms (e.g., worms), as well as mechanisms that could specifically be used by a hacker to penetrate a targeted system that has been located and found to have a known weakness (e.g., security holes in peer-to-peer networking [P2P]). Known weaknesses in operating systems and specific applications are the primary means by which hackers (and presumably terrorists and extremists) attack systems.

The existence of known weaknesses is why keeping security-related operating system and networking patches up to date is so important. There is always a race going on between hackers, finding yet another hole, and vendors, supplying a plug for (patching) that hole. Many SCADA system owners take an attitude toward patches of "If it ain't broken, don't fix it." They are loath to touch anything if the system is working properly. This attitude usually derives from past experience with (or anecdotal stories about) SCADA systems that, upon being patched or upgraded, failed to work properly until the prior version of software was reinstalled. After all, who needs to fear a hacker when the IT group or your vendor is even more likely to shut down the SCADA system? But ignoring the management of security patches is a dangerous risk. Often a SCADA vendor will review patches and updates from operating system and application vendors and make a determination regarding which patches are or are not essential. Those they decide are essential generally ought to be installed. If a development or support system is available, it can be used to test patches (and software updates) prior to releasing them to a production system.

Known Vulnerabilities to Windows Systems in 2004

- Internet Information Services (IIS)
- Microsoft SQL Server (MSSQL)
- Windows Authentication
- Internet Explorer (IE)
- Windows Remote Access Services
- Microsoft Data Access Components (MDAC)
- Windows Scripting Host (WSH)
- Microsoft Outlook and Outlook Express
- Windows Peer to Peer File Sharing (P2P)
- Simple Network Management Protocol (SNMP)

- MS Messenger
- Blaster virus
- Slammer virus
- Slanner virus
- Iraqi Oil
- Bugbear
- Instant Messenger ID
- P2P Control
- SSH
- Netsky
- MyDoom

- Nimda Worm
- Liotan Worm
- Sasser Worm
- Opaserv Worm

Known Vulnerabilities to UNIX/LLINUX Systems in 2004

- BIND Domain Name System
- Remote Procedure Calls (RPC)
- Apache Web Server
- General UNIX Authentication Accounts with No Passwords or Weak Passwords
- Clear Text Services
- Sendmail
- Simple Network Management Protocol (SNMP)
- Secure Shell (SSH)
- Mis-configuration of Enterprise Services NIS/NFS
- Open Secure Sockets Layer (SSL)

FIG. 7–3. *Most common methods of attacking computer systems in 2004*

Probability of Attack

The effort you need to expend in securing your systems and networks and training your personnel is directly proportional to the probability of being attacked and the potential damage caused by an attack. If there were little chance of ever being subject to an attack or if the results of a successful attack were of little consequence, then it probably would not be worth taking any efforts to improve your security. The fact of the matter, though, is that attacks—at least nontargeted attacks—are very likely to occur, and depending on the critical nature of the infrastructure controlled by a SCADA system, that system could become a target for a directed terrorist attack. DHS has concluded that there is a distinct possibility that critical automation systems, such as SCADA systems, could be the target of a terrorist attack.

Setting aside the possibility of terrorists for the moment, in this age of cost-cutting, downsizing, rightsizing, and outsourcing, the possibility of insider attacks cannot be dismissed. There are a lot of disgruntled employees—and really angry ex-employees—with significant insider knowledge and a serious grudge (see table 2–2). If a terrorist wanted to improve his chances of success dramatically, he could find these individuals, befriend them, and convince them to aid his efforts, in order to exact revenge (or maybe to make some money). This is another reason for nondisclosure and confidentiality agreements (to make employees understand their legal exposure)—although a really angry person might choose to disregard the legal consequences of violating such agreements.

How do you decide if you are a likely target of a cyber attack? The best way is to consider the various categories of attacks and of threat agents, as well as what they hope to achieve. We will ignore natural and man-made disasters for the moment and assume that your organization has taken reasonable steps to safeguard critical systems against these threat agents. That leaves nonspecific and directed attacks by a variety of threat agents.

Nonspecific attack probabilities

- If you have a connection to the Internet, or to a network that in turn has a connection to the Internet, then it is almost guaranteed that you will be assaulted, possibly multiple times each year, by the plague of worms regularly launched onto the Internet. However, if you have strong firewall and NIDS technologies in place (and policies restricting transport of removable media), the odds are good that these assaults will not affect you.

- Likewise, those same conditions, or the use of either incoming dial-up over telephone lines or WiFi WLANs, make you highly likely

Type of attack	Type of damage caused	Impact on SCADA system	Impact on process
Non-targeted worm virus gets into the network and various computers	Infected computers need to be reloaded and rebooted	Worse case is short duration outage while system is reloaded. Alternate site could take over. May only be partial loss if mixed OSs	Probably none due to the short duration of the potential outage
Hacker 'discovers' your systems and breaks into your network and computers	May plant a Trojan or root kit. May just look around. May try to kill the computer he has broken into	NIDS/HIDS will detect these activities, redundant system probably not discovered, reloading and rebooting will recover	None, as unlikely that hacker realized the system was redundant or got into both sets of servers prior to discovery
Insider decides to cause damage because they feel they were not treated fairly by the organization	May try to intentionally introduce virus or worm, may try to corrupt or delete important data, may try to cause control malfunctions	Reloading (possibly from off-site backup) and rebooting should restore the system. Could be partial outages and disruptions	Anywhere from none to the possibility of control malfunctions
Extremist group targets your organization to 'teach you a lesson'	Probably seeking damaging confidential information or to cause company financial losses. May try to shut system down	Reloading (possibly from off-site backup) and rebooting should restore the system. Could be partial outages and disruptions	Depends on objectives, may try to create damage but probably seeking to discredit your organization
Terrorist/extremist group targets your organization and they have the assistance of a former insider	Taking operational control of the system so as to command plant/process equipment into unsafe states	Legitimate users locked out while terrorists use the system themselves. Alternate site (if any) would have to take back control	Assume the worst

TABLE 7–2. *Example scenarios of various threats and potential outcomes*

to be probed by a hacker from time to time (at least every couple of years and quite possibly more often). Again, if you have strong and well-maintained defenses (including up-to-date patches), have the necessary protections on all telephone lines and wireless APs, and train your personnel about social engineering and information protection, the odds are good that the hackers will go off in search of easier prey.

• Undoubtedly, if your SCADA systems are monitoring and controlling critical infrastructure, such as a major gas pipeline or part of the electrical grid, then you have already taken steps to increase the robustness and reliability of your system. The typical approach is to have some level of redundancy for all key components of the system. If your facilities are in an area that is subject to threats of a natural origin—earthquakes, floods, forest fires, hurricanes, and so forth—then you have probably also taken steps to harden your facilities against those threats and may even have established a remote backup control center with a duplicate SCADA system and communications subsystems.

Directed attack probabilities

• If your SCADA system is monitoring and controlling a process that would be a tempting target for a terrorist, then you have a nonzero probability of being subjected to a cyber attack. Whether that probability is 0.000001% or 50% over the next N years is more a subject for the Central Intelligence Agency than for this book. The safe strategy would be to take all reasonable precautions to ensure that if an attack were to occur, you could limit its chance and degree of success and recover quickly, before any serious damage could occur. Not surprisingly, one of the best strategies to thwart a terrorist's cyber attack is also used to thwart an attack by Mother Nature: namely, having separate, redundant operational systems and facilities and robust, high-availability systems architectures. If even with all of your protective technologies, a terrorist got control of your primary SCADA system, you could take back control by killing power to the invaded system and bringing the backup site online. Of course, this assumes that systems at the backup site are insulated and isolated from possible cyber attack and that, during their interval of control, the terrorists did not manage to cause irreparable or irrecoverable damage.

- It is also possible that your systems could be subject to routine attacks from extremists, terrorists, or even gangsters, who don't expect or want to capture headlines and create havoc but just want to cause you pain (or at least threaten to cause some). It is well known that certain types of e-commerce Web sites have been subjected to DoS attacks by groups who demanded blackmail in exchange for halting the attacks. E-blackmail and e-terrorism both stand to increase in popularity and frequency in the coming years. Nevertheless, if you have adequately designed and maintained your defenses and have used high-availability architectures for your SCADA systems, the chances are good that any such attacks might make your IT staff crazy but will probably not reach the point of disrupting ongoing SCADA operations.

- An attack by an angry current or former insider is always a possibility. In Australia, a former insider caused the dumping of millions of gallons of raw sewage by going around and remotely opening valves at various treatment plants and lift stations. He didn't want to shut down the SCADA system, he wanted to take control of it and had the confidential information required in order to launch a successful attack (actually several dozen successful attacks over an eighteen-month interval). Implementing a *separation of duties* scheme can thwart many of the actions that could be taken by an insider. Immediate deletion of accounts, IDs, passwords, digital certificates, and physical access rights—along with recovery of company materials, information, and equipment—will go a long way toward preventing a former insider from launching an attack. It is also wise to inform all coworkers that their former colleague is no longer authorized and to remind the former insider of obligations under confidentiality agreements. Policies and procedures sometimes play as strong a role as technical solutions. Taking these steps drastically reduces the possibility of an attack and the chances of its success. NIDS and HIDS can be useful in detecting and flagging abnormal activity by insiders, which could be the first stage of an attack.

- Although it would seem an unlikely possibility from the standpoint of a SCADA system, another threat agent could be an outsider who is attempting to obtain confidential corporate information. More dangerous still would be an insider attempting the same thing, because of their probable access to networks and systems. This confidential information could be marketing, production, scheduling, or other business-related information that could offer a competitive advantage. It could also be information of a legal nature—for use in green-/blackmail schemes or for release to the public to discredit the corporation. Fortunately, properly configured and maintained protective measures, including up-to-date firewall and N/HIDS technologies and properly organized and assigned access rights, would make the success of such an attempt very unlikely, even for an insider.

Guesstimating the Impact of a Successful Attack

To evaluate the impact of a potential attack (in terms of loss of life, injuries, damage, financial losses, etc.), it is necessary to make a guess at the possible outcome of an attack, which will vary based on the actual threat agent. What a terrorist wants to achieve by attacking your SCADA system is probably quite different than what a greedy or angry insider wants to achieve. Table 7–3 summarizes a range of threat agents and what their probable/possible objectives would be in staging an attack. Spending the manpower and dollars on implementing countermeasures against all possible threats is a losing proposition from a strictly business point of view. The objective of performing a risk assessment is to gauge the probability that potential threats ought to be addressed, the impact of a successful attack by the various threat agents, and the costs involved in mitigating the impact to an acceptable level. Realistically, reducing the probability of an attack (or the consequences of an attack) to zero is probably cost prohibitive from the standpoint of a cost-benefit analysis. Implementing cybersecurity countermeasures, whether they be procedures, PC software, or locks on the door, has to have a supportable business case in order to receive funding in most organizations. The problem facing most organizations is the lack of hard data that can be used to quantify probabilities and consequences. Most organizations that perform risk assessments use qualitative rather than quantitative evaluations. In a qualitative assessment you use terms like "not very likely," "somewhat likely," or "all too likely," rather than precise probabilities. You can assess the consequences of a successful attack in similar terms: "devastating," "very costly," "expensive," or "insignificant." It is up to you to decide on how many graduations you should make from one extreme to the other, but most people find that four or five are more than adequate. Although these terms have no specific numeric value, you can still use them to perform budgetary math. If a threat/attack is very probable and has devastating consequences you can multiply them together to justify a large expenditure for countermeasures. If the threat/attack is unlikely and its consequences are insignificant, then multiplying them shows that no countermeasure is justified, unless it has a negligible cost. The real budgeting challenges occur when a threat/attack is not very probable but has a devastating consequence. In this case your investment in countermeasures will probably be directed toward reducing the consequences of a successful attack, since the threat probability is already determined to be minimal.

For each of the possible outcomes, it is important to determine if that outcome is relevant—and if so, what would be the magnitude of the damage if such an attack were successful. In addition, it is important to determine both the steps necessary to recover from a successful attack and the steps you can take, and countermeasures you can put in place, to prevent (or at least lower the probability of and consequences from) such an attack. We have already discussed many of the technologies and technical measures available to protect your systems. In the following chapters in this section, operational and physical security measures, as well as policies and procedures, are discussed.

Risk Assessment

Risk assessment is the process of determining what threats you feel to be credible and what actions (if any) you need to take to counter those threats. In effect you are performing risk management wherein you are balancing

Increasing seriousness of actions →

↓ Increasingly dangerous threat agents

	Steal information	Use system resources, RAT kit	Make a zombie	Destroy critical files	Shut systems down	Issue command to RTUs	Take control of system
Greedy Insider	✔						
Angry insider	✔			✔	✔	✔	
Angry ex-insider	✔	✔		✔	✔		
Greedy ex-insider	✔	✔					
Ordinary hacker		✔	✔				
Malicious hacker	✔	✔	✔	✔	✔		
Greedy outsider	✔						
Extremist group	✔			✔			
Extremist group with former insider	✔			✔	✔		
Extremist group with insider	✔			✔	✔	✔	
Terrorist group	✔			✔	✔	✔	
Terrorist group with former insider	✔			✔	✔	✔	
Terrorist group with insider	✔			✔	✔	✔	✔

✔ **Most likely actions**   ✔ **Possible actions based on skills, training, knowledge plus access and authority level**

TABLE 7–3. *Threat agents and most probable objectives from an attack*

the cost of countermeasures against the potential impact to employees, the environment, the public, your customers, and your shareholders. There are several methodologies being used in various industries for the purpose of performing a formal risk self-assessment. Some organizations like the ISA have published guidelines and suggestions for this process (TR99.99.01) and governmental organizations like NIST have published guidelines as well (NIST SP-800-26 Security Self-Assessment Guide for Information Technology Systems). (NIST is an impressive source of information on a whole range of security related topics.) Major corporations, like Dupont, have devised their own methodologies and formalized them with the acronym: DNSAM (Dupont Network Security Assessment Methodology). There is no one single way to perform a security self assessment, and the specific one you use needs to be tailored to the business methodologies and budgeting procedures used in your particular organization, because in the end you are building a business case to justify the manpower and capital outlay required to implement the countermeasures you have concluded to be necessary. Remember also that implementing a security program (if you don't already have one in place) is not a one-shot deal and includes implementing policies and procedures that will have a distinct and ongoing manpower impact. A properly done security assessment needs to address cybersecurity (including communications), but also operational and physical security (which are discussed later in the book).

The first step in doing a self assessment is to put together a team, preferably one with representatives from various key departments and organizations including operations, engineering, IT, legal, human resources (HR), etc. Not everyone on the team will be actively involved at every step; some (like legal and HR) will mainly be there to insure that your plans and suggested polices and procedures don't violate laws or regulations. The next step is to collect information about your critical cyber assets: systems, communications, information, software, facilities, infrastructure, etc. Since this book deals with SCADA systems, it is assumed that we are referring specifically to those assets required for the SCADA system to remain properly operational. Appendix E provides a set of checklists and tables that can be used for identifying and inventorying these assets. Once the critical assets are enumerated it is then possible to review them for vulnerabilities, both of a physical nature and of a cybersecurity nature, and to assess what realistic threats exist that need to be countered. The final step (in the self assessment process) is to select (and cost justify) the countermeasures being proposed, showing the basis for the decision. Table 7–4 shows a simple example of the threat assessment and countermeasure selection for a key asset.

	Critical asset	Threat agent	Attack/ threat	Probability of attack	Consequences or cost	Countermeasure	Cost to implement
1.0	Office PC (work computer)	Accident	Physical destruction	Possible	$5000.00 plus $50k in lost productivity	Surge arrestor Backup disk	< $500
1.1		Evil insider	Theft	Possible	$5000.00 plus $50k in lost productivity	Door lock on office	< $200
1.2		Evil outsider	Plant Trojan, gain network access information, use to attack SCADA	Possible	Very costly, possible legal consequences	Firewall and malware scanning SW	< $100/yr
1.3		Evil insider	Business secrets to competition	Possible	Very costly, sales decline	File encryption SW	< $300
1.4		Malware	Loss of files, data, rework	Very Possible	$50k in lost productivity	Virus scan SW Backup Disk	< $100/yr

TABLE 7–4. *Threat assessment and countermeasure selection example*

8

Classifying Cyber Attacks and Cyber Threats

As has been mentioned, there are many different kinds of attacks that can be launched against your systems, and there are many types of attackers or threat agents. The most serious threat (a terrorist attack taking control of your SCADA system) is posed by the lowest-probability threat agent. Conversely, the least serious threat (getting infected by a virus or worm) is posed by the highest-probability threat agent (random software infection). This is not to imply that a malware infection is not dangerous. Quite the opposite; it can definitely shut down your SCADA system. But if you take the appropriate precautions with firewalls and N/HIDS and virus-scanning software, your chances of software infection are low. If you make and keep adequate software backups and practice recovery procedures, the impact of a successful infection will be minimized.

If terrorists chose to attack your systems, they would have most likely gone to great lengths to determine what type of system and computers you have and to learn as much as possible prior to launching an attack. If you take steps to prevent them from obtaining critical information (particularly from a former insider), uphold strong and properly maintained defenses, and establish procedures and policies that further safeguard your systems, then the chances of a successful attack are small. Again, if you make and keep adequate software backups and practice transfer (to a redundant system and/or an alternative operational site) and recovery procedures, the impact of a successful attack can be minimized.

By contrast, if a hacker stumbled across your systems and decided to probe and play, that person would not know in advance of breaking in what type of systems you have. To a hacker, such mystery is part of the fun—posing an enjoyable technical challenge. We have previously discussed the types of tools used by hackers to probe and learn about your systems, mainly to identify vulnerabilities. There are other types of general attacks that hackers employ to invade your systems.

Using downloaded hacker tools, even unskilled individuals surfing the Internet may mount an attack. There are lots of computer enthusiasts and amateurs who lack the advanced programming skills of a real hacker but, for whatever reasons, seek the thrill of playing hacker games. Those individuals obtain software and do-it-yourself instructions, on writing viruses and worms and launching a range of attacks, from various hacker Web sites. Hackers call these amateurs *script kiddies* because they follow a cookbook script, rather than inventing their own attacks. Hackers speak of these people with disdain, yet provide the tools and instructions they use.

Again, with properly established and maintained protective measures and the use of N/HIDS technologies, the chances of a hacker (and certainly a script kiddy) playing with your systems while remaining undetected is quite low. The following are the most prevalent types of attacks used by hackers and script kiddies.

WEB Site/SQL Attacks

Although most SCADA systems don't have actual Web servers offering up real-time data to the Internet, a fair number use Web technology for the operational HMIs on their LAN. A good number also interact, through intermediate relational databases, with corporate Web servers that offer information within the corporate WAN and the Internet. Those Web servers may possibly also support XML data exchanges with the equivalent business-to-business (B2B) Web servers of major customers, suppliers, and partners. Web sites that interact with back-end relational databases to obtain requested information, or even to look up a user's ID and password for login purposes, are vulnerable to a technique called *SQL injection*. In this technique, specially formulated text is put into data entry fields on

Web pages (Web forms), such that the logic behind the Web page (usually some script written in a language like JavaScript, VBScript, or Perl) is tricked into either revealing unauthorized data or believing that the user has some level of access rights (fig. 8–1). In effect, the specially constructed text, entered into the data entry field, has the effect of modifying the query made to the relational database. This could be to cause the lookup of a user's ID and password to appear to be successful, to cause other database tables to be revealed, or to cause the extraction of data from a table that is not supposed to be exposed for external access.

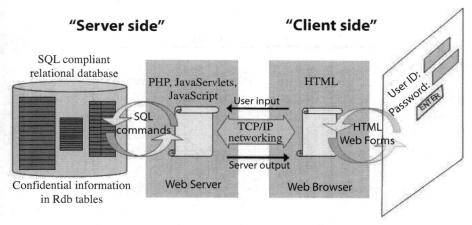

Attacker enters text that causes the logic of the interactive script to make an SQL query that is different than what was intended by the programmer. Poor (or no) validity checking on user input to web forms enables SQL injection attacks.

FIG. 8–1. *Logical relationship between relational database and Web pages*

SQL injection is successful mainly with Web pages that have poor validity checking on their data entry fields. If a person's name is expected, then an input like "UNION SELECT Card_No FROM CARDLIST WHERE ' ' = ' ' " is probably an attempt at SQL injection and should be rejected (and a log entry should be sent to the N/HIDS package). Hackers have been able to extract an amazing amount of confidential information from corporate databases that were linked to the corporate Web server. If stealing company information is the objective of an attacker (e.g., of an internal attacker) and if your SCADA system passes data through a common relational database and uses Web server/browser technology to distribute information, then SQL injection could be used to access other information on that shared relational database. Fortunately, there are commercial products that can scan your Web pages and identify places where an SQL injection attack could be used. Addition of suitable input validity checking to the Web pages will generally prevent SQL injection attacks.

E-mail Attacks

Delivery of malware—in particular, script viruses—to employee computers is most frequently accomplished via e-mail. Commonly used e-mail clients (e.g., Microsoft Outlook) include some capability for filtering e-mail, but they also have a feature to offer a preview, which can cause the execution of script viruses embedded in the e-mail message. Script kiddies were having fun for a while with e-mail attachments written in various programming languages—especially Microsoft Visual Basic. Double-clicking (running) these attached programs triggered them to cause damage to your PC. Today most people know not to click on attachments from people they don't know.

Individual PCs can also be equipped with virus-scanning software that checks every incoming message. Of course, that approach could mean having to manage the routine updating of a large number of PCs. Most corporations place a centralized e-mail server on the network and pass all e-mail, both internal and external, through that server, where virus scanning and attachment sequestration are performed. Of course, this can cause problems when people need to send legitimate large attachment files or when the e-mail server decides that a legitimate e-mail source is now a spam site and refuses to accept their mail. As long as the virus-scanning software is kept up to date, the odds of an infected e-mail getting through are reasonably low. Of course, there is always the danger of a *day-zero virus* getting in, because it is not yet known to the virus-scanning software.

Malware

Malicious software generally falls into one of the following four general categories.

Software that mindlessly reproduces and consumes resources

The terms *virus, bacteria,* and *worm* are used for software of the first category. Hackers and script kiddies create and launch these types of software just for the thrill of seeing how many systems can be infected and how far the software gets before it is eradicated. The term *day zero* implies the date/time of the first detection of any new software of this type (the date the person who developed the malware released it onto the Internet). The terms *time bomb, Easter egg,* and *Trojan* are used for the second type of software—even though Easter eggs don't usually do any serious harm (many are quite cool), and Trojans, based on their secret function, may be more correctly grouped in the next category.

Software that inflicts harm once a programmer-specified trigger condition is met

A surprising percentage of the apparently useful shareware available on the Internet falls into this category, including time bombs and Trojans. There are Web sites that track and list shareware that has been found to contain time bombs and Trojans. Use of shareware is always a dangerous proposition in critical systems. Many a script kiddie has discovered that the neat hacker tools they downloaded from the friendly hacker Web site ended up being a time bomb or Trojan.

Software that allows a remote party to (re)enter your systems and (re)use your resources

The third category of software includes remote access toolkits and rootkits, as well as some types of Trojans. The basis for this type of tool is the replacement of legitimate system software modules with hacker versions that perform the original functions, but also provide a back door that bypasses normal authentication processes so that a hacker gains high level access and authority without actually going through the checks. By planting any of this software into your systems, a hacker will probably obtain the ability to come and go as he or she pleases—nearly undetected. That "nearly" is critical. N/HIDS software is normally quite effective at detecting the anomalous conditions generated by a hacker playing these games. By contrast, if a hacker, working with a terrorist group, got any of this software into your systems, the results could be very, very bad because the intended damage could be inflicted before a N/HIDS observed enough indications to trigger an alarm.

Software that finds and collects sensitive information

The fourth category of malware includes spyware, adware, traffic sniffers, and keystroke loggers. The general purpose of all of these variants is to gather confidential information and send it out, probably over the Internet, to a third party who will then make use of the information. Hackers have gotten very clever about disguising the communications between such spyware and the hacker's remote computer. Often such message traffic is tunneled inside of protocols used for email and web browsing, so as to hide it from detection. A well designed NIDS will tend to notice the new traffic, even if tunneled. One way that hackers break into systems is to plant keystroke loggers in people's PCs by offering some shareware utility that seems really useful but that actually records and transmits keyboard entries to the hacker's computer. Looking through the transmitted data, the hacker generally finds IDs and passwords, as well as other data that will be used subsequently to stage an actual attack. A traffic sniffer is a program that watches IP and Ethernet packets and records and forwards those that match a given type (e.g., e-mail or IM) to the hacker's computer. Again, the recorded messages usually contain a wealth of information useful for setting up an attack. N/HIDS packages are usually able to detect the presence of this category of malware, but often only after a given amount of data has been released. Virus/Trojan scanners can often detect the presence of these particular types of malware. When a local Ethernet LAN is created using switches (and possibly sub divided into VLAN segments), this also aids in thwarting traffic/packet sniffers, since this makes it nearly impossible to find a single connection point where all traffic flows past. But this doesn't prevent a strategically placed sniffer from watching specific traffic, such as between a system administrator's PC and the central SCADA server.

Remote Control/Usage

The typical hacker (if such a person exists) breaks into systems to show off technical prowess and to prove that he or she can beat your defenses. Once in, a hacker might just *plant a flag* (i.e., place some obvious message in your system that proclaims that a breakin has been made), do some damage (delete critical files or plant a virus), or ensure that he or she can come back and use your systems for his or her own purposes. In that case, the hacker will attempt to plant a *rootkit* or a remote access Trojan (RAT). Variations on rootkit/RAT software for Unix/Linux and Microsoft operating systems are readily available from hacker Web sites and usegroups.

A hacker might wish to be able to use your computing power, use your storage, or use your systems as a relay point (to cover their tracks) for attacking other systems. One way that legitimate e-mail servers end up on spam site–blocking lists is that hackers set up an e-mail relay on your e-mail server and then use your e-mail server to send out their spam attacks. (Spam is undesired, unsolicited e-mail—the junk mail of the Internet that fills your in basket every day.)

Zombie Recruitment

One of the biggest problems on the Internet today is the existence of several networks of computers that have been infected by hackers and that can be brought together to participate in a hacker-coordinated attack. There is no way to be sure, but federal authorities think that at least four such networks exist. Hackers break into any poorly defended computer that is permanently connected to the Internet and implant remote control Trojan software, which allows them to send the computer commands that will be executed as instructed.

In hacker terms, such a computer is now a zombie (or a 'bot' which is a shortened form of robot), meaning that it is under the inconspicuous control of the hacker. Then, on a given date and time, a huge number of these zombie computers will participate in an attack either by making constant and repeated Web page access requests to a targeted Web site or by sending specially designed messages (e.g., the "ping of death") over and over to the designated target. Distributed denial of service (DDoS) attacks and ping-flooding attacks are staged using such zombie networks.

If you have proper firewall, protection, perform regular malware scans, and employ N/HIDS technology, it is unlikely that your systems will be infected with any of the types of malware described previously. Your systems could still, however, become the target of one of these distributed zombie attacks. As with all possible threats there needs to be a probability assessment, and the probability of a DDoS attack on a SCADA system's web server seems improbable, as it would not necessarily effect the basic operation of the SCADA system. But, nothing says that a DDoS attack has to focus on a web server.

In the past, SCADA systems were highly unlikely to be directly connected to the Internet—and they might not even have been connected into the corporate LAN/WAN. In the future, though, it is more likely that the Internet could serve as a communications subsystem for linking SCADA systems to their field-based remotes and to other SCADA systems. In this case, DDoS attacks cannot be discounted as a possibility. Such attacks are unlikely to shut down a SCADA system, but they could seriously degrade the system's ability to communicate with field equipment. If RTUs were using IP networking to communicate with their SCADA system, even if using VPN technology to protect their communications, a massive DDoS attack against the SCADA system, just making IP requests (which will be rejected in the VPN authentication process) would eat up processing power and communications bandwidth needed by the SCADA system.

Firewall Configuration

In an optimally configured SCADA system, there will be at most one connection between the SCADA system's network and the corporate network (with the assumption that this also provides a path to the Internet.) As has been mentioned previously, that may not be possible due to the need for interconnections to other systems, which may themselves have interconnections to the Internet. The best line of defense in these instances, to keep malware and cyber attackers at bay, is a strong and well configured firewall at each connection point. A poorly or improperly configured firewall is the hacker's best friend. All of the attacks described earlier in this chapter assume that an attacker can get into your systems and on your network. Using VPN technology, or at least link encryption technology, has been discussed for protecting communications with other systems. These strategies don't prevent attackers from going through these external systems to attack your SCADA system. They merely keep the interconnection channel secure. (Imagine having two office buildings linked with a steel encased, fully enclosed, air conditioned hallway. People could travel between the buildings, using this hallway, and be safe and secure from weather or outside threats. But this doesn't stop an attacker from entering either building through other entrances and then going to the hallway and passing through to the other building!) All interface points to other systems [using IP protocol] and networks need to be secured with firewall technology (which is like placing a guard who checks IDs at each end of our metaphorical inter-building tunnel.) A firewall may be an optional function available within the communications device that provides the interface to the communication link [e.g., the router]. We are focused on connections that use IP networking and messaging only because an attacker coming in through the Internet (the external entrances to our metaphorical buildings) requires this in order to reach your SCADA system.

If your SCADA system exchanges data with another system (e.g., a plant DCS) using something else, such as serial Modbus protocol [but not the IP version], then an attacker can't use this channel to stage conventional cyber attacks. (Of course that doesn't mean that the serial link couldn't be compromised and used to send false data/control information in either or both directions using a protocol test set.) As has been mentioned, firewall software comes in different levels of capability, based on the data it checks in making its allow/deny decision on each message. At the lowest level a firewall can check the IP address and TCP/UDP port number in each packet (going in and out through the firewall) and block or allow based on this data. A basic requirement for using such filtering is that all communicating computers have fixed, *static IP addresses*, rather than ones that are temporary and changeable (assigned by some gateway computer using DHCP [dynamic host configuration] protocol.)

Since the interconnections between systems can usually be restricted to a very limited set of known services, and the IP addresses for the specific computers in those systems can be known, it is possible to have a firewall block all messages (in both directions) except for a very specific, limited set. It is always a good idea to start with a firewall approach that blocks *everything*, and then to "open" the firewall for the restricted set of IP addresses (computers) and well-known port numbers (applications and services) that are actually needed. Here we are talking about message traffic that is leaving or entering the SCADA system's network, not the messages that stay within the SCADA system network itself. There may be protocols and services, such as OPC, that are difficult to firewall because of their dynamic use of port numbers, but such traffic normally stays within the computers on the SCADA network (e.g., between a SCADA workstation and a historian or real-time data server.) If you require OPC to exchange data with an external system/computer, then you do have a bit of a firewall problem. Firewalls can be more sophisticated and be application/protocol aware (such as a type of firewall called an application proxy server) but this is normally only available for well known protocols. (None currently are on the market support ICCP, IP-DNP3, IP-Modbus, OPC and other specialized protocols, although there is discussion about developing such versions.) These firewalls actually "read" the messages to see if they make sense based on the protocol (helpful for spotting message traffic hidden within [tunneled] a standard protocol.) Some of the frequently used IP-based protocols for data exchange (or other purposes) with a corporate IT system, or other types of systems include the following. There are lots of other IP based protocols, but this list covers the majority that are typically used for inter-system/network interfaces with SCADA systems:

- FTP — File Transfer Protocol allows the reliable computer-to-computer transfer (copy) of one or more files, with no regard to file type and size. This is a very commonly supported and well used protocol for the automated, periodic transfer of specified data files. It lacks any form of security and sends user ID/password information in ordinary text format that is all too easily captured. It is often used to deliver (over-write and replace) software/program files as well. In general it is not too dangerous to use it for out going data files. But it presents a high security risk if allowed for incoming files. There are known vulnerabilities in FTP implementations that can be exploited by hackers. (Remember that here we are discussing a permanent interconnection with other systems for the purpose of delivering data. If a vendor needs to provide remote support to your system, and send you new software, you should establish a temporary VPN connection for this purpose.)

- TFTP—Trivial FTP is a stripped down, version of FTP that is less often used because of its lack of login requirements. It should not be used in most cases and should be at least replaced with FTP.

- SSH—Secure Shell is a mechanism for a remote user to have login access to a computer, typically for remote administrative and development purposes. Allowing this message traffic to come into a SCADA system opens up a possible way for an attacker to break in as well. IT support folks who need administrative access to a SCADA system can also use VPN tunnels (or physically come to the SCADA system facility) just like a vendor would.

- HTTP—Hyper Text Transfer Protocol is the protocol used between Web browsers and Web servers. If corporate personnel are allowed Web browser access to the SCADA system (or if data exchange is via XML data files) then this protocol would be used. Unfortunately this protocol is not secure and has many exploitable vulnerabilities. Its use implies that there is a Web server in the SCADA system poised to respond to a request for an XML document (or other type of Web page) from a client on the other end of the connection. If the SCADA system needs to provide

Web-based data access, it would be best if a separate server were used for this purpose, and isolated in a DMZ arrangement, between the SCADA network and the other network.

- HTTP/S—A more secure version of HTTP that allows for authentication. Wherever possible this should be used rather than HTTP and the authentication features enabled for both the client and server components.

- SMTP—Simple Mail Transfer Protocol is used to deliver e-mail, including attachments, from one computer (a client) to another computer (the e-mail server). Some SCADA systems send e-mail alerts and alarms to specified individuals (on the corporate/ enterprise WAN) when various specified conditions are detected. Outgoing mail traffic from the SCADA system is not generally the issue, but rather incoming traffic, which normally should not be permitted. If e-mail (and IM) is used between SCADA personnel and the corporate network, then separate PCs, only connected to the corporate network, should be used for this purpose (and the same is true for web browsing.)

- Telnet—This is a less secure version of SSH and should not normally be permitted into the SCADA system from an external system.

- SNMP—Simple Network Management Protocol messages are used to monitor various network components, and provide remote administrative support. Some N/HIDS packages use this protocol to communicate with the central monitoring client. Unless the SCADA system is being administered remotely, there is no reason for allowing such message traffic into the SCADA system network. If remote administration is being used, then at least the v3 level of SNMP, with its added levels of security features, ought to be required. Earlier versions have wide range of known vulnerabilities.

- ICCP—The Inter Control Center Protocol was designed for SCADA to SCADA system exchange of real-time data, supervisory control commands, information (such as schedules) but it did not (at least initially) incorporate any security features or functions. There are now extensions for authentication functions.

• DCOM—This is the messaging protocol used by OPC. As was already mentioned, OPC uses random ports for its functions and is thus difficult to manage in a firewall. Although some implementations allow ports to be limited to a defined range, it is still dangerous to use OPC for data exchanges with external systems. If this protocol must be used, then an approach, as with HTTP, of using a semi-isolated server, specifically for this data exchange (and using a more controllable protocol between the SCADA system and this server) is one way to increase the security.

• SQL—Standard Query Language clients and servers communicate across networks using an application-level protocol called Tabular Data Stream (TDS) which is available for most operating system platforms. In a Microsoft environment the connectivity might be via ODBC which uses a different messaging scheme and protocols such as TDS, TNS [Transparent Network Substrate] and DRDA [Distributed Relational Database Architecture]. The biggest threat with an SQL connection is that of malicious messages, causing damage to, modification of, or deletion of, the database tables. SQL implementations today support client-server authentication, which should be implemented for security purposes.

• IP-DNP3.0 —The IP version of the popular serial communications protocol was essentially created by packing DNP messages into an IP message frame, and thus no additional security features were provided with this transition. DNP has no authentication or encryption functions, although the committee that manages its evolution and specifications, is looking at such enhancements. There have been successful SCADA projects where SSL-based authentication and encryption were combined with IP-DNP for secure IP based communications, but these efforts were proprietary implementations and not based on DNP committee approved specifications or standards.

- IP-Modbus—The comments are essentially the same as those concerning the IP version of DNP3.0, except no plans have yet been announced regarding expanding the protocol for security purposes and the writer is unaware of any implementations where security features, other than those which can be added as part of generalized IP networking, have been developed and deployed.

Note again that these issues relate to the IP-based network interface(s) between a SCADA system and an external system/network, and not to communications on the SCADA system's LAN/WAN among and between the computers and assorted devices that compose the SCADA system (including links with alternate operating sites and with network-connected field sites.) Those connections, when based on IP networking, also need to be considered for allowed and disallowed traffic. For example, should a user at a field site be able to telnet into the main SCADA system and perform administrative functions, just as they might if they were in their office at the central facility? When IP networking is extended out to the field sites, this offers a lot of conveniences, but also opens up a whole new range of security issues and vulnerabilities.

9

Physical Security

The topic of internal threats and insiders as potential attackers was discussed earlier in this section. As already stated, an insider is a person who has some level of physical access to your facilities and who may also have some level of authorized electronic access and access to critical information. If we assume that an insider is a threat agent, then one of the ways to defend against such a threat is to use physical security mechanisms.

A basic tenet of security is the concept of least privilege, whereby a person is assigned only the access rights required to perform his or her duties. Access rights are supposed to be reviewed routinely and whenever a person's duties are modified. For example, just because Fred was allowed SCADA control room access last week, to fix a wiring problem, doesn't mean that such access permission should continue after he has fixed the problem. Unfortunately, for a variety of reasons, personnel tend to collect access rights over time and never lose them. If someone decided that Fred was to be trusted in the control room once, obviously he can be trusted there again, so why go through the effort to change his access rights? In many organizations, physical security is rather loose. Once you make it past the guard at the front door, nothing prevents you from going wherever you please. Social engineering has shown that walking around boldly and being obvious makes you seem more legitimate, rather than sneaking about quietly.

Physical security deals with the physical protection of critical systems and their interrelated subsystems, as well as the protection of confidential and critical materials, of personnel, and of actual facilities. Today physical security even extends to the protection of portable or mobile devices owned by the corporation. This book is focused on the security of critical cyber assets, specifically those that are part of a SCADA system. Thus, we will not address issues of physical security relating to natural and man-made disasters or issues not immediately relevant to securing the critical cyber assets—even though these threats still need to be addressed. (A SCADA system can be knocked out by a hurricane or a facility fire just as completely as by a cyber attack.)

Access Controls

On the assumption that different personnel will have different levels of access to facility areas, there needs to be a means for enforcing those restrictions. The first level of access control is at the entrance(s) to the facility. SCADA systems are often housed in facilities with multiple purposes. It may be a corporate headquarters, an engineering facility, or just an office building shared by multiple organizations. That being the case, there needs to be public access, and you cannot prevent people from coming and going at will. It is therefore generally necessary to create one or more layers of physical protection around your critical cyber assets, internal to the facility itself, to address this issue (fig. 9–1).

NERC describes the need to establish a physical security perimeter around critical systems. This is not always easily done, especially with consideration for fire codes and personnel safety, but it is important to place a physical barrier between unauthorized personnel and your critical SCADA systems. Hallways can be blocked with one-way, solid-core doors. Windows can be secured with wire mesh, bars, or even shatter-resistant polycarbonate laminates.

The important issue is to carefully review the physical security perimeter and watch out for such weaknesses as suspended ceilings, large air ducts, and other inconspicuous ways in which your perimeter can be breached. The objective is to limit the number of entry points (without compromising personnel safety) so that you can then establish

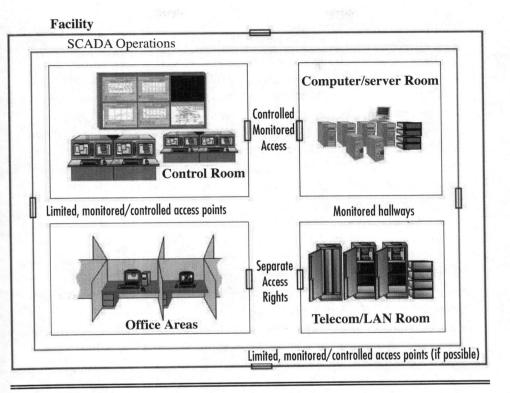

Facility

SCADA Operations

Computer/server Room

Controlled Monitored Access

Control Room

Limited, monitored/controlled access points

Monitored hallways

Separate Access Rights

Office Areas

Telecom/LAN Room

Limited, monitored/controlled access points (if possible)

FIG. 9–1. *Physical security layers for added security*

access controls (and monitoring) at those few points of potential ingress. However, because of fire codes and personnel safety, you may not be able to restrict egress via the same small number of locations: you cannot require people to go through authentication procedures if the fire alarm is going off. It is usually assumed that people leaving a restricted area are not as big a concern as people entering, since they must have had access rights to enter in the first place. Of course, if an insider were trying to remove critical equipment or materials or make a quick getaway, the best approach would be to pull the fire alarm and head for a egress point (ideally one that is not monitored). Access-control mechanisms themselves can be totally manual, totally electronic, or a hybrid of both.

Manual access controls

At the lowest level, in many organizations, manual access control amounts to using locks and keys (possibly electronic) as a means for restricting access to only authorized personnel. If a person has a key, they are obviously authorized. This is a dangerous assumption and lacks a critical component: an audit trail of who entered and exited and when. And let's face it, keys can be stolen and locks picked. An acceptable totally manual system would employ guards to check credentials and refer to access-control lists (and who know the company's access policies and procedures) to determine if a given person is allowed entrance beyond that point (and under what conditions they may bring materials in and out and escort unauthorized people). Nonforgeable credentials are a very important provision in such a scheme, so that the guard can be assured that the person offering the credentials must have gotten them legitimately. Most states now issue driver's licenses that are extremely difficult to forge or modify. They contain holograms, photographs, and florescent dyes that stymie the counterfeiter. Employee credentials need to be of the same caliber, particularly if verification is strictly through visual inspection by a guard. This is because the credentials are all the guards can use as the basis for their decision (allow entrance) and because guards are frequently changed. Under such a system the loss of credentials and especially the theft of credentials need to be treated as serious matters, because an attacker may be trying to obtain credentials to modify or to learn their features and construction. Don't forget that the vendors who sell you the equipment to produce your credentials will sell the same equipment to others.

Electronic access controls

Since employment of guards has both pluses and minuses (mainly overall cost and retraining issues when guards are replaced), many organizations have switched to fully electronic access controls. We have already covered many of the technologies used for personnel authentication by a computer system: passwords, biometrics, magnetic-strip cards, smart cards, RFID, and so forth. These are generally a superset of the same technologies used for electronic remote access authentication.

A computer can't yet (but likely soon will) look you in the eye and then look at your photographic ID to decide whether they match. In the meantime, you need electronically readable credentials of some sort. Since we want little or no chance of forged or stolen credentials being used for entrance, multiple authentication factors will normally be required: a magnetic or smart card plus a password or code number (a PIN). Biometric authentication would be the best, but there are still reliability issues with these technologies. (Biometric scanners usually employ some form of recognition threshold that can be set higher or lower. If you get too many false positives, you can raise the setting; if you get too many false negatives, you can lower the setting.) Granting people access to sensitive areas incorrectly is unacceptable, but refusing access to authorized personnel is also a problem. Biometrics tend to work best in a hybrid arrangement, in which a human guard can use other authentication methods to resolve issues of false negatives. Noncontact RFID smart cards with an integrated photographic ID (and possibly a manually entered code number) are the most prevalent technology used today for fully automated, electronic access control. However, as biometric technologies improve and decrease in cost, expect these to gain market acceptance and wider general usage.

Hybrid access controls

As the term implies, a hybrid system uses a combination of human guards and electronic access controls. In a typical hybrid strategy, an electronic mechanism of credential validation, such as a magnetic-strip or RFID card reader, is placed at each entry point and connected to a site computer that contains access information. Use of any reader to scan electronic credentials automatically informs a guard that someone wants access (and, in the most current systems, probably pops up a stored image of the person whose ID was scanned on the guards console display).

Usually, in place of a guard at every entry point, a single guard, centrally located, uses video camera technology to observe the access points and to view the person requesting entrance (see fig. 9–2). The guard will be equipped with a CRT display linked to the card reader computer and to the video camera system, and will be able to the access control and personnel databases. The security system will normally provide a stored image of the employee in question, as well as any access restrictions and issues (not allowed to bring anyone else into the facility, not allowed weekend access, not allowed evening access, etc.). The live image from the close-circuit video camera will also be displayed on the guard's CRT screen. The guard makes the decision to allow the person access and sends a command to unlock the door (and momentarily disable the alarm mechanism), based on his visual inspection of the person, the information in the access control database, and the information from the person's electronic credentials.

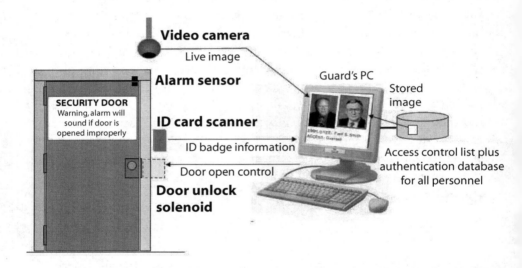

FIG. 9–2. *Typical hybrid access-control system architecture*

With biometric scanners, a false negative (refusing entrance to a valid, authorized person) can be resolved by having the guard compare the stored image to the live camera image of the person and possibly demanding additional ID. Biometrics can make the need for a guard to verify a person's credentials unnecessary, except when the biometrics generate a false negative. To eliminate false positives, however, the acceptance settings on biometric scanners usually need to be at a level that will guarantee a moderate number of false negatives.

Access Tracking

Security professionals will also generally recommend that you keep track of the entrance and exit of personnel who have access to secure areas. Just as an NIDS or HIDS package identifies cyber threats by watching for unusual and anomalous activities inside your computers and on your networks, keeping an audit of personnel access can aid you in spotting anomalous personnel behavior, which might be an indication that an insider is planning something.

Access tracking can be manual or electronic. If a guard is the means for access control, a sign-in log is often the means of access auditing. With almost any electronic access-control technology, the systems used maintain an electronic log file for auditing purposes. Both types of logs, physical and electronic, should be considered as containing sensitive and confidential information and accorded appropriate protections. A physical log book would provide a potential attacker with names, departments and typical access times/days for authorized personnel. An electronic log could contain a lot more data, including employee ID numbers, telephone numbers, and other credential-related personnel information. A potential attacker would be aided by getting their hands on such information. A hostile insider would be aided in covering up illicit activities by destroying such information. Procedures should be developed to secure the access logs and protect the information they contain—for example, making multiple daily backup copies and storing them somewhere secure (even off site).

Illegal-Entry Alarms

Access-control mechanisms keep out the honest people, but the dishonest will try to circumvent such controls—by getting the necessary credentials through illicit means, disabling (or attempting to bypass) the access-control mechanism, or by finding holes in your perimeter (an unsecured window, a service tunnel, a false ceiling, etc.). We have already discussed using nonforgeable credentials to prevent their illicit use if lost or stolen. But what about people gaining access through other unauthorized means?

From a security standpoint, it is good practice to place sensors (separate from the access-control mechanisms) on doors, windows, and other access ways that can detect their opening—particularly if such access ways cannot be visually monitored. An illegal-entry alarm is triggered when such an access way is used, but no access-control authorization was given (and who authorizes access through a window anyway?). Another scheme is to use motion sensors in rooms and areas containing critical equipment or materials and to generate an alarm if motion is detected when no authorized access has been granted to the room or area.

The idea is to make it as difficult as possible (preferably impossible) for any potential threat agent to gain access to your critical systems and confidential materials and information. If they do gain entry to those areas, you want to detect this immediately, so that you can minimize the time available to them to inflict damage or access materials. A very important procedure for an organization with critical systems and information is to develop, test, and practice responding to illegal-entry alarms and ensuring that everyone knows their role in such a situation.

Physical Isolation of Assets: Layers of Defense

In the design of the physical security perimeter that will protect key computing systems, personnel, and confidential materials, it is wise to follow the old dictate not to place all your eggs in one basket. It is unideal to create one, big enclosed area and assume that once inside, you and all of your systems and confidential materials are secure. It is also probable that there will be differing levels of access authority required for subareas within your perimeter. It is still fairly standard to stage large computers and their peripherals in a computer room with environmental controls, raised flooring, and a UPS. The separate environmental controls require that this area be enclosed and isolated from the general office environment and have limited points of ingress/egress. With this design as a basis, it is easy enough to add electronic access controls on the entry points and to require a higher level of authorization to enter the computer room than is needed to enter the general office area. This same approach can often be taken with the operational consoles and associated display and annunciation equipment. These are usually placed in a physically separate control room with its own access ways.

We have already discussed the typical job classifications of people working with and around a SCADA system—from operator trainee to senior system administrator. We can set physical access rights by job category, so that the operational staff can't directly enter the computer room and the computer support staff can't directly enter the operations control room (and the general office staff can't enter either). The same can be done with the telecom and LAN/WAN equipment if it is located in separate, controllable spaces. Physical segregation by job category doesn't mean that people *can't* go into other areas, just that they can't do it without the knowledge and approval of someone with sufficient authority. In this manner, a sort of generalized separation of duties can be created. Even though this may seem to be just a bureaucratic strategy—making it harder to get your job done and frustrating reliable, honest, dependable employees—it also frustrates the illicit efforts of those insiders who are not so honest and reliable.

Physical Protection of Materials and Information

Owning and operating a SCADA system to monitor and control your distributed processes isn't the same as being a government agency in charge of spying on enemy agents. You're not likely to have sensitive information of a top secret level lying around. However, you do have sensitive information like your personnel IDs and passwords, drawings and designs related to your communications system, backup copies of the system configuration files, and many other such materials that need to be kept away from the unauthorized and protected from theft, destruction, or tampering. Potential attackers would be greatly aided in their efforts by such information. Surprisingly, you may also have information that is considered relevant to the Sarbanes-Oxley (SOX) Act of 2002 (which addresses all information related to business processes) and which, therefore, needs suitable protection mechanisms, audit trails, access controls, lest you and your organization be subject to the fines and legal prosecution allowed under that law. [It would be quite unusual for a SCADA system to contain and present information relative to the health insurance portability protection act (HIPPA), but you ought to make sure!]

In accord with the layered defense strategy outlined above, physical materials—whether documentation, manuals, drawings, or computer-readable media—need to be protected as well and housed in storage that affords some level of access control. Locked cabinets can be effective in keeping people without adequate authorization (as indicated by being issued a key or combination) away from materials to which they have no access rights.

There ought to be procedures for tracking materials and ensuring their timely (and unaltered) return when they are removed from safe storage. If materials are very confidential, it may also be necessary to take approaches to ensure that they cannot be duplicated without proper authorization or discarded without ensuring their adequate destruction (shredding paper documents, smashing disk drives or CDs to bits, etc.). For materials essential to recovery from a system failure (e.g., backup tapes or disks), merely locking up a set of media in a cabinet in the computer room is probably not sufficient (although it is a good start). The best practice for handing such essential materials is to keep a queue of backups, made at some time interval (e.g., daily or weekly), as well as before and after any software or configuration changes to the system.

Since restoration of the systems from these backups will be necessary if the systems suffer a hardware failure or a software corruption (or a successful cyber attack), it is important to know that the backup images will actually be usable and correct (which means that they need to be tested and checked when made, and actually used to do a restoration, as part of an annual training and retraining exercise.). It is also important for there to be multiple levels of backup available, going back a good length of time, in case a software problem or configuration error was introduced but not identified for a period of time over which additional backup images have been made.

Complete system backup images once required reels of magnetic tape and a lot of shelf space. Today, with recordable DVD media and ultrahigh-density tape systems, a complete backup may fit in your coat pocket (which also makes them easier to filch). Making and verifying backups is a critical procedure and needs to be done properly and in a secure manner. History includes too many examples of organizations that either had no backup images or discovered that theirs were incomplete or unreadable. A security-oriented approach would dictate that, although some number of backup images are needed on site so that restoration can be initiated immediately after any system failure, a second copy of each should be securely stored off site, and probably going back in time over a much greater interval than the locally maintained backup images (fig. 9–3).

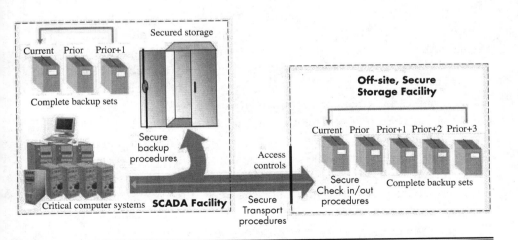

Fig. 9–3. *On- and off-site storage of critical system backup materials*

CYBERSECURITY FOR SCADA SYSTEMS

Since a backup image would afford a potential attacker with a wealth of information about your systems (they can be restored onto other systems and examined), their transport, storage, and production all need to be managed in accordance with good physical security procedures. An acceptable off-site storage facility ought to also follow security procedures. (If it is too hard to steal backups from an operating facility, just get a job at the place where they are stored!) For backup storage and retrieval, the storage facility should require your credentials (they might provide you with a key), and their personnel should not have access to your materials without your presence. Banks have figured out this procedure; look at their methodology for handling safe-deposit boxes. Actually, with backup now being possible on rugged, high density (and physically small) media, such as recordable DVDs, it isn't inconceivable to use a bank safety deposit box for off-site storage. That is certainly better than not having an off-site backup cache, but the problem is that you still need an audit procedure and credential verification procedure (maybe requiring a call back to the SCADA facility to verify that backups have been requested) and most banks don't provide that additional level of security. If you are on the approved list and have suitable ID, you get the safety deposit box and privacy to do whatever you want with its contents.

For secure transport between the operational facility and the off-site storage facility, banks have again figured out a way: armored-car companies. Of course, today, for the off-site storage of digital information (which is all that the backup images contain), you need not physically transport anything. It is possible to have *electronic vaulting*, whereby you send your critical backup images over a leased, encrypted (preferably authenticated) communication circuit to a commercial storage facility. This type of service was originally designed for backing up the system software, electronic transactions, and database changes occurring on huge corporate servers, so that data recovery could occur. (A store wouldn't want its computers to forget about orders or invoices because of a computer failure.) These same service providers don't really care what it is they are recording and holding for you and can provide off-site storage of your backups. In effect, as you copy your files to a local backup device, the same files are sent over the line to the service provider, who makes an additional copy at his facility. Electronic vaulting is an option worth considering for maintaining a critical SCADA system backup.

Critical Ancillary Subsystems

For identification of the boundaries of your physical security perimeter, it is important to make sure that it extends to the subsystems that are essential to the operation of your SCADA system and facility. A SCADA system without communications to the field is useless. The same is true of one without electrical power.

Environmental factors like electrical power, telecommunications, and heating, ventilation, and air-conditioning (HVAC) are essential for a SCADA system to operate. In the same vein, the people who use and operate the SCADA system also need an acceptable environment comprising HVAC, water, lighting, and sewer. An extremist group could probably shut down your SCADA operations (or at least force you to activate an alternative facility) by tossing a dead skunk (or a chemical agent) into the building air intake or breaking your water supply main. There are ways to eliminate this possibility (using chemical filters and positive-pressure rooms), but they tend to be costly and are much more easily done as part of an initial facility design, rather than as add-ons or as modification to an existing facility.

Fire suppression

Most modern facilities have some form of fire-detection and abatement system (usually smoke detectors and sprinklers). If the sprinkler system in the computer room isn't designed properly, shutting down and seriously damaging a computer system can be accomplished by setting off the sprinklers. The use of Halon as a fire suppressant had replaced most sprinkler systems in computer rooms, but the risk to human life—and to the ozone layer (Halon contains chlorofluorocarbons)—proved to be too great. Today a computer room (control room) full of electronic equipment is best protected against fire by a Halon substitute; however, if this is not viable owing to local fire safety codes, then the sprinklers at least ought to be set up with independent zones, and the computer room(s) should be separate from other areas. It is also useful to have a programmed delay in sprinkler activation to permit cancellation of activation owing to a false alarm.

Telecommunications

Many SCADA systems use leased telephone lines provided by the local telecommunications service provider. Somewhere in the building where the SCADA system is located will be a *telecom room*. Too often this room and the equipment it contains will be neglected when a security perimeter is defined, possibly because it is separate from the computer and control rooms or because the room is thought of as belonging to the telephone company. This is one place where an attacker could get access to all of your RTU communications.

These days, this room may also house your routers, switches, and other LAN/WAN equipment. It is essential that this equipment be protected from physical access by anyone not properly trained and authorized. The telephone company might object, but it is in your best interest to ensure that even their personnel have to be escorted by an authorized employee with the necessary credentials, to access these areas. For SCADA systems that use radio communications, the same need for physical protection applies to the master radio equipment, access to the cable from computers to the transmitter, the cable from the transmitter to the antenna, and the antenna/mast itself.

LANs

A potential attacker can also gain a lot of confidential information by sniffing the IP packets traversing your internal LAN, as these will contain e-mail and IM, remote login sequences, and file transfers, for instance. Make sure that your LAN equipment (hubs, switches, and routers) is inside your physical security perimeter. This should even extend to the cabling used to connect hubs and switches to the computer equipment. This pertains to WLANs as well, and the need to implement suitable protective measures on all wireless access points has already been discussed. It has been mentioned that using the intelligence available in (Ethernet) switches to create VLANs, and the message isolation provided by switched Ethernet, add a level of security against packet sniffing. This is true, but if an attacker can get physical access to the switches, it would be possible to alter the configuration so that all message traffic was replicated on a given switch port so that a packet sniffer plugged into that port would have the desired message access.

Electric power

Electric power is essential to run the SCADA system and the communications equipment, as well as the lighting, the HVAC, and even the access controls and monitoring subsystems. Cutting electrical power is an obvious way to take out a SCADA system. Most facilities have a UPS or a standby generator or a combination of both. (The combined approach is best, owing to the time required in order to bring a standby generator up to operating levels once power has been lost.) Obviously, you ought to provide physical protection for the generation and UPS equipment. But you also need to think about the electrical distribution system and equipment, as well as the fuel supply for the standby generator (fig. 9–4). Eliminating the fuel source for the generator, prior to knocking out the power feed from the local utility, would be a good way to kill power to a facility.

If the direct-current (DC) supply to the UPS is accessible, then it could be severed, disabling the UPS. It is also possible to damage the distribution and circuit breaker panels to shut off power to critical systems. The electrical infrastructure for your critical (sub)systems needs to be considered as a potential vulnerability and ought to be inside your physical security perimeter.

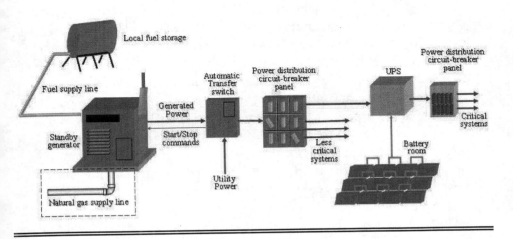

FIG. 9–4. *Power supply typical configuration and equipment interconnections*

Remote and Field Sites

SCADA systems include the electronic equipment located in the field that is used to establish the I/O interface, to measure and control the distributed process and plant equipment. In most instances, this means some type of RTU or PLC device with serial communications to the SCADA system. Otherwise, depending on the industry segment, this may mean a small DCS, a PLC system, or a substation automation system.

It might appear trivial to consider the issue of physical security (of the SCADA system components) at a field site. For someone to get access to that equipment, they would already have gotten into the site and could just as easily smash things or manually operate the local process equipment. Field sites usually do have some level of physical access controls, even if just a chain-link fence with a padlocked gate. The more critical or essential the site is, the greater will be the protective measures employed. Normally, physical security measures around a field site will be implemented to keep out the curious, the vandals, and those looking for something to steal. Physical security is intended just as much to keep people from getting hurt or killed as it is to protect the plant and equipment. A determined and skilled attacker would find it reasonably easy to break into most field sites.

It has already been mentioned that in many cases, leased telephone lines (or digital communication circuits) are often terminated outside the facility, by the communications supplier, and are then routed into the site. This holds true for electrical substations in particular. Such a configuration makes it possible for an attacker to gain physical access to the telecommunication circuit without having to break into the site. An attacker with a laptop PC, a modem (or the digital equivalent), and a protocol test set could then take control of the communications link and send commands to the equipment at that field site. If the circuit is a multi-dropped circuit and the attacker selects the first drop site, then he or she would be able to send commands to the field equipment at all of the sites that share the multi-dropped circuit. The damage that can be inflicted by taking over one or a few field sites depends on the nature of the site and of the process. Tripping a particular circuit breaker, taking out a selected transformer, closing a particular valve, or starting a selected pump can have minor or major impacts.

IP networking in the field

Some industries have begun running TCP/IP networking to their field sites. This is happening in part because of the disappearance of traditional analog telephone service and in part because IP networking offers a lot of additional functionality and can be implemented with commercially available hardware and software. The same telephone line that could only support 1,200-baud analog communications can be replaced with a DS0 digital line that supports 64 kbps data transmission. A single circuit can be used for voice and data and can support multiple, concurrent traffic streams.

Personnel who go to field sites could, in theory (though limited by available bandwidth), be linked into the corporate e-mail system, access files, drawings, and manuals and even be bridged into the corporate phone system and the Internet (fig. 9–5). This may sound great, but the problem is that this also means that a remote field site could, if not adequately protected, be the point of access for an attacker who wants to get into your systems. Breaking into a remote field site is probably a lot easier than breaking into corporate headquarters and the SCADA control room.

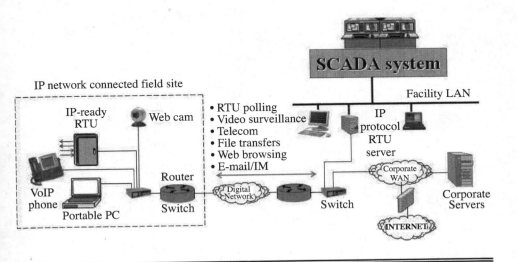

FIG. 9–5. *Extending IP networking to the field*

And with IP networking, making a connection at one field site could, in theory, provide direct network access to all of the other field sites and interconnected systems, PLCs, and RTUs. This is another reason to consider having digital certificate/VPN–based authentication and encryption across all of the computer equipment (including RTUs and PLCs). An attacker who connects into your network in the field but who has no valid digital certificate still won't be able to interrogate and control anything, and the damage would be limited to whatever he could do at the one field site.

10

Operational Security

Policies and Administrative Controls

As has been mentioned, maintaining the security of your critical systems, information, and infrastructure is not based totally on the application of technical remedies, such as video cameras, firewalls, and intrusion-detection systems. Security begins with the process of establishing a corporate culture that identifies security as a primary goal and that provides incentives to encourage employee acceptance and active participation in achieving that goal. It is essential that security not be seen as some bureaucratic program that management has forced on employees for the sake of avoiding legal hassles but as something critical to the success and well being of the organization. Security needs to be a top-down objective, supported at the highest levels of the organization. If top management doesn't take security seriously, then neither will middle management or the rest of the employees. They may give it lip service, but they won't really adopt it as a necessary and critical aspect of the way they perform their duties.

Real security requires a proper mind-set: the sincere acceptance of the need for security-oriented habits and procedures. For a SCADA system operation—particularly one that supervises and controls a critical, essential, or dangerous process—proper security could be a matter of life and death.

The starting point for security is the establishment of written policies that define the organization's goals, intentions, and rules with regard to security. Written policies are crafted to address the business requirements of the organization, as well as to address the legal and regulatory issues facing the organization. The challenge is to have well-considered policies that don't go overboard while also limiting the number of policies, so as not to create a policy manual that looks like the telephone book for New York City.

It is also important to understand the difference between a policy and a procedure. A policy states beliefs and objectives, whereas a procedure defines how those objectives will be implemented. Normally every policy will have one or more procedures that are used to implement the policy. Management must lead in setting policy. However, it is usually best to have active employee participation in developing, testing, and revising the procedures that carry out the policies. For the purposes of overall security, including cybersecurity, there need to be written, enforceable policies that address issues such as

- Protection of critical and confidential information

- Protection of critical cyber assets

- Use of corporate computing and networking resources

- IM, e-mail, and Internet access

- Use of cell phones, PDAs, and mobile devices

- Use of WiFi and other wireless technologies

- Discarding of equipment and confidential materials

- Information access control and categorization

- Management's role and responsibility for security

- Personnel training and security familiarization

- Personnel hiring and termination practices

- Physical access control and monitoring

- Use of removable electronic media

- Systems management and administration

- Personnel physical and electronic surveillance

- Software updating, testing, and patching

- SCADA configuration management

- Application development, testing, and maintenance

- Third-party application software use and maintenance

This list is by no means intended to be comprehensive, but is merely a good starting point for policy definition. Policies don't have to be especially verbose. Actually, a clear, concise policy is more likely to be understood and followed than one tortuously crafted by a team of lawyers (although your legal and human resources staffs should review and approve your policies). For example, a policy regarding adding software to a company computer could be as simple as the following:

All computers owned by the company and used by employees in the execution of their assigned duties will be configured with company-approved operating system and application software, which will be installed and maintained by the company IT department. No employee shall add, remove, or modify the software on their company-supplied computer, including downloading of software from the Internet or installing software owned by the employee. Employees who believe they require additional or different software in order to accomplish their assigned duties will contact the IT department and define their requirements. Only the IT department may modify the approved set of software on individual computers. Employees must use only company provided computers and software in the execution of their assigned duties.

Policies, particularly those aimed at cybersecurity, need regular review and frequent updating to match the current threat and technological environment (e.g., a policy regarding use of floppy disks should probably be replaced with one regarding [re]writable CDs or DVDs and Universal Serial Bus [USB] *flash drives*). For the electric utility industry, the NERC recommendations for cybersecurity state that someone in upper management must be assigned to oversee and enforce the policies; that there be written procedures governing authorization of exceptions/ deviations to any policy, including justifications for the exception; that there be an audit trail of such events, as well as of any modifications to any policy; and that there be an annual review and evaluation of the policies and related procedures.

Although government regulations change over time, every organization currently has to be concerned also about cybersecurity issues related to SOX and HIPPA compliance (and NERC 1200/1300 [now called CIP-002 through 009] if you are an electric utility). Thus, these regulations must be considered when establishing policies. Although the types of business and personal information specifically targeted for protection by SOX and HIPPA are unlikely to be stored on a SCADA system, the interconnection of the SCADA system to the business/corporate LAN/WAN makes a possible access path to that data—a flaw that must be addressed to be in compliance with the requirements of those laws. Although policies ought to be customized to meet your particular business and operational goals and objectives, there are numerous sources for prewritten, example policies that can provide a good starting point. (A Google search will yield a number of potential sources of example policies.)

Policies, no matter how well crafted, are meaningless unless known and understood by the employees and backed up by consequences. Employee understanding ought to go beyond rote memorization; employees need to understand the threats and consequences of not having the policies in place and enforced. When people understand the reasons for a policy, they tend to adopt it and support it, which is particularly vital when many of the policies (and resultant procedures) may seem to introduce time-consuming and counterproductive requirements that add to an employee's workload.

Procedures

Once policies are established (written), procedures that implement the policies must be crafted. These procedures need to be carefully considered, because long and excessively complicated or laborious procedures tend to be ignored or bypassed. A procedure is like cooking with a recipe; it contains a clear set of steps and directions for executing a process, so that the process is done properly and so that no critical step is forgotten or done out of order. Participation from employees is essential in development and testing of procedures, since they are the people who will have to follow the procedures. Personnel are far more accepting of procedures if they have a hand in developing and validating them. Procedures need to be reviewed on a routine basis—to improve, streamline, and correct them, as well as to keep them current. Similarly, procedures (and policies) should be retired when they no longer serve a purpose.

One reason for the development of good procedures is to encapsulate and document the expertise and experience of the personnel. Procedures can be written at many differing levels of detail, depending on who is to follow them. If everyone following a given procedure will have an advanced degree in mathematics, then a procedural step could merely state "Compute the standard deviation of the data set." If this is not the case, you will have to put in the details of how to make that calculation. Well-developed and documented procedures can double as training materials for new employees. Emergency procedures that are (hopefully) not required on a routine basis—such as restoring the SCADA system from the backup media—need to be especially clear, detailed and complete *and* these procedures need to be validated through testing.

Procedural validation

Procedural validation is merely walking through the procedure, like a dress rehearsal for a play, to insure that it actually includes every necessary step, in the correct order, plus any potential variations that might be necessary and that all required materials and resources are actually available and functional. If the procedure requires using backup CDs that are locked up in a secure, fireproof cabinet and obtaining the key from an authorized individual isn't part of the procedure, then the procedure is a failure. If the procedure requires making a voltage check and the necessary test equipment isn't available, then the procedure is a failure. It is generally a good idea for someone not involved in developing a procedure to be selected to perform procedural validation. Excessive familiarity with a procedure and process can cause the procedure writers to miss a critical step that needs to be documented. Because they are so familiar with the process, they automatically perform that step without thinking, and thus don't put it in the document. Again, the level of detail needed in a procedure will depend on the frequency of its use and the training and experience level of the personnel who follow the procedure.

Critical procedure sets

It is worth enumerating here some of the procedure sets that are critical for SCADA system security, as well as the issues that each addresses.

- **Employment initiation and termination.** This includes procedures regarding the requirement of drug tests and financial and police background checks on prospective employees, as well as periodic rechecks on employees with high access levels; procedures for having employees sign nondisclosure agreements (NDAs); and procedures for collecting company property, canceling access rights and credentials, and reviewing ongoing legal obligations under the NDA during exit interviews.

- **Contractor supervision and management.** This is similar to the previous procedure set, except dealing with contractors. This includes procedures for verifying that a contractor organization meets (or exceeds) the minimum acceptable security standards of your organization (e.g., that the contractor organization also does background checks and drug testing).

- **Credentials, password, and account management.** This includes issuance and cancellation of accounts and credentials, upgrading and downgrading of access right as duties change; procedures for dealing with lost and stolen credentials; and personnel password guidelines.

- **Security-patch/virus-scanning management.** This includes installing and testing security patches, distribution of patched software, and making backups of new versions, as well as procedures for routine virus scanning and updating of virus-scanning software.

- **Software-update validation and testing.** This is the methodology used to update, track, and test operating system, networking, application, and third-party software in the off-line environment, prior to release to production system.

- **Installation of modifications to the production system(s).** This establishes who is to perform the work, as well as what sequence is to be followed for redundant and alternative site configurations. This also includes procedures for reverting to the prior version (*rollback*) if problems arise during the modification process. Operational conditions under which this is or is not to occur are outlined, with attention to required coordination and approval from all necessary parties.

- **SCADA system start up and shut down.** This is probably provided by the SCADA system vendor and includes normal steps taken and sequence followed to gracefully bring the system up or down—primarily for use before and after hardware replacements, repairs, or software upgrades.

- **SCADA system restoration.** This is used when the system has crashed or been otherwise disabled. Assumptions regarding possible hardware failures and/or software corruption are outlined. Procedures include performing necessary visual inspection and unit tests of equipment, replacement of damaged equipment, power-up sequence, required restoration media and correct version, overwriting of damaged/infected software, and proper sequence of software installation, as well as restoration of configuration, restarting the various servers and other computers, restoration and verification of RTU polling, initial alarming override, restarting operator functions, restoring links to other systems, and so forth.

- **Employee security training.** This addresses the types of training needed for given levels of access, the frequency at which retraining will be required, and metrics for determining training efficacy.

- **Electronic security incident response and reporting.** This includes possible symptoms or indications of attack, actions to take and their order and priority based on incident type, personnel who need to be informed, and reporting requirements.

- **Physical security incident response and reporting.** This includes personnel safety issues, facility and equipment safety issues, actions to take and their order and priority based on incident type, personnel who need to be informed, and reporting requirements.

- **Firewall and N/HIDS updating.** This outlines who is authorized, reasons for updating, periodicity of updating, processes used to ensure security during updating, audit log of updates, and validation and testing of updates.

- **Sensitive/confidential material management.** This includes identification and classification of materials, methodologies for physical protection and backup, and mechanisms for access control, duplication control, and modification control, as well as procedures for storage and destruction of materials.

- **SCADA system backup generation and storage.** This addresses events that should trigger a backup, periodicity for backups, who can make a backup, on-site and off-site storage rotation, access to on-site and off-site backups, secure transport mechanisms, remote storage access procedures, authority level for access, and approvals for access, as well as validation of backups and creation of an audit trail of backups.

- **Communications subsystem restoration.** This includes contacting the telecommunications supplier to report problems, checking the status of and restarting the telecommunications equipment, as well as understanding equipment diagnostic indicators.

- **Electrical power restoration.** This outlines how to manually (re)start the backup generator, how to enable or bypass the UPS, and how to configure the necessary switch gear and circuit breakers.

- **Access to secure areas.** This establishes the access-level authority required for each category of restricted area, requirements for entry and exit, requirements for bringing materials in or out of a restricted area, and procedures for accompanying quasi-authorized personnel (people who occasionally have a need for physical access such as a vendor maintenance or facility maintenance employee) into restricted areas.

- **Remote electronic access.** This includes setting up electronic credentials, establishing a VPN connection, strong-authentication procedures, dial-in telephone mechanisms, corporate WAN mechanisms, and Internet mechanisms. It should also address the periodic re-issuance of credentials and changing of passwords.

- **Collection and retention of logs and audit files.** This addresses frequency of collection, verification of logging, storage duration, storage media, and their handling and physical protection.

- **Addition and retirement of computing equipment.** This includes installation of baseline operating system and application software; establishment of network settings and user accounts; installation of virus-scanning and firewall software and settings; installation of N/HIDS software and electronic-access monitoring and surveillance software; and disposition, destruction, and/or disabling of key components.

- **Fire alarm response and reporting.** This includes evacuation of the area, verification of the validity of the alarm, personnel safety, notification of and coordination with police/fire departments, and shutoff of gas and electric service. If key equipment needs to be shut down or critical materials moved to safety, this should be addressed as well, including authorizations needed, who must be contacted, etc.

- **Social engineering incident response and reporting.** This outlines official response to a perceived social engineering attempt, telephone and e-mail guidelines for social engineering ploys, requirements for request verification, and necessary credentials and credential validation.

Undoubtedly this seems like a lot of procedures (and it isn't even a comprehensive list), but keep in mind that your personnel are inventing informal, undocumented, and unofficial procedures all the time. They have to in order to do their jobs. The problem is that two employees, with similar responsibilities and duties, will generally come up with two different (though probably successful) procedures to accomplish the same task. By formalizing procedure development, you can apply best practices and end up with a standardized yet optimized methodology that can be passed on to new employees. With proper periodic reviews, the procedures can be improved and modified to meet current environmental (business, legal, and regulatory) demands.

Operational Differences

Supporting a SCADA operation is different from supporting a computer service bureau, an application/Web server farm, or a software development environment. For that reason, some of the policies and procedures that would be typical in those environments are not typical (or even practical) in a SCADA system operating environment (e.g., you won't find a help desk, and rarely will there be any policy regarding performance and capacity management). All of the aforementioned operations, including SCADA, involve a lot of computers and networks and software. However, the main purpose of a SCADA system is to monitor and control a well defined, infrequently (if ever) changing process (the process itself, not the condition/state of the process), so there is little motivation to make some of the changes that would be typical in other environments.

Once a SCADA system is operational and fully debugged, most owners/operators are loath to make even slight changes, owing to the all too true possibility of breaking something as a result. In other environments, it would be commonplace to keep operating system, networking, Web server, and commercial application software up to the latest and greatest versions—and not because of security alone (although that is a *big* part of it today). If a Web site doesn't support the latest features of PHP scripting, Perl, or JavaScript or if a server farm isn't running the latest update of Microsoft Office, then they are not fulfilling their mission. Also, their procedures for installing updates are generally in the form of "load and run the service pack." For a SCADA system operator, there has to be a very good reason to allow software, configuration, equipment, or application changes. The only reasons for changing software that are usually considered acceptable are because there is an intolerable bug in the software and/or because the vendor is dropping its support of the old version of the software or hardware.

For big SCADA systems, supervising critical processes, the update process must involve trying it out on an off-line (non-production) system first. Today, as SCADA systems are linked into LANs and WANs and exchange information with other systems and as corporate IT groups are called on to supply technical support for the computer portions of these SCADA systems, there can be a conflict between the perceived mission of the IT group and that of the SCADA/operations group. Clearly written policies and procedures that are jointly crafted by these two groups represent a way to bring these two cultures together while addressing the unique requirements of both. And like it or not, SCADA systems today need security patches every bit as much as (or even more than) an IT server farm does. On the other hand, the IT group needs to understand the operational differences that are unique to a SCADA environment. It may be undesirable and have a revenue impact to take down an e-commerce Web site for an hour to install patches and upgrades, but it is potentially life threatening to do so with a SCADA system. Worse still, restarting a SCADA system is not just a matter of rebooting the computers (which may solve a lot of conventional IT problems, but it can be a last resort to a SCADA operation). SCADA systems control physical processes and, in order not to send out dangerous or damaging control commands, a SCADA system needs to scan the field devices, determine their status and configuration, and that of the process, in order to be ready to support supervisory control and alarming functions. If RTUs have to be reinitialized (or even reloaded with configuration information and control logic) that adds another level of complexity. During the recent electrical blackout in the northeastern United States, the process of bringing the various regional SCADA systems back online and piecing the electrical grid together again took several days of continuous work. Bringing a long-haul product pipeline back into operation is similarly complicated. IT personnel providing support to SCADA system organizations need to propose all activities and actions in advance, have them discussed with the operational team, and then perform and coordinate their work using mutually developed procedures. On the other hand, it is no longer realistic for a SCADA system owner/operator to take the position that security related patches and updates can be ignored.

Training

Your own personnel are normally the first line of defense against certain types of security threats, particularly the current or former hostile insider and an attacker attempting to gather information (or gain unauthorized access) using social engineering tricks. (Pretending to be an ex-employee returning, just for a moment, to pick up some forgotten personal effect is a typical social engineering ploy.) Nevertheless, for your personnel to be effective, they must not be denied appropriate training. Certainly, part of that training includes being familiarized with company security policies and learning the procedures relevant to all employees (e.g., fire safety) and those procedures associated with their particular duties. (E.g., you wouldn't teach every employee how to make a SCADA system backup, because not every employee will be authorized to perform that task, but you should consider some level of cross-training so that there is always someone available who knows how to perform any critical, essential operation.) Part of training is to educate personnel about how serious the company values security and how important it is to everyone who is part of the organization.

It is highly recommended that all employees in an organization that owns and operates a SCADA system take part in an initial security-training seminar immediately on starting employment, just as a new employee at a chemical plant or refinery would attend a plant safety seminar. The key points that all employees need to know follow:

- Awareness that cyber threats do exist and awareness of the potential threat sources

- Awareness of the means used by attackers to plan and stage attacks and gather confidential information (malware, hacking, social engineering, etc.)

- Awareness of basic practices that support and enable an effective security policy (passwords, access control, information security, etc.)

- Awareness of the potential damage/impact, both to the organization and to the outside world, of a successful attack

- Awareness of management support for the necessary policies and procedures

One problem with security training is that it becomes outdated as technology and hacking methods evolve. Thus, there needs to be a mechanism for updating people's training and for keeping people apprised of new threats. One problem with security awareness is that, like anything that isn't used on a regular basis, it fades over time. Consider the threat-alert color scheme adopted by the DHS to advise the population—and the appropriate military, civil defense, and law enforcement agencies—of the terrorism threat level. Because nothing noteworthy has happened in the United States since 9/11 (even though the public would not be aware of attacks that have been *prevented*), many people now basically ignore the color system and any announcement of an increase in the threat level.

Keeping people interested and focused on security is not an easy task, given all that they normally have to deal with in their jobs. It's kind of like safety training; the day after someone is seriously injured or killed in a plant, everyone suddenly takes the time to follow the recommended safety practices, even though the prior day they were bypassing them. There is no single solution to this problem, but different organizations have used the following strategies to keep security in the forefront of employees' attention:

- Quarterly employee meetings, to reaffirm the need for security

- Metrics that track compliance, offering rewards for the best performance

- Annual retraining/training-update seminars

- Bonuses to managers who meet security objectives

- E-newsletters that provide information on new threats and actual events

- Security certification program, offering rewards at various levels (up to black belt) of certification

- Computer penetration testing (pen testing), sharing the results with staff

- Physical penetration testing, where the attacker leaves visible indicators in areas successfully penetrated

Recovery Procedures

As has been previously mentioned, well-documented and validated system recovery procedures are essential to a SCADA system operation. Most SCADA systems, once commissioned and stable, tend to operate 24/7 for years without mishap. This is obviously a good thing, but it does mean that personnel responsible for performing a system restoration, if one is ever required, have little or no opportunity to practice their duties. This makes it even more important that the procedure be very clear, well-documented, and fully validated. Unfortunately, full and complete validation of the restoration procedures may not be possible, because no one wants to bring the system back down, once it is fully operational, for procedure validation purposes.

If there is a *test and development system* available, separate from the production system, then this might be usable for procedure testing. However, it is common for such test and development systems to include a minimum set of hardware and software, usually in a nonredundant configuration. Thus, such a system may only approximate the true system architecture and would thus limit the ability to do a complete procedural validation.

Developing well-documented and validated procedures may require the assistance of the SCADA vendor, who normally has systems on their factory floor, or training facilities, that can be used for this purpose. If the SCADA system is fully redundant, then it may be possible to do a good bit of the validation (and training) on the standby equipment. If the system is supported by an alternative facility, then the SCADA system at that alternative facility can be used for procedure validation and training. Vendors can usually provide generic training (and maybe documentation) on system recovery and restoration, but the site/customer–specific and application-specific portions of the procedure will still have to be documented and added into the recovery procedure by the SCADA system owner. Even if a full procedural test cannot be performed, due to the lack of backup or alternate facilities, it is possible to do a *structured walk-through* or a simulated execution of the procedures. In these cases, the knowledgeable experts in each area of the procedure follow along as the testing/training personnel follow the steps of the procedure (without actually doing the disruptive things like turning equipment on or off, loading software, etc.) with the experts verifying that the individual steps and actions, as described in the procedures, are complete, in the right sequence, and technically accurate. A structured walk-through is a good way to test a procedure, prior to its issuance, as well as being used for the training of personnel in the use of the procedure, once formally issued.

Annual Review

Various governmental agencies and industry standards organizations recommend that critical procedures be practiced, and policies and procedures be reviewed, on at least an annual basis. The objective here is to ensure both that personnel remain competent and capable of performing these procedures and that the procedures remain accurate and up to date. If there is no reason to make significant revisions to a procedure (e.g., the SCADA system underwent a major upgrade or was replaced), then total procedure revalidation generally isn't necessary.

The annual rehearsal (for retraining purposes) of critical procedures can be performed on one of several levels. The procedures can actually be performed on backup equipment; they can be simulated; they can be subjected to a structured walkthrough; or they can just be given a checklist review. On the one hand, the latter alternatives are less involved and nondisruptive but don't provide the same training experience as actually performing a procedure or at least simulating its performance. On the other hand, a structured walkthrough or checklist review should be performed by non-experts, and be audited by those experts who developed the procedures; thus, these review levels afford an opportunity for expert oversight (and revision if needed) of the procedures.

Background Checks

As objectionable as it may seem to inquire into someone's private life as a requirement of employment, it makes sense that people placed in positions of trust ought to be trustworthy. Today, if just to avoid the legal liabilities, most companies now require preemployment drug testing and random drug and alcohol tests for all current employees (and possibly for contractors performing sensitive or vital activities). Government positions dealing with secret matters require a security clearance that necessitates a detailed background check. Thus, if a person is going to be allowed to operate, program, or maintain a SCADA system, it makes sense that he should be willing to accept some level of background check, both as a requirement of employment and on an annual basis. (Of course, a company should also remember to impose a drug and alcohol policy on these individuals.)

The recommended policy for people with top-level access is to have criminal and financial checks performed. The reason(s) for doing a criminal check ought to be obvious, but why require a financial check? Insiders in various government and private organizations have been compromised by financial motivation since the beginning of civilization. A person who has gotten into financial trouble previously—or is just plain greedy—would be a perfect target for an external threat agent seeking the means for staging an attack. Whether by giving out an ID and password or providing a set of access-control credentials, people have been known to "join the dark side" for the right amount of money. By reviewing the overall financial history of an employee, it is often possible to distinguish those who might be good candidates for recruitment (and for company-provided financial counseling) from those who don't, and even to identify those who have inexplicable income. If an employee is aware that financial and criminal checks will be made on an annual basis, that provides added incentive to avoid temptation. Of course, personal financial and criminal information needs to be held confidential and treated with proper discretion, as should any other personal information maintained by the company. It is important that policies and procedures related to background checks be reviewed by your legal and human resources departments, for compliance with laws and regulations.

11

Electronic/Systems Security

In the same way that you need to establish and maintain a security perimeter that physically protects and isolates your critical systems, sensitive and confidential materials, and personnel from threat agents, you need to establish and maintain an electronic security perimeter that protects and isolates your systems, software, and electronically stored data and confidential information from threat agents. As with physical security, you need to define and limit the number of electronic access points through this electronic perimeter, protect them by using access-control technologies, and monitor them for suspicious activity and attempted/successful intrusions.

In essence, we are talking about protecting the communication paths into the critical computing platforms of the SCADA system. We have already enumerated and discussed the five common electronic communication paths, as well as their protection:

- Telephone connections (dial-in or leased)

- LAN connections

- WAN connections

- The Internet

- Wireless connections (WiFi and Bluetooth)

(Although the Internet is the world's biggest example of a WAN, it is worth separate mention owing to its unique properties and architecture.) In addition to those five obvious electronic communication paths, we need to recognize the continued existence of the original computer networking technology, the *sneakernet*. That is the adorable name used to describe the manual transport of removable electronic storage media as a means for delivering data and software from one computer to another (fig. 11–1). Back when computers ran on coal, that meant carrying boxes of punched cards or reels of magnetic tape from one computer facility to another. Today it can mean carrying a key-chain flash drive or a CD in your pocket or carrying portable electronic devices with up-/download capability, such as a laptop, a PDA, a cell phone, or even an MP3 player or digital camera.

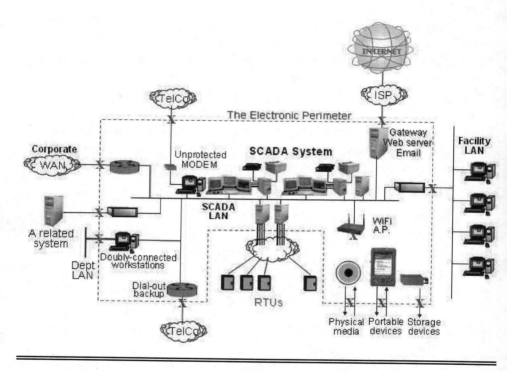

Fig. 11–1. *Identifying APs through your electronic perimeter*

Here, we refer to devices that can be used to physically transport files, data, and programs from point A to point B, regardless of how they electrically (wired/wireless) interface in order to up-/download this information. From a security standpoint, it is vital to remember that sneakernet delivery, whether intentional or accidental, represents a breach of your electronic security perimeter. All sorts of malware can be introduced into critical systems through the use of removable media and portable devices as a delivery mechanism. Further, no firewall is going to detect and protect against such a delivery, since the use of sneakernet bypasses such devices (although any good N/HIDS package ought to detect the infection once it has occurred).

It can be argued that, since we are talking about the physical transport of physical materials, this is a physical security issue. However, it is not the physical materials that pose the risk, but rather the electronic information that they carry. Still, regardless of where you address it, there needs to be a security policy that outlines the care and use of transportable media and of electronic devices that can be used for that same purpose, as well as procedures to protect such media and devices and safeguard their usage.

Removable Media

The biggest problem with removable media is that today it is indeed removable and, in general, physically small. Both Microsoft and Unix/Linux have made the use of removable media a plug-and-play event, requiring no computer expertise or system administrative intervention. You can insert a CD, a DVD, a flash drive, or a memory card into most computers, and the operating system will detect the media and attempt to either boot from it and/or read its file directory and offer a list in a file manager window. If you can't do it through a computer, plugging a flash card into many printers will make their content available to you over the network. The same is true for making a USB connection to a modern digital camera or MP3 player. If malware is planted in the boot sector or file directory, then it is already delivered and on its way to do its intended damage. If malware is just a file on the media (with a seemingly innocuous name), clicking on the icon will make it run before you realize that it was the wrong thing to do. With luck, if your virus-scanning software is ready and up to date, it will catch and block the malware before it can do anything. A good policy regarding removable media is that if you didn't personally place the files on the media in question, always run a virus scan on them and have your virus protection running prior to inserting the media. The types of removable media that need to be considered and addressed include

- Floppy disks (although these are fading away)

- Zip disks (and variations like Jaz—also fading away)

- CDs

- DVDs

- Smart cards and removable flash cards

- USB flash drive storage devices

There are other, older forms of removable and bulk storage media, such as magnetic (digital) tape cartridges. For the most part, however, older media devices tend not to be supported with plug-and-play capabilities— many because they predate the introduction of plug-and-play and others because of their relatively limited capacity. It would certainly be possible to put a virus on a magnetic tape cartridge, but since it normally can't be automatically activated just by having the tape read, few would bother. In most instances, tape cartridges will be used merely as a backup media, and you should have control over the process of both making and restoring from them. It is highly improbable (although not impossible) that someone would bring in a tape from home and load it onto their PC, thus infecting the network. If it were a CD or floppy disk, the probability would increase dramatically, unless proper precautions were taken.

Aside from the risk of something being brought into a secure SCADA facility on removable media, there is also the risk of the same types of media being used to take confidential or sensitive information out of a facility. Unless you intend to perform a full body search of every employee and also search their belongings as they exit the physical security perimeter, you need to address this concern in some other manner. One strategy is to disable the CD/DVD drives and USB/PCMCIA ports on all computers that have access to secure information (e.g., are on the same VLAN as the servers containing the information). Another strategy is to encrypt all sensitive information and strictly limit the number of personnel with decryption keys. If system logging and monitoring functions are enabled and if you have a N/HIDS package in place, then you can track and log all accesses to designated files and directories; most people are less likely to take an inappropriate, disallowed, or illegal action if they know in advance that there is a good chance of being discovered.

Mobile Electronics

More insidious and more difficult to protect against is the transport and delivery of malware via common electronic devices. This is especially true because, for easy use and compatibility, these devices generally come with standardized interfaces and plug-and-play capabilities. The range of devices that are capable of being used as a delivery mechanism is both surprising and appalling. Moreover, as with removable storage media, there is also the problem that these devices may be used to remove sensitive or confidential information from the facility. Remember that even a simple digital camera has a USB interface and a file-downloading capability (and probably removable storage media), so that it is, in effect, a plug-in, mobile, file-storage device. One would hope that all the files in a camera's storage are images, but the camera software probably doesn't differentiate as long as the file has a JPG extension. Portable MP3 players have the same liability. The types of electronic devices that can be used to deliver malware (or transport confidential electronic files) include

- USB or FireWire plug-and-play external hard drives

- Cell phones with Bluetooth or USB

- Media players (e.g., MP3 or video) with USB or FireWire connectivity

- Laptop PCs, with or without Bluetooth and/or WiFi

- Digital cameras with removable media or USB

- High-quality (photo-quality) color printers with removable media slots

- PDAs with Bluetooth and/or WiFi

- PCMCIA plug-in storage devices

There are documented cases of virus introduction into systems from PDAs and laptops when brought into communication with other computers or a network. Unfortunately, with wireless communications, especially Bluetooth (because of ad hoc mode), the establishment of communication requires no obvious, physical connection. In the last two years, organizations that track malware have noted an increase in the number of viruses and worms that are designed specifically for PDAs and cell phones, taking advantage of their Bluetooth capabilities and the embedded operating systems they run. It can be expected that more cross-species (PDA to PC and cell phone to PC) viruses and other types of malware will be showing up in the near future. There are even documented examples of viruses that have spread through networked printers (which incorporate pretty powerful computing platforms these days).

Bluetooth

Bluetooth wireless technology belongs to a category called mobile ad hoc networking. This means that unlike WiFi, no action is required in order to establish or terminate a communication connection, other than getting within physical range of the radio (which is a few meters). With WiFi you may, at the least, have to click a button to accept a connection, type in an SSID, or perform some other overt act, even in ad hoc mode.

What makes Bluetooth so cool (and so dangerous) is that, unless specifically reconfigured not to do so, a Bluetooth-enabled device will automatically establish a connection with any other Bluetooth devices within range. The other problem with Bluetooth is that, although the standard incorporates a lot of layered protective measures, it is possible to make a partial implementation that works but doesn't include all of the protective measures defined in the standard. *Bluesnarfing* is a new and popular game in which a person with a Bluetooth device and hacker software (downloaded from various Web sites) connects with cell phones and PDAs that don't fully implement all of the protective measures. In most cases, all that happens is that messages pop up on the device being probed. However, there have been recent instances in which items like telephone/address lists and notes were extracted from the cell phones of (in)famous personalities, using these techniques. The next time it could be user account and password information or a confidential telephone list from the company-issued cell phone of one of your employees.

With portable electronic devices, as with removable media, an important objective should be the education of employees about the possibilities for misuse of these devices—even by accident—and the damage that could result. With wireless devices, particularly those with Bluetooth, the safest strategy is to disallow their use in secure areas and to disable Bluetooth functions on any PC that is also network connected to your LAN via conventional Ethernet. For WiFi devices, if the appropriate configuration steps have been taken with your APs, then they should be secure; nevertheless, the ad hoc mode of the WiFi cards in all of your mobile devices should be disabled, so that a direct connection to them, from another WiFi device, is not possible. Most of the other devices mentioned pose a threat mainly when someone attempts to connect one to a PC. Thus, one possible strategy, in addition to installation of good virus-scanning and -blocking software in each PC (and an N/HIDS package), would be to keep all non–SCADA system PCs on the other side of a good firewall. In addition, security policies ought to preclude bringing any of the listed devices inside the physical security perimeter of the SCADA control room, computer room, or any room containing essential computing equipment and ought to preclude connecting any of these types of devices to critical PCs.

Computer Systems

SCADA systems are indeed computer systems (just with applications that perform SCADA functions, rather than, e.g., accounting functions) and, as such, need to be protected with the same types of technology as any other type of computer. In a SCADA system, there will be one or more computers assigned to perform several categories of functions including

- Polling of RTUs and processing of data returned

- Converting, alarming, and storing of the field data values and status

- Data archiving, trending, and storage

- Running process-specific applications, models, and calculations

- Generation of logs, reports, and operational summaries

- Generation and updating of operator displays

- Alarm annunciation, notification, and tracking

These computers tend to be servers (possibly redundant, multi-processor arrays with Redundant Array of Independent Disks or RAID storage) that sit in a separate computer room, interface a high-speed LAN (possibly redundant), and interact with the operators, programmers, and system administrators via their individual PCs or workstations. If you walked into the computer room of a modern SCADA system, you might not be able to tell the difference between the equipment there and the equipment, supporting business and accounting functions, at the company's server farm. One of the pathways through the electronic perimeter and into the computer room is the high-speed LAN (which is almost guaranteed to be some form of Ethernet). Other potential routes include WAN and telecommunication connections to the SCADA system for remote communications and connectivity (fig. 11–2).

An interesting set of statistics have been generated by the folks at the BCIT (British Columbia Institute of Technology) Computer Science lab regarding how automation systems have been attacked and infected. By this we mean the communication mechanism by which attackers, whether in a directed or non-directed attack, gained access to the automation system. As of 2005, the breakdown of statistics fall into the following percentages:

Path into the automation system	% of incidents
Via corporate WAN interconnection	49%
Via direct connection to the Internet	17%
Via trusted third-party system connection	10%
Via remote user VPN connection	7%
Via dial-up modem connection	7%
Via leased Telco network connectivity	7%
Via wireless networking/access points	3%

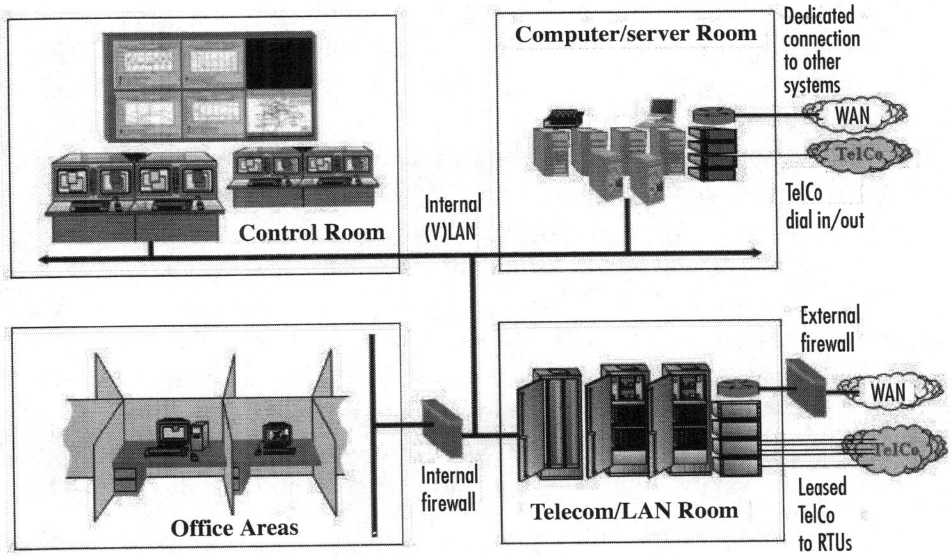

FIG. 11–2. *Communication connectivity to the SCADA computers*

A potentially surprising statistic to some is the fact that VPN connections can be used for an attack. Keep in mind that a VPN tunnel protects the communications between computers and authenticates computers to each other, but if I have a virus on my laptop PC and make a VPN connection to a remote system, there is nothing in the VPN technology that prevents that virus from being sent (albeit very securely) to the remote system. This vulnerability is the result of not having a suitable firewall and virus scanner rather than the fault of VPN technology.

Among the computers that form the SCADA system will be those that manage the communications with the field devices and support the necessary RTU protocols. These computers will usually be redundant, as they represent a single point of potential failure. These computers will have interfaces with the communications equipment (radio, leased telephone lines, etc.) and probably with the high-speed LAN. (Some earlier SCADA system designs used a dedicated front-end processor for each of the redundant host computers, with a proprietary high-speed connection; however, this design is now unnecessary, owing to the data-transmission speed available with fast Ethernet.) If these computers use serial character-oriented RTU protocols, then they will probably have a bank of modems (one per polling circuit) for interfacing the communications equipment. These circuits are not a viable way for an attacker to penetrate the computer system or network, as these protocols are not routing protocols and are not IP based. Later in this chapter we discuss options for securing the communications on these circuits, but this is to prevent an attacker from sending false data and/or commands to the SCADA system or RTUs. If the SCADA system uses an IP-based protocol for communications to the field (e.g., IP-DNP3.0, UCA2, IP-Modbus, or ICCP), then this connection *is* subject to conventional cyber attacks and is a potential entry path for a cyber attacker. Fortunately, conventional cybersecurity technologies—routers with firewall and encryption features enabled and even IP$_{SEC}$ (if the SCADA system and RTUs can both support this capability)— can be applied to secure these links.

In some larger SCADA systems (in particular, electrical EMS systems), there may be a need to have a real-time connection to one or more regional control centers, often using the IP-based ICCP. Also, if an alternative operating site has been established, continuous synchronization of the alternative site's systems require that a high-speed link be maintained between the primary and alternate sites. Both of these cases present the opportunity for an attacker to find a path into the SCADA system, particularly since the physical communication circuits used will most likely be leased from the local public telephone company. (Some brave souls may use the actual Internet for these connections, but that isn't common practice today.) Again, since these will most likely be IP-based communication links, using the firewall and encryption functions of the routers at each end of the connections will generally provide adequate protection of the communication path.

It was very common, prior to the events of 9/11, to have remote, direct, dial-in telephone access to SCADA systems, either by company personnel (or contractors) who needed to view system information remotely (e.g., from a field site) or by vendor personnel, for remote diagnostic and support activities. Today, because of the widespread availability of the Internet—with ISPs of local dial-up access almost everywhere, even via cellular telephone systems—many vendors (and your own employees) prefer to use the Internet (over a long-distance telephone call) as their mechanism of communication with your SCADA system. The best means for providing this access, while protecting your SCADA system, is to use VPN technology, including the issuance of *temporary* digital certificates to anyone who needs remote access. (For an overview of VPN technology and architecture, see fig. 6–15.) With VPN technology, you can prevent anyone from accessing your system via the Internet, unless they have proper credentials (in the form of a digital certificate), for authentication and encryption purposes.

PCs

Today a typical operator's console, engineering workstation, or administrator's workstation on a SCADA system is probably just a high-performance PC, running either Microsoft Windows or Unix/Linux. The processing power, memory, and video display capabilities of the average PC today are much greater than the custom display generation hardware and software that SCADA vendors had to develop for these purposes over the period extending from the 1970s to the mid-1990s, prior to the time when PCs reached the necessary capability levels.

Today a PC can support huge video image spaces and render these as one or more video displays with panning capabilities if the image space is greater than the display area available. The color resolution and pixel resolution of PCs, particularly those with high-performance video cards, allows for video and animation, as well as static images. The video game industry has fostered the development of high-performance PC multimedia capabilities, which can be used in SCADA operator-console applications as well (the ultimate video game?).

SCADA system operator-console display functions tend to come in two general architectures: centralized and distributed (fig. 11–3). In a centralized architecture, the operator-console equipment basically acts as a semipassive display device and is driven by display software running on the central server(s). All of the display definitions and logic to change/update displays, on the basis of data and alarm changes, resides in the central server. One advantage to such an architecture is that displays and associated logic can be changed in one place and all operator consoles will

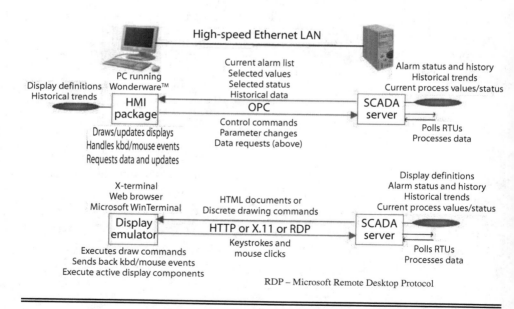

Fig. 11–3. *Centralized and distributed operator–console architectures*

be presented with the revised version the next time the modified display is requested. There are three common examples of technologies that support the centralized operator-console architecture:

- Web browser–based operator consoles (all displays offered as Web pages)

- X-terminal–based operator consoles (consoles acting like X-terminals)

- Microsoft remote desktop application–based consoles ("remote terminals" in Microsoft terms)

The first technology has the advantage of working on any operating system platform and in mixed platform environments (a mix of Unix/Linux and Microsoft Windows computers.) The second technology is a defined standard that comes from the Unix world, and although Microsoft (and third-party vendors) can support X-Window functions, this technology seems to work best in Unix/Linux environments. The third technology is Microsoft's response to the X-Window System—that is, a proprietary capability that does roughly the same things but works only on Microsoft platforms (and is thus a de facto standard because it's from Microsoft).

Centralized operator-console architectures depend upon a high-speed link between the consoles and the central server, to provide rapid-display presentation and updating, as well as responsiveness to operator actions. In a centralized scheme, the central server really needs to be fully redundant, since all operator consoles will be nonoperational if there is no central server to drive them. There will be extensive message traffic over the LAN—between the various consoles and the central server. These messages will be sent using the respective (well-known and documented) protocols defined by each of the technologies listed.

Anyone with access to the LAN and an easily downloaded packet sniffer program could learn a lot by recording the message traffic between consoles and the central servers. It would also be possible to launch a man-in-the-middle or session-hijack attack if the attacker had access to the message traffic crossing the LAN. One way to prevent this is to implement a VPN among all of the console PCs and SCADA servers, using IP_{SEC} and digital certificates. This would mean that all traffic would be encrypted and that an attacker couldn't employ those two attack methodologies without a valid digital certificate. Depending on physical protective measures taken to secure the LAN wiring and switches, it could also be useful to employ Ethernet switch VLAN functions to keep critical message traffic from being available to any Ethernet port other than those connected to the servers and the console PCs.

The alternative to centralized operator-console architecture is a distributed architecture, wherein each operator console is an independent computer with local display definition, storage, and generation. Each console acts with relative independence, but does still require a source for the SCADA data updates, alarms, and events. When a display is requested by the operator, it is locally generated, but the console must request current data from the central server to fill in the data areas of the display (and set color and display modes in accordance with alarm and status conditions). Then, on a periodic basis, data updates must be requested from the central server so that operator displays can be updated. Some systems use a report by exception or *publish-subscribe* mechanism to handle data updates, so that the server pushes data to the consoles as needed, rather than having them make continuous requests.

A distributed scheme reduces the message traffic over the LAN and can eliminate many of the dangerous messages (e.g., login messages), depending on what functions are still relegated to the central server. This also makes them better for applications where a remote operator console is needed and where the connection will have to be a lower-bandwidth WAN (as opposed to a high-bandwidth LAN).

Most SCADA systems that use this architecture either have a proprietary design and messaging scheme (which does make them more difficult to sniff and attack) or use one of the small number of interoperability API standards, such as UCA2.0 or OPC. When based on these standards, the possibility of having sensitive messages sniffed and of being vulnerable to the attacks previously discussed is just about the same as for the centralized architecture. The same protective measures that can be used with a centralized architecture can be employed to secure the message traffic in a distributed architecture.

For the administrative and programming functions associated with a SCADA system, the desktop PC is also the common interface device today. A system administrator sitting at his or her desk can open up a window on their PC screen and interact (after logging in with a suitable ID and password) with the system utilities, running on the SCADA servers, that are used to maintain the SCADA system. The same is true for application and system programmers. The system administrator may be running an X-terminal session or acting as a remote desktop to a Microsoft application. The same may be true for the system programmers, or they may be using a telnet session or a secure shell (ssh) session to communicate with the server.

Once again, the best way to protect sensitive LAN traffic from being sniffed is to implement a VPN that includes these computers. VLAN configuration of the LAN can also be somewhat useful in protecting (isolating) the sensitive message traffic. Although ssh is better from a security standpoint than telnet, both possess known vulnerabilities.

RTUs

RTUs and other field-based electronic devices either communicate using a serial protocol designed for conventional, analog communications systems (e.g., telephone and radio) or are capable of interfacing an IP network (by virtue of being IP ready). Serial (analog) communications normally implies relatively slow communications (baud rate) and a conventional, bit- or character-oriented RTU protocol. In both cases—using conventional analog telephony (whether leased from a telephone carrier or privately constructed and operated) and using conventional analog radio—there will normally be modems at each end of the communication circuit that convert the EIA-232 serial signals into audible modulations suitable for a voice-grade (analog) circuit or radio channel.

It is unlikely that RTUs designed for analog communications would be able to have strictly firmware upgrades, to add some level of secure communications. That is because most of these RTUs will have memory and CPU limitations that make implementing even a basic level of encryption impossible. Therefore, addition of communications security to an analog polling circuit usually requires an external device. Today, for replacement of existing modems, vendors offer *encrypting modems* (fig. 11–4), which provide communications security across the analog circuit.

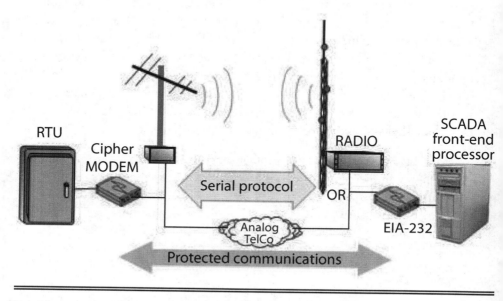

FIG. 11–4. *Securing serial (analog) communications with encrypting modems*

Radio communications in use may or may not include modems, depending on the age of the equipment. Starting in the late 1980s, most radio equipment designed specifically for data communications incorporated an integral modem and offered an EIA-232 serial interface to the RTUs and the SCADA systems. On the one hand, if the analog radio equipment requires an external modem, then (as with voice-grade telephone circuits) the existing modems may be replaced with encrypting modems to secure the communications. Modern encrypting modems use *out-of-band* communications (at startup and periodically thereafter) to perform key exchanges and authentication sequences; also, so that there is no noticeable delay introduced by their presence, they either perform encryption using stream ciphers or treat each octet of protocol message as a block for block encryption. Unfortunately, few if any current product offerings have been designed to work with legacy bit-oriented protocols. (They expect all protocol messages and data to be asynchronously exchanged as some integral number of octets.) In instances where the radio equipment incorporates the modem, it may still be possible to insert an encryption device in the EIA-232 serial connection between the radio and the RTU/SCADA system. In this case, however, the device is providing encryption only, not acting as a modem. Since their manufacture requires merely leaving out the analog circuitry found in modems, these *bump-in-the-wire* encryption devices are usually available from the same sources.

If a SCADA system supports IP for RTU polling and if the corresponding RTUs are IP ready, then there is a high likelihood that the RTU/SCADA system will interface with some minimal Ethernet LAN (probably just a couple of ports on a switch or router) provided by the communications equipment that manages the connection to the WAN or the digital communications circuit. This equipment will often be a router, a FRAD, or a *channel service unit/digital service unit* (CSU/DSU) of some other type. Most such devices today have the ability to support a link-level encryption mechanism in concert with their counterpart at the other end of the channel, on all communications passing between them. Thus, if the RTU and the SCADA system use an IP-based protocol that has no security features (e.g., IP-Modbus), there can still be communications security. By contrast, if the RTU equipment and SCADA system can use secure IP (e.g., certain extended versions of IP-DNP3.0), then encryption need not be enabled on the communications equipment, and the security extends from the RTU to the SCADA system without the problem of nonsecure local IP message traffic on the Ethernet LAN at each end of the link (e.g., other Ethernet ports on the switch or router). In theory, these other ports could be disabled or made unavailable by setting up a VLAN.

VLANs are created by configuring the logic of LAN (Ethernet) switches such that they route only certain ports to other selected ports—thus creating the effect of an isolated subnetwork, physically separated from the rest of the LAN (fig. 11–5). However, someone who obtained physical access to the site and the equipment could potentially reconfigure the switch settings to allow full access. Of course, this doesn't change the settings of switches at other field sites, but it might enable access to the central LAN and WAN from the compromised field site. The security issues associated with running IP networking to the field are discussed in greater detail in section III.

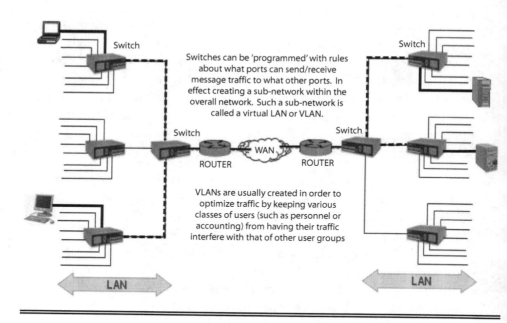

FIG. 11–5. *Using Ethernet switch configurations to create a VLAN*

Because many users of SCADA systems are migrating away from traditional analog communications (whether leased or owned) and instead are adopting digital networking technologies, the very real possibility exists that non–IP-enabled RTUs and SCADA system central hosts will need to operate over a digital network during the transition process. Fortunately, available technologies can *encapsulate* a serial protocol and carry it across a digital (maybe IP) network for real-time delivery at the other end (fig. 11–6). Encapsulation devices make it possible to create the illusion of a dedicated, serial, point-to-point, asynchronous communication circuit that is somehow operating through a digital network. Such devices are available for both frame-relay networks and IP-based networks (as well as Ethernet LANs). As with a true IP networking setup, the encryption functions of the network interface equipment (e.g., within a router) could be enabled for link-level security across the WAN. Alternatively, if the encapsulation devices support encryption, then they can be used for securing the serial communications (fig. 11–7). (In some instances, as

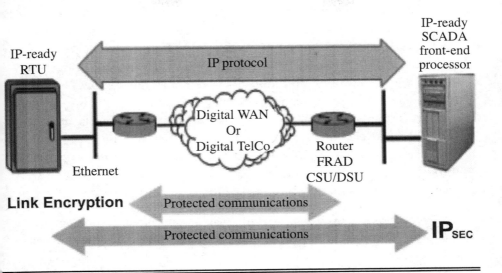

FIG. 11–6. *Securing IP-based communications at the link or* IP_{SEC} *level*

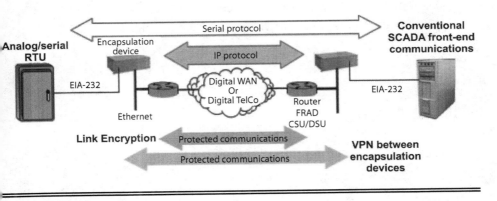

FIG. 11–7. *Encapsulating and transporting serial communications over a secure WAN*

with frame relay, the encapsulation device includes the communications interface, so that a physically separate device is not required.) A good deal of the high-end digital communications equipment on the market today (such as routers) support IP version 6, which extended the prior version (IPv4) including extensions specifically designed to allow for communications security. Two IPv6 end devices (such as routers) can, in theory, provide a secure tunnel for transporting non-secure messages (including IPv4 packets) by implementing IP_{SEC} features: authentication, encryption, and credential/key exchange. It is worth remembering that various digital networking technologies (like Frame relay, ATM, FDDI, etc.) do *not* use IP protocol, although they can carry IP (including IPv6) packets as their data. If a SCADA host supports IP protocols and has RTUs that likewise support such protocols, even though those protocols don't incorporate any security measures, the messages will normally pass through a communications device (router) at each end and these devices may support IPv6 and thus IP_{SEC} capabilities.

Most currently available serial message encapsulation technology has the same constraints as most encrypting modems—that is, it works well with asynchronous serial communications that use octet-based messaging designs. In other words, the serial interfaces work with character-oriented serial protocols, but generally do not work with legacy bit-oriented protocols. This is usually because the serial ports incorporate a Universal Asynchronous Receiver Transmitter (UART) circuit, which is a device that only deals in octet-based asynchronous data transmission.

12

Electric Utility Industry–Specific Cybersecurity Issues

The electric utilities were one of the first to use—and continue to be a major proponent of—computer-based supervisory control. Electric power transmission systems were being monitored and controlled by computer-based SCADA systems as far back as the early 1960s, when only very expensive mainframe computers were available. Part of the reason for this early adoption is that scheduling, optimizing, and controlling electric power generation and transmission requires very complex models and advanced applications that can't be performed—in anything approaching real time—except by rather powerful computers.

SCADA systems initially provided a way to keep track of and manipulate the available power being produced by an electric utility's various generating facilities, as well as a way to match that power with real-time demands over their large geographic service areas. As SCADA technology advanced in parallel with computer technology, the applications running on electric utility SCADA systems became more diverse. SCADA systems could keep track of historical power demands, over each service day, on the basis of what type of day was being experienced (in terms of weather, time of year, weekday vs. holiday, etc.). This information allowed electric utilities to predict the hour-by-hour power demand for the next day and to schedule their generation assets appropriately. In addition, regional SCADA systems were established to coordinate the various utilities and to manage the overall national power grid. This enabled utilities to buy and sell their generation capabilities to better match supply and demand.

Electric utilities have historically been—and continue to be—major purchasers of RTU equipment and have played a major role in developing many of the protocols still in use today. (Some legacy protocols are even named for the utility that sponsored the development, like PG&E protocol.) Electric utilities have industry-specific requirements both for their RTUs and for their advanced application programs. In section I, we explored some of these unique requirements.

Although electric utilities were one of the first adopters of SCADA technology, they have also been the most hesitant—or possibly just the least able—to integrate changes and adopt new technology (for a variety of operational and economic reasons). Many electric utilities have continued to use obsolete legacy communications protocols because they have a huge installed base of old RTUs—and a maybe even a SCADA system that may not be capable of being upgraded to support other protocols (because the vendor is long gone). There are RTU manufacturers who produce RTUs specifically for the electric utility market because of their unique requirements and legacy protocols. Electric utilities are also a major user of leased analog telephone lines, because that is what many of the older RTUs were designed to utilize. It is not unusual for major electric utility SCADA systems to still be using legacy protocols running at 1,200- and 2,400-baud data rates (1.2 and 2.4 kbps, respectively) over several dozen analog leased telephone lines.

Furthermore, unlike the two other major industry segments that use SCADA technology (water/wastewater and pipeline industries), electric utilities have generally used only the most basic RTU capabilities (analog, pulse, and contact inputs and contact outputs), even though RTUs have progressed to become quite powerful and flexible. Nevertheless, over the past few years, market forces and technology developments have driven the electric utilities to rethink their notions about communications and what an RTU comprises. In addition, as the cost of SCADA technology has dropped owing to the development of low-cost yet highly powerful PCs and servers, electric utilities have extended SCADA applications into their power distribution systems. This same market drive has also made SCADA systems available to small electric utilities (e.g., rural cooperatives and small municipalities) that previously couldn't afford to own and operate a SCADA system.

A major electric power transmission SCADA system can be quite a large and sophisticated system—with full automatic redundancy, several interconnections to other systems, and often a backup alternate operating site, where a (nearly) duplicate system waits, ready to take over in the event of a disaster (fig. 12–1). Electric utilities have tended not to directly interface the DCS systems that run their respective generating plants; rather, RTUs placed on site and momentary contact outputs send ramping commands to these systems and return a select set of real-time measurements. When they are interfaced it is usually because the plant DCS system can provide an RTU emulation and communicate in the same serial RTU protocol used by the actual RTUs.

Industry architectural differences
Electrical Transmission System Architecture

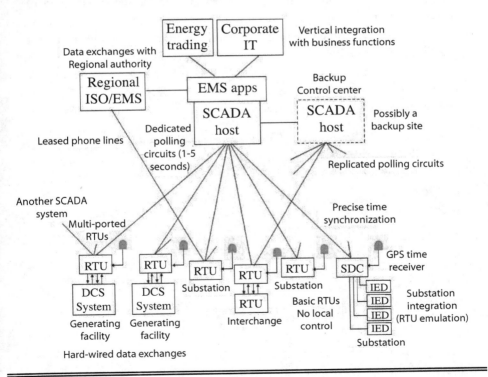

FIG. 12–1. *Generalized block diagram of an electric utility SCADA system*

It is very common for electric utility SCADA systems (or EMS systems) to have real-time communication connections with regional coordinating authorities (e.g., a power pool, or today an ISO, or even an RTO.) These connections are usually via leased telephone circuits (possibly digital) and utilize either the ICCP protocol (discussed later in this section) or an RTU protocol. For forecasting purposes, there may be data links to weather information suppliers, and for coordination purposes, there may be data links to the SCADA systems of adjacent electric utilities.

Unlike in other industries, things happen very quickly in the electrical world. A power transient can travel at nearly light speed and can trip protective relays (and the circuit breakers they control) in several electrically adjacent substations in just small fractions of a second. Thus, in electric utility SCADA systems, it is more and more common, especially with the availability of low-cost GPS receivers, to have high-precision time synchronization (to the millisecond or better) and local time tagging of recorded events. Because conditions can change fairly rapidly, electric utility SCADA systems tend to use individual polling circuits to each RTU, rather than using a multi-drop (multiple RTUs on a shared circuit) approach to reduce the number of polling circuits. This results in a system architecture with a large number of RTU polling circuits, as compared to a pipeline or water/wastewater system with a comparable number of remote units.

Geographic distribution of substations and generating facilities might also make line sharing impractical. Electric utility SCADA systems tend to make use of multi-ported RTUs to provide simultaneous access from multiple systems. In the past few years, RTUs have begun to be replaced with *substation data concentrators* (SDCs), which emulate RTU protocols and collect real-time data from multiple sources within the substation.

Substation Back Doors

To understand the unique attributes of electric utility SCADA systems and the corresponding cybersecurity issues, it is necessary first to consider the main application of SCADA technology within electric utilities. The overwhelming majority of RTUs interfaced into an electric utility SCADA system will be located in electrical substations, for the purpose of controlling switch gear and transformers and making electrical measurements. Others will be located at generating facilities, for the purpose of issuing generation controls (to ramp generating units up or down) and making local electrical measurements. Still other RTUs will be located at key locations in the power transmission system, such as at interconnection points (*inter-ties*) with geographically adjacent utilities. (The majority of RTUs are in substations because there are usually a lot more substations than generating plants and system inter-ties.)

Although *generator ramping* is an important task, it is the control of switch gear and transformers that can have the greatest impact on the electric power grid. To a certain degree, the components that form the electric power grid are like a row of dominoes, and like a row of dominoes, if you set one falling, it can take down the next, which takes down the next, and so on. Protective relays and switch gear are positioned at various key points in the grid to break the chain and thereby limit damage (a process called *islanding*); the Northeast blackout in August 2003, however, demonstrated that this process doesn't always work as intended. Thus, it is vital for an attacker to be prevented from gaining communications access to substation RTUs, because that would provide the ability to control and operate switch gear and transformers.

In a traditional electrical substation, the RTU monitors the status of circuit breakers, re-closers, switches, transformer tap changer position, capacitor banks, and other equipment (fig. 12–2). It also typically has momentary contact outputs for controlling and operating much of the same equipment. In addition, the key bus and feeder currents and voltages are brought into the RTU for transmission to the SCADA system.

In parallel with the RTU will be protective relays (and other devices) that make many of the same measurements and operate the same equipment, for the purpose of preventing severe damage to the plant equipment and the power grid. In the past, these protective relays were dumb electromechanical devices. But for the past decade or so, they have become microprocessor-based devices capable of some level of serial (and today even Ethernet) communications.

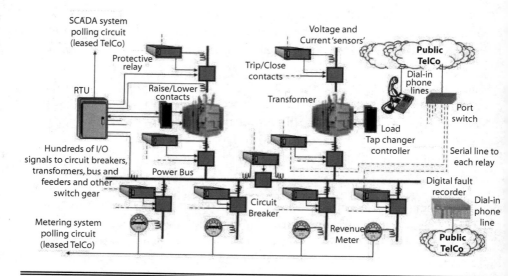

FIG. 12–2. *Small traditional electrical substation*

Electric utilities, particularly large ones, have often organized their internal personnel into groups responsible for different aspects of the operation:

- One group would be responsible for the protection of the system and equipment and would handle all of the protective relaying. This group would engineer, install, and configure the relays and would be responsible for examining the data collected by these relays, and other monitoring devices, when a fault occurred.

- Another group would be responsible for measuring (metering) the power/energy being bought and sold. This group would install and calibrate revenue meters and operate a separate data collection system designed specifically to collect meter data and compute billing information.

- A final group would handle the real-time operation of the transmission system. This group would own and operate the SCADA system and place the RTUs into the substations, inter-tie points and other necessary sites.

It is common for substations to have numerous, parallel communication (telephone) circuits: one or more for each department or group—and even one for an actual telephone!

The primary danger if an attacker were to gain communications access to an RTU would be that the attacker could then operate critical switch gear—for example, a circuit breaker controlling a major power delivery circuit—or trip a transformer, thus causing a domino to fall in the analogy invoked previously. To accomplish this, however, a knowledgeable attacker would not have to penetrate the SCADA system or wide area communications system. Most large substations have a back door that can be used for the same purpose (i.e., to control equipment). The protective relay groups in most large electric utilities want quick access to the data captured by relays whenever a fault occurs (e.g., a momentary outage due to a lightning strike) to identify the type of fault, to evaluate the potential damage to equipment, and to determine the effectiveness of the protection scheme.

Today, a typical protective relay is capable of continuously recording voltage and alternating-current (AC) waveforms on all three phases, over several dozen or more cycles. This information, along with precise data on contact event timing, provides tremendous insight into the causes and effects of faults and the efficacy of the protective schemes. Also, the logic and calculations performed in a relay, to determine when to take a protective action, can be adjusted by changing any number of settings. Often, for various reasons (e.g., expansion of the physical system or seasonal changes), these settings need to be adjusted.

Furthermore, since substations are distributed over large geographic areas, it is understandable that with digital (microprocessor-based) relays, the protection organizations would seek to establish remote communication mechanisms. In most instances, this amounts to placement of a *port switch* on an incoming dial-up telephone line and connection of the communication/configuration ports of all of the relays to this switch. With such a scheme, a relay engineer (or a hacker with a war dialer program) can dial into the desired substation from his desk, using a PC and a modem, and then send a short character sequence that causes the port switch to select the desired port/relay. Security is provided by having each relay require a password. Of course, most relays are set to the same password for convenience (often the factory default; e.g., "otter tail," which was used by a major relay manufacturer). If the passwords have been changed, it is common to use the name of the substation as the password. Most relays place no limit on the number of times you could try to log in and enter the password—which is a very convenient feature for an automated password cracker program.

If one is communicating to these relays, there is no need to bother with the SCADA system or RTUs, as the relays also control the circuit breakers (and other switch gear) and can, depending on make, model and configuration, be commanded to trip or close the breakers via the dial-in port. This dial-in relay connectivity is one of the greatest vulnerabilities in the electric power grid, and most utilities are taking steps to close this back door to their substations. Port switches have gotten smarter, and manufacturers have added levels of access control and authentication; some can now even perform encryption. Undoubtedly, though, a large number of substation back doors remain vulnerable.

With changes in technology, the design of substations has also evolved, and most modern substations are now filled with intelligent electronic devices (IEDs). Many IEDs support some form of communications and also measure the same signals and values that are monitored by the RTUs. In an effort to reduce costs associated with a substation, some utilities have embarked on "*substation automation*" (a bit of a misnomer). This process entails changing the RTU from a device with lots of physical I/O to one with a lot of serial ports and little or no physical I/O. If a relay or power meter is already measuring the voltages and currents (probably with greater accuracy than the RTU), then why absorb the high costs for double-wiring those same measurements into the RTU, when a simple point-to-point serial communications link would allow the RTU to poll and fetch that data from the relay or meter?

Today it is not uncommon for an RTU (or an SDC) to support 16–64 serial ports and a variety of IED protocols, just for the purpose of collecting and concentrating data from the various substation IEDs (like a small SCADA system within the substation; see fig. 12–3). In the vast majority of these instances, the data collected are normally only the simple, real-time data (e.g., real and reactive power, currents, and voltages). Many substation IEDs also contain a lot of other types of data (e.g., time-sampled AC waveforms and SOE logs) not typically collected by the RTU or the SDC. This is because the RTUs (and SCADA systems) usually don't support such exotic data. (Few if any SCADA systems have an application for viewing AC waveforms.) Moreover, the protocols used for communications between an RTU and a SCADA system generally don't support the transportation of such complex, compound data (except by playing tricks). For these reasons, most substations still require a separate dial-in telephone line, so that protection engineers can access their relays and fault recorders, upload fault records, and change settings.

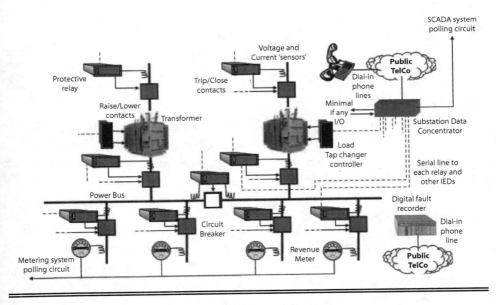

FIG. 12–3. *Substation information consolidation (substation automation)*

In some instances, the SDC may be substituted for the port switch, to offer a *pass-through mode,* whereby a dial-in connection to the concentrator would allow the caller to temporarily take over any one of the links to the various relays (or other IEDs). In effect, the SDC would act like a port switch for connections made via the separate dial-in telephone line. When the caller hangs up, the ports are reclaimed by the SDC and polling of the IEDs resumed.

The use of a dial-in telephone line still presents a potential back door through which the substation could be attacked. This separate dial-in telephone line might be replaced by a network WAN connection in some instances, and the SDC might be capable of supporting some form of cybersecurity, such as link encryption or even full VPN with authentication. SDC technology is still in its infancy, and the product capabilities and architectures vary widely from vendor to vendor.

IP to the Substation

With most telecommunications companies trying to phase out analog telephone lines, it has become difficult for some electric utilities to lease additional circuits, and it has become more expensive to maintain the circuits they already have. For this reason—and in an effort to consolidate communications onto a single circuit into the substation—various utilities are migrating toward WAN technologies. Small electric utilities, such as small municipal utilities (*munis*) or rural electric cooperatives (*co-ops* or *RECs*) often have an easier time migrating to networking technologies, as they have a small number of substations and can often string fiber-optic cables along their lines and rights-of-way because of the comparatively short lengths and limited numbers involved.

Many munis are multiple-service utilities (supplying, e.g., power and gas or power, gas, and water) and use their fiber-optic bandwidth to offer telephone and Internet services, as well as providing the municipality itself with networking and communications. In these instances, the IP to the substation is over a private network (a fiber-optic one to boot) and thus is already somewhat physically secure. The major threat would come from network interconnections between the SCADA system and the other business and IT systems which might have Internet connectivity.

Another threat would be that such a system will have communications hubs at various points around the municipality, possibly in public buildings. Access to the equipment at these hubs must be protected and monitored. These hubs would need to be considered as belonging within the physical security perimeter of the SCADA system.

Getting physical access to the communications and networking equipment could provide an attacker with communications access to all substations. Of course, if VPN technologies (including authentication via digital certificates) were employed at all substations, mere physical access to a network communications node would not afford the attacker with exploitable communication access. Regardless of whether the WAN connection to the substation is private or public, the main issue is having IP connectivity to substation equipment (e.g., an SDC) that is designed for IP connectivity and networking (fig. 12–4).

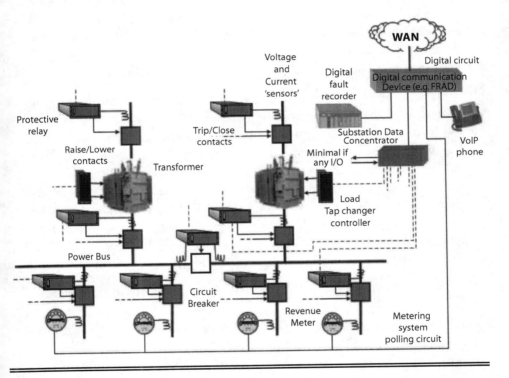

FIG. 12–4. *IP networking to the substation*

For larger utilities, which cannot reasonably construct and maintain their own communications infrastructure or need to convert from leased analog telephone lines to leased digital circuits, the challenge is to use public networks in a secure manner. Telecommunications providers can offer a range of wired and wireless digital networking alternatives including (full and fractional) T1/T3 circuits, ISDN circuits, frame relay, X.25 packet switching, and even DSL technologies (xDSL). (These last circuits route your communications onto the Internet, however, which is something few utilities would risk.)

A digital circuit requires different types of electrical connectivity than an analog circuit. (You can't hook your telephone modem (analog) to a digital circuit and expect it to work.) Nevertheless, a digital circuit merely transports bits from one place to another, and the security of that data transmission needs to be ensured by something other than the digital communications infrastructure. (Your cell phone is actually a node on a wireless digital communications system, but to ensure the confidentiality of your conversations, the cellular system uses message packet encryption.)

The most popular choice of digital communication circuit for electric utilities is frame relay, because it is the digital technology that is most like a conventional analog circuit and because existing analog circuits can usually be converted to frame-relay circuits with a minimum of effort (usually using the same wires). Most telecommunications providers can supply frame-relay service, and even a minimal frame-relay circuit offers data transmission rates of 56 kbps, and rates of 128, 256, and 512 kbps and much higher are available if needed. Since most data acquisition from existing substation RTUs is done at 1.2 or 2.4 kbps (1,200 or 2,400 baud, respectively), even a low-speed digital circuit is quite a bit faster.

The main problems with frame relay, from the standpoint of replacing conventional analog telephone circuits, is that digital circuits can't be interfaced with existing analog modems, and for optimal use of the digital circuit (to justify a cost savings by going digital), it may need to be shared by several applications or devices (which previously had their own individual analog circuits). Even a low speed digital circuit will generally provide 56–64 Kilobits per second of bandwidth. Since the majority of the IEDs that have support analog telephone connectivity only support 9.6 Kilobits per second (or slower) data transmission rates, sharing a digital circuit (if possible) has a strong financial attractiveness. Another problem associated with going digital is that the protocols usable over a digital circuit have only recently become available in typical IEDs, so the vast majority among the installed base of IEDs (including RTUs) cannot support them. Fortunately, vendors have risen to the challenge and now supply frame-relay access devices (FRADs), which provide the equivalent of multiple, dedicated serial (RS/EIA-232) communication channels, by multiplexing the bandwidth of the frame-relay circuit (fig. 12–5). Since most IEDs (except RTUs from the 1970s) connect to their analog modems via an EIA-232 serial port, these connections can be made directly to a port on the FRAD in the substation. (Of course the electric utility industry has the largest percentage installed base of obsolete 1970s-era RTUs that have built-in analog modems.)

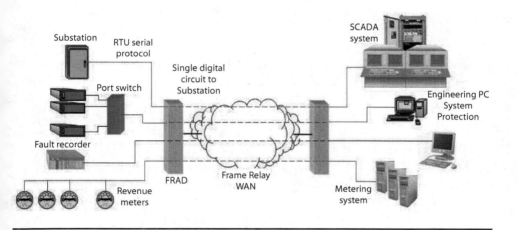

FIG. 12–5. *Frame-relay networking and virtual circuits*

Even though FRADs and frame relay networking may create the effect of multiple, dedicated, point-to-point EIA-232 circuits between the substation and the various locations where systems and PCs need a connection to the substation equipment, the truth is more complex. Used in this manner, the digital communications link is not an IP connection, but is instead a frame-relay circuit that is carrying serial protocol character streams from several systems/devices to other corresponding systems and computers. This is *not* what is meant by "IP to the substation." (In fact, frame-relay networks have their own protocols—in the same way that an Ethernet LAN does—and don't use IP messaging.) This architecture simply employs a digital network to transport multiple asynchronous character streams, just like a multiplexer would over a conventional (analog) telephone circuit. This approach generally allows electric utilities to maintain their legacy (serial) communications strategy while offering the option of link encryption across the digital WAN (if the FRAD vendor supports this capability). No IP messages are exchanged (frame relay uses its own protocols); furthermore, because all communication paths within the frame-relay network are preset in the system (as PVCs) at network configuration time, no dynamic routing is required. This type of architecture, although it does little to enhance the communications capabilities available to the substation, provides reasonably good cybersecurity (if link encryption is enabled) and provides for efficient use by multiple devices of the single frame-relay circuit. Since there are no IP communications happening, an attacker breaking into a remote site would gain no access to the SCADA system or corporate networks.

There are now RTUs and SCADA systems capable of supporting IP-based protocols and LAN (Ethernet) interfaces. The commonly used IP networking protocols are primarily the IP version of DNP and Modbus, but there is also a growing implementation base of systems and devices that support UCA2.0 and ICCP. Extension of IP networking to the substation (fig. 12–6) implies that there is a LAN (invariably Ethernet) in

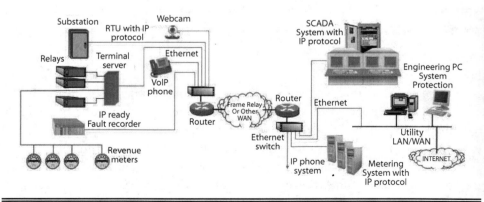

FIG. 12–6. *IP networking at the substation level*

the substation along with IP routing hardware and software, plus a WAN interface outside the substation such that devices that "speak" IP can be connected to that substation LAN and communicate over the WAN. IP messages are used locally, on the office LAN (carried by Ethernet); are then potentially transported through the WAN; and are finally regenerated onto the remote LAN, where they can be routed to other destinations. (And the intermediate WAN may be something like frame relay which, as has been noted, does not use IP as its protocol.)

With IP to the substation, a person at a substation could, in theory and unless prohibited via technical countermeasures, connect to the SCADA central computer, corporate servers, send and receive e-mail, and even browse the World Wide Web, just as if they were in their office on the corporate WAN (or across the Internet to which the corporate WAN has a connection). Likewise, a person in her office at headquarters could browse to a substation—and even a specific IED—and have access equal to being present in the substation. When true IP networking is deployed to the substation, there are benefits (e.g., immediate access to fault data and relay settings from the engineer's desktop), as well as dangers (an attacker who gains network access could find his way to the substation IEDs). However, with IP networking, there is the option of employing all available IP cybersecurity technologies: firewalls, VPN, IP$_{SEC}$, SSL, digital certificates and authentication, and link encryption. Still, these are the very technologies that hackers work toward penetrating and defeating.

TASE.2/ICCP Connections

Electric utility SCADA systems often have to interconnect with the SCADA systems of adjacent utilities and with regional coordination and grid management systems (including ISOs and Regional Transmission Organizations [RTOs]). These interconnections are used for data exchanges of real-time data, generation of scheduling data, and even control commands. Many years ago, an effort began to develop a standard protocol for use in establishing these data interchanges. The results of many years of work is the ICCP, also called TASE.2 (or IEC60870-6 TASE.2). This protocol was initially designed to ride on top of (be transported by) an ISO/OSI network, but as that protocol was put to rest in an early grave by TCP/IP, most if not all current implementations of ICCP are IP networking based (although there may be OSI messages carried by IP, since some vendors took a shortcut in converting their implementation to run over IP networks). At present ICCP does not incorporate comprehensive security measures (aside from application authentication using association control service element [ACSE] functions, which older versions may not support). Because the ICCP messages are transported by IP, however, other security mechanisms can be used to protect the communications.

Efforts are under way to expand ICCP and include full security features and functions. Since most ICCP connections are made over leased communication lines, with routers at each end of the line, protection can be implemented by enabling link-layer encryption and firewall functions between the two routers. Even though the ICCP specification defines eight basic function blocks for ICCP, not every implementation configures all eight. (Some are quite sophisticated and are used for things like the exchange of scheduling/planning information.) In fact, the vast majority hardly implement more than the basic measurement exchange blocks—such as blocks 1 and 2 and possibly data set support blocks 4 and 5. What is to be supported is defined in the *bilateral agreement* established between the two SCADA systems. Thus, any attack on an ICCP communications link (or through one from a back door in the interconnected system) would be constrained, if firewall settings excluded all but ICCP message types, resulting in an attacker's merely abusing the function blocks actually supported.

RTUs have become more powerful, and some now support ICCP as an available IP protocol. In this case, the block(s) associated with supervisory control will generally have been included in the ICCP implementation. Thus, an attack on such a connection could make field equipment (circuit breakers, transformer LTCs, etc.) vulnerable, unless some form of additional cybersecurity (such as VPN with authentication) were incorporated.

UCA2.0 (IEC61850)

Over the past 10 years, another communications architecture and set of standards have been under development, for communications between and among IEDs in a substation and between SCADA (and other) systems and those substation devices. The results of this work are the utility communications architecture (UCA; currently version 2 [UCA2.0]). UCA2.0 and ICCP are related: both build on the object-oriented manufacturing messaging service (MMS) protocol and object set (which were originally part of the failed efforts to establish MAP as a factory-floor manufacturing protocol architecture and standard.) Some people now refer to ICCP as UCA1.

UCA2.0 (in a substation) is designed for a high-speed (100 Mbps) switched Ethernet LAN (possibly redundant), to support very high-speed messaging (called GOOSE messages) between protective relays (as a replacement for hard-wired I/O signals). Because of the need for high speed, switched Ethernet hardware support as well as either OSI or TCP/IP networking software (within a substation LAN UCA2.0 may use OSI over Ethernet), many simple substation devices [IEDs] still do not support UCA2.0, or they support it via an external protocol converter device (that may cost more than the IED itself). These devices still tend to support serial protocols, such as Modbus or DNP3.0 (see the next section). But, market demand for plug-and-play device compatibility is driving the acceptance of UCA2.0 and its European counterpart, IEC61850.

The UCA2.0 protocol architecture does not, in and of itself, incorporate any comprehensive cybersecurity features or functions. However, because the protocol requires significant bandwidth (partly owing to the IP underpinnings) and IP networking to the substation, it is not as frequently used to communicate outside the substation. For munis and coops that create their own fiber-optic WANs, UCA2.0 can be used for all of the communications between and among their SCADA systems and substations. In that event, physically securing the communications equipment and using IP security mechanisms would be necessary. To move data from a UCA2.0-compliant substation to a SCADA system, where a high-speed WAN is not available, it would more common to use a protocol like ICCP, and such a connection (as was discussed previously) can be secured with various IP security mechanisms. It would also be common to see a SCADA system communicate to such a substation through a protocol translator that provided only the necessary information and control points (a subset of all of the available data) through a standard, low-speed serial protocol, such as DNP3.0.

DNP3.0

DNP3.0 is a serial, character-oriented asynchronous RTU protocol initially introduced into the public domain by the Harris Corporation and has been expanded, by the committee that controls its definition, to incorporate a multitude of data types and functions. In recent years, an IP version has been defined (which mainly looks like the same messages being carried as data in IP packets). Currently, DNP is one of the most commonly implemented serial protocols used in IEDs by the electric utility market. (Modbus is the other.) Although it is a useful and well-proven protocol, it remains essentially an RTU protocol based on the predefined data and command types it supports.

DNP supports and defines three communication modes: polled, polled report by exception, and unsolicited report by exception. The IP version does not currently include any authentication or encryption functions, but as a protocol in the IP suite, it can be carried within a VPN tunnel or an IP_{SEC}-protected network. Many utilities have converted to DNP for their RTU communications, in an effort to use standards and to replace older, less feature-rich legacy protocols. DNP3.0 works well over slow-speed analog communication circuits. Because it is a well-defined, published standard, DNP3.0 protocol test sets and protocol analyzers are readily available and can be used to monitor and record ongoing communications and to create and transmit simulated messages to either an RTU or a SCADA system. As a character-oriented protocol, it is generally possible to use encrypting modems on a DNP polling circuit. DNP popularity postdates the era of RTUs with built-in analog modems, so if an RTU supports DNP (even via an add-on protocol converter), it probably uses a conventional modem that could be replaced by an encrypting modem.

NERC 1200/1300 Compliance

After 9/11, in cooperation with various governmental organizations and laboratories (e.g., The National Institute of Standards and Technology [NIST]), the NERC embarked on the development of recommendations and standards to make the SCADA systems and related electrical power grid infrastructure more secure against terrorist threats, cyber and physical. Its first effort was the Urgent Action Standard 1200 (released in August 2003), which defined 16 areas of concentration, ranging from physical security and electronic security to incident reporting and recovery planning.

In short order, that document was updated and replaced by Standard 1300—Cyber Security (released in September 2004). Standard 1300 consolidated the 16 areas of concentration into 8, added definitions, and eliminated redundancies. In early 2005, the 8 sections of Standard 1300 were individually reissued as CIP-002-1 through CIP-009-1. NERC only deals with issues relating to electric utilities and the reliability of the electric power grid, although other agencies and organizations are providing similar recommendations in other industry segments.

SECTION 3:
INDUSTRIAL SECTORS

13

Water/Wastewater Industry–Specific Cybersecurity Issues

The water and wastewater industries are also major users of SCADA technologies (fig. 13-1). As the collection, transportation, treatment, storage, and distribution of potable water usually involves a large geographic area, SCADA technologies offer the ideal means for supervising and controlling the set of processes and operations involved. Wastewater (sewage, rainwater, industrial effluent, etc.) collection, transportation, and treatment systems also involve a lot of equipment and sites scattered over a large geographic area (usually the same as or a subset of the geographic area served by the potable water system). Not surprisingly, these geographic areas tend to be municipalities, ranging in size from small towns to large cities.

Both water and wastewater systems involve distributed storage sites interconnected by pipelines with pumping facilities to move the liquids through the pipelines (sewers and mains). They both also utilize processing/treatment facilities located at key points in the network. After that, the similarity ends, but from a SCADA standpoint, the system architectures are pretty much the same. There are obvious differences in the supervisory applications employed, but those don't tend to influence the overall SCADA system architectures.

The supervision and control of water/wastewater processes is not generally an activity that requires high speed and rapid data updating. It is

Industry architectural differences
Water Distribution System Architecture

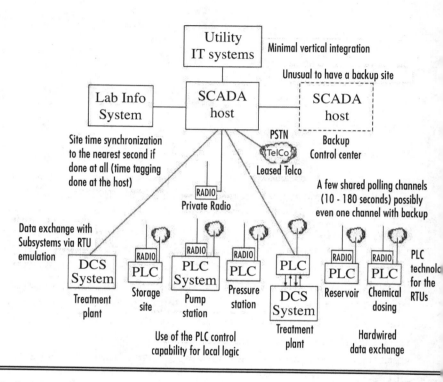

FIG. 13–1. *SCADA system block diagram for the water/wastewater industry*

very common for water/wastewater utilities to use private radio systems for communication with their RTUs and to have polling cycles (the amount of time required for a complete update of field data from all RTUs) of multiple minutes (as compared to multiple seconds in electric utility applications and multiple tens of seconds in the pipeline industry). Large numbers of RTUs (or even all of the RTUs) may share a single, common, low-speed communication channel. Communications between the SCADA system and other systems, such as the control systems running the treatment facilities, are usually via dedicated links, possibly leased telephone lines. SCADA systems may or may not be integrated into higher-level business systems and IT applications.

As a municipal utility, the water/wastewater organization often will share a common WAN/LAN with other city departments and organizations. This opens up the possibility of an IP connection that can be an entry point for a cyber assault, particularly if there is an Internet connection at some point (which is virtually guaranteed these days). The necessary firewall protection should be in place on any IP connections from a SCADA system to or from any other network or system.

Communications to critical RTU sites may be backed up with alternative communications technology, such as a dial-up telephone line. Thus, if the radio system fails, the SCADA system can poll key sites by going through a telephone number dial-out sequence to each such site, one at a time, to obtain updated data values. This might be slow, but it is often sufficient to keep the water/wastewater system operating. Some such utilities use the opposite approach: telephone leased lines are the primary communications mechanism, with the system falling back to private radio if any or all of the telephone connections fail.

Water/wastewater utilities, like electric utilities, are major users of leased analog telephone circuits. We have already discussed the issues related to security (or lack thereof) on analog telephone circuits. Leased telephone circuits might be used to connect with RTUs or to remotely located master radios, geographically distant from the SCADA facility, usually because of the topology or size of the service area. (The topology might not allow radio communications to all points from a single master radio, so additional master radios can be remotely located, with leased telephone circuits connecting them to the SCADA system's polling channels.) Water/wastewater utilities sometimes use hybrid communication schemes involving both radio and leased telephone lines (not as a backup for each other but in combination as the primary communication mechanism). Water/wastewater utilities have the same problem with obtaining and maintaining their leased analog telephone lines as do electric utilities, and some have similarly been forced to migrate to digital networking and communications.

Licensed Radio Communications

Because the water/wastewater operations are usually geographically constrained to a metropolitan area, a radio communications system can usually provide the necessary communications coverage. Conventional, single-frequency, half-duplex, licensed radio systems can easily cover an area within a 20–30-mile radius, depending on topology, the transmitter power, and the height and type of the antennas. Often there are portions of the water system (e.g., wells and reservoirs) that may lie outside the normal service area of a metropolitan telephone company; radio provides a way for the water utility to establish communications with those sites. Water utilities often have elevated finished water tanks (e.g., "golfball" tanks) situated along the water main lines for storage and pressure maintenance purposes. These make ideal places to mount radio equipment (and to attract lightning strikes) because they tend to tower above all but the highest structures, and, of course, the water utility owns them. If a repeater based radio system is used, these tanks make ideal spots for the geographically distributed repeater stations.

An analog (voice grade) radio can usually provide the same data rates as a poor-quality telephone line (1,200 or 2,400 baud). Most serial protocols that work over telephone lines will work equally well over a radio system (particularly because the vast majority of these protocols are half-duplex in nature). Here we are talking about conventional licensed UHF/VHF radio.

All RTUs are equipped with radio transmitter-receiver equipment (also frequently called a *transceiver*) that are tuned to the same frequency (channel) and essentially share the channel in a logically multi-dropped manner. The equipment used for radio communications is sold by numerous vendors and is totally compatible as long as you know the assigned frequency. Because the frequency is exclusively assigned (licensed) to this application (in this geographic area), it is registered with the FCC and maintained in their records. There are only a limited number of frequency bands and subchannels available for voice and/or data communications (also called *radio spectrum*), and in major metropolitan areas, these are coveted by police and fire departments, taxi companies, and other emergency response organizations and utilities. The upshot of this is that it isn't difficult to find out the frequency (channel) assigned to a water/wastewater utility and to buy commercial radio equipment that will let you monitor RTU polling activities. With such radio equipment and a computer running a serial protocol analyzer application, it is easy to capture and view the message traffic between a SCADA system and its RTUs.

In a basic radio-based system the central SCADA system normally has an omnidirectional antenna, whereas the individual RTUs usually have directional (yagi) antennas pointed toward the main antenna of the central SCADA system. (A more complex system might have multiple locations where a master radio and antenna are located, each serving the geographically adjacent RTUs, and each master radio probably using a different frequency channel.) An eavesdropper might only hear half (the central SCADA system's polling messages) of the message traffic, unless they were physically in between a given RTU site and the SCADA main antenna site. Since radio equipment and laptop PCs are readily portable these days, a drive around a metropolitan area would eventually lead to the successful capture of complete message traffic. Since most water/wastewater utilities have been migrating to a small number of standardized serial protocols, a knowledgeable eavesdropper would not have too much difficulty identifying the protocol in use. Once that is known, the appropriate protocol test set software and the necessary portable radio equipment would allow the reception and interpretation of polling messages, as well as the generation of syntactically valid messages or responses. There are well-documented cases of this approach being used to issue controls and commands to field equipment by sending false messages to the respective RTUs. Conventional analog radio equipment incorporates no protective or security measures, and the most commonly used RTU protocols don't incorporate any either. Thus, a major cyber vulnerability of water/wastewater industry SCADA systems is the hijacking of RTUs that use conventional, licensed analog radio communications (fig. 13–2).

Today there are other wireless technologies available, including unlicensed (frequency hopping or direct sequence) spread-spectrum radio and digital radio, although they may not provide the distances needed or be compatible with the RTU protocols being used. There are also smart packet radio networks that store and forward message traffic and

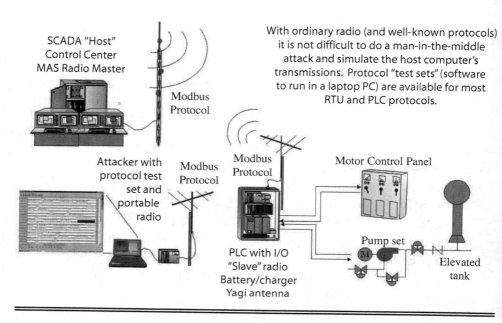

With ordinary radio (and well-known protocols) it is not difficult to do a man-in-the-middle attack and simulate the host computer's transmissions. Protocol "test sets" (software to run in a laptop PC) are available for most RTU and PLC protocols.

FIG. 13–2. *Using portable equipment to hijack a remote site*

use (somewhat more secure) digital communications. However, these are also often incompatible with the poll-response data-updating modes and protocols of most RTUs (particularly those based on PLC technology). Such radio systems usually want unsolicited report-by-exception data updating (where RTUs initiate message transmission, without being polled, when they determine that they have new information required by the SCADA system). Fortunately, the same types of encrypting modems that can be used on a multi-drop analog telephone circuit will generally work with analog radio equipment. These may represent the most straightforward means for securing legacy radio communication channels. Encrypting modems need to work in a manner that does not cause the introduction of transmission delays, because most RTUs and SCADA systems have timeout logic in their protocol software that will decide that messages have failed to be delivered if they are excessively delayed and will automatically initiate retransmission of the previous message (fig. 13–3). This is why new encrypting modems tend to use stream ciphers, rather than block ciphers, in their designs. Block ciphers that worked by capturing, encrypting, and then retransmitting an entire message at a time could introduce delays that might cause timeout errors to occur, and would definitely reduce the effective data transmission rate. A hybrid approach, which treats each message octet as a block, would probably not add excessive delays, but could not be used with legacy bit-oriented serial protocols.

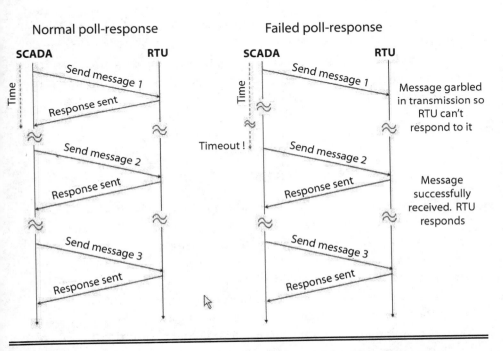

Fig. 13–3. *Poll–response timing for communication between RTUs and SCADA systems*

Nonsecure Protocols

As was mentioned previously, the vast majority of all water/wastewater RTU communications—regardless of the underlying communications technology or RTU technology—will employ a well-known serial communications protocol designed for efficiency and compact message size, rather than for communication security. The Modbus protocol is widely adopted by the water/wastewater industry throughout the United States. In part, this is because the Modbus protocol is in the public domain and is simple and easy to implement; also, the water/wastewater industry has adopted PLC technology for use as RTUs, and all major PLC vendors offer the Modbus protocol as either a standard feature or a readily available option. In municipalities where a high-bandwidth IP-based WAN has been created and made available to the water/wastewater utilities, utilities have occasionally used IP-based protocols, including UCA2, IP-DNP, and IP-Modbus. As was discussed in the chapter on electric utilities, these protocols do not currently incorporate comprehensive security features, but since they are transported by IP messages they can be protected by employing such standard IP cybersecurity technologies as router-based link encryption, IP_{SEC} and VPN tunnels.

PLC Equipment as RTUs

During the 1970s and 1980s (and even the 1990s), a lot of SCADA vendors entered the market, targeting at least one of the three main industry segments; unfortunately, most of these vendors eventually disappeared. This left a large number of installed-base SCADA customers without any support or the ability to expand or modify their systems. At the same time, in industrial automation (and factory automation), PLC manufacturers were introducing and expanding their product lines and slowly adding to their capabilities. Many water/wastewater SCADA system owners discovered that they could successfully apply PLCs to the monitoring, automation, and control problems at their treatment plants (in place of the much more expensive and complicated DCS systems), and this eventually led to placing the same kind of PLC equipment at field sites where RTUs would traditionally have been installed. To capture the RTU replacement business, PLC vendors and their partners manufacturing product accessories were willing to implement other legacy (serial) protocols. Eventually the vast majority of water/wastewater utilities adopted as standard one of the major brands of PLC equipment and, for use as their RTUs, one of the de facto protocol standards (often Modbus serial protocol). If you look at the public-bid procurement specifications issued today by most water/wastewater utilities, you will find technical specifications taken directly from the product literature of their preferred PLC manufacturer.

PLCs are very capable devices that over time have evolved into flexible, user-configurable, autonomous monitoring and control computers, with a wide range of sequential and regulatory control functions and features (fig. 13–4). Since they were initially sold as independent, stand-alone devices, vendors had to develop programming and configuration utilities that provided for the downloading of control logic and configuration information, either through a direct physical connection to the PLC or via the communication link to the PLC. When PLCs were originally introduced, they were targeted for factory-floor automation, so it was no big deal to physically reach a given PLC to establish a communication connection to its programming port, for downloading logic and configuration changes. As PLCs were scattered to remote sites, with only the polling channel available for communications, it became necessary to provide protocol messages/codes that supported logic and configuration downloading into the PLC via the same communication channel used for the polling, to avoid the logistical nightmare of going to numerous, widespread PLC sites to make changes.

In many SCADA applications in the water/wastewater industry, the PLC manufacturer's programming and configuration utilities are included with the SCADA software and can be used to remotely change PLC logic and configuration data by temporarily usurping the RTU-polling communication channel (see Fig. 13–4). For the most part, commercial PLCs have not incorporated any communication or configuration security measures. If you send syntactically correct messages to the PLC, it will accept them and process them. Because these PLC configuration tools are readily available on the open market (from PLC vendors and third-party suppliers) and because they work independently of the SCADA system, there is a possibility that an attacker could gain access to a polling channel (leased analog telephone or licensed radio) and corrupt, modify, or just disable the logic of the PLC. This includes the ability to shut off I/O scanning and processing, causing the PLC to report falsified data. It could also include the ability to control outputs that operate pumps, valves, and other process equipment.

Over the past decade, the IEC601131-3 standard has emerged for the definition of control logic for the PLCs. All major PLC vendors support compatibility with this standard, which makes third-party development of configuration and programming utilities possible. Some of the commercially available programming tools also allow existing control

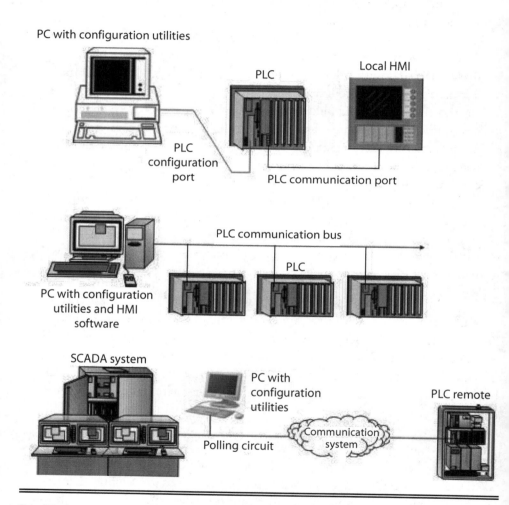

FIG. 13–4. *Evolution of PLC programming and configuration downloading*

logic in the PLC to be uploaded and examined. This capability would provide a potential attacker with a great deal of insight into how to modify the existing logic for the worst possible impact. Uploading logic in this manner would interrupt the normal polling of the PLC (and others on the same channel), but because SCADA users are accustomed to momentary communication outages, such a disruption might go unnoticed if polling activities recovered after the upload.

All of these remote support capabilities (uploading and downloading logic and configuration settings via the polling channel) were wonderfully convenient back in the days when we didn't suspect the need for cybersecurity. PLC manufacturers and third-party utility vendors are working on ways (if only through password access controls) to add security to these processes. However, a huge installed base of legacy PLCs are out there operating with no restrictions on their remote reprogramming and configuration. The hijacking scenario described earlier (using portable radio equipment) could also be used to download revised programming logic into PLC-based RTUs, rather than merely sending them a control command. Therefore, a number of PLCs could be implanted with malicious control logic that would await activation (e.g., a specific date/time), in the same way that logic bombs can be implanted in your PC by a virus or a hacker. In truth, this would be difficult to execute without inside knowledge. (Since the malicious logic would have to be appended to the real logic, an attacker would need to know what I/O signals were for controlling what equipment and fit in available memory.) The events of 9/11 show that we cannot discount the extraordinary amount of time and effort that some groups will invest in putting together a serious attack. Although this book deals with SCADA systems, this same type of threat exists for plants that use PLC-based automation systems (which includes a lot of water and wastewater treatment plants!).

Supervisory and Local Control Applications

The electric utility market makes great use of industry-specific application software, but little of that software actually initiates closed-loop (automatic) control. Sending out generator unit raise/lower commands is the major type of closed-loop supervisory control in the electric utility industry. There is also little local autonomous regulatory control, other than load tap changers, voltage regulators, and a capacitor bank here and there. Further, the control logic for these types of devices is usually embedded and not remotely alterable.

By contrast, the water/wastewater industry frequently uses supervisory and local control applications to make decisions about starting and stopping pumps, opening and closing valves, and performing other closed-loop autonomous operations. Many operations in the water/wastewater industry are time-of-day based, or are triggered by alarms/events, or are initiated by operator command. The actual control logic may be a program (or supervisory control script) that runs in the SCADA central computer, or it may be control logic residing in the PLC(s). If an attacker can cause the right signals to be sent to a PLC, the local control logic can be triggered; if an attacker can cause a simulated alarm/event to be sent to the SCADA system, supervisory control logic can be triggered; and if an attacker can get programming access to the SCADA system (as an insider might have), then a malicious supervisory control program could be added to the system and initiated by events or conditions defined by the attacker (e.g., waiting for a high-demand/high-load situation or delaying until the attacker has had adequate time to abscond).

Most SCADA systems have no mechanisms (and many utility organizations have no procedures) for ensuring that supervisory control programs are authorized, validated, and unaltered. Most supervisory control logic programming is usually simplistic in design and sequential in nature: once initiated by a false alarm/event, few programs incorporate any subsequent checks to revalidate the triggering condition(s). A supervisory control program will often send a large number of control commands to the respective RTUs and then wait for a time interval to elapse or a measurable condition to be reached (e.g., a pressure or level reaching a specified value). If the human operators are observant and act quickly, they might be able to detect and cancel a supervisory program or at least stop or reverse some of its commands. If it is an intentionally malicious program, then its designer might include code that overrides operator inputs and even creates numerous alarms to distract the operators. (In a previous chapter of the book the need for application development tools that enforce security policies and procedures was discussed. To date no such tools exist.)

Local automatic control has been a particular strength of PLCs. Often a local PLC will have preprogrammed emergency shut down and start-up logic that can be triggered by conditions it is monitoring or by *flags* set by the operators. There is no authentication between the PLC and the operator; if a syntactically valid message arrives, the logic will be triggered, regardless of where the message actually came from. Some logic designers, recognizing the possibility of human error, will include a requirement for a second, confirmation message (within a given time window) in order for the logic to be triggered. (For a discussion of select-check-operate message sequences from early dumb RTU technology, see section 1.) A patient attacker can eavesdrop on unsecured RTU/PLC communications and eventually record such sequences. Simple serial protocols, such as Modbus, are highly vulnerable to a replay attack whereby the previously recorded message is merely regenerated on the communication circuit, a capability standard in most protocol analyzers or protocol test sets.

It might be possible to improve on communications and control security, even without resorting to full link encryption, by using additional application logic (which would require additional logic at the host level and within each PLC). As an overly simplistic example, if the PLCs and the host are kept within a reasonable time synchronization by having the host send out time broadcasts on a periodic basis, then it could be possible to require current date/time to accompany control messages. The PLC could compare its time to the time in the message, and if they differed too much (as in a replayed message recorded earlier), it would discard and ignore the message. (In reality, this specific approach would be a poor defense, since an attacker could either send a fake time sync message first, to set PLC time to the time in the recorded message, or edit the time portion of the recorded message before replaying.)

Currently, the only truly secure strategy is to encrypt the communications. With PLC equipment, as with conventional RTUs, this can be accomplished using external encrypting modems (fig. 13–5). Some PLC product lines also support plug-in communication modules that can be used to add other protocols to the PLC. A secure communications protocol could be implemented using such a plug-in module, but the SCADA host computer would have to be modified to support the same protocol, or a protocol converter would have to be added in front of the SCADA host. Today there are no commercially available serial protocols that incorporate security features, although the AGA has proposed a design basis for developing one (refer to Appendix C). This means that integrating an external encryption device (at both ends of each polling circuit) is the only available solution for securing the huge installed base of RTU and PLC devices.

Efforts to develop secure, low-speed, serial communications protocols are under way, and the resulting commercial products should become available in the near future. Meanwhile, if communications are converted to digital networks that support IP protocols, then security technologies are readily available already. However, it is assumed that such a wholesale migration is neither realistic nor viable in the short term. Also, although link encryption is a good first step, an overall solution should include authentication methodologies as well. It is good to know that forging a message will be made difficult because of encryption, but it is better still to know for certain that the messages are coming from the SCADA system and not some attacker's PC. The latest PLC equipment, introduced in the past few years, supports Ethernet LAN connectivity and IP networking. Still, that doesn't mean that it supports any aspects of IP security (e.g., encryption, digital certificates, key exchange, or authentication), nor is this equipment of any value if the existing SCADA systems still need to use nonsecure legacy (serial) protocols and analog communications technology, such as leased telephone lines and radio.

The results of an attacker invading a water/wastewater SCADA system might not be as newsworthy as a major electrical power outage or a major pipeline leak. Nevertheless, damaging a water-delivery system, cutting off water to a major metropolitan area, and causing a major sewage spill are all possible outcomes of an attack on a water/wastewater SCADA system. Thus, the potential exists to alarm—and even harm or kill—a large number of people.

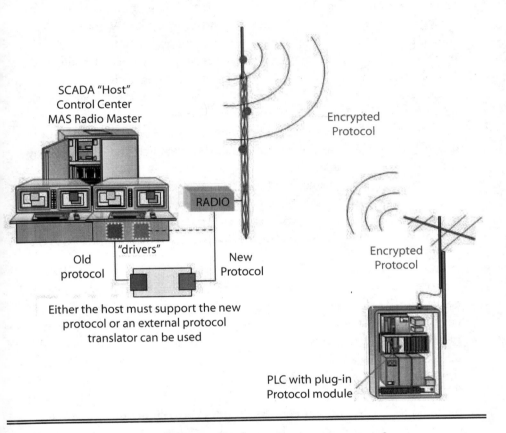

SCADA "Host"
Control Center
MAS Radio Master

Encrypted
Protocol

RADIO

"drivers"

Old protocol

New Protocol

Encrypted
Protocol

Either the host must support the new protocol or an external protocol translator can be used

PLC with plug-in
Protocol module

FIG. 13–5. *Using additional hardware for conversion to secure protocols*

Municipal LANs and WANs

Water/wastewater utilities, as was already mentioned, mostly exist for the support of residents and businesses of the municipalities in which they are based, as well as for the municipal government and its facilities. Therefore, they frequently share the communications infrastructure that supports the municipality, especially if that infrastructure was funded and constructed by the municipality. It is not uncommon to see municipalities that have invested in high-speed municipal area networks (MANs) using fiber optics. The bandwidth of such a WAN may be sufficient to offer telephone, networking, Internet, and even cable TV services. The municipality can often fund the cost of creating and maintaining a MAN by the sale (lease) of these various services, leaving plenty of bandwidth available for their own voice and data communications needs. A municipal water/wastewater utility is equally likely (as is the municipal electric utility) to utilize communication services over such a WAN, even if that addresses only part of their overall communications requirements. One cybersecurity-related problem with such an arrangement is that many times the MAN will have communication nodes in public buildings or commercial buildings shared with public companies (see fig. 13–6). As was mentioned in the section on municipal electric utilities, this places physical access to the network equipment into locations that need to be protected and included within the physical security boundary of the SCADA system.

Another problem is that the MAN will often interconnect with conventional IT systems for both the municipality and major utility customers/suppliers, and somewhere out on the MAN an attached system will make a connection to the Internet (and probably to the public telephone system as well). The security issues—and the strategies to meet those challenges—are essentially the same as those of a municipal electric utility. (For details, see chapter 12.) One aspect of a MAN that wasn't included in the discussion of electric utilities is that there may very well be sub-multiplexed voice-grade channels (e.g., analog PLC communications traffic) passing through the MAN and interfaced to public, leased telephone lines to reach outlying sites. These interfaces are a point of vulnerability, unless the serial communications are encrypted (at the host and the PLC ends), and thus require physical security to prevent access by unauthorized personnel. When a portion of the bandwidth of a digital network is sub-multiplexed to create voice grade channels (for actual telephone service or for data communications), those channels must be treated no differently, from a security standpoint, than telephone lines leased from the local telephone company.

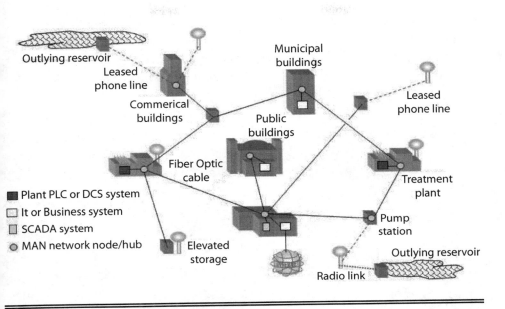

FIG. 13–6. *Simplified example MAN shared by a municipal utility SCADA system*

Control Interfaces to Plant Control Systems

Another difference between water/wastewater and electric utilities is that treatment plants in a water/wastewater SCADA system may be tightly coupled and interfaced to the SCADA system, with significant remote control and adjustment capabilities, because the status and operational level of a given treatment plant can have a significant impact on the overall operation of the water/wastewater utility. (An off-line, or load-restricted, treatment plant can result in the inability to meet water demands or the need to allow sewage to accumulate.) The level of automation in a modern water/wastewater treatment plant can be quite high, nearly eliminating the need for on-site supervisory or operational personnel—except during peak-load hours and in the event of plant problems. Therefore, it is common for the interface between the SCADA system and the individual treatment plant control systems to include a large volume of real-time operational data from the plant and a good number of supervisory controls and adjustable parameter settings going back to the plant control system from the SCADA system (fig. 13–7). This is so that SCADA personnel can monitor and (to a degree) remotely adjust/control the treatment plant, if necessary.

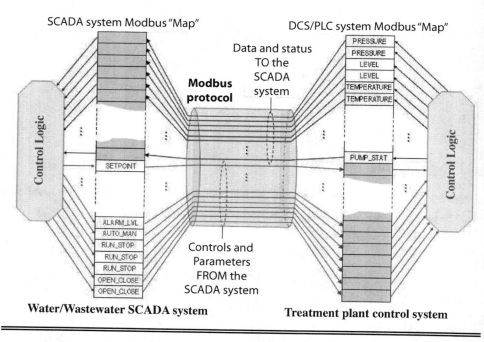

SCADA system Modbus "Map"

DCS/PLC system Modbus "Map"

Data and status
TO the
SCADA
Modbus system
protocol

Control Logic

SETPOINT

PRESSURE
PRESSURE
LEVEL
LEVEL
TEMPERATURE
TEMPERATURE

PUMP_STAT

Control Logic

ALARM_LVL
AUTO_MAN
RUN_STOP
RUN_STOP
RUN_STOP
OPEN_CLOSE
OPEN_CLOSE

Controls and
Parameters
FROM the
SCADA system

Water/Wastewater SCADA system

Treatment plant control system

FIG. 13–7. *Data and control exchange between plant DCS and SCADA system*

There may be a serial communication link between the SCADA and plant control systems, using a conventional protocol such as Modbus, which delivers important control system process measurement and status data to the SCADA system and delivers supervisory control flags and parameter value changes to the treatment plant control system. The main point is that an attacker who obtains communications access to the link between the SCADA system and the treatment plant control system would have an extremely high level of control access into the treatment plant, almost equivalent to physical (or electronic) access to the treatment plant control system itself. (Further, unlike physical or electronic access, there will be no form of controls or authentication—e.g., password or key card—on the communication link.) If supervisory control of the treatment plant is implemented in this manner, the data exchange between the two systems will usually include control-loop *set points*, alarm limit settings, alarm enable/disable flags, pump and other equipment controls, flags to open and close *control-loop cascades*, flags to set the *automatic or manual mode* of control loops, and possibly even the ability to adjust valve positions.

This is quite different from the way in which electric utility SCADA systems interact with their respective generating facilities. Often the only interface between a generating plant and the respective SCADA system is an on-site RTU that returns a few assorted electrical measurements and affords remote ramping (up or down) of the individual generating units. Depending on the computer technology of the water/wastewater treatment plant control system, there may be remote viewing and control capability provided in the form of remote console support (X-terminal in the Unix/Linux world and, more recently, Web browser–based access in both the Unix/Linux and the Microsoft worlds.) If remote console access is implemented as an application protocol layer on top of a TCP/IP network then this type of remote access can usually be safeguarded using the various IP security technologies already discussed: link encryption, IP_{SEC}, VPN tunnel, and so forth. If such security measures are not employed, then an attacker who gains access to the communications channel has a reasonably good chance of gaining full operational access to the control system. If a remote operator has an X-window session to the remote control system and has already been authenticated, then an attacker who hijacks the session has the same control authority (and sees the exact same displays) as the operator.

IP to the Field

Because the PLC equipment being installed at remote sites as RTUs and the treatment plant control systems are generally available with IP networking capability these days (although not necessarily with any security features) and because water/wastewater utilities face the same telecommunications challenge posed by slowly disappearing analog telephone circuits as do electric utilities, water/wastewater utilities are also making the transition to digital technologies and IP networking.

With an IP connection between a SCADA system and a treatment plant control system, there may be no need for the exchange of supervisory flags and variables. The SCADA system operators may be able to call up Web-based, remote console–based (or X-Windows–based) operational displays—just as if they were physically at the treatment plant itself. Of course, any attacker who gained IP network access would have the same capabilities. At that point, the only line of defense between an attacker and the discharge of sludge into a river might be the user ID/password mechanisms of the plant control system. All of the currently available remote console technologies are based on well-known and standard technologies (e.g., X-Windows, Web servers, and Microsoft's remote console support). Thus, if an attacker were able to establish an IP connection with the plant control system, it is highly likely that they would be able to see the same console displays offered to a legitimate remote operator/user, unless some protection were provided.

IP to the field allows for remote configuration and reprogramming of PLCs and PLC systems. It also opens up the possibility of an attacker launching DoS attacks on the SCADA master and/or the remote sites. Security testing of IP enabled PLCs at a university lab showed that the process of running a readily available, standard port sweeper utility (nmap) against the PLCs often caused them to hang (not the control logic, but the communications). An attacker who obtained network access, regardless of encryption and authentication, could in theory blind the SCADA system by port sweeping all of the remote sites. It is highly probable that many IP-ready devices and IED will be found to have similar problems with communications robustness.

Pipeline Industry–Specific Cybersecurity Issues

The pipeline industry can be decomposed, at the highest level, into liquid and gas pipelines, and those two broad categories can be further decomposed. Gas pipelines carry natural gas (methane) or other gases, such as carbon dioxide (CO_2). Natural gas pipelines are often quite long and can run halfway across the United States, whereas a CO_2 pipeline might just run a few miles between the plant where it is produced and another plant that needs it as feedstock. Liquid pipelines can carry crude oil to a refinery from a production field or an unloading terminal. Liquid pipelines may carry a single refined product, multiple refined products (in batches), or liquids produced from the processing of natural gas (NGL).

There are obvious differences between the various types of pipelines, particularly in the operation of the lines and the control strategies and supervisory applications (one major difference being the high compressibility of gases versus the near incompressibility of most liquids). However, from a generalized communications and SCADA viewpoint, these different types of pipelines tend to be quite similar: they will have measurement and control points distributed along the pipeline and locations where the transported medium is injected into the pipeline and where it is extracted from the pipeline. Both liquid and gas pipelines also need occasional booster/pump/compressor stations to maintain the required flow rates and pressures along the line. A SCADA system for a pipeline will usually have RTUs located along the line to make measurements and provide remote control of pumps, valves, and other equipment. Normally, some number of these RTUs will be situated at measurement points with no power source and thus will have to be solar (or alternate method) powered and designed for very-low-power operation, including their radio equipment.

One particular variation in production field SCADA systems is the offshore (oil/gas) production field, where the RTUs are located on platforms out in the ocean and thus have to survive in this environment. Communications to RTUs located offshore can be disrupted by storms, fog, and hurricanes; thus, the RTUs have to be able to operate independently of the SCADA host for long periods of time. The RTUs used in pipeline applications tend to incorporate more (and higher complexity) calculations and regulatory and sequential control logic, as compared to those used in water/wastewater applications (and in electric utility applications, they generally have no such features).

Pipeline SCADA systems also normally interface with the control systems used to automate the pump/booster/compressor stations and may even provide remote control (or at least adjustment) of such systems (fig. 14–1). For liquid lines, there will also be storage areas (tank farms) at the injection and extraction points. Gas lines may move gas to or from production and storage well fields. Optimization of pipeline operations usually requires that the entire pipeline be modeled; this can be achieved only at a supervisory level, at which continuously updated real-time data is available for the entire pipeline. The output of pipeline models may initiate either the direct remote operation of pipeline equipment (e.g., to start/stop pumps and open/close valves) or the adjustment of operational set points within the booster/pump/compressor station control systems. Because energy trading and delivery schedules are an integral aspect of the business enterprise that rely on current operational information, pipeline SCADA systems are often tightly interfaced with other business systems across the corporate WAN (the term *vertical integration* is often used for the business segments, but applies to data integration as well). Although pipelines can be used to transport many types of gases and liquids and can come in many lengths, the focus here will be on the long-haul pipelines used for delivery of hydrocarbon fuels (gas and liquids), since disruption (or disabling) of one of these pipelines would have the greatest impact on the United States.

Industry architectural differences
Product Pipeline System Architecture

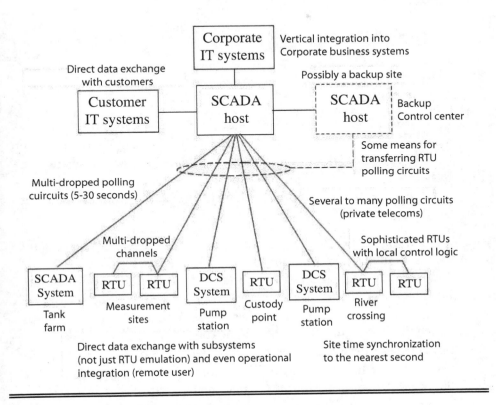

Fig. 14–1. *Generalized architecture of a pipeline SCADA system*

Radio Communications

By their nature, hydrocarbon pipelines tend to run long distances through rural (or sparsely populated) areas—from the source of hydrocarbon fuels (the Gulf Coast) to places where such fuels are needed (e.g., the East Coast and the West Coast). Because they tend to be located away from public infrastructure, and may cross through the service areas of multiple utilities and telecommunication providers, pipelines have almost always incorporated private communication systems. Until the introduction of fiber-optic cable, in the 1980s, communications were radio based, utilizing three types of radio technology:

- Analog point-to-multipoint radio

- Microwave radio point-to-point links

- Satellite uplinks and ground stations

As mentioned previously, pipeline companies typically borrowed their communications technology from the telephone company. Thus, a pipeline built in the 1970s would probably have included a series of microwave relay towers located along the pipeline right-of-way and used to provide voice-grade telephone communication circuits (for voice and data) along the pipeline and back to the SCADA system (fig. 14–2).

Starting in the late 1980s (and continuing thereafter), microwave towers were replaced by a fiber-optic cable that could be buried in the same trench as the pipeline. (Here I am talking about new construction. Pipeline operators didn't go out and tear down the existing microwave infrastructure. Hybrid systems, where expansions were made with fiber optics, can also be found.) Although the communications used fiber-optic technologies, they were, however, undoubtedly still based on voice-grade telephone circuits generated by de-multiplexing the bandwidth of the fiber-optic cable (in the same way that the microwave signal would have been de-multiplexed).

Today that very same fiber-optic cable can be used to carry IP networking (including VoIP telephone service) by replacing the telephone multiplexer equipment with Ethernet switches. The placement of microwave relay towers (or fiber-optic repeaters) is dependent on a source of power. Because this equipment needs to be protected from the elements and tampering, its physical positioning cannot always be adjacent to every point of measurement and control. (Microwave towers also need line-of-sight relationships with up- and downstream towers—something that isn't an issue with fiber-optic cable. But when you get to a river crossing microwave regains the advantage.)

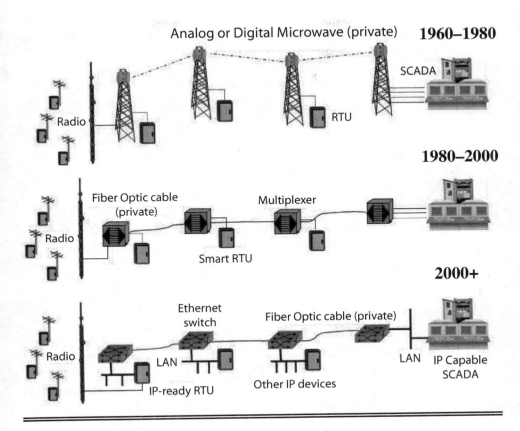

Fig. 14–2. *Evolution of pipeline communications technologies*

With pipelines, it has been typical to combine conventional radio communications with a microwave/fiber-optic backbone, to extend communications to geographically adjacent areas. The susceptibility of radio communications to tampering (hijacking) has already been discussed; unlike in the water/wastewater industry (where radio is often the primary communications mechanism); however, along a pipeline, radio communication *spurs* are generally used only to bridge lower-priority measurement sources onto the (microwave/fiber-optic) communications backbone. Unlike conventional, broadcast radio, satellite and microwave communications tend to be more physically secure from attack: to tamper with or disrupt communications, you have to have physical access to the equipment or get in line with the highly directional/focused radio signal.

(Still, this is a possibility, since many pipeline facilities are located in the middle of nowhere and are not under constant supervision.)

Along a pipeline, the facilities provide physical security in the form of fences, walls, and buildings that house the communications equipment. (Also, much of the pipeline itself is buried, which gives added physical protection, especially when fiber-optic cables are used.) In theory, you could erect a temporary tower between two microwave repeaters and intercept or disrupt the communications, but this would require significant and rather obvious effort. Disruption of communications would probably be unsuccessful (unless initiated on a widespread basis) in that most microwave systems are designed in a looped configuration that permits communications to continue (by reversing direction around the loop) if any repeater station goes down or if local weather conditions disrupt any section of the backbone. With the advent of fiber optics to replace microwave towers, it is theoretically possible for someone to excavate along a pipeline and reach the fiber cable. Once this were accomplished, the cable could be cut and an additional (de-)multiplexer (or Ethernet switch) could be inserted to gain access to the communications. However, this would be a technically daunting task requiring a lot of insider information to be successful. It would be much easier to merely breach the excavated pipeline with explosives and ignite the gas/liquids therein.

Smart RTUs

The pipeline industry has made extensive use of microprocessor-based RTUs since their introductions in the early 1980s. SCADA vendors who serve the pipeline industry have incorporated many pipeline-specific measurement and control functions in their RTU products, along with general sequential and regulatory control functions. As with the water/wastewater industry, locally and remotely (re)programmable RTUs are used and often contain downloaded calculations and control logic, enabling them to perform autonomous control functions. It is not uncommon for RTUs to handle the opening and closing of valves, the regulation of pressure and flow, and the operation of pumps and compressors. Volumetric metering of gas/liquids for billing and leak-detection purposes is also a common function in pipeline RTUs.

If the control logic of an RTU were replaced with malicious code, it would be possible for an RTU to cause physical damage to the pipeline equipment or to cause intentional product leakage. With a product pipeline, tampering with RTU logic could cause the wrong products to be routed to designated storage tanks, thus rendering the products unusable without reprocessing. All of these scenarios would require communications (or physical) access to the RTUs (or the SCADA host computer), as well as application knowledge to which only an insider would have access.

The pipeline industry (for obvious reasons), unlike the water/wastewater industry, has been more inclined to use separate, hardwired safety equipment to prevent malfunctions of the normal controls (e.g., the RTUs) from initiating a catastrophe. Much of the control logic running in the RTUs (or separate safety systems) is designed to make a determination of safety, based on local measurements, and opt for the safest strategy. Thus, totally disabling a pipeline SCADA system might not have as much of an impact as taking control of such a system and using it maliciously. Taking control of an RTU and trying to use it to cause damage might cause external hard-wired logic to be triggered in order to block or limit the actions of the RTU.

RTU Program Logic

As with water/wastewater SCADA systems, the need to change program logic in a number of remotely located RTUs led the pipeline industry to adopt centralized programming and configuration of pipeline RTUs as early as the late 1970s. To stay competitive, most SCADA vendors serving that market had to roll out smart and remotely configurable RTUs and had to extend their RTU protocols to support these capabilities. Since this technology emerged prior to the widespread adoption of PLCs (and PCs), the programming tools tended to be developed as integral components of the SCADA host system software, not as independent utilities that could be purchased separately. This also meant that there was little or no compatibility between vendors, which eventually led the industry to push for cross-platform standards. Standardization in the pipeline industry has not reached the same levels as it has in the water/wastewater industry, but it is headed in that direction.

On the positive side, security wise, to use the RTU programming and configuration tools, one would normally have to have access to, familiarity with, and a valid user ID/password on the SCADA system. Today more and more pipeline SCADA systems are based on commercial SCADA packages, much like those used in the water/wastewater industry and are using both RTUs and PLCs as remote units. PLCs can now be programmed to perform functions that were once exclusive to industry-targeted RTUs (AGA gas volumetric calculations, tank volume strapping tables with specific gravity and temperature corrections, etc.). This means that the pipeline SCADA industry now is encountering the same problems with securing RTU configuration and programming as did the water/wastewater industry. Programming tools are commercially available to anyone, and RTUs (or PLCs) have no authentication mechanisms to detect and prevent unauthorized programming and configuration changes.

Supervisory Control Applications

Because pipelines are complex and need to be modeled for a variety of reasons, it is commonplace to use supervisory applications, running on the SCADA system, for autonomous, automatic control of the pipeline. Depending on the pipeline operator's operational philosophy, the supervisory control applications may or may not request permission from a human operator prior to sending control messages to RTUs and local control systems. Importantly, these applications seek operator authorization only because they have been specifically programmed to do so. In most SCADA systems (except those in which device tagging is supported), there is nothing in the system design that prevents a supervisory program from sending a control command to an RTU. It is usually up to the application developers to add specific program logic to request operator authorization (possibly with a timeout that allows program continuation if no human responds to the request for authorization). This means that if a malicious supervisory application could be introduced into the SCADA system, such a program could send commands out to the field devices. The risks posed by malicious supervisory applications and the need for insider access to create and install such applications are the same as have already been discussed in chapter 12, in regard to electric utilities.

IP along the Pipeline

In the communications architecture evolution shown previously (see fig. 14–2), the most recent step is the conversion of the high-bandwidth backbone into a WAN, by replacing the multiplexing equipment with network components such as switches and routers. This step has made possible the use of the WAN for a variety of applications. With IP-enabled SCADA systems and RTUs, the WAN provides real-time data and command exchanges for the basic SCADA functions.

If the local control systems in the pump/booster/compressor stations are likewise IP-enabled, the WAN offers remote access to these systems for control, maintenance, and support functions. Personnel working at or dispatched to the various sites along the pipeline could even be allowed e-mail and Web browser access to the corporate servers. Various corporate business and asset/maintenance management systems have direct communications with corresponding subsystems along the pipeline. VoIP and *Webcam* technologies can be integrated into the WAN for voice communications and for visual supervision and monitoring of the various pipeline facilities.

In other words, as with the other industries that employ SCADA systems, numerous technical and operational advantages are gained when the underlying communications are based on IP networking. Further, just like those other industries, deploying IP networking to the field, without adequate technical safeguards, offers the opportunity for hackers and other threat agents to gain access to those IP-enabled systems and devices. Unlike the water/wastewater and municipal electric utilities, however— where networking equipment could be located in readily accessible public buildings—with a pipeline, the communications equipment would normally be housed in (reasonably) secured facilities (along the pipeline) and would not be readily accessible to the public. Nevertheless, if an attacker were to gain physical access to a remote pipeline facility that was part of the WAN, they could potentially access any other WAN-connected system or equipment, if adequate cybersecurity protective measures were not implemented. Physical security is never a substitute for appropriate cybersecurity and electronic security measures; it is just part of a comprehensive *defense-in-depth* security strategy.

Web Browsing and E-mail Integration

A pipeline SCADA system built on a private communications network along the pipeline right-of-way still requires a control room somewhere, staffed with operational and supervisory personnel. It is quite common that this control room be located in the headquarters of the pipeline company, since as long as communications are available, there is no real restriction on its location. (This is much the same as in the electric power industry.) The people who operate and supervise the pipeline SCADA system need to communicate with other corporate personnel and provide data to related corporate systems (e.g., asset management systems, accounting systems, billing systems, and even maintenance management systems).

It used to be that when a SCADA system was implemented, it was a stand-alone system that wasn't interconnected with a company LAN/WAN. For many years, concern over the security of corporate networks—and the Internet—kept SCADA systems physically isolated. It remains common to see separate PCs in a control room connected to the corporate network, for e-mail and Web access by the operational personnel. This was easy to justify when SCADA systems were built from computer equipment that markedly differed from the average desktop PC, but today there is little difference (other than in name) between a person's desktop PC and the operator console attached to the SCADA system or one of its servers. It has become more usual to see the SCADA system's LAN bridged onto the corporate network via some form of firewall that permits bidirectional e-mail and Web browsing directly from the operator's console. The only intended purposes of this integration might be to enable internal e-mail (within the corporation) and to provide Web access to corporate servers. However, somewhere on the corporate network, there is a connection to the Internet, because others in the corporation do require World Wide Web and e-mail access. For a long time, no one viewed this *creeping integration* as particularly dangerous, and it was convenient for operational personnel to have these facilities. Today such functional interconnectivity poses a security risk to the SCADA system because of malware, which can be attached to or embedded as part of an e-mail message or implanted while Web browsing. As already discussed, the danger of creating an electronic path for threat agents is always present when a SCADA system is connected to other systems and networks that are connected to the Internet. Most SCADA-knowledgeable security experts would agree that functions such as e-mail and Web browsing, if required, ought to be relegated to separate PCs on a separate network, which is not connected to the SCADA system's network (and the dangers of dual homed PCs, even if via integral wireless networking, have already been presented).

The Emerging Cyber Threat to SCADA Systems

Supervisory control systems had never been designed and constructed with consideration of the need to defend against and withstand intentional attacks and tampering, prior to the events of 9/11 (and that fact has not fundamentally changed in the intervening time). As with computer systems in general, it was assumed that designing them to be fault tolerant and deal with simple human error was sufficient.

Although much research has been done and many proposals have been made, the basic construction and design of SCADA systems has not fundamentally changed since the events of 9/11. There is a large installed base of SCADA systems, ranging from current levels of technology back to technologies from the 1980s (and possibly even older). As large as the installed base of SCADA systems is, the installed base of RTUs (including PLCs used as remotes) is many times as large, and this includes RTU technologies going back to the 1970s. Surprisingly, it is not the older SCADA systems that are the primary concern, at least at the central host level, because many predate IP networking and are built upon legacy operating systems that are far less known today than those that are the focus of attacks by hackers.

SCADA system vendors have rushed to incorporate add-on protective measures, primarily those already in use in the IT world. SCADA system vendors now offer third-party intrusion-detection packages, firewalls, and virus-scanning software. Some vendors have added biometric scanners and other forms of strong authentication, for user login verification. Where possible, vendors now offer serial line encrypting modems for

RTU communications and enable IP link encryption in the routers on all network interconnections. Off-the-shelf VPN software is used to secure remote operator and maintenance connections to the SCADA systems. All of this is obviously good, and it represents what can be done quickly, without making significant design changes in the basic SCADA system software and hardware. Since SCADA systems today are built upon commercial hardware and operating systems, most SCADA system vendors are counting on Microsoft, Intel, and other manufacturers to implement integral security measures, from which they will benefit.

The owners/operators of SCADA systems are taking steps to determine their vulnerabilities and are implementing physical and operational security practices to augment the cybersecurity enhancements offered by the SCADA vendors. In the long run, however, there will need to be basic changes in the design and construction of SCADA systems (including the RTUs) if they are to be made intrinsically secure. Possibly the greatest vulnerability in SCADA systems today is the assumption that threats come from the outside and that anyone working for the organization (an insider) can be assumed to be trustworthy.

Much of the protection being put into place for SCADA systems (and operational organizations) is in the form of building a security perimeter (both physical and electronic). This denotes an outward-looking siege mentality. The problem is that the most dangerous (although admittedly least frequent) threats come from trusted insiders that decide to use their powers for evil or who unwittingly aid in breaching the security perimeter. An incautious insider can accidentally bring malware inside the electronic security perimeter and introduce it into the SCADA computers.

A particularly virulent worm or virus can rapidly multiply and spread to all interconnected computers, including the backup computers in a redundant SCADA configuration. If an organization routinely practices recovery procedures and maintains backup system copies, such a breach may mean only a temporary loss of part (or possibly all) of the SCADA system. If a full backup site is standing by, then the overall effects may be minimal. However, since most backup sites have some form of data link to the primary site, for synchronization or updating purposes, the alternative site could also be threatened and infected.

There are well-documented cases of certain worms spreading across the Internet in just hours, infecting thousands of computers. The Sapphire worm (also called Slammer) was the fastest computer worm in history as of the day it hit the Internet. As it spread throughout the Internet, the number of infected computers doubled every 8.5 seconds. It infected more than 90% of vulnerable hosts within 10 minutes by targeting a buffer-overflow vulnerability in Microsoft's SQL Server. Worms like Code Red I and II, Nimda, and Slammer can rapidly spread across a LAN or WAN and shut down all of the networked computers.

Temporary loss of the SCADA system may or may not cause widespread damage, depending on the duration of the outage and the process being controlled. On the one hand, losing the SCADA/EMS system controlling a large power grid during a peak-load condition could lead to a blackout. On the other hand, temporarily losing a water-distribution monitoring system might not cause any noticeable problems. Of course, generic malware is designed only to disrupt and shut down computers and communication networks.

By contrast, intentionally malicious supervisory control application programs or downloaded RTU control logic could pose the most significant threat to plant facilities and processes. Few if any SCADA systems have integral technical controls (and not all organizations have procedural controls) that would prevent an insider from installing and running such applications. SCADA systems themselves don't have any mechanisms for differentiating authorized and unauthorized applications. Although the vast majority of SCADA systems still use nonsecure, legacy (serial) protocols for their RTU communications, work has begun to define requirements for a new generation of field devices and protocols that would make such communications secure. Meanwhile, addition of external link encryption devices—if that can even be done—remains the only available strategy for securing these communication links. Possibly the best news for SCADA system owner/operators is that the external hackers and malware that might be trying to breach your system defenses are going to be using techniques and technology that is understood by your IT organization (and by the IT community as a whole), and for which there are available, reasonably effective countermeasures. The bad news is that implementing these countermeasures takes time and money and trained resources. The further bad news is that an internal attacker can bypass most of these technical countermeasures. At that point, nontechnical countermeasures, in the form of well designed and enforced policies and procedures, are your next line of defense.

The remainder of this section focuses on review of current security capabilities and discussion of future security needs and alternatives.

SECTION 4:
SCADA SECURITY ARCHITECTURES

16

Commercial Hardware and Software Vulnerabilities

The manufacturers of computer and networking equipment and software are well aware of the existing cybersecurity threats, since these have had an impact on their business and their customers for many years. Hackers have been attacking from across the Internet since the early 1990s, (and via dial up phone lines since the 1980s), and the pace and volume and sophistication of cyber attacks (including the launching of malware) has been increasing steadily since that time.

Certain manufacturers' products, particularly those from Microsoft and Cisco, have born the brunt of a large percentage of these attacks, if for no other reason than that they are the proverbial "800-pound gorillas" of the computer world. It didn't help that their products were (initially) woefully lacking in security features and chock full of vulnerabilities. (To be fair, this can be said about almost all competitive products in the same time frame.) But in the past few years, both companies, as well as their competition, have made great strides in eliminating vulnerabilities and shoring up their cybersecurity capabilities (at least if you kept up-to-date with the continuous stream of patches). Nevertheless, it remains true that vulnerabilities still exist and that the business objectives and development priorities of the manufacturers are directed at much broader commercial and consumer markets, and not at the industrial automation market. The amount of computer hardware and software purchased for the production, repair, and/or upgrading of SCADA (and even DCS) systems represents a very small fraction of the total market. Thus, the particular cybersecurity needs of the SCADA community may well have to be addressed within that vendor community. In the past, SCADA vendors devised mechanisms for providing fully automatic redundancy, when computer vendors had no such provisions. The same is true for HMI interface and display hardware. There have always been hardware and software requirements for automation systems that could not be addressed with the commercially available products. Although the percentage of an overall SCADA system represented by such requirements has dropped, at least two obvious areas remain. First, SCADA system vendors need to make their configuration and application development tools far more secure, and incorporate self-checking features that verify the integrity of critical databases, applications and data. The next most obvious area would be in devising new RTU protocols, or extensions to existing ones, that provide for authentication and encryption. In the meantime, the commercial vendors that provide the hardware and software platforms on which automation systems are built need to continue addressing their vulnerabilities as well.

Operating System

A computer's operating system is the collection of software that "own" the full set of computer resources (CPU, memory, storage, communications, and peripheral devices) and make them available to application programs and users on the basis of a defined set of rules. Those rules may include assigning all applications a priority value and then allocating resources according to the relative priorities of the competing applications. The rules may define a given set of time-critical applications that *must* be granted resources when requested, with the remaining resources parceled out on an equal sharing basis. Regardless of the rule mix and structure, there will be some mechanism that decides who gets what resources and when. In a multi-user environment, it is also a task of the operating system to ensure that the resources allocated to one user are not accidentally or intentionally made available to another user (or that any single user can usurp all of the available resources).

To make this possible, computer hardware designs usually incorporate special features that enable the operating system to enforce security provisions. The computer hardware may restrict the memory area that a given program can actually address (the range of memory locations program instructions can read and write) and make I/O devices (e.g., disk drives and Ethernet network interface cards [NICs]) invisible to programs, so that they have to ask the operating system to send commands to these I/O devices when they want to use them. A real time hardware clock can be used to control which program gets to use the CPU, including the programs that comprise the operating system, and for how long. Similarly, these protective hardware features can make it possible to isolate one program from another, even though they reside in adjacent memory areas. However, just because a particular CPU has hardware to support these protective capabilities, that doesn't mean the operating system will actually make use of them. Some of the vulnerabilities in commercial operating systems stem from not being designed to take advantage of the available hardware protective features designed into commercial CPUs.

Another security-related concept that needs to be understood is that of a *user*. People can't *use* a computer. A person at a workstation or terminal or PC is interacting with a program (or multiple programs) written to provide mechanisms by which human beings submit requests to the operating system (and receive responses when appropriate). With any luck these programs are designed to accommodate human error and limit human maliciousness. When you click on a directory tree and get presented with a tabular list of the files in the selected subdirectory, what has actually happened is that your click was translated into a call to the file manager of the operating system, requesting that the information about the files in the selected (sub)directory be returned for graphic display on your terminal/PC. This activity should include a check of your user ID, to verify that the directory selected is available to you (and if not, to return a message essentially saying "Sorry, you are not allowed to see this information"). When you click on an icon to run a program, you actually cause a request to be sent to the operating system to allocate to the program indicated the resources (at least memory and CPU) needed for it to run—again presumably with a check of your ID, to verify that you are allowed to run that program.

In a modern operating system, every user is given an *account* (the right to use system resources) with specific levels of access rights. Inside the operating system, your ID and password have an associated *access-control list* (ACL), which enumerates what you can and can't access. Typically, unless you have administrative rights (in Unix, being root or the superuser), you can't access the programs that set up new (or that modify existing) user accounts. Likewise, you can't normally access the files of other users. The mission of a typical hacker is to end up with an account that has administrative rights. This will typically be accomplished by stealing the ID and password of someone who has administrative rights (by using social engineering, sniffing a LAN or WiFi AP, or using a password cracker, among other methods). We have already discussed many of the techniques used for this purpose. Once granted administrative rights, the hacker can replace valid system utility programs with a hacker version that incorporates a back door, so that the hacker can gain access to the system any time thereafter. The term *rootkit* is used for this sort of replacement software, as it allows a hacker to gain system access as a root-level (administrative) user at any time.

Current operating systems do not have any mechanism for authenticating the source and validity of programs loaded into them. If you have administrative rights and overwrite the file that contains system utility X with a hacker version, the operating system will assume that this is fine and will allow you to do so. In the future, operating systems will be more protective of their critical software modules and will implement an authentication/validation process prior to allowing the replacement of any system-level software modules (and maybe incorporate mechanisms that allow third-party software suppliers, including the SCADA vendors, to authenticate theirs as well). In addition, the process of logging onto an operating system and being authenticated will become ever more based on biometrics and strong-authentication methods, so that stealing a user ID becomes nearly impossible (unless, as in the James Bond™ movies, a thief is willing to cut off a finger or extract an eyeball). This still doesn't address the problem of a high-level insider (who actually has administrative rights) as the threat agent; however, possible solutions that address this particular vulnerability include the addition of operating system *critical utility* authentication/validation and the requirement that a *second* administrative-level user enter his or her ID/password (or be biometrically scanned) before the replacement of a critical utility is effected (similar to the two-man rule used in the military for authorizing dangerous actions).

Inside the operating system, there are usually different levels of access rights, based on the authorization level assigned to a program. Just as users may have more or less access, programs may also have different levels of access. When a user runs a given program, that program may be given the same rights as the user, or if it is a system utility program, it may have much higher access rights (but will be carefully designed to perform only predefined, well-tested functions). Thus, if a user develops and runs a program, that program can access the files of the user only and not those of other users. However, if the user (a hacker) can fool the operating system into thinking that their application is a system utility, then the application might access files and programs for which the user lacks access rights.

Hacker attacks like buffer overflow are intended to take advantage of these rules. If a hacker can corrupt a system program, by sending it too much data and overwriting its program logic, then the modified system program, which has high-level access rights, can do things that the user (hacker) couldn't do directly (e.g., cause a file in the user's account area to be written over a file in the operating system area, thus implanting a back door). The current strategy of fixing programs, once their vulnerability to a buffer overflow attack by hackers has been proven, is totally reactive. In the future, operating systems will need to be designed with protective measures that are proactive, so that critical programs/files can't be so easily replaced or modified (and if replaced or modified, so that the replacement is detected and the bad file is automatically quarantined).

One of the problems with protecting an operating system is that authentication and validation processes generally rely on the use of hash codes (with a resultant message authentication code or *message digest*), ciphers, and encryption keys. To be used, they need to be accessible to the operating system and its applicable utilities, which has typically meant having them stored in the computer somewhere. If they are in the computer, then they are subject to being found, read, and potentially modified, which make them a significant vulnerability. In the past couple of years, CPU chip makers have introduced the trusted platform module (TPM), a chip that incorporates a built-in factory installed encryption key and encryption algorithm. The operating system does not have access to the key and can merely submit data to the chip for encryption. Adoption of the TPM (or competing technologies) can aid in making operating systems more secure.

From a SCADA standpoint, the vulnerabilities of the operating system are not something that can easily (or ever) be corrected by the SCADA software provider. They rely on the operating system and the computer hardware platform to incorporate sufficient security. To date (and into the near term), this has been a potentially dangerous dependency. Thus, SCADA vendors rely on architectural strategies (e.g., full duplication) to attain the necessary reliability. Unfortunately, such strategies are mainly addressed at improving availability primarily based on the assumption of hardware failures. Mere duplication of equipment will not prevent a virulent worm from shutting down the primary system computers and then jumping over to the backup computers and doing the same. SCADA vendors need to take a very hard look at their redundancy schemes in light of the current range of potential cyber attack methodologies and malware.

Since attacks can come from the inside and since operating systems are not yet to the point of being self-defending, it is still a good idea to utilize virus scanning and N/HIDS technologies as a means to identify and eliminate various types of cyber threats.

TCP/IP

When the Internet was being initially developed and expanded (as [D]ARPANET), there was no need to make TCP/IP secure, since the network was government controlled and access was limited. [And hey, who wants to mess with the Department of Defense?] Even in the early 1990s, when the newly designated Internet was just beginning its exponential growth, there was little recognition of the eventual security vulnerabilities that would be exploited and of the evolution of an Internet subculture intent on abusing this technology. Since the early 1990s, there have been great strides made in securing IP communications and, as a result, in securing the Internet. Nevertheless, making IP secure doesn't happen by default.

Technologies such as advanced firewalls, VPN, public key encryption, and digital certificate-based authentication all require that someone design, implement, and maintain the necessary architecture and security configurations. As discussed previously, the use of digital certificate-based computer-to-computer authentication and session-based encryption keys (in other words, creating a VPN) can provide a very high level of security within a set of computers on a given network. Still, this means that every computer will need a digital certificate; that there are procedures for renewing, issuing, and revoking certificates; and that communication with other computers outside the VPN, will require special considerations. And VPN technology is powerless to prevent a DoS attack from clogging the network and bogging down the various computers. It also won't stop a worm or virus that gets into one of the VPN member computers from spreading the malware to the other members. (But firewalls might!)

TCP/IP networking is basically a message-transport and -delivery mechanism. The purpose of security, in this context, is to ensure that we don't accept messages from those with whom we don't need to communicate and that we make it nearly impossible for anyone not authorized to do so to read our messages. That is exactly what a VPN is intended to provide. If all of the computers in a SCADA system, including workstations, PCs, and servers (primary and backup) were participating in a VPN, it would be very difficult for an outsider to attack that system across the network. Since SCADA systems often have to interface with other systems (which may not be feasibly incorporated into the VPN of the SCADA system), firewall technologies are needed in order to secure those interconnections. Finally, even though these technologies make it very difficult for an attacker to succeed, it is still a good idea to utilize NIDS technologies—in particular, to detect insider attacks.

Where TCP/IP networking is taken to the field, the same basic security issues have even greater relevance. Unfortunately, the TCP/IP implementations in many of the IP-ready field devices (e.g., RTUs and PLCs) were done in a hurry, either by adding additional hardware that implements the protocol (essentially a single-board computer that functions as a protocol translator) or by patching in a third-party protocol stack. Such implementations may not be capable of supporting authentication and encryption functions and may be very vulnerable even to outmoded attacks (e.g., the ping of death or SYN flooding). In these cases, the protective measures described earlier (establishing a VPN) would have to be implemented within the router/firewall communications equipment that manages the communications interface to the field site. Many IP ready IEDs (including RTUs) do not have the robustness to survive various types of attacks and may be susceptible to DoS attacks and even the mere act of probing them with hacker tools.

Web Site/Server

A Web server is, by its very nature, intended to be connected to a network (up to and including the Internet) and made available to anyone who wishes to access the information (Web pages) it contains. A person accessing the Web site/server does not typically go through the same level of authentication and ID/password validation as a person attempting to log in to a computer system. In effect, a Web site is like a community bulletin board. Anyone who passes by can take a look. (A more secure variation of Web server/browser technology, based on a protocol called S-HTTP, does exist. But it is not as commonly used as ordinary HTTP.)

A great deal of attention has been focused on active content exploits that can be used by a malicious Web site to place malware onto the computer of a person browsing that Web site. When you browse a Web site, you actually are asking the Web server to send you a hypertext document (Web page) that your browser will display for you. A Web page can drag along a range of software that will be loaded into and executed by your browser, to add animation and interactivity to the Web page. It is common for a Web page to use Java applets, ActiveX controls, JavaScript, and Macromedia Flash to make the Web page more entertaining (and just as often, more annoying). Although these technologies (especially Java applets) are supposed to have security constraints, hackers have found ways to use such technologies to plant malware and spyware on your PC. In other words, these techniques are used by the malicious Web site to attack the visitors to that Web site. Since this book deals with SCADA systems, we are concerned with ways that an attacker could, via Web browser technology, penetrate a SCADA system that uses such technology to offer a user interface and system access. It is not likely that someone would set up a malicious SCADA system Web site to attack the system users.

Some SCADA systems interface with a separate (or corporate) Web server, to provide data to customers, clients, and partners. In these cases, selected data are used to update one or more Web pages, and the connection between the SCADA system and the Web server is (presumably) constrained to passing the specified data. There may be a firewall separating the Web server and the SCADA system in this configuration, or an intermediate relational database server may be used to isolate the two systems. Nevertheless, some mechanism is used to send updated information from the SCADA system to the Web server and needs to be secured. Typically, such an arrangement involves data flowing only *from* the SCADA system to the Web server; thus, the intervening firewall can often be configured to exclude incoming message traffic and connection requests. When Web sites are used to query backend systems (as might be the case with a SCADA system) and present requested data to a user, then there is always the possibility of badly designed Web pages that allow for SQL injection, Server Side Include injection, cookie poisoning (modification), and even HTML injection. These techniques can be used to send undesirable commands from or reveal supposedly inaccessible data to a suitably skilled attacker.

Some SCADA systems have incorporated Web technology as a means for providing operational HMI access to both local and remote users. SCADA systems often have one or more servers on a LAN: one might contain the real-time data from the RTUs; another server would store the historical data; and yet another server would hold the data from a process model or other advanced application. Getting all of these data onto a single HMI display is a complex task—made even more complex if multiple HMIs, some remotely located and communicating across a low-bandwidth WAN connection, need to have the same data. In the Unix world, the X-window standard offered a potential solution, although it wasn't initially designed to simultaneously connect to multiple servers concurrently; the same is true of Microsoft's remote console capability.

Now enter the World Wide Web. Web server and browser technologies offer a platform independent solution that easily supports all of the popular operating systems and computers (see fig. 16–1). In addition, a workstation can easily open multiple browser windows, or a multi-pane window, displaying Web content from different servers, concurrently. (A Web server is, by its very nature, designed to serve multiple clients concurrently.) Different SCADA vendors have implemented Web technologies, with varying degrees of integration, and some offer full-function HMIs (including operator alarming and controls) via Web displays and technology.

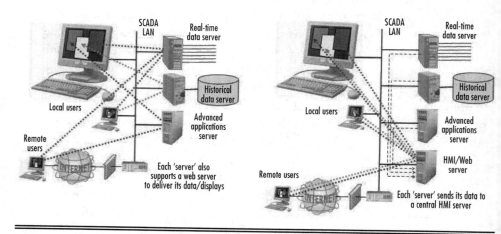

Fig. 16–1. *Distributed and centralized Web-based operational HMI architectures*

Unfortunately, conventional Web browser/server technologies, in and of themselves, are not very secure. Unless some means is provided to restrict the clients who can connect to a Web server, anyone with LAN/WAN access and a browser could, in theory, call up the same displays as a legitimate operator. Some SCADA vendors implement an ID/password scheme on their Web server, with scripting languages (e.g., PHP, VBScript, and/or JavaScript) and user account information stored in relational database tables on the server. Such schemes are susceptible to SQL injection attacks or to plain old password cracker software.

There are also numerous documented exploits that can be used to bring down most of the popular Web servers (thus blinding the operators). However, since Web browsing depends on IP networking, the technologies that secure IP networks (authentication, encryption, and VPN) can also be used to protect Web-based HMI servers. If all of the operator workstation/PC clients are part of a VPN with the Web server, it would be nearly impossible for an outsider (a workstation/PC outside the VPN) to access the Web server, because its attempts to establish a communications connection would be rebuffed. Still, this doesn't provide protection against an insider attack, because the insider would have access to workstations/PCs that were included within the VPN.

Protecting the SCADA system from abuse of the operator interface/HMI by an insider is a totally different problem and deserves specific discussion. The general issue of operator console/access security is addressed later in this section. Use of VPN technology provides authentication of the workstation/PC, as well as security (through encryption) of the message traffic. (It is assumed that the user of the workstation/PC would have already been authenticated in some strong manner.) The exchange of messages between a Web server and browser is generally done using HTTP, which is not in and of itself secure.

There are two available enhancements for securing Web browser connections: HTTP/S and S-HTTP. The first, HTTP/S, is actually just HTTP sent across a connection that has first been made secure via SSL (only with a temporary, 40-bit or 128-bit session encryption key); in HTTP/S, the Web server will supply the browser (client) with a digital certificate for authentication purposes (and for delivery of the public encryption key), but the browser does not have to reciprocate, providing no proof of whether the browser/client can be trusted. The second, S-HTTP, is similar except that both the browser and the server provide certificates for authentication purposes; that is equivalent to the requirements for a VPN and thus is much more suitable for securing the Web server. If Web browser technology is part of the operator console mechanisms of a SCADA system, then it needs to be secured.

Relational Databases

SCADA system vendors have also adopted commercial relational database packages as a means to store historical trend data, in addition to the numerous other types of data, logs, events, and alarms that are accumulated in a SCADA system. Relational database packages readily accommodate huge amounts of data and make it easy to organize and search such data. In many SCADA systems, the relational database is actually relegated to a separate server on the SCADA LAN, and data are exchanged via messages sent between various applications and the relational database server. Because of the popularity of Microsoft operating systems, their SQL Server relational database package (specifically targeted by the Slammer worm) has gained wide acceptance. In the Unix world, there are also many relational database packages, including open source packages such as MySQL.

The connection between relational database packages and the applications that send them data (request data from them) is made via messages exchanged across the LAN. Depending on the operating system platform and the programming language used, the API may be Microsoft's ODBC (or OLE DB), Java's JDBC, or even via XML. In any case, these messages are not specifically secure and can be sniffed and forged. The messages usually contain commands in SQL going to the relational database server and ASCII text messages (containing the results of the query) being returned (see fig. 16–2). Usually, at system startup, there will also be messages sent to the relational database server to establish connections. These usually carry ID/password information in clear ASCII text. If the connection between the relational database server and the various servers running applications that generate/require data are not secured, then there is ample opportunity for an attacker (particularly an evil insider) to eavesdrop on and record database transactions and user ID information. (It should be noted that most relational database vendors have recently added levels of authentication and encryption to their products, but legacy systems may not always be able to incorporate and make use of these new capabilities.)

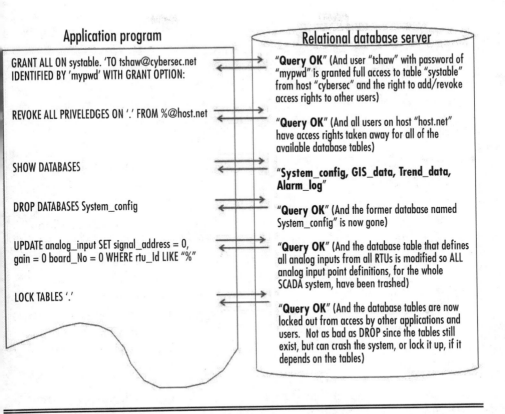

FIG. 16–2. *SQL message formats and database response messages*

This connection provides a weakness that can be exploited by a skilled attacker, who could create and send to the relational database server a set of messages causing it to erase or modify important data. Although they were discussed earlier, in the section on Web server technology, SQL injection attacks are actually a means for getting into a relational database through the connection between the Web pages and the associated relational database. Many Web sites offer displays that are populated by data extracted from a relational database. Web server scripting languages like PHP make it easy to create interactive Web pages that accept user inputs, use these inputs to query a relational database, and then return the results of the query for display on the Web page. An SQL injection attack is a means for sneaking SQL commands past the validity checking logic of a Web site, so that these commands are handed over to the relational database to execute. Never forget that a simple SQL command ("DROP DATABASE *name*;") can wipe out the specified database and all of the data and tables therein. (So making and retaining regular, frequent backups is a very good way to insure your ability to recover.)

This raises an important point: it may seem highly unlikely that a SCADA system can be taken out of operation because of the corruption or loss of data in its historical/relational database server. This would be true except in cases in which essential system configuration information is also maintained in relational database tables. Some SCADA vendors have taken full advantage of the power and flexibility of relational databases and have begun maintaining other information (database tag information, user ID/password information, system hardware configuration settings, etc.) in these databases. If an attacker were able to corrupt the appropriate files and then force a system restart, the SCADA system could be shut down until suitable uncorrupted backup files could be located and used to restore the proper data settings.

Advanced applications also use relational databases to hold their current information set, as well as the results of their computations. In SCADA systems that have HMIs based on GIS maps (as do many electrical EMS systems and some pipeline control systems), the enormous quantity of geospatial information used to draw the maps and of position information within them is usually stored in relational database tables. Thus, there are numerous potential SCADA system operational dependencies related to the integrity and availability of information maintained within relational databases. Relational databases can be protected by duplication (shadowing) and/or by making backup copies on a regular basis. (This doesn't actually protect the databases, it just makes it possible to recover if one is damaged or destroyed.) Attackers can be kept from recording and reading messages by the use of encryption and can be prevented from sending false messages by the use of encryption and by host authentication (VPN technology).

In setting up access rights and privileges, it is also wise to severely restrict the users and applications that are granted the right to use dangerous SQL commands, such as DROP and GRANT. There have been vulnerabilities discovered in the underlying technologies used for connecting application programs to relational databases, such as Microsoft's ODBC and ActiveX controls. Microsoft and other vendors continue to implement security patches and enhancements in an effort to eliminate vulnerabilities. Keeping the SCADA system up to date with the latest vendor software patches is a tiresome but critical activity.

OPC

In the SCADA market, there are off-the-shelf, commercial software packages that run on a Microsoft (so-called Wintel) operating system platform and provide a range of SCADA functions and capabilities. Likewise, there are field devices—such as RTUs, PLCs and other smart instruments—that have data to offer these software packages. To connect the two, the OPC interfacing standard was developed in the 1980s. As the full name (OLE for Process Control) implies, a major technology underlying this interface standard was the object-linking and -embedding (OLE) mechanism for allowing one application to be called upon by another to process data and deal with the data objects for which the application called upon was designed. This technology also relied on Microsoft's DCOM as a communications protocol for applications to use in negotiating with one another (which used Microsoft RPC0 remote procedure calls which have known vulnerabilities). OPC has evolved over the years and currently includes several classes of servers that can offer differing types of data (see fig. 16–3). In a SCADA system based on OPC, there will be clients (e.g., an HMI display running on a PC) that need data and servers (e.g., a server that is polling RTUs and maintaining a real-time database of values) that can provide data.

OPC (using the underlying DCOM services) allows these clients and servers to locate each other, resolve names, request services, establish a persistent connection, and transfer data as appropriate or as requested. OPC was designed to be efficient, reliable, and flexible. If a connection

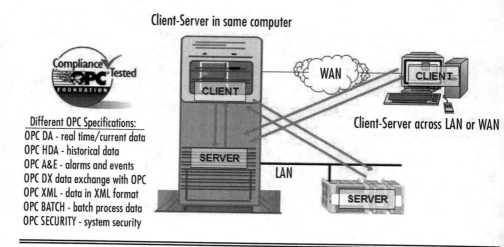

FIG. 16–3. *Classes of OPC servers and client/server relationship*

is lost, it should automatically be restored. If a client uses a nonstandard TCP port number, it will be allowed anyway. Unfortunately, these very attributes make OPC (and DCOM) far too easy to subvert. Numerous viruses and worms have targeted DCOM services, and when those underlying processes are disabled, they take OPC down with them.

Any application with appropriately written code can issue requests to identify and connect with most available OPC servers, because of a lack of rigorous application-to-application authentication (as opposed to computer-to-computer or domain-to-domain authentication). In fact, a DoS-style attack can be created by making continuous server requests to one or more OPC servers. (This was discovered by accident, owing to badly written code containing an infinite loop.) The committee responsible for OPC, the OPC Foundation, is earnestly working to correct these vulnerabilities, but much of that effort is contingent on the assumption that Microsoft will add the necessary security features. The OPC Foundation has been moving their technology away from the DCOM platform and toward the Microsoft.NET architecture for many of these reasons. (In addition, because they are tied to Microsoft, they thus have to follow where Microsoft goes.) Finally, it must be remembered that even though future versions of OPC will undoubtedly incorporate more security mechanisms, there exists a large installed base of systems and applications that will take time and effort to upgrade (assuming that upgrading is possible).

DCOM

DCOM was developed to allow the sharing of distributed objects and provide a range of services among distributed applications. DCOM requires a number of TCP ports for locating and identifying computers and applications, resolving names, requesting services, performing authentication functions, and sending and receiving data, among other activities. If these ports are not available, DCOM—in an effort to be robust, flexible, and reliable—will automatically search for other ports.

DCOM also supports remote procedure calls (RPCs), which give a program on computer A the ability to call a software function located on computer B. Although this capability represents a very powerful mechanism for distributed computing architectures, it is a significant security vulnerability. DCOM is so widespread as the underlying communication mechanism for Windows-based functions that it is difficult to adequately monitor and control (from a cybersecurity standpoint). Because there is no guarantee which ports DCOM will use (although a standard default set are defined for every application that uses DCOM), communicating through firewalls can become a problem, causing NIDS packages to initiate alarms. Moreover, since many functions share a common set of ports, firewall and NIDS packages can't tell the difference between allowed and disallowed ports.

Since Microsoft has based all of its advanced object linking and embedding on the underlying functionality of DCOM and since DCOM is well documented and available for custom application development, DCOM has been an obvious target for hackers. (Numerous attacks against a wide range of Microsoft-based systems have exploited DCOM vulnerabilities.) Microsoft is well aware of the issues and, in the most recent versions of the Windows operating systems, has been migrating away from DCOM and toward their .NET architecture (which supports features that address many of the extant security issues).

Having capabilities and properly implementing and configuring them are two different things. Never forget that security features need to be enabled and properly configured (setting up the rules in a firewall) in order to do their job.

X-Window

In the Unix world, one of the basic technologies for user interaction with a computer is the X-Window HMI. (This is a slight misnomer since the actual interactions take place between the window manager—e.g. Motif, FVWM, Sawfish, or Blackbox—and the user. The X-Window functions constitute the underlying technology that enables the window managers.) The X-Window System allowed for the separation of the physical workstation/terminal hardware and the HMI software, by defining a virtual abstraction level that could be emulated by any reasonably modern terminal device.

Another aspect of the X-Window System decomposes user-system interactions into two components: clients and servers (although they did get the definitions of these two components backward.) An especially powerful result of this decomposition was that clients and servers did not have to be running on the same computer; they could be separated by a network connection. The result is that in nearly every Unix-based SCADA system, the operator HMI will be an X-Window–based device, whether an actual X-terminal, a PC, or a workstation running X-Window software. This is a powerful and flexible design, because X-Windows based workstations can be local (on the LAN) or remote (over a WAN connection) and can be redirected from a primary sever to a backup (for redundancy purposes), either automatically or with a simple command.

Unfortunately, as with so much of the important technology, the X-Window System does not include any integral security features. The communications are in a nonsecure, X11 protocol (unless launched via an SSH session), and because it is assumed that a user will need to log in with an ID and password (or use those facilities within SSH), there is no integral authentication process. X11 sessions are easy to sniff and to hijack.

If X-terminal devices (*thin client*—in other words, dumb) are used, then there is no way to implement any VPN functions (or support for SSH) within that device. (An X-terminal device typically implements TCP/IP and the X11 protocol, but not the full IP suite of protocols and applications.) If the X-terminal device is remotely located, the WAN, equipment (routers) can be used to implement a VPN tunnel. If on a LAN, the X11 packets will be available for all to see and sniff. If full-function workstations are used as operator consoles, then these can implement SSH (or participate in a VPN), and their X-Window functions/communications will be secured (although operator access may still be protected merely by an ID/password login process).

Firewalls

As has been mentioned, any time there is a connection between the SCADA system's LAN/WAN and an external network or computer, that connection needs to be guarded and the proper technology for this purpose is the firewall. Firewalls are not specifically a physical device, but rather a set of functions that can be implemented in a device like a router or cable modem. That doesn't mean that you won't find firewalls sold as a specialized stand-alone network appliance, just that it isn't a requirement. But, depending on the vendor, a network appliance may use a proprietary operating system, which makes them far more immune to being attacked by a hacker or virus. Firewalls look at message traffic (individual IP packets) and make the basic decision to allow or disallow the passage of each such packet. In an earlier section of the book the seven layer ISO/OSI model was discussed and described. Firewalls are often differentiated based on how much of an inspection they can perform on a given packet. They will be described as a layer 3, layer 4, layer 5, or layer 7 firewall. All this means is that as you go to higher levels, the firewall knows more about IP and IP connection status, about specific protocols and port numbers, and about valid message syntax. Today you will even hear about deep-inspection firewalls that receive the entire message (not just the individual packets) and reassemble it and then check it for malicious content before sending it on to the destination. Note that as firewalls get to higher levels of analysis, they use more processing power and introduce more communications latency (delay). Unfortunately as hackers have gotten ever more clever, firewalls have needed to do the same. Firewalls need configuration in order to work properly and they need updating to stay up with the latest attacks. If you don't deal with both of these issues, then your firewall can end up looking like Swiss cheese, rather than an impregnable wall, to a talented hacker. Firewalls that know about protocols (application proxy) don't exist for the specialized IP protocols used by SCADA systems, like ICCP, UCA2, and IP-DNP.

Placement of firewalls is critical as well. If you have a shared server, as part of a SCADA system, that needs to be accessed by the SCADA system and an external system (for example a historian or Web server), a good strategy is to always create a hackers no-man's land by placing the server outside the SCADA system network, on the other side of a firewall, and then placing yet another firewall on the side of the server that connects to the external network. This bookend-like arrangement (called setting up a DMZ) is popular with IT folks (and manufacturers of firewall technology) because when properly done it gives you the ability to safely communicate with the shared server, while keeping your network well isolated. If the shared server has totally separate network interfaces and all routing is disabled, then security is further improved. In other cases where there is no shared server, just a dedicated connection to an external system, then a single firewall (preferably at *each* end of the link) will have to suffice. It may be enough to just have a firewall on the SCADA system end, but dual firewalls should prevent malware or an attacker from reaching your system by going through the system at the other end of the link (and vice versa!). Never forget that firewalls have been around for a while, and yet hackers and malware keep getting through. There is a constant battle and it would be foolish to believe that a firewall, no matter how expensive and well maintained, is the only protection you require.

Traditional Security Features of SCADA Systems

Traditionally, SCADA systems (and DCS) have incorporated few, if any, security features. As was briefly mentioned in the introduction, the computer automation community (vendors and users both) didn't even recognize the need for security—other than to protect against human error, tampering, and accidental misuse—prior to the events of 9/11. Some industries do deal in proprietary and confidential information within their automation systems, such as product formulations and power generating schedules, but many do not. The SCADA vendor community has been scrambling to catch up ever since the sad and tragic events of that day and still has a long ways to go before SCADA systems can claim cybersecurity to be a central, integral function and capability. As a general rule in SCADA system operations, if you are an insider (an employee of the organization or even a contractor), then you are considered to be trustworthy; the security of most SCADA systems is, to a large degree, dependent on the veracity of that assumption.

Procedures and Policies

Because SCADA systems have not been designed with integral security features and technologies, the actual security of such a system and facility, at least for the time being, depends heavily on the training, alertness, diligence, and intelligence of the operational personnel. The vast majority of SCADA systems that monitor and control critical infrastructure have been operating successfully, day in and day out for many years, without problems. However, that fact can be attributed to luck alone; had these SCADA systems been subject to an actual attack, the results might not have been acceptable, either from the purely financial standpoint or from the impact on society.

Aside from a cyber attack, such operations need to be ready to deal with the loss of essential personnel owing to such normal events as job changes, promotions, sickness, and retirement. This is where the development of policies, standards, baselines, and training programs, in addition to the documentation of procedures, comes into play. If an essential procedure is well documented and practiced at least occasionally, then the loss of any individual from the company, for whatever reason, should not seriously threaten the viability or security of a SCADA operation. Hiring policies and practices (e.g., background checks) can aid in establishing the trustworthiness of a prospective employee, and regular training can make all employees better able to deal with the changing threats. While SCADA vendors are working on technical solutions to make SCADA systems more robust, organizations can use procedural and managerial strategies to augment their cybersecurity.

User Access

In almost all SCADA systems, the task of ensuring that only authorized personnel have access to and use of the various utilities and services that compose the system, falls to the user login process. This has typically been a simple user-specific or job-category based ID/password sequence. Many SCADA vendors allow for job-category-based user accounts. Thus, all operators log in with the user ID and password assigned to "operator." In many control rooms, the operator workstations remain logged in for long periods of time, and users don't bother logging on to, or off of, the system. Many SCADA systems have had the same user IDs and passwords since the systems were initially installed. You can go into some control rooms and find ID/password information stuck to a convenient surface, scribbled on a Post-it note. Few if any SCADA systems place limits on the number of login attempts by operational personnel, since the danger of locking out an operator is unacceptable. (This may not be the case for other classes of system user, such as an application programmer.) Some systems might generate an alarm if excessive login attempts are detected. In the past couple of years, some SCADA vendors have added optional capabilities to support strong authentication (e.g., a magnetic ID card in addition to a password, or possibly biometric devices) for user login.

User access for system administration, system configuration, and application program development is usually protected in the same manner—that is, with a user ID and password. However, these may be operating system logins, rather than SCADA system logins, and thus will be governed by the user permission settings of the operating system (some of which do support account lockout triggered when a user makes an excessive number of failed login attempts). Some SCADA system vendors provide *operator tracking,* which is a function that maintains an audit log of the actions taken by operational personnel ("started a pump at time X:XX"; "acknowledged alarms and silenced the annunciation at time Y:YY"; etc.). If a N/HIDS system is added to a SCADA system, it can be important that this log be part of what the H/NIDS application monitors.

For the other categories of user access (programmer, administrator, etc.), there may or may not be entries created in the operating system's audit log(s), depending on the actions taken and the authority level of the individuals. Note that with administrative rights, a user can access and edit/delete the system logs, thus bypassing this protective measure; such a user could also delete critical files and programs and shut down the system. The N/HIDS application, if added to a SCADA system, should definitely monitor the system logs of all SCADA system computers and workstations and watch for suspicious activity such as logs being deleted.

System Configuration

In most SCADA systems, the utilities that set and modify system configuration data are restricted by user ID (or job classification), because they can modify, corrupt, or even destroy the system's configuration tables if used improperly. Configuration utilities are the programs that establish all of the customer-specific system settings: I/O points, calculations, alarms and alarm presentation, custom graphic and configurable displays, trending assignments, communication channels and RTU scanning priorities, user login accounts, and so forth. Most SCADA system vendors provide extensive customer training and user documentation on these utilities, even when the vendor takes the responsibility for implementing the (initial) system configuration.

The system configuration data are usually stored in multiple files or tables, based on the type of data involved and the utility program that manipulates that data. There may be linkages between the data in various files/tables such that making a modification to one type of data requires making a change to others. A good example would be defining input points, a process which includes assigning them *tag names* (which would be stored in a single table/file). Once defined, those database point tag names could then be used in the creation of dynamic graphic displays or in user-defined computations (which would be stored in other tables/files). Depending on the SCADA system vendor, such data relationships and dependencies will be managed either automatically or through a great deal of manual effort. (E.g., attempting to delete a database point that is being referenced in computations might cause an alert to the user, asking for verification: "Do you *really* want to delete this point definition?")

The crux of the matter is that maintaining the integrity of these configuration data repositories,—and ensuring their coordinated modification—is critical to the proper functioning of a SCADA system. Most vendors will place as many error checks and warning messages as possible into the utilities used for system configuration maintenance, primarily to defend against human error (typing errors, spelling errors, etc.). Some systems will make the requested changes but provide for a limited *rollback* capability so that these configuration changes can be undone. (This rollback facility may not be available, however, with all of the various configuration utilities of a given SCADA system.) With other SCADA systems, the vendor-recommended procedure is to make changes to the off-line (standby) system and then, before rolling them out to the production system, to check and verify these modifications as thoroughly as possible. Some vendors will strongly advise making a backup of system configuration files on a frequent basis, during times when configuration changes are being made, so that errors can be corrected by reloading the prior copy. The problem with erroneous configuration data is that the errors may not be obvious or detectable by the system. Such errors have existed in running systems for years, prior to anyone eventually noticing. About the only way to find such errors is to perform a signal-by-signal end-to-end test of the system; something that can be done on the manufacturer's factory floor, but not once the system is in operation. If the SCADA system's various configuration utilities don't or can't provide reasonability and validity checks on change requests, then the next best strategy is to have a procedure that has a second individual verify and review the changes to be made. This also makes it far more difficult for an evil insider to intentionally corrupt the configuration data files and tables.

Organizations with large and complex SCADA systems often establish procedural strategies to minimize the possibility of fouling up the running system with improperly implemented configuration changes. (As with all procedures, they achieve their goal only if properly followed.) Some systems support both online configuration changes and off-line configuration changes. Online means that the changes take effect immediately, as they are entered into the configuration utility. Off-line means that the changes to be made are recorded in some manner, and the actual implementation will be done, as an additional step, at some preferable future time (e.g., the middle of the night). During the initial commissioning of a SCADA system, the online mode is highly useful and expeditious. However, once a system is operationally stable, the off-line mode of making configuration changes, with a manual verification by a second person inserted in the middle of the two steps, may be preferable (and less risky).

All of these approaches assume the good intensions (and proper training) of the personnel using the configuration utilities and provide no additional restrictions to usage once a suitably authorized user ID and password have been supplied. The protective mechanisms provided exist so that a well-intentioned user can undo a mistake, rather than to identify and prevent modifications that could damage the system (e.g., deleting all of the configuration information).

Application Development

The development, testing, and deployment of application programs is a sophisticated process that requires both programming skills and process knowledge. Use of the SCADA system's application development tools is usually restricted to trained personnel by means of suitably authorized user ID and password access. (Again, these tend to be operating system user IDs and not SCADA system user IDs; thus, operating system access controls come into play.) Most SCADA systems provide some mechanism that enables user-written programs to access the SCADA information (e.g., current real-time values for all I/O points)—for example, either a subroutine library used in the programs or a system service (e.g., OPC) *called* to acquire the specified data.

Most systems also offer a means for application programs to issue supervisory control commands to the field devices, much as can be done through the operational HMIs. Some systems provide a very wide range of access to application programmers: access configuration files, communication drivers, HMIs, and alarms and logs, among other things. It is assumed that the programmers' skills and experience will be sufficient to keep them from causing damage. In many major SCADA operating environments, application programming is done on the backup system, and new applications are rolled out to the production system only once they have been thoroughly tested. Still, even the best-written and -tested application program can have bugs (or worse still, an intentionally embedded time bomb) that might appear after the application has been in use for a while.

Some SCADA vendors provide high-level scripting languages for user-defined applications, to control and restrict the supervisory control and information access of application programs. These scripting languages place restrictions on what an application can do and what it can access, and they eliminate a lot of the bugs that occur in programs written in lower-level languages. To be useful, however, these scripting languages need to provide supervisory control access and access to relevant system data sources. Scripting languages are generally used to make application programming less complex and less buggy, but not to keep the applications from being useful. Of course, if the SCADA system's operating system vendor includes generalized programming tools (a text editor, a C compiler, a linker, a debugging utility, etc.), then a suitably skilled programmer could still develop application programs that perform actions beyond what is supported by the scripting language.

Some SCADA end-user organizations establish procedures for the design, peer-review, testing, and rollout of application programs, to eliminate (or at least minimize) application programming problems. Too many organizations lack the staff to implement such procedures, regardless of written policies calling for their observance. Most SCADA systems don't have any built-in automatic mechanisms that control or audit the installation of new application programs or the modification of existing ones.

System Physical Security

Most owners and operators of SCADA systems have upgraded their physical security so that the control room and the computer room (if separate) are physically isolated from the rest of the facility. It is not uncommon to see electronic key card systems used to control access to these rooms/floors. It is less common to see the key card system differentiate between categories of employees. There is a good chance that the same key cards that let employees of an organization into the building will also allow them into restricted areas. In cases where such a distinction is made, the procedures for the granting and revoking of access rights are not rigorous. When individual access rights are upgraded to provide temporary entry to the restricted areas, it is rare for those rights to be reviewed and revoked in the future.

Some SCADA system owners have adopted the recommendations of the NERC with regard to the establishment of a physical security perimeter by placing supervision (guard or closed-circuit television) on all entrances to the restricted areas. If entrances aren't supervised, then it may be possible for unauthorized personnel to gain access through the aid of authorized personnel (using social engineering tricks). Essential

SCADA support subsystems—such as electrical power, HVAC, and communications—are not always protected from physical access, because they are situated in common/public areas (or are not considered during security planning). In too many instances, it is possible to shut down the SCADA operation by merely pulling the fire alarm and setting off the overhead sprinklers. Information that would be invaluable to an attacker, like database dumps and backup copies of the system's configuration files, might be found in plain sight, on bookshelves in a corridor or piled up in the corner of an employee's office, where no physical security is present. Physical security has been heavily dependent on the general trustworthiness of organizational personnel and contractors.

Communications

In a SCADA system, communications security encompasses the communications among the computers that form the SCADA system, communications between the primary SCADA site and any alternative site, communications between the SCADA system and other systems, and outgoing communications from the SCADA system to the field sites.

In most large organizations, there is an IT department that is responsible for the cybersecurity of firewalls, Web sites, internal servers, and the company LANs/WANs. In smaller organizations, where such an organization might not exist, and the problem of communications security will fall on the SCADA system staff, who may have to rely on outside vendors to supply the necessary skills and expertise.

Many IT people have little experience with SCADA systems and do not comprehend the operational differences between corporate IT systems and a SCADA system (and based on the convergence of the underlying technologies, that is somewhat understandable). Solutions that work in the IT world may be incompatible with the SCADA system. For example, in the IT world a matched pair of encrypting modems, which perform message-by-message encryption and use out-of-band messaging to negotiate encryption keys, might be applied to secure a serial communication circuit (and the modems would be set to run at the maximum possible baud rate). By contrast, the RTU protocol of a SCADA system might not tolerate the time delays introduced by such modems (and because of the problem of operating at 1,200 baud, there would be little bandwidth available for out-of-band messages). In general, most IT groups have a basic and adequate knowledge of LAN technologies, but may not have any serious depth of experience in WANs and particularly in old-fashioned analog telecommunications. Serial protocols, RTUs, and analog telephony are all topics that tend to be unknown in the IT world. These are essential to SCADA systems and, as corporations reorganize and down size, there is often an assumption that anything technical can be handled by IT.

Another issue with communications security is that any security technology applied (firewalls, digital certificates, intrusion-detection systems, etc.) will require maintenance and ongoing support for updates and modifications. You can't just put up a firewall and then forget about it. If nothing else, you need someone knowledgeable to review the logs and alarms that most of these technologies generate and to install updates as new malware threats are identified. If a N/HIDS package is added to the SCADA system then these protective devices need to be included in the data gathering and analysis process as well.

Most SCADA systems today will have no communications security on the LAN for message traffic among the SCADA system's various computers. If there is a backup operating site, the communication link to that site may have some level of security, such as link encryption between the routers at each end of the circuit. Many SCADA systems don't even have that in place, because of the assumption that a leased telecom circuit is supposedly secret and thus impossible to attack. Very few SCADA systems have any form of security on the serial communications (polling circuits) to the field devices (RTU/PLC), although specialized encryption devices have come onto the market in the past two years. Where SCADA systems have to interface other networks and other systems, a firewall will generally be in place to protect the SCADA system. The efficacy of these firewalls is debatable, and many are not kept up to date with security patches, especially in organizations that brought in outside vendors or contractors to initially set up such equipment and that lack an internal group with the expertise to provide ongoing support.

When a SCADA system migrates to IP-based protocols and networking for field equipment (e.g., IP to the substation), the same technologies that can be used to secure any IP network connection can be applied to securing the field equipment. Although most of the IP-ready RTUs and PLCs on the market today can't support such advanced features as the protocols used to set up a VPN, the routers that invariably are placed in the field to receive the telecommunication link *can* be equipped for a VPN (although this may require upgrading the router).

Remote Access

In the 1990s, it was very popular for SCADA system vendors to provide remote access over telephone lines (and eventually over the Internet), as a means to offer technical support and perform diagnostic activities without having to rush to an airport and fly across the country. Purchasers of SCADA systems often required a technical-support response-time guarantee in their procurement contracts, and the only practical way to meet that requirement was to offer remote dial-in (telephone) connectivity. For these reasons, a lot of SCADA systems were supplied with an auto-answer telephone modem that was connected into the customer's telephone system. With X-Terminal devices (or remote console support), it was possible to connect to a remote SCADA system and see the same HMI displays as the operators or to access the system utilities available to a local user.

SCADA system owners were quick to realize that the capability for remote access allowed them to connect to their own system from home when they received that inevitable call for help at 1:00 AM. So they added more dial-in circuits. This capability was further enhanced with the advent of the Internet. However, remote access represents a very dangerous vulnerability that cyber attackers might exploit.

Unfortunately, SCADA system owners still rely on remote support from their vendors and need occasional remote access themselves. The problem with these connections is that if a hacker finds the modem, all that protects the system is a user login process (for details, see the discussion of war dialing in chap. 6). Strategies to secure these remote access facilities include using dial-back modems (which can be thwarted by call forwarding), instituting procedures for manual connection of modems when connectivity is needed (which inevitably get left connected and forgotten), and switching to encrypting modems (which can be a problem if multiple remote users share a common dial-in connection).

It is usually possible to convert the telephone connection to an IP-based LAN-to-LAN connection by using commercially available routers that support dial-out and that incorporate authentication and encryption (see fig. 17–1). This approach at least provides end-to-end authentication (between the routers) and message encryption, in addition to the user login requirement (i.e., it creates a VPN tunnel). This approach also works for the remote user who connects across a network, including the Internet. Then again, if this equipment falls into the wrong hands (or an insider turns to the dark side of the force), you are back to having nothing but the user ID/password process to keep an attacker at bay.

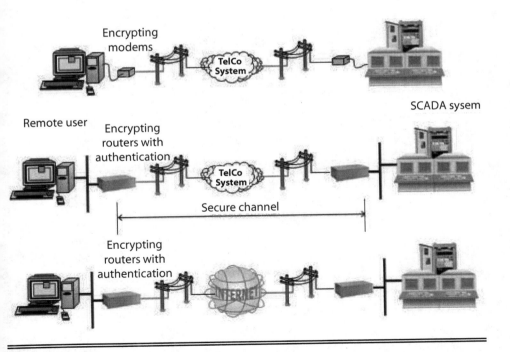

FIG. 17–1. *Securing remote user access to SCADA systems*

Interoperability

SCADA systems often interface other systems, to receive data and/ or to provide data to those other systems. Those other systems might be business systems, such as a billing or inventory management system, or operational support systems, such as a work order management or (electric power) outage management system. SCADA system owners have long understood the risks of connecting a production SCADA system to other systems, even when the perceived risk was just based on possible programming errors or electrical/communication problems that could have an impact on the SCADA system.

Today it is understood that the number of threats—and the number of types of threats—is much greater and that targeted threats could be specifically aimed at SCADA systems. Connections to other systems (and networks) are potential points of entry for attacking a SCADA system. The kinds of connectivity used to interoperate between a SCADA system and other systems fall into three broad categories (see fig. 17–2):

- Proprietary application-specific interfaces

- Interfaces based on standard protocols other than IP or networking protocols

- Interfaces using IP and/or other networking technologies (such as Ethernet)

Older SCADA systems (from the 1970s and 1980s) may have custom-developed interfaces that were put in place prior to the widespread adoption of Ethernet LAN and TCP/IP WAN technologies. These are usually point-to-point connections using either a serial port or bidirectional parallel port to make the electrical connection and using custom-developed applications to exchange data. These interfaces are not generally a risk, as they can't be subverted to other purposes. Nevertheless, the application program in the other system could, in theory, be replaced with one that attempts to send data in a manner that crashes the SCADA system's corresponding application (and maybe the SCADA system itself); that is a very low-probability scenario, however. (Partly because it is doubtful that anyone

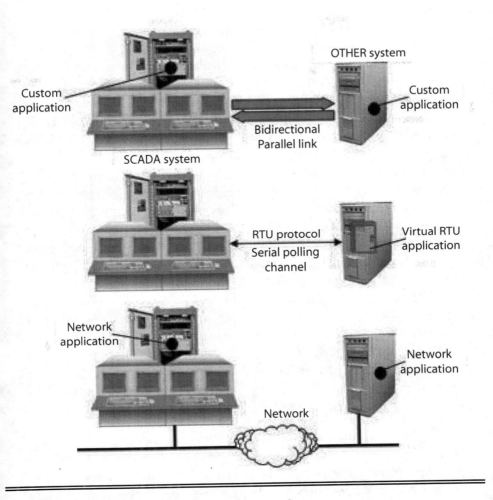

FIG. 17–2. *Three approaches for intersystem data exchange*

could even locate a copy of the source code for both of the custom-developed application programs.) But, older programs of the type described were usually developed without any logic to check the amount and validity of data being transferred. (This poor programming style has led to the problem of buffer overflow attacks used by hackers today.) As unlikely as it might seem, there is potential for a buffer overflow attack, if anyone still remembers how to make program changes on the other system.

A fair number of SCADA systems use RTU protocols as a means for exchanging data with other systems. That makes sense because the protocol drivers and the ability to receive and process the data already exist in the SCADA system. The other system merely implements a protocol driver and pretends to be an RTU (acts as a virtual RTU). The functions and capabilities of that type of interconnection are restricted by the specific protocol used, but other than taking over the link and sending bad data, there is nothing much an attacker could do to threaten the SCADA system through such a connection. Most protocols had very specific error checking and maximum data buffer sizes limits that would preclude an attacker from attempting to do much more than· send bad data to the SCADA system. Having said that, if the SCADA system were equipped to send out emergency shut down commands of some type, based on receiving some type of data over this link, then an attacker could theoretically trigger this action, if they knew enough about the data link to know how to do this, and knew that such a function existed in the SCADA system (a lot of "ifs" that make this type of attack a low probability). Here we are assuming that the connected system is *not* a control system itself (such as a pump station or treatment plant DCS). If it were, then the attacker might be trying to control that system by attacking the interconnection. This discussion deals with attempting to damage the SCADA system by manipulating the messages going across the inter-system data link.

By contrast, any time you use a networking technology to connect a SCADA system to another system, you create the possibility for that network connection to be used by someone other than the intended party. Also, a general purpose network often supports remote access to operating system services, something you definitely do not want to allow.

With a network connection, it becomes possible for an attacker to get physically connected (from his own computer) to the network or run utilities or applications on the other system, to connect through the network to the SCADA system. Remember that a network connection usually allows multiple simultaneous communication sessions. Thus, while the SCADA system and the other system exchange data, the attacker will be sitting on a terminal attached to the other system and playing with the file manager on the SCADA system.

In current SCADA systems, where a network connection is used, the main protective measure is to place a firewall between the two systems (really between the SCADA system and the network), to block unwanted message traffic (from untrusted IP addresses and/or to ports that are not allowed). A stronger mechanism to protect the network itself would be to set up a VPN with the other system and use authentication and encryption for the message traffic between the two systems. This doesn't prevent the situation described above of an attacker (who is allowed on or has gained access to the connected system) using the connected system to break into the SCADA system. This assumes that the network is TCP/IP based, which is probably true of any system produced in the past decade. For older SCADA systems, however, the network connection could be via a legacy network like DECnet, SNA, or Token-Ring. These network technologies are problematic, because they have essentially been abandoned and nobody is developing security solutions for them. Here SCADA systems have to depend on the concept of *security due to obscurity*. By contrast, little capability exists with these proprietary networking architectures for remote access via message routing; therefore, an attack across such a network would have to be launched by an evil insider who has access to a computer that is part of the proprietary network (which may not provide sufficient comfort for most managers). Ideally, such connections ought to be replaced with ones that can be defended with current technology.

18

Eliminating the Vulnerabilities of SCADA Systems

Technical Security Strategies

In order for SCADA systems to ultimately attain a high level of cybersecurity and be resistant to cyber assaults—in particular, against insider attacks—more needs to be done to change the basic way in which these systems work. To date, most efforts aimed at improving cybersecurity have been on the level of *accessorization*—add a NIDS, erect a firewall, and/or run a virus scanner. This is understandable since major enhancements require significant redesigning of the software in a SCADA system. A large number of organizations are working on ways to improve the cybersecurity of SCADA systems and DCS. (For a list of these organizations, see app. F.) The following recommendations are intended to support their work and provide additional perspectives on ways to improve such systems.

The electronic perimeter

The term *electronic perimeter* is generally used to mean communication channels through which an attacker can reach the system, for the purpose of implanting malware or sending messages/commands that cause the system to fail. Under that definition, the securing of removable media connection points (USB and FireWire ports; floppy, CD, and DVD drives; etc.) ought to be included, along with wireless communications technologies. On a higher level, though, the issue is that it ought to be nearly impossible for new software to be added or for existing software to be modified without multiple levels of authorization, accompanied by strong-authentication methods. This would not truly represent an inconvenience, because in most cases, once SCADA systems are up and operating in a stable manner, it is highly desirable that no such changes be made unless there is a critical need because of an operational impact or security vulnerability being corrected.

It is far too easy to modify the critical software set of a SCADA system. The operating systems that underlie SCADA systems were designed for user convenience, not for self-defense. In a control system environment, it ought to be difficult to replace a program with a new version (i.e., essentially what happens when a virus attaches [appends] itself to a program file or when a hacker installs a replacement program with an embedded back door or Trojan). File read/write operations, as well as the file manager utility itself, need much more rigorous security restrictions. It is also worth considering a change in the way that *autorun* and *auto_boot* functions occur when removable media is inserted. These are convenient features, but too dangerous for critical systems. In effect, programs on the SCADA system, once tested and verified, ought not to be able to be modified, and new programs ought not to be added (or executed) without a rigorous procedure. Operating systems need security mechanisms that enable them to be able to detect any such software modifications or replacements (and those mechanisms need to be secure from tampering themselves).

Operational access

Since high-level user access to a SCADA system would be the ideal goal of an attacker (unless they just wanted to shut down the system), making it difficult to gain illegitimate user access ought to be a design priority. Features and capabilities that could be added to SCADA systems to further secure user access include

- *Dead man timers* on user login sessions, such that a user is automatically logged off the system after a given amount of time passes with no user activity (with an alert generated to supervisory personnel).

- Ability to schedule operator change-over times (e.g., at 5:00 p.m. every day) and require that a new login (or a re-login) be performed once those specified times are reached.

- Ability to predefine the operational personnel who should be logged on for given shifts and to generate an alert to supervisory personnel if actual user logins deviate from this plan.

- Use of biometrics (in conjunction with passwords or other mechanisms) for user identification/authentication, to eliminate the problem of compromised user information.

- Ranking of certain operational supervisory control functions as critical and requiring a second (possibly supervisory) authorization prior to execution. For safety's sake, such operations could initiate a supervisory alert and have a time-out that overrides the requirement for a second authorization.

- Making passwords expire after a given amount of time. (Unlike in business systems that use this sort of scheme, an expired SCADA password would still be accepted [until replaced], again for safety's sake, but its continued use would initiate a notification process alerting management personnel that the password is overdue to be changed and warning the user that this has occurred.)

- Although account lockout (after n failed login attempts) is a viable strategy for preventing password hacking/guessing, it probably would not be considered as safe for a SCADA system operator (although it would be a good strategy for other classes of SCADA system users). However, a strategy that initiates an immediate alert to supervisory personnel after n login attempts by an operator, possibly accompanied by audible annunciation, could improve system security. Having an alarm go off when thieves are detected trying to break into your home doesn't prevent the thieves from continuing their efforts, but the odds are good that they won't.

System programs and supervisory applications

All programs (including those that compose the operating system and the SCADA system functions) are normally stored on a computer as disk-based files. As such, they have descriptive information for users and the operating system to utilize in identifying, protecting, and managing those files/programs. A data structure containing this information for every file is also maintained on the system disk and is accessible (in theory) only by the operating system. These data usually include the file creation date/time, size, location, and so forth. It is possible to compute the equivalent of a message authentication code (MAC) for every program's initial load image and to retain these as a secure, encrypted cache. Then, the process of loading and executing a program could include recomputing that MAC value for verification. Modified or substituted programs would fail such a test. (The availability of a hardware security chip makes the encryption and key secure, so they can't be hacked.) Computer systems today are certainly fast enough to support making such a test without a noticeable loss in performance (degradation), especially if CPU vendors add special hardware features to support those calculations. Other steps that could be taken, as alternative approaches, include the following:

- The process of installing a new or modified application program should include multiple intermediate verification steps in which a third-party, preferably supervisory personnel, must authorize the completion of that step or the progression onto the subsequent step. Authorizations should involve (strong) authentication of the third party and their explicit, logged permission to proceed. This process would also generate and store the MAC for the program.

- If possible, an encrypted file system should be used for all critical system and application programs. Again, hardware support for encryption/decryption would make this transparent to the user and would prevent performance degradation.

- Application programming development tools should include a simulation mode in which application programs are supplied with real (or simulated) inputs but the control commands or parameter/setting changes that would normally occur are merely recorded and logged for later review.

- The running (production) SCADA system should not include any program development tools or utilities. All applications must be developed and tested elsewhere and added to the production system through a secure process based on documented procedures.

- Application program scanning tools could be used to identify the existence of code that is waiting for events or specific future times (time bombs) and could categorize the control and parameter-changing actions present in the program. These tools could also look for logic that would cause bulk changes (changes to a large number of settings of a given category or type) in configuration parameters.

- User application development tools could enforce calls to security (authorization) checking routines and safety/validity checking routines and inject mandated operator confirmation procedures whenever critical control actions are to be issued. In the same manner, access to system level objects and resources could be forced through security checks as well. In effect, this makes the tools available for user-written supervisory applications such that creating a malicious application is nearly impossible.

Configuration data

The current security mechanisms for system configuration changes generally amount to requiring a suitably authorized user ID and password. After that, all bets are off. Configuration settings are vital to proper system operation, and once established and suitably tested, they should not be easily modifiable. Actions that can be taken to secure the configuration settings include the following:

- All configuration utilities need to be a bit smarter in regard to changes that cause bulk modifications (e.g., that reset *all* analog input point engineering unit conversion scale factors to 0.0). They also need to have validity checking on all user input and require that exceeding the specified value range involve a second authorization, particularly on critical control values.

- All configuration utilities ought to incorporate an audit trail facility that can be used to undo (roll back) the changes they effect, preferably with that audit trail stored in the most secure manner possible, requiring several levels of authorization in order to be accessed.

- Certain types of configuration operations ought to require a second authorization (possibly even a supervisor's) in order to be permitted, particularly if they are being made in online mode.

- The configuration process should be broken into two phases: first, define the changes to be made; then, audit those changes prior to making them. Require that the two phases be carried out by different personnel. In effect, once the system is stable, force configuration changes to be made only in off-line mode, and insert a validation and authorization step in the middle.

- Store all backup/initialization data on configuration settings in an encrypted form, with a MAC to validate the integrity of the data. In many systems, there is a cold start/restart set of configuration settings, used to bring the system up from a nonoperational state, and a running set of configuration settings (initially set from the cold start/restart set.) If the running set becomes corrupted, it is essential to be able to restore them from the restart set.

- Where Web-based HMI technology is used, it should be possible to develop a standardized client-side and/or server-side function that checks user Web-form input values and either discards unacceptable characters or properly encodes them to be transparent and not interpreted as either SQL or HTML or any of the scripting languages. If the Web browser vendors don't do this, then the Web developers can and procedures can be enforced to verify that all Web pages that incorporate user data inputs incorporate this function. The basic problem with Web server vulnerabilities is that they depend on good programming practices by the Web developers to keep them secure. This should be automated and not left to the Web developer, at least when used in critical automation systems.

Intersystem and intrasystem data exchanges

VPN technology—including authentication and message encryption, with occasional renegotiation of session encryption keys—can be applied to all of the computers that form a SCADA system, even extending outward to computers at the backup site. However, since these data exchanges are actually occurring between application programs running on the SCADA system and those on other systems, authentication ought to be supported at the application level; otherwise, a hostile application, running on a computer that is part of the VPN, could hijack the connection. ICCP now offers an authentication service for this purpose (although it is optional and may not actually be used in many installations). It is also important to employ conventional cybersecurity methods to lock down (and monitor access to) unused ports. System security could be enhanced by having the SCADA vendor adopt the Kerberos technologies and use those to authenticate and control the running applications and the users of the system.

RTU communications

The issue of securing RTU communications is principally one of authentication—verifying the source and integrity of a received message, so that falsified control commands cannot be issued and critical data cannot be altered. Preventing unauthorized access to the information being exchanged is the secondary consideration, although in market-driven industries (e.g., electric power generation), this could also be a high concern.

The fundamental problem with securing RTU communications is the huge installed base of existing (and old) field equipment that can't quickly or easily be replaced and can't be reprogrammed. The only viable solution for this equipment is the addition of external hardware with the required security features. For the latest RTUs and field devices, it should be possible to implement new protocols (serial and IP based), if a standard can be adopted. SCADA hosts can be upgraded to support these new protocols, or front-end protocol converters can be used to accommodate them. Nevertheless, that won't fix the problem in the installed base. Actions that could be taken to move forward are as follows:

- Extension of selected standard serial protocols (e.g., DNP3.0 and Modbus) to include functions for authentication and message encryption. The AGA has proposed an encryption algorithm (for additional details, see app. C) designed for integration into existing serial protocols. As authentication would occur only at startup (and may be repeated once every 24 hours), it shouldn't affect system polling and updating speeds.

- Authentication (to the level of the actual configuration utility itself) of any messages used for the purpose of changing configuration or programming within the RTU. It should not be possible for anyone with a copy of a commercial programming tool to tap into the communication channel and send new programming down to an RTU or PLC.

- Development of bump-in-the-wire add-on encryption hardware for byte- and bit-oriented protocols (including multi-dropped configurations). This is potentially the best solution for the installed base, although the really old RTUs still used in the electric power industry may still present a problem.

- Conversion to IP-based communications and adoption of available VPN, authentication, and encryption technologies. IP-ready field devices would need to support the additional protocols and functions required for these capabilities. Most devices currently do not incorporate such protocols and would require new firmware at the least.

- Robustness testing of the IP communication capabilities of IP-ready devices to confirm their ability to survive a DoS attack or probing by typical hacker tools. Too many such devices have unknown reactions to unexpected communication traffic.

Nontechnical Approaches

Everything mentioned so far in this chapter is a possible technical solution (a program change, a piece of hardware, or an operating system enhancement), but of course, it remains essential to address the nontechnical aspects of cybersecurity (i.e., the personnel and organization) and to identify and quantify the risks being mitigated. The need for policies, procedures, training, and management involvement has already been addressed in detail. Improved SCADA technologies do not necessarily eliminate the need for these management strategies and operational measures. Better technology can certainly close some of the gaps, but as long as people support, maintain, and operate SCADA systems, there will be a need for managerial controls in addition to the technical controls.

Furthermore, SCADA systems are usually owned and operated by a business entity—and such entities are in the business of making profits and increasing shareholder equity. Therefore, any investment in a capital asset improvement, especially a large, probably unbudgeted investment, will have to pass through the financial mechanisms and be approved on the basis of a range of factors. If making a SCADA system secure is an expensive proposition and there is no return on the investment, then few organizations would bother, unless required by laws or regulations (and in some instances this is exactly what is happening). The risk of not making a SCADA system secure and the liability of the officers and corporation, if the worst came to pass, must be taken into account—as do the implications toward business liability insurance underwriting and potentially increased insurance costs.

As with any business decision, there needs to be a well considered business case, including a risk assessment and gap analysis, before any steps are taken. This is not so that taking an action to reduce risks can be put off or delayed, but rather so that a cost-effective plan can be developed and given full management support on the basis of the real priorities and vulnerabilities.

Training, incentive programs, and employee involvement are all essential if security is to become a basic component of every employee's responsibilities. Management involvement and support is critical and must demonstrate the corporate commitment to security. When security issues and security readiness become a KPI (Key Performance Indicator) in management business reporting, then senior management is sending the right message to the overall organization.

Appendix A:

Department of Energy's "21 Steps to Improved SCADA Security"

In an effort to provide some initial guidance and basic recommendations, for securing automation systems (specifically SCADA) shortly after the initial recognition by DHS of the vulnerability of the national infrastructure, DOE issued its bulletin regarding twenty one actions that could be taken to greatly improve the security of a typical SCADA system. These recommendations are still as valid today as they were when initially issued and thus are worth reviewing:

1. Identifying all connections to SCADA networks

2. Disconnecting unnecessary connections to the SCADA network

3. Evaluating and strengthening the security of any remaining connections to the SCADA network

4. Hardening SCADA networks by removing or disabling unnecessary services/ports

5. Avoiding reliance on proprietary protocols to protect the system

6. Implementing security features provided by device and system (SCADA/computer) vendors

7. Establishing strong controls over any medium that is used as a back door into the SCADA network

8. Implementing internal and external intrusion-detection systems (IDS) and establishing 24-hour-a-day incident monitoring

9. Performing technical audits of SCADA devices and networks and any other connected networks to identify security concerns

10. Conducting physical security surveys and assessing all remote sites connected to the SCADA network to evaluate their security

11. Establishing SCADA "Red Teams" to identify and evaluate possible attack scenarios

12. Defining clearly cybersecurity roles, responsibilities, and authorities for managers, system administrators, and users

13. Documenting network architecture and identifying systems that serve critical functions or contain sensitive information that require additional levels of protection

14. Establishing a rigorous, ongoing risk management process

15. Establishing a network protection strategy based on the principle of defense-in-depth

16. Identifying clearly cybersecurity requirements

17. Establishing effective configuration management processes

18. Conducting routine self-assessments

19. Establishing system backups and disaster recovery plans

20. Establishing expectations for cybersecurity performance and holding individuals accountable for their performance

21. Establishing policies and conducting training to minimize the likelihood that organizational personnel will inadvertently disclose sensitive information regarding SCADA system design, operations, or security controls

Appendix B:

NERC 1300 – Recommendations for Electric Utilities

Following are key technical and operational points related to SCADA system security, as presented in "Standard 1300—Cyber Security" (version 1.0), a draft as of September 2004 of recommendations by the North American Electric Reliability Council (NERC). (This information is reprinted with the permission of the NERC.) The points extracted break down the various aspects of physical and electronic security and the actions that need to be taken to secure a SCADA system, develop a security program and maintain an acceptable level of ongoing security. Certain electric industry–specific portions of this document, and legal/regulatory sections, have been intentionally excluded. Since its issuance the document has been replaced by a set of individual [CIP-002-1 through CIP-009-1] standards that essentially take the individual section of 1300 and make them separate items. But, the technical content essentially remained the same and so here we present the important materials extracted from the NERC document. Although NERC specifically intended these recommendations for the Electric utility industry, these recommendations, in whole or in part, are being widely adopted by standards organizations in other industrial segments and therefore are well worth review, regardless of the industry.

Standard 1300 — Cyber Security
Page 1 of 35 Draft Version 1.0
September 15, 2004

DEFINITIONS

Cyber Assets: Those systems (including hardware, software, and data) and communication networks (including hardware, software, and data) associated with bulk electric system assets.

Critical Cyber Assets: Those cyber assets that perform critical bulk electric system functions such as telemetry, monitoring and control, automatic generator control, load shedding, black start, real-time power system modeling, special protection systems, power plant control, substation automation control, and real-time inter-utility data exchange are included at a minimum. The loss or compromise of these cyber assets would adversely impact the reliable operation of bulk electric system assets.

Bulk Electric System Asset: Any facility or combination of facilities that, if unavailable, would have a significant impact on the ability to serve large quantities of customers for an extended period of time, or would have a detrimental impact to the reliability or operability of the electric grid, or would cause significant risk to public health and safety.

Electronic Security Perimeter: The logical border surrounding the network or group of subnetworks (the "secure network") to which the critical cyber assets are connected, and for which access is controlled.

Physical Security Perimeter: The physical border surrounding computer rooms, telecommunications rooms, operations centers, and other locations in which critical cyber assets are housed and for which access is controlled.

Responsible Entity: The organization performing the reliability function, as identified in the Reliability Function table of the Standard Authorization Request for this standard.

Incident: Any physical or cyber event that:
• Disrupts, or could have lead to a disruption of the functional operation of a critical cyber asset, or
• Compromises, or was an attempt to compromise, the electronic or physical security perimeters.

Security Incident: Any malicious or suspicious activities which are known to cause, or could have resulted in, an incident.

Standard 1300 — Cyber Security
Page 2 of 35 Draft Version 1.0
September 15, 2004

1300 — Cyber Security

1301 Security Management Controls

1302 Critical Cyber Assets

1303 Personnel & Training

1304 Electronic Security

1305 Physical Security

1306 Systems Security Management

1307 Incident Response Planning

1308 Recovery Plans

Purpose: To reduce risks to the reliability of the bulk electric systems from any compromise of critical cyber assets.

1301 Security Management Controls

Critical business and operational functions performed by cyber assets affecting the bulk electric system necessitate having security management controls. This section defines the minimum security management controls that the responsible entity must have in place to protect critical cyber assets.

(A) Requirements

(1) Cyber Security Policy
The responsible entity shall create and maintain a cyber security policy that addresses the requirements of this standard and the governance of the cyber security policy.

(2) Information Protection
The responsible entity shall document and implement a process for the protection of information pertaining to or used by critical cyber assets.

(i) Identification
The responsible entity shall identify all information, regardless of media type, related to critical cyber assets. At a minimum, this must include access to procedures, critical asset inventories, maps, floor plans, equipment layouts, configurations, and any related security information.

(ii) Classification
The responsible entity shall classify information related to critical cyber assets to aid personnel with access to this information in determining what information can be disclosed to unauthenticated personnel, as well as the relative sensitivity of information that should not be disclosed outside of the entity without proper authorization.

(iii) Protection
Responsible entities must identify the information access limitations related to critical cyber assets based on classification level.

(3) Roles and Responsibilities
The responsible entity shall assign a member of senior management with responsibility for leading and managing the entity's implementation of the cyber security standard. This person must authorize any deviation or exception from the requirements of this standard. Any such deviation or exception and its authorization must be documented. The responsible entity shall also define the roles and responsibilities of critical cyber asset owners, custodians, and users. Roles and responsibilities shall also be defined for the access, use, and handling of critical information as identified and classified in section 1.2.

(4) Governance
Responsible entities shall define and document a structure of relationships and decision-making processes that identify and represent executive level management's ability to direct and control the entity in order to secure its critical cyber assets.

(5) Access Authorization

(i) The responsible entity shall institute and document a process for access management to information pertaining to or used by critical cyber assets whose compromise could impact the reliability and/or availability of the bulk electric system for which the entity is responsible.

(ii) Authorizing Access

The responsible entity shall maintain a list of personnel who are responsible to authorize access to critical cyber assets. Logical or physical access to critical cyber assets may only be authorized by the personnel responsible to authorize access to those assets. All access authorizations must be documented.

(iii) Access Review

Responsible entities shall review access rights to critical cyber assets to confirm they are correct and that they correspond with the entity's needs and the appropriate roles and responsibilities.

(iv) Access Revocation/Changes

Responsible entities shall define procedures to ensure that modification, suspension, and termination of user access to critical cyber assets is accomplished within 24 hours of a change in user access status. All access revocations/changes must be authorized and documented.

(6) Authorization to Place into Production

Responsible entities shall identify the controls for testing and assessment of new or replacement systems and software patches/changes. Responsible entities shall designate approving authorities that will formally authorize and document that a system has passed testing criteria. The approving authority shall be responsible for verifying that a system meets minimal security configuration standards as stated in 1304 and 1306 of this standard prior to the system being promoted to operate in a production environment.

(B) Measures

(1) Cyber Security Policy

(i) The responsible entity shall maintain its written cyber security policy stating the entity's commitment to protect critical cyber assets.

(ii) The responsible entity shall review the cyber security policy at least annually.

(iii) The responsible entity shall maintain documentation of any deviations or exemptions authorized by the current senior management official responsible for the cyber security program.

(iv) The responsible entity shall review all authorized deviations or exemptions at least annually and shall document the extension or revocation of any reviewed authorized deviation or exemption.

(2) Information Protection

(i) The responsible entity shall review the information security protection program at least annually.

(ii) The responsible entity shall perform an assessment of the information security protection program to ensure compliance with the documented processes at least annually.

(iii) The responsible entity shall document the procedures used to secure the information that has been identified as critical cyber information according to the classification level assigned to that information.

(iv) The responsible entity shall assess the critical cyber information identification and classification procedures to ensure compliance with the documented processes at least annually.

(3) Roles and Responsibilities

(i) The responsible entity shall maintain in its policy the defined roles and responsibilities for the handling of critical cyber information.

(ii) The current senior management official responsible for the cyber security program shall be identified by name, title, phone, address, and date of designation.

(iii) Changes must be documented within 30 days of the effective date.

(iv) The responsible entity shall review the roles and responsibilities of critical cyber asset owners, custodians, and users at least annually.

(4) Governance

The responsible entity shall review the structure of internal corporate relationships and processes related to this program at least annually to ensure that the existing relationships and processes continue to provide the appropriate level of accountability and that executive level management is continually engaged in the process.

(5) Access Authorization

(i) The responsible entity shall update the list of designated personnel responsible to authorize access to critical cyber information within five days of any change in status that affects the designated personnel's ability to authorize access to those critical cyber assets.

(ii) The list of designated personnel responsible to authorize access to critical cyber information shall be reviewed, at a minimum of once per quarter, for compliance with this standard.

(iii) The list of designated personnel responsible to authorize access to critical cyber information shall identify each designated person by name, title, phone, address, date of designation, and list of systems/applications they are responsible to authorize access for.

(iv) The responsible entity shall review the processes for access privileges, suspension and termination of user accounts. This review shall be documented. The process shall be periodically reassessed in order to ensure compliance with policy at least annually.

(v) The responsible entity shall review user access rights every quarter to confirm access is still required.

(6) Authorization to Place into Production

Responsible entities shall identify the designated approving authority responsible for authorizing systems suitable for the production environment by name, title, phone, address, and date of designation. This information will be reviewed for accuracy at least annually. Changes to the designated approving authority shall be documented within 48 hours of the effective change.

1302 Critical Cyber Assets

Business and operational demands for maintaining and managing a reliable bulk electric system increasingly require cyber assets supporting critical reliability control functions and processes to communicate with each other, across functions and organizations, to provide services and data. This results in increased risks to these cyber assets, where the loss or compromise of these assets would adversely impact the reliable operation of critical bulk electric system assets. This standard requires that entities identify and protect critical cyber assets related to the reliable operation of the bulk electric system.

(A) Requirements

Responsible entities shall identify their critical bulk electric system assets using their preferred risk-based assessment. An inventory of critical bulk electric system assets is then the basis to identify a list of associated critical cyber assets that is to be protected by this standard.

(1) Critical Bulk Electric System Assets
The responsible entity shall identify its critical bulk electric system assets. A critical bulk electric system asset consists of those facilities, systems, and equipment which, if destroyed, damaged, degraded, or otherwise rendered unavailable, would have a significant impact on the ability to serve large quantities of customers for an extended period of time, would have a detrimental impact on the reliability or operability of the electric grid, or would cause significant risk to public health and safety. Those critical bulk electric system assets include assets performing the following:

    (i) Control centers performing the functions of a Reliability Authority, Balancing Authority, Interchange Authority, Transmission Service Provider, Transmission Owner, Transmission Operator, Generation Owner, Generation Operator, and Load Serving Entities.

        (a) Bulk electric system tasks such as telemetry, monitoring and control, automatic generator control, real-time power system modeling, and real-time inter-utility data exchange.

    (ii) Transmission substations associated with elements monitored as Interconnection Reliability Operating Limits (IROL).

    (iii) Generation:

        (a) Generating resources under control of a common system that meet criteria for a Reportable Disturbance (NERC Policy 1.B, Section 2.4).

        (b) Generation control centers that have control of generating resources that when summed meet the criteria for a Reportable Disturbance (NERC Policy 1.B, Section 2.4).

    (iv) System Restoration:

        (a) Black start generators.

        (b) Substations associated with transmission lines used for initial system restoration.

    (v) Automatic load shedding under control of a common system capable of load shedding 300 MW or greater.

(vi) Special Protection Systems whose misoperation can negatively affect elements associated with an IROL.

(vii) Additional Critical Bulk Electric System Assets

(a) The responsible entity shall utilize a risk-based assessment to identify any additional critical bulk electric system assets. The risk-based assessment documentation must include a description of the assessment including the determining criteria and evaluation procedure.

(2) Critical Cyber Assets

(i) The responsible entity shall identify cyber assets to be critical using the following criteria:

(a) The cyber asset supports a critical bulk electric system asset, and

(b) The cyber asset uses a routable protocol, or

(c) The cyber asset is dial-up accessible.

(d) Dial-up accessible critical cyber assets, which do use a routable protocol require only an electronic security perimeter for the remote electronic access without the associated physical security perimeter.

(e) Any other cyber asset within the same electronic security perimeter as the identified critical cyber assets must be protected to ensure the security of the critical cyber assets as identified in 1302.1.2.1.

(3) A senior management officer must approve the list of critical bulk electric system assets and the list of critical cyber assets.

(B) Measures

(1) Critical Bulk Electric System Assets

(i) The responsible entity shall maintain its critical bulk electric system assets approved list as identified in 1302.1.1.

(2) Risk-Based Assessment

(i) The responsible entity shall maintain documentation depicting the risk-based assessment used to identify its additional critical bulk electric system assets. The documentation shall include a description of the methodology including the determining criteria and evaluation procedure.

(3) Critical Cyber Assets

(i) The responsible entity shall maintain documentation listing all cyber assets as identified under 1302.1.2.

(4) Documentation Review and Maintenance

(i) The responsible entity shall review, and as necessary, update the documentation referenced in 1302.2.1, 1302.2.2, and 1302.2.3 at least annually, or within 30 days of the addition or removal of any critical cyber assets.

(5) Critical Bulk Electric System Asset and Critical Cyber Asset List Approval

(i) A properly dated record of the senior management officer's approval of the list of critical bulk electric system assets must be maintained.

(ii) A properly dated record of the senior management officer's approval of the list of critical cyber assets must be maintained.

1303 Personnel & Training

Personnel having access to critical cyber assets, as defined by this standard, are given a higher level of trust, by definition, and are required to have a higher level of screening, training, security awareness, and record retention of such activity, than personnel not provided access.

(A) Requirements

Responsible entity shall comply with the following requirements of this standard:

(1) Awareness
Security awareness programs shall be developed, maintained, and documented to ensure personnel subject to the standard receive on-going reinforcement in sound security practices.

(2) Training
All personnel having access to critical cyber assets shall be trained in the policies, access controls, and procedures governing access to, the use of, and sensitive information surrounding these critical assets.

(3) Records
Records shall be prepared and maintained to document training, awareness reinforcement, and background screening of all personnel having access to critical cyber assets and shall be provided for authorized inspection upon request.

(4) Background Screening
All personnel having access to critical cyber assets, including contractors and service vendors, shall be subject to background screening prior to being granted unrestricted access to critical assets.

(B) Measures

(1) Awareness
The responsible entity shall develop and maintain awareness programs designed to maintain and promote sound security practices in the application of the standards, to include security awareness reinforcement using one or more of the following mechanisms on at least a quarterly basis:

    (i) Direct communications (e.g., e-mails, memos, computer based training, etc.);

    (ii) Security reminders (e.g., posters, intranet, brochures, etc.);

    (iii) Management support (e.g., presentations, all-hands meetings, etc.).

(2) Training
The responsible entity shall develop and maintain a company-specific cyber security training program that includes, at a minimum, the following required items:

    (i) The cyber security policy;

    (ii) Physical and electronic access controls to critical cyber assets;

    (iii) The proper release of critical cyber asset information;

    (iv) Action plans and procedures to recover or re-establish critical cyber assets and access thereto following a cyber security incident.

(3) Records
This responsible entity shall develop and maintain records to adequately document compliance with section 1303.

(i) The responsible entity shall maintain documentation of all personnel who have access to critical cyber assets and the date of completion of their training.

(ii) The responsible entity shall maintain documentation that it has reviewed its training program annually.

(4) Background Screening

The responsible entity shall:

(i) Maintain a list of all personnel with access to critical cyber assets, including their specific electronic and physical access rights to critical cyber assets within the security perimeter(s).

(ii) The responsible entity shall review the document referred to in section 1303.2.4.1 quarterly, and update the listing within two business days of any substantive change of personnel.

(iii) Access revocation must be completed within 24 hours for any personnel who have a change in status where they are not allowed access to critical cyber assets (e.g., termination, suspension, transfer, requiring escorted access, etc.).

(iv) The responsible entity shall conduct background screening of all personnel prior to being granted access to critical cyber assets in accordance with federal, state, provincial, and local laws, and subject to existing collective bargaining unit agreements. A minimum of Social Security Number verification and seven year criminal check is required. Entities may conduct more detailed reviews, as permitted by law and subject to existing collective bargaining unit agreements, depending upon the criticality of the position.

(v) Adverse employment actions should be consistent with the responsible entity's legal and human resources practices for hiring and retention of employees or contractors.

(vi) Update screening shall be conducted at least every five years, or for cause.

1304 Electronic Security

Business and operational requirements for critical cyber assets to communicate with other devices to provide data and services result in increased risks to these critical cyber assets. In order to protect these assets, it is necessary to identify the electronic perimeter(s) within which these assets reside. When electronic perimeters are defined, different security levels may be assigned to these perimeters depending on the assets within these perimeter(s). In the case of critical cyber assets, the security level assigned to these electronic security perimeters is high. This standard requires:

• The identification of the electronic (also referred to as logical) security perimeter(s) inside which critical cyber assets reside and all access points to these perimeter(s),

• The implementation of the necessary measures to control access at all access points to the perimeter(s) and the critical assets within them, and

• The implementation of processes, tools, and procedures to monitor electronic (logical) access to the perimeter(s) and the critical cyber assets.

(A) Requirements

(1) Electronic Security Perimeter
The electronic security perimeter is the logical border surrounding the network or group of sub-networks (the "secure network") to which the critical cyber assets are connected, and for which access is controlled. The responsible entity shall identify the electronic security perimeter(s) surrounding its critical cyber assets and all access points to the perimeter(s). Access points to the electronic security perimeter(s) shall additionally include any externally connected communication end point (e.g., modems) terminating at any device within the electronic security perimeter. Communication links connecting discrete electronic perimeters are not considered part of the security perimeter. However, end-points of these communication links within the security perimeter(s) are considered access points to the electronic security perimeter(s). Where there are also non-critical cyber assets within the defined electronic security perimeter, these non-critical cyber assets must comply with the requirements of this standard.

(2) Electronic Access Controls
The responsible entity shall implement the organizational, technical, and procedural controls to manage logical access at all electronic access points to the electronic security perimeter(s) and the critical cyber assets within the electronic security perimeter(s). These controls shall implement an access control model that denies access by default unless explicit access permissions are specified. Where external interactive logical access to the electronic access points into the electronic security perimeter is implemented, the responsible entity shall implement strong procedural or technical measures to ensure authenticity of the accessing party. Electronic access control devices shall display an appropriate use banner upon interactive access attempts.

(3) Monitoring Electronic Access Control
The responsible entity shall implement the organizational, technical, and procedural controls, including tools and procedures, for monitoring authorized access, detecting unauthorized access (intrusions), and attempts at unauthorized access to the electronic perimeter(s) and critical cyber assets within the perimeter(s), 24 hours a day, 7 days a week.

(4) Documentation Review and Maintenance
The responsible entity shall ensure that all documentation reflect current configurations and processes. The entity shall conduct periodic reviews of these documents to ensure accuracy and shall update all documents in a timely fashion following the implementation of changes.

(B) Measures

(1) Electronic Security Perimeter
The responsible entity shall maintain a document or set of documents depicting the electronic security perimeter(s), all interconnected critical cyber assets within the security perimeter, and all electronic access points to the security perimeter and to the interconnected environment(s). The document or set of documents shall verify that all critical cyber assets are within the electronic security perimeter(s).

(2) Electronic Access Controls
The responsible entity shall maintain a document or set of documents identifying the organizational, technical, and procedural controls for logical (electronic) access and their implementation for each electronic access point to the electronic security perimeter(s). For each control, the document or set of documents shall identify and describe, at a minimum, the access request and authorization process implemented for that control, the authentication methods used, and a periodic review process for authorization rights, in accordance with management policies and controls defined in 1301, and on-going supporting documentation (e.g., access request and authorization documents, review checklists) verifying that these have been implemented.

(3) Monitoring Electronic Access Control
The responsible entity shall maintain a document identifying organizational, technical, and procedural controls, including tools and procedures, for monitoring electronic (logical) access. This document shall identify supporting documents, including access records and logs, to verify that the tools and procedures are functioning and being used as designed. Additionally, the document or set of documents shall identify and describe processes, procedures and technical controls and their supporting documents implemented to verify access records for authorized access against access control rights, and report and alert on unauthorized access and attempts at unauthorized access to appropriate monitoring staff.

(4) Documentation Review and Maintenance
The responsible entity shall review and update the documents referenced in 1304.2.1, 1304.2.2, and 1304.2.3 at least annually or within 90 days of the modification of the network or controls.

1305 Physical Security

Business and operational requirements for the availability and reliability of critical cyber assets dictate the need to physically secure these assets. In order to protect these assets, it is necessary to identify the physical security perimeter(s) within which these assets reside. This standard requires:
• The identification of the physical security perimeter(s) and the development of an in-depth defense strategy to protect the physical perimeter within which critical cyber assets reside and all access points to these perimeter(s),
• The implementation of the necessary measures to control access at all access points to the perimeter(s) and the critical assets within them, and
• The implementation of processes, tools and procedures to monitor physical access to the perimeter(s) and the critical cyber assets.
When physical perimeters are defined, different security levels shall be assigned to these perimeters depending on the assets within these perimeter(s).

(A) Requirements

(1) Documentation
The responsible entity shall document their implementation of the above requirements in their physical security plan.

(2) Physical Security Perimeter
The responsible entity shall identify in its physical security plan the physical security perimeter(s) surrounding its critical cyber asset(s) and all access points to the perimeter(s). Access points to the physical security perimeter(s) shall include all points of physical ingress or egress through the nearest physically secured "four wall boundary" surrounding the critical cyber asset(s).

(3) Physical Access Controls
The responsible entity shall implement the organizational, operational, and procedural controls to manage physical access at all access points to the physical security perimeter(s).

(4) Monitoring Physical Access Control
The responsible entity shall implement the organizational, technical, and procedural controls, including tools and procedures, for monitoring physical access 24 hours a day, 7 days a week.

(5) Logging Physical Access
The responsible entity shall implement the technical and procedural mechanisms for logging physical access.

(6) Maintenance and Testing
The responsible entity shall implement a comprehensive maintenance and testing program to assure all physical security systems (e.g., door contacts, motion detectors, CCTV, etc.) operate at a threshold to detect unauthorized activity.

(B) Measures

(1) Documentation Review and Maintenance
The responsible entity shall review and update their physical security plan at least annually or within 90 days of modification to the perimeter or physical security methods.

(2) Physical Security Perimeter
The responsible entity shall maintain a document or set of documents depicting the physical security perimeter(s), and all access points to every such perimeter. The document shall verify that all critical cyber assets are located within the physical security perimeter(s).

(3) Physical Access Controls
The responsible entity shall implement one or more of the following physical access methods.
- Card Key: A means of electronic access where the access rights of the card holder are pre-defined in a computer database. Access rights may differ from one perimeter to another.
- Special Locks: These may include locks with non-reproducible keys, magnetic locks that must open remotely or by a man trap.
- Security Officers: Personnel responsible for controlling physical access 24 hours a day. These personnel shall reside on-site or at a central monitoring station.
- Security Cage: A caged system that controls physical access to the critical cyber asset (for environments where the nearest four wall perimeter cannot be secured).
- Other Authentication Devices: Biometric, keypad, token, or other devices that are used to control access to the cyber asset through personnel authentication.

In addition, the responsible entity shall maintain documentation identifying the access control(s) implemented for each physical access point through the physical security perimeter. The documentation shall identify and describe, at a minimum, the access request, authorization, and de-authorization process implemented for that control, and a periodic review process for verifying authorization rights, in accordance with management policies and controls defined in 1301, and on-going supporting documentation.

(4) Monitoring Physical Access Control
The responsible entity shall implement one or more of the following monitoring methods.
• CCTV: Video surveillance that captures and records images of activity in or around the secure perimeter.
• Alarm Systems: An alarm system based on contact status that indicated a door or gate has been opened. These alarms must report back to a central security monitoring station or to an EMS dispatcher. Examples include door contacts, window contacts, or motion sensors.
In addition, the responsible entity shall maintain documentation identifying the methods for monitoring physical access. This documentation shall identify supporting procedures to verify that the monitoring tools and procedures are functioning and being used as designed. Additionally, the documentation shall identify and describe processes, procedures, and operational controls to verify access records for authorized access against access control rights. The responsible entity shall have a process for creating unauthorized incident access reports.

(5) Logging Physical Access
The responsible entity shall implement one or more of the following logging methods. Log entries shall record sufficient information to identify each individual.
• Manual Logging: A log book or sign-in sheet or other record of physical access accompanied by human observation.
• Computerized Logging: Electronic logs produced by the selected access control and monitoring method.
• Video Recording: Electronic capture of video images.
In addition, the responsible entity shall maintain documentation identifying the methods for logging physical access. This documentation shall identify supporting procedures to verify that the logging tools and procedures are functioning and being used as designed. Physical access logs shall be retained for at least 90 days.

(6) Maintenance and Testing of Physical Security Systems
The responsible entity shall maintain documentation of annual maintenance and testing for a period of one year.

1306 Systems Security Management

The responsible entity shall establish a System Security Management Program that minimizes or prevents the risk of failure or compromise from misuse or malicious cyber activity. The minimum requirements for this program are outlined below.

(A) Requirements

(1) Test Procedures

All new systems and significant changes to existing critical cyber security assets must use documented information security test procedures to augment functional test and acceptance procedures.

Significant changes include security patch installations, cumulative service packs, release upgrades or versions to operating systems, application, database or other third party software, and firmware.

These tests are required to mitigate risk from known vulnerabilities affecting operating systems, applications, and network services. Security test procedures shall require that testing and acceptance be conducted on a controlled nonproduction environment. All testing must be performed in a manner that precludes adversely affecting the production system and operation.

(2) Account and Password Management

The responsible entity must establish an account password management program to provide for access authentication, audit ability of user activity, and minimize the risk to unauthorized system access by compromised account passwords. The responsible entity must establish end user account management practices, implemented, and documented that includes but is not limited to:

(i) Strong Passwords

In the absence of more sophisticated methods, e.g., multi-factor access controls, accounts must have a strong password. For example, a password consisting of a combination of alpha, numeric, and special characters to the extent allowed by the existing environment. Passwords shall be changed periodically per a risk based frequency to reduce the risk of password cracking.

(ii) Generic Account Management

The responsible entity must have a process for managing factory default accounts, e.g., administrator or guest. The process should include the removal or renaming of these accounts where possible. For those accounts that must remain, passwords must be changed prior to putting any system into service. Where technically supported, individual accounts must be used (in contrast to a group account). Where individual accounts are not supported, the responsible entity must have a policy for managing the appropriate use of group accounts that limits access to only those with authorization, an audit trail of the account use, and steps for securing the account in the event of staff changes, e.g., change in assignment or exit.

(iii) Access Reviews

A designated approver shall review access to critical cyber assets, e.g., computer and/or network accounts and access rights, at least semiannually. Unauthorized, invalidated, expired, or unused computer and/or network accounts must be disabled.

(iv) Acceptable Use

The responsible entity must have a policy implemented to manage the scope and acceptable use of the administrator and other generic account privileges. The policy must support the audit of all account usage to and individually named person, i.e., individually named user accounts, or, personal registration for any generic accounts in order to establish accountability of usage.

(3) Security Patch Management
A formal security patch management practice must be established for tracking, testing, and timely installation of applicable security patches and upgrades to critical cyber security assets. Formal change control and configuration management processes must be used to document their implementation or the reason for not installing the patch. In the case where installation of the patch is not possible, a compensating measure(s) must be taken and documented.

(4) Integrity Software
A formally documented process governing the application of anti-virus, anti-Trojan, and other system integrity tools must be employed to prevent, limit exposure to, and/or mitigate importation of email-based, browser-based, and other Internet-borne malware into assets at and within the electronic security perimeter.

(5) Identification of Vulnerabilities and Responses
At a minimum, a vulnerability assessment shall be performed at least annually that includes a diagnostic review (controlled penetration testing) of the access points to the electronic security perimeter, scanning for open ports/services and modems, factory default accounts, and security patch and anti-virus version levels. The responsible entity will implement a documented management action plan to remediate vulnerabilities and shortcomings, if any, identified in the assessment.

(6) Retention of Systems Logs
All critical cyber security assets must generate an audit trail for all security related system events. The responsible entity shall retain said log data for a period of ninety days. In the event a cyber security incident is detected within the 90-day retention period, the logs must be preserved for a period of three (3) years in an exportable format, for possible use in further event analysis.

(7) Change Control and Configuration Management
The responsible entity shall establish a Change Control Process that provides a controlled environment for modifying all hardware and software for critical cyber assets. The process should include change management procedures that at a minimum provide testing, modification audit trails, problem identification, a back out and recovery process should modifications fail, and ultimately ensure the overall integrity of the critical cyber assets.

(8) Disabling Unused Network Ports/Services
The responsible entity shall disable inherent and unused services.

(9) Dial-up modems
The responsible entity shall secure dial-up modem connections.

(10) Operating Status Monitoring Tools
Computer and communications systems used for operating critical infrastructure must include or be augmented with automated tools to monitor operating state, utilization, and performance, at a minimum.

(11) Back-up and Recovery
Information resident on computer systems used to manage critical electric infrastructure must be backed-up on a regular basis and the back-up moved to a remote facility. Archival information stored on computer media for a prolonged period of time must be tested at least annually to ensure that the information is recoverable.

(B) Measures

(1) Test Procedures

For all critical cyber assets, the responsible entity's change control documentation shall include corresponding records of test procedures, results, and acceptance of successful completion. Test procedures must also include full detail of the environment used on which the test was performed. The documentation shall verify that all changes to critical cyber assets were successfully tested for potential security vulnerabilities prior to being rolled into production, on a controlled non-production system.

(2) Account and Password Management

The responsible entity shall maintain a documented password policy and record of quarterly audit of this policy against all accounts on critical cyber assets. The documentation shall verify that all accounts comply with the password policy and that obsolete accounts are promptly disabled. Upon normal movement of personnel out of the organization, management must review access permissions within 5 working days. For involuntary terminations, management must review access permissions within no more than 24 hours.

(3) Security Patch Management

The responsible entity's change control documentation shall include a record of all security patch installations including: date of testing, test results, management approval for installation, and installation date. The responsible entity's critical cyber asset inventory shall also include record of a monthly review of all available vender security patches/OS upgrades and current revision/patch levels. The documentation shall verify that all critical cyber assets are being kept up to date on OS upgrades and security patches or other compensating measures are being taken to minimize the risk of a critical cyber asset compromise from a known vulnerability.

(4) Integrity Software

The responsible entity's critical cyber asset inventory and change control documentation shall include a record of all anti-virus, anti-Trojan, and other system integrity tools employed, and the version level actively in use. The responsible entity's critical cyber asset inventory shall also include record of a monthly review of all available updates to these tools security patches/OS upgrades and current revision/patch levels. The documentation shall verify that all critical cyber assets are being kept up to date on available integrity software so as to minimize risk of infection from email-based, browser-based, or other Internet-borne malware. Where integrity software is not available for a particular computer platform or other compensating measures that are being taken to minimize the risk of a critical cyber asset compromise from viruses and malware must also be documented.

(5) Identification of Vulnerabilities and Responses

The responsible entity shall maintain documentation identifying the organizational, technical and procedural controls, including tools and procedures for monitoring the critical cyber environment for vulnerabilities. The documentation will also include a record of the annual vulnerability assessment, and remediation plans for all vulnerabilities and/or shortcomings that are found. The documentation shall verify that the responsible entity is taking appropriate action to address the potential vulnerabilities.

(6) Retention of Logs
The responsible entity shall maintain documentation that index location, content, and retention schedule of all log data captured from the critical cyber assets. The documentation shall verify that the responsible entity is retaining information that may be vital to internal and external investigations of cyber events involving critical cyber assets.

(7) Change Control and Configuration Management
The responsible entity shall maintain documentation identifying the controls, including tools and procedures, for managing change to and testing of critical cyber assets. The documentation shall verify that all the responsible entity follows a methodical approach for managing change to their critical cyber assets.

(8) Disabling Unused Network Services/Ports
The responsible entity shall maintain documentation of status/configuration of network services and ports on critical cyber assets, and a record of the regular audit of all network services and ports against the policy and documented configuration. The documentation shall verify that the responsible entity has taken the appropriate actions to secure electronic access points to all critical cyber assets.

(9) Dial-up Modems
The responsible entity shall maintain a documented policy for securing dial-up modem connections to critical cyber assets, and a record of the regular audit of all dial-up modem connections and ports against the policy and documented configuration. The documentation shall verify that the responsible entity has taken the appropriate actions to secure dial-up access to all critical cyber assets.

(10) Operating Status Monitoring Tools
The responsible entity shall maintain a documentation identifying organizational, technical, and procedural controls, including tools and procedures for monitoring operating state, utilization, and performance of critical cyber assets.

(11) Back-up and Recovery
The responsible entity shall maintain a documentation that index location, content, and retention schedule of all backup data and tapes. The documentation shall also include recovery procedures for reconstructing any critical cyber asset from the backup data, and a record of the annual restoration verification exercise. The documentation shall verify that the responsible entity is capable of recovering from the failure or compromise of critical cyber asset.

1307 Incident Response Planning

Security measures designed to protect critical cyber assets from intrusion, disruption or other forms of compromise must be monitored on a continuous basis. Incident Response Planning defines the procedures that must be followed when incidents or cyber security incidents are identified.

(A) Requirements

(1) The responsible entity shall develop and document an incident response plan. The plan shall provide and support a capability for reporting and responding to physical and cyber security incidents to eliminate and/or minimize impacts to the organization. The incident response plan must address the following items:

(2) Incident Classification
The responsible entity shall define procedures to characterize and classify events (both electronic and physical) as either incidents or cyber security incidents.
(3) Electronic and Physical Incident Response Actions
The responsible entity shall define incident response actions, including roles and responsibilities of incident response teams, incident handling procedures, escalation and communication plans.
(4) Incident and Cyber Security Incident Reporting
The responsible entity shall report all incidents and cyber security incidents to the ESISAC in accordance with the Indications, Analysis & Warning Program (IAW) Standard Operating Procedure (SOP).

(B) Measures

(5) The responsible entity shall maintain documentation that defines incident classification, electronic and physical incident response actions, and cyber security incident reporting requirements.
(6) The responsible entity shall retain records of incidents and cyber security incidents for three calendar years.
(7) The responsible entity shall retain records of incidents reported to ESISAC for three calendar years.

1308 Recovery Plans

The entity performing the reliability authority, balancing authority, interchange authority, transmission service provider, transmission operator, generator, or load-serving entity function must establish recovery plans and put in place the physical and cyber assets necessary to put these recovery plans into effect once triggered. Recovery plans must address triggering events of varying duration and severity using established business continuity and disaster recovery techniques and practices. The recovery plans and the physical and cyber assets in place to support them must be exercised or drilled periodically to ensure their continued effectiveness. The periodicity of drills must be consistent with the duration, severity, and probability associated with each type of event. For example, a higher probability event with a short duration may not require a recovery plan drill at all because the entity exercises its response regularly. However, the recovery plan for a lower probability event with severe consequences must have a drill associated with it that is conducted, at minimum, annually.
Facilities and infrastructure that are numerous and distributed, such as substations, may not require an individual Recovery Plan and the associated redundant facilities since reengineering and reconstruction may be the generic response to a severe event. Conversely, there is typically one control center per bulk transmission service area and this will require a redundant or backup facility. Because of these differences, the recovery plans associated with control centers will differ from those associated with power plants and substations. There is no requirement for recovery plans for substations and generation plants that have no critical cyber assets.

(A) Requirements

(1) The responsible entity shall create recovery plans for critical cyber assets and exercise its recovery plans at least annually.

(2) The responsible entity shall specify the appropriate response to events of varying
duration and severity that would trigger its recovery plans.

(3) The responsible entity shall update its recovery plans within 30 days of system or procedural change as necessary and post its recovery plan contact information.

(4) The responsible entity shall develop training on its recovery plans that will be included in the security training and education program.

(B) Measures

(1) The responsible entity shall document its recovery plans and maintain records of all exercises or drills for at least three years.

(2) The responsible entity shall review and adjust its response to events of varying duration and severity annually or as necessary.

(3) The responsible entity shall review, update, document, and post changes to its recovery plans within 30 days of system or procedural change as necessary.

(4) The responsible entity shall conduct and keep attendance records to its recovery plans training at least once every three years or as necessary.

Appendix C:
Security Recommendations of the Instruments, Systems, and Automation Society and the American Gas Association

The ISA (Instruments, Systems, and Automation Society [formerly the Instrument Society of America]) is actively involved in attempting to develop guidelines for improving the security of automation systems, including SCADA systems, DCS, and PLC-based systems. As part of this effort, they have created and issued a technical report entitled "Integrating Electronic Security into the Manufacturing and Control Systems Environment" (ANSI/ISA-TR99.00.02-2004). This is a working document, subject to periodic review and modification, if required, that has been issued not as a standard, but rather as a set of recommendations (a Technical Report). The ISA's recommendations were developed by soliciting the input of industry experts and the end-user community (companies that employ computer-based automation systems). This document names vendors, end-users, and industry experts that participated in the development of the document.

A very important aspect of the creation of this report is the participation of people who are also active with other organizations attempting to develop equivalent standards and recommendations. To date, there are at least a dozen groups working, in parallel and independently, on standards and recommendations to achieve the same end result: cybersecure automation systems. These groups are listed in appendix D.

The work being done by most of these groups is somewhat redundant—with a high degree of overlap and, in some cases, contradiction. In other instances, the work being done is targeted to a specific area of need, such as the AGA's recommendation for a light-weight encryption standard for secure serial communications to field devices (AGA Report No. 12 includes a specific section entitled "Low Latency Cryptographic Protection for SCADA Communications" [a separate discussion of this document follows]). In many cases, the general recommendations of these groups are essentially an amplification and detailed expansion of the initial recommendations by the NERC in 2003.

In the summer of 2005, an effort was made to bring all of these different groups together, to coordinate their work, establish lines of communication, and standardize terminology. This first International Standards Coordination Meeting was cosponsored by the Department of Homeland Security and is planned as an annual event. The ISA is already coordinating with many of the groups listed previously and has made an effort, in its technical report, to incorporate much of the work being done by these different groups.

The technical report clearly distinguishes cybersecurity issues, practices, and solutions appropriate in a classical IT environment from those that would be suited to a control system environment. This distinction is critical, since certain standard IT practices (e.g., taking a system out of service during off hours to install new patches and software updates) don't translate well into a process/production plant environment where control systems operate 24/7. The technical report also discusses the process of developing a security program and the process of getting management to buy in—for the effort and costs—by developing a business case. This is where the involvement of actual end users is invaluable, as they are aware of the corporate blockades that must be surmounted and are aware that, because you can't circumvent them, they have to be addressed. The report recognizes the business realities of obtaining funding for (cyber)security programs and acknowledges that the goal should be adequate electronic security, rather than the creation of the perfect or the most sophisticated security program. Part of this is the process of doing a security assessment, which includes weighing the possibility and consequences of various threat agents and determining the cost justifiable range of countermeasures that ought to be implemented.

The major topics addressed in the technical report include:

- Development of a security program with a business case justification

- Enumeration of risks and their probabilities and costs

- Performing a risk assessment and gap analysis

- Selecting appropriate countermeasures for the key vulnerabilities

- Implementing the selected counter measures

- Developing and executing test plans

- Establishing and maintaining an operational security program

- Setting up a change-management program

- Developing disaster recover and response plans

The report addresses a wide range of topics, but it does not offer a how-to solution for most of them. Rather, the report generally lists the issues and the tasks that should be performed, but leaves the details of implementation to the reader. In some instances, where a suitable ISO standard exists, the report will direct the reader to that applicable ISO standard. The report does include a range of examples and templates for documentation such as summarizing a plant's critical control/computer/automation assets, defining and assessing risk, and writing a security policy.

Because the report covers all types of computer-based automation, including continuous, batch and discrete manufacturing automation, it addresses critical assets that would not typically apply in most SCADA applications. A bar-code scanner might prevent a truck from being loaded with boxes at a discrete manufacturing plant, but it would be a rare SCADA system that depended on such a device. By contrast, the report excellently describes the differences between an insider and an outsider as a possible threat agent. It also offers a very good general outline of the special considerations that make automation cybersecurity different from conventional IT cybersecurity:

- The risks involved include loss of life, facilities, and plant equipment; endangering the public/public health; and damage to product.

- It is not normally corporate information that must be protected (although that is a factor in some SCADA systems) but the plant and process. The fact that specialized automation devices (e.g., PLCs and RTUs) may be more critical than the central SCADA server/computer.

- Automation systems require nearly perfect availability and may control processes that are unstable without constant supervision (this is less the case in SCADA applications than in process control applications, but still true to some degree).

- Control systems (and the processes they control) often involve time-critical responses that preclude making procedural changes that introduce delays (e.g., having an operator enter a password before a command is sent). However again, this is less of a factor in SCADA applications.

- Communications may involve proprietary protocols and networks, or at least non–IP-based communications, such that common IT tools (e.g., an Ethernet packet sniffer) are ineffective or useless.

- Information integrity may be more critical in a control system where a bad value could cause a process upset or plant shutdown.

- Software maintenance and change management may—and really should—involve the control system vendor, since patches to the underlying operating system software could affect the operation of the control system software. Such updates and patches should be applied and tested by the SCADA system vendor and should not be applied until approved by the vendor.

Recommendations of the AGA

AGA Report No. 12, "Cryptographic Protection of SCADA Communications—General Recommendations," addresses the issue of securing the existing communication channels in a SCADA system between the central host and the field-based remotes. The basic assumption of the AGA is that these low-bandwidth communication channels, with their slow-speed, serial, asynchronous communications protocols, are probably not going away any time soon and thus need to be protected. The subject of hijacking an RTU has been discussed in great detail in the present book; suffice it to say, this is a real concern.

Unfortunately, much of the technology available for securing an analog communication circuit is either very expensive (as is a telephone *scrambler,* which can protect voice communications) or not compatible with serial protocols (as are encryption modems that buffer, encrypt, and then retransmit, introducing excessive time delays). The AGA has recommended an encryption standard that could be implemented in commercial products and that is designed to be compatible with low-bandwidth/low-baud-rate protocols. The scheme proposed addresses mutual authentication, certificate authentication, session keys, and link encryption. The actual standard has four sections (12-1 through 12-4) and each takes a slightly different view of SCADA communications security, including security over digital networks, although to date only the initial two sections have been completed.

Of course, this cannot be retrofitted directly into the programming and hardware of older RTUs. It would require external hardware placed in front of the RTU on the communication circuit. However, the latest RTUs, with Pentium-class CPUs, could potentially be reprogrammed to incorporate all of these functions and features. It will be interesting to see how many vendors elect to adopt and implement the recommended standard, either as add-on hardware or directly within their RTU products.

Furthermore, the central host end of the communications circuit has to support these same functions. Again, this could be handled either as an external hardware fix or as a software enhancement to the SCADA system itself. The major accomplishment of the AGA report (and the proposed encryption standard) is that it is supposedly designed to function within the real-world constraints of typical SCADA polling channels. As of this date there is actual testing going on to verify this assumption and there are commercial products in the works that will be based on this standard.

Appendix D:

Industry and Government Security Recommendations

The following is a list of various governmental, industry, and international organizations that are developing or have published security recommendations related to SCADA systems.

- Instruments, Systems, and Automation Society (ISA)—TR1, TR2, and SP99 Standards

- Process Control Security Requirements Forum (PCSRF)

- International Electrotechnical Commission (IEC)—TC 57 and 65

- U.S. Department of Homeland Security (DHS)—Process Control Systems Forum (PCSF)

- Institute for Information Infrastructure Protection (I3P)—SCADA Initiative

- U.S. Department of Energy (DOE)—National SCADA Test Bed

- U.S. National Institute of Standards and Technology (NIST)—Industrial Control Systems Test Bed

- Control Systems Security Center—INL

- Center for SCADA Security—SNL

- U.S. CERT Control Systems Center

- International Council on Large Electric Systems (CIGRE)

- Institute of Electrical and Electronic Engineers (IEEE)—Power Engineering Society (PES)

- North American Electric Reliability Council (NERC)—Standard 1300

- Electric Power Research Institute (EPRI)

- Process Control Systems Cyber Security (PCSCS) Forum

- Chemical Industry Data Exchange (CIDX)

- American Petroleum Institute (API) 1164

- American Gas Association (AGA) Report No. 12

- American Water Environment Federation (WEF)

- International Standards Organization (ISO)

  - ISO 17799

  - ISO 15408

- Applicable NIST 800-series documents:

  - 800-48: Wireless Network Security

  - 800-41: Firewalls

  - 800-40: Security Patches

  - 800-31: Intrusion Detection

- American Water Works Association (AWWA)

As can be seen, there is a lot of ongoing activity and a lot of work being done by various groups that may end up replicating the efforts of others. Out of all of this activity it can be presumed, will emerge new standards and recommendations.

It is worth specifically noting the excellent work being conducted by NIST and that NIST is a good source for a wide range of recommendations and technical information on a wide range of cyber security topics.

Appendix E:
SCADA System Security Assessment Checklists

The following checklists are intended to assist an organization with a SCADA system, or those responsible for assuring SCADA system security, with the process of collecting and evaluating the information relevant to cyber security. Many of the checklists are based on the overall recommendations documented by NERC in Urgent Action Standard 1200 for SCADA system security.

Even though multiple, separate tables are shown for the various security-related information to be tracked and recorded, note that this information (as with most of these tables) will in actual practice probably be implemented in an electronic form (spreadsheets or database applications) in which the multiple tables can be integrated into a single compound form or implemented as linked database tables.

These checklists are provided only as examples of the type of information to be recorded and tracked. The actual details and mechanisms used will vary by organization.

CATEGORY:	Security policies and procedures

WRITTEN POLICIES

No. assigned	Description/requirement	Initially issued on	Manager responsible and title	Current revision no.	Last updated on	Nex revie dat
POL-001	Corporate policy on information management, protection, disclosure, and confidentiality,					
POL-002	Use of company systems and networks					
POL-003	Passwords, user accounts, and account maintenance					
POL-004	Telephone usage including personal cell phone					
POL-005	Internet usage and prohibited Web sites					
POL-006	Software licensing policy					
POL-007	Portable computing policy					
POL-008	Personal computer equipment and software					
POL-009	Removable media policy					

L-010	E-mail and IM usage and content					
L-011	Facility access policy and electronic credentials					
L-012	Background checks prior to and during employment					
L-013	Monitoring of computer usage by employees					
L-014	Handling and care of confidential information					
L-015	Classifications for information protection and access					
L-016	Downloading of data, software, or files					
L-017	Virus scanning of computer equipment and media					
L-018	Performance reviews and employment termination					
L-019	Use or possession of personal electronic devices on company property					
L-020	WiFi- and Bluetooth-equipped devices					
L-021	Spam, restricted e-mail list, and e-mail attachments					

POL-022	Remote access and VPN usage					
POL-023	Duplication of and removal of sensitive documents					
POL-024	Video surveillance and physical searches of persons, possessions, and office area					

The policies listed above are provided as examples and are not to be considered a comprehensive list

INSTRUCTIONS: Create and maintain an accurate list of all published company policies related to information management, confidentiality, computer usage, account management, confidentiality communications, Internet access, equipment and software validation and approval, baseline requirements, standards, and anything associated with critical computing systems, networks, and associated regulations such as HIPPA and SOX. A senior manager should be assigned responsibility for each policy, and policies should be reviewed and updated as/if needed, on an annual (or more frequent) basis. All written policies should include an audit log of changes and written approvals for issuance. Policies that relate to others should list those dependencies and relationships in a specific document section. Policies that have been identified as necessary, but not yet written or completed should at least be enumerated in this list above and assigned both a unique ID number and a manager with the responsibility for policy completion. This list itself should be treated as an essential document and reviewed monthly, to schedule and organize impending policy reviews, or whenever a new or revised existing policy is generated.

Are all fire doors set up with alarms?			
Does the fire alarm sprinkler system have a delay on release of water for manual alarm pulls?			
Does the fire sprinkler system have separate, independently activated zones?			
Are employee credentials of a form that is very difficult to forge?			
Does unattended access control include multiple factors (e.g., ID card and PIN number)?			
Is there a differentiation in the access credentials for different areas and categories of personnel? (Are access credentials universal, or are they area/employee specific?)			
Is attended video surveillance in effect for the most critical areas?			
Is the recorded video routinely collected and stored in a secure manner?			
Are visitor logs verified by a guard (or an authorized employee) and collected and stored ona routine basis?			
Are electrical supply systems and HVAC controls for critical systems and areas protected from tampering?			
Are entry/exit logs created by the access control system, and are they reviewed and preserved on a regular basis?			
Are fire-proof storage cabinets available for on-site storage of critical information and backup?			

Does your business liability and fire insurance provide adequate coverage for the loss and restoration of critical systems, business interruption, and potential legal liabilities if confidential information is improperly disclosed as a result of a cyber attack?		
Are backups made on all computer systems on a regular (daily to weekly) basis, and are multiple copies on a storage rotation scheme with off-site storage?		
Are there procedures to ensure that backup copies cannot be claimed by unauthorized personnel?		
Is there a suitable UPS in place for critical systems (including habitability considerations and communications subsystems)?		

ELECTRONIC SECURITY

Does the company have a policy prohibiting WiFi access points on the LANs of critical systems?		
Does the company have a policy regarding removable media?		
Does the company have an e-mail server that scans and sequesters attachments and blocks identified SPAM sites?		
Does the company have a policy regarding use of the Internet, IM, and e-mail for nonbusiness purposes?		
Does the company require that only approved, properly licensed software be loaded onto personal computers?		
Does the company prohibit the use of personal computer and peripheral equipment or their attachment to company systems and networks?		

Is there a NIDS monitoring traffic on the critical LAN/WAN segments?			
Is there a HIDS monitoring the resources and applications on the set of critical hosts and servers?			

STEM MAINTENANCE

Are all computers equipped with the latest virus-scanning and firewall software and configured to receive automatic updates?			
Is there a department/person responsible for ensuring that relevant security updates and patches are installed on all systems on a regular basis?			
Do your system vendors perform functional testing of operating system, networking and third party software updates and patches and provide integrated updates that incorporate all of these items?			
Do your critical vendors have a 24/7 support capability that includes trained, competent help desk personnel who are familiar with your specific systems?			

SASTER RECOVERY

Does the company have a written disaster recovery plan?			
Is this plan reviewed, tested, practiced, and amended on an annual basis?			
Does the company have an alternative site of some form, which can be put into operation if the primary site or systems are unavailable?			

Does the disaster-recovery planning include and address telecommunications requirements?			
Does the disaster-recovery plan address obtainment of necessary equipment and software resources?			
Does the disaster-recovery plan address the return to the primary place of business and termination/disposition of the alternative site?			
Is there a senior manager with responsibility for assuring the viability of the disaster-recovery plan and procedures?			

GLOSSARY

A2D: Analog-to-digital conversion. The electronic circuitry that generates a binary numeric value that varies in value over a predefined range, directly in relation to a voltage signal being varied over a corresponding voltage range.

ACL: Access-control list. The list of access rights assigned to a given user or program by association to their user ID. This defines the resources (utilities, files, CPU time, etc.) and usage priority available to the particular user, within the operating system of a given computer or a defined network of computers.

AGA: American Gas Association.

AGA calculations: A series of ever more precise volumetric (or caloric) calculations for natural gas, based on the available instrumentation and analytical measurements.

Alarm acknowledgment: A specific action (usually a keyboard function of display target mouse click) taken to indicate to a SCADA system that newly detected and specially annunciated alarm indications have been reviewed, so that special annunciation (visual and audible) can be terminated

ANSI: American National Standards Institute. (See also *ISO* [1] and *SQL*.)

AP: (Wireless) access point. A WiFi (wireless Ethernet) transceiver connected to a conventional Ethernet LAN, providing wireless, broadband bridging of the LAN to devices within range that have a compatible wireless card.

API: Application program interface. The explicitly defined set of subroutines or library functions (or object methods) offered to an application program(mer) to access capabilities of the operating system, other applications, or system resources.

ARP: Address Resolution Protocol.

ARP cache: The locally stored list of Ethernet (and corresponding IP) addresses for all of the other computers on a LAN. Each computer on a LAN maintains its own such list, which is updated by special ARP messages.

Asymmetric: Unbalanced/unequal, usually in reference to the subdivision of communication bandwidth into a full-duplex channel. (E.g., an asymmetric DSL circuit has much greater incoming bandwidth than outgoing bandwidth.)

ATM: Asynchronous transfer mode. (See also *SONET.*)

Authentication: Exchanging and validating credentials (often issued through a trusted third party) to prove an identity. In computer terms, this means exchanging and verifying X.509 digital certificates and possibly validating them with a CA elsewhere on the network.

Automatic/manual mode: Placing a periodically executed control calculation, used to manipulate a physical process parameter and control equipment (as a valve), under the manual control of a human operator or allowing the computer to continue the automatic execution of the calculation and logic.

B2B: Business to business. An automated exchange of data between the business systems of company A and company B, often using XML technologies (e.g., automated ordering from a vendor on the basis of inventory levels).

Back door: An undocumented, unauthorized, secret mechanism for gaining access to a computer system, such as a hard-coded ID/ password or a Trojan horse program that relays information around the protective mechanisms of the operating system.

Bacteria: A self-replicating type of malware that multiplies and consumes all available memory, CPU, and disk resources until the operating system is disabled.

Baseline: The minimum set of (obligatory) technical requirements. Add-ons are available to address variable and differing needs.

Battery backup: A power source that can nondisruptively continue to supply DC power to operate computer equipment or protect volatile storage in the event of the loss of normal power sources.

Biometric scanner: Any device that makes one or more physical measurements of features unique to an individual (e.g., fingerprints, retinal pattern, and/or hand geometry), for confirmation of identity.

Bit-oriented protocol: A legacy serial protocol that predates the development of UART technology and microprocessor-based RTUs, using asynchronous messages with frame lengths that are not definable as an exact multiple of eight-bit octets but rather some specific fixed bit-length (e.g., 35 or 47 or 58 bits per message frame) defined in the protocol specification.

Bluetooth: A wireless LAN technology for short-range, ad hoc communications connectivity between computer devices and peripherals and for use in cell phones.

Boolean logic: Predicate logic equations based on the two-state (true/false) combinational algebra defined by George Boole in the 1800s. Inputs are acted on by the operators AND, OR, NOT, and XOR to produce a true/false result.

Buffer overflow: A type of hacker attack in which programs that accept data input are given more data than they expect. The excess data (which is actually carefully crafted computer instructions) target the program logic in the memory region that follows the end of the memory storage area allocated to hold the data input, overwriting legitimate computer instructions and replacing them with instructions selected by the hacker.

CA: Certificate authority. A third party that provides (sells) X.509 digital certificates for authentication purposes, also providing online authentication (or rejection) of certificates that are alleged to have been issued by that CA. The CA acts as an impartial third party that can verify that the credentials offered for identification to computer A by computer B are valid and were issued by the CA to computer B.

Calculated variable: A numeric or Boolean value that is computed by the computer system, from other physical inputs, manually entered inputs, or other calculated variables, and that is subsequently treated by the SCADA system as if it were an actual physical input.

Character-oriented protocol: A protocol that uses messages composed of one or more ASCII characters or eight-bit octets, thus making the messages suitable for use over asynchronous serial communication circuits on the basis of conventional computer serial-port UART hardware designs.

Cipher: A scheme for encrypting messages (plaintext) into a nonreadable form (ciphertext) and then back into plaintext.

Ciphertext: The encrypted form of a message, once it has been subjected to a cipher or encryption algorithm.

Circular buffer: A fixed-length (e.g., n elements) data storage area where, once filled, each subsequent incoming data element overwrites the oldest data previously stored into the buffer area, so that the buffer always holds the most recent n elements.

CLI: Command-line interpreter. An operating system utility program that interacts with a human user to allow the entry of commands, from a predefined set, in human-friendly form, to be executed by the operating system. The Microsoft DOS window is an example of a CLI.

Closed-loop control: A computer-based control algorithm. The computer makes a measurement, computes the need for (and magnitude of) a control adjustment, and automatically sends the necessary commands to the respective control device, to effect an adjustment without the need for human intervention.

COM: Common Object Model. The Microsoft equivalent of CORBA. COM was intended for applications running on the same computer and was supplanted by DCOM. COM messages allow application programs to share data and provide processing services to each other.

Compiler: A program that converts human-readable commands (high-level programming language) into the actual computer command code numbers (machine language) used by a specific type of computer. This is different from an Interpreter which is a program that accepts a high-level, machine independent program as its data and performs the functions called for in that data as if it were a real set of machine instructions for that specific computer.

Console port: The interface, in most operating systems, through which an authorized user is given direct access to the CLI (as opposed to a port that is owned by an application program through which a user would interact only with that application program). In older computers, this might be a physical port, but today it is more likely a logical port (e.g., the DOS window that can be displayed under the Microsoft Windows operating systems).

Control-loop cascade: In complex, multivariable regulatory control schemes, there may be two or more control loops, the output of one (the upper loop) being the set point of the next (the lower loop). The data connection that passes the value of the set point from the upper loop to the lower loop is the cascade.

CORBA: Common Object Request Broker Architecture. In Unix, the technology for allowing objects to be shared by applications running on different computers, even on different operating systems.

CPU: Central processing unit.

Cracker: A hacker who uses computing/programming knowledge and skills to cause damage and harm to, or gain the unauthorized use of, the computer systems and networks of others.

CRC: Cyclic redundancy check. A binary polynomial calculation used to generate a unique binary number for a unique sequence of binary data provided as input.

CRC code: Code number carried along with transmitted messages to verify the message integrity at the receiving end. A form of one-way hash algorithm used in most modern communication protocols.

CSU/DSU: Channel service unit/digital service unit. The electronics and logic needed to interface with both the communications equipment and the end digital device requiring connectivity. FRAD is an example of a CSU/DSU device, as is an ISDN modem. A CSU/DSU is commonly used to connect to a T1 telephone circuit.

CSV: Comma-separated value.

CSV file: An ASCII text file in which data values are written as ASCII character sequences with a comma character separating each subsequent data element. Commonly used for data exchange between Microsoft applications, such as Excel spreadsheets.

Daemon dialer: A hacker tool (program) for detecting modems. A daemon dialer will sequentially automatically dials all telephone numbers within a defined range or pattern, recording the numbers answered by a modem.. Some daemon dialers do additional probing when a modem answers, to glean additional information for the hacker.

Database point: In a real-time control system, each piece of information that is part of the real-time database, updated on a regular basis either by RTU polling or via calculations. A database point (also called a tag) is usually a specifically named data structure that includes a current value that can be used in displays and reports and tested for alarm limit violations. A point (or tag) is usually a collection of data elements, in a defined structure, including the actual (most recently updated) value of the point. The other data elements describe the point and how it is to be displayed and processed by the control system.

Datagram: A self-contained data packet carrying its own address information, so it can be independently routed from the source to the destination computer without reliance on earlier exchanges (between the source and destination computer and the transporting network). In TCP/IP architecture, IP packets are the basic datagrams sent through a network, carrying UDP or TCP packets as their data.

Data mining: The process of looking for previously unrecognized patterns or statistical relationships among huge data sets by use of statistical, neural network, or other means.

Day-zero virus: A new virus that has just been launched onto the Internet and thus is not known to and may not be recognized by the current virus-detection software. Heuristic virus-detection programs attempt to identify such viruses by similarities to known viruses; IDS packages attempt to identify such viruses by their actions once they enter the IDS-monitored system.

DCOM: Distributed Common Object Model. The extension of the Microsoft COM architecture for applications running on network-connected computers, as well as applications running on the same computer.

DCS: Distributed control system. An automatic process control system composed of multiple, independent control computers, each responsible for only part of the overall plant/process. (In theory, a partial DCS failure will not take down the entire plant/process.)

DDoS: Distributed denial of service. (See DoS.)

Dead-man timer: Hardware and/or software that monitors operator activity and initiates some action if no activity is detected within a predefined time interval.

Decryption: The process of undoing the encryption of a ciphertext message to recover the original plaintext message.

Deep inspection firewall: A firewall that looks at the message content of IP packets and is knowledgeable of defined protocols and malware, to verify that the IP packets do not contain a known virus and conform to the protocol specifications. (See also *stateful inspection* and *application proxy*.)

Demand scan: A SCADA supervisory function whereby an operator can force the immediate polling of one or more RTUs, thus preempting the scheduled RTU polling activity.

DHCP: Dynamic Host Configuration Protocol. A protocol in the IP suite that is used to incorporate a computer into an IP network by assigning it a temporary (reusable/dynamic) IP address from an available range of addresses.

Dictionary attack: Attempting to break (guess) the password of a target computer system by going through a previously compiled list of words (the dictionary) and trying them is succession. The word list is usually oriented around a given theme, such as sports teams or city names.

Digital certificate: A set of data that can be used as electronic credentials to verify a computer's identity by another computer. A digital certificate typically contains identification information, a digital signature' validity dates, and a unique serial number, as well as the sender's public encryption key and information about the issuing CA (including their digital signature). The ISO specifies a standard for digital certificate structure and content, currently X.509v3.

Digital signature: An encrypted data element that cannot be forged (using reasonable means) and that uniquely verifies the sender of a message and confirms that the message has not been altered. Usually included as part of a digital certificate.

Digital-to-analog conversion: An electronic circuit that produces a voltage output that corresponds to the binary numeric value input to the circuit. Occasionally abbreviated as A2D.

Digitization: Taking sequential samples of an analog signal and converting them to a sequence of numbers, with an A2D converter, such that the numeric sequence adequately reproduces the analog signal when sent back through a digital-to-analog converter circuit at the same sampling rate. For digitization and transmission of the human voice/speech, the telephone company uses 8,000 samples per second (stored as eight-bit integers).

Display drill down: Going from a high-level overview display to a more focused and detailed display by using poke points and navigational targets built into an HMI application.

Display hierarchy: Logical structuring of navigational relationships among a large number of available display pages, facilitating the location of the desired display page in an intuitive manner by use of the fewest possible intermediate steps..

Display navigation: Switching from display page to display page by using the navigational poke points and keyboard functions (e.g., soft keys or function keys) provided by the operational HMI.

DLCI: Data link connection identifier. The communications interconnection address/circuit address used to interface with a frame relay network. An end point node on a frame-relay WAN is uniquely identified by its DLCI, much as an IP address identifies a computer connected to the Internet. The DLCI is included in all messages and is used for routing within the frame-relay WAN.

DMA: Direct memory access. Special hardware/circuitry that allows the writing of bulk data directly into a contiguous range of random-access memory (RAM), without passing through the CPU under program control. Commonly used for reading and writing blocks of data to/from bulk storage devices (e.g., hard drives).

DNP3.0: Standardized serial protocol for use with RTUs and other IEDs. Supports a reasonable range of strong data types, as well as polled and unsolicited report-by-exception modes. Widely used in the electric utility market. An IP version has also been defined.

DNS: Domain name server. The computer that provides URL-to-IP-address conversion, when requested by a Web browser or an e-mail client/server. Like a telephone directory, but converting a URL, rather than a name, into an (IP) address.

DNS cache: The local storage of a limited number of recently accessed URLs and their corresponding IP addresses, eliminating the need to go to a DNS. A point of attack by hackers, who overwrite the IP addresses with different values.

Domain name: A uniquely assigned, registered name (e.g., mywebsite. com) that is added to the applicable DNS, so that URL requests will be directed to the Web/e-mail server of the registered organization.

DoS: Denial of service. An attack in which communications with a computer or device are blocked, typically by overloading the bandwidth of the communication channel and/or the computing power of the computer/device. A common mechanism is to have a large number of zombie computers concurrently deluge the designated computer/device with a constant stream of messages; this is called a distributed DoS (DDoS) attack.

Drill down: See display drill down.

DS0 circuit: The lowest-bandwidth digital communication circuit offered by the telephone company. Offers the bandwidth defined by the telephone company as needed to deliver the digitized human voice (i.e., 8,000 samples per second × 8 bits per sample = 64 kbps).

DSL: Digital subscriber line.

DSSS: Direct-sequence spread spectrum. A type of spread-spectrum radio that uses a pseudorandom chipping code, combined with the actual data being transmitted, to make the resultant signal appear as random noise to any receiver that can't undo the effect of the chipping.

Dual ported: An RTU that has two (or more) serial ports that can be independently used by separate SCADA systems to poll and retrieve data. Commonly used in the electric utility industry. Dual ported RTUs are occasionally used for the purpose of protocol conversion where different protocols are used on the ports, and the RTU has no physical I/O hardware.

EGU conversion: The mathematical computation of a process engineering unit value Y (e.g., volts, cubic feet per minute, degrees Fahrenheit, etc.) from a binary integer X returned by an A2D converter circuit. Often (but not always) a linear relationship in the form of $Y = MX + B$.

Electronic vaulting: Sending critical data from one computer over a network to another computer, where it can be stored as a backup in the event that the first computer is damaged or the data it contains are lost.

EMI: Electromagnetic interference. A category of electronic noise that can alter (introduce errors into) a message transmitted over a communication circuit. (Additional usage: entity-machine interface—for the extremely politically correct, who don't wish to risk offending nonhumans by using the term HMI.)

Encapsulation: Transporting one type of message (e.g., individual ASCII characters or serial protocol messages) as the data portion of another type of message. Specifically, using TCP/IP messages to carry non-IP messages across an IP network.

Encryption: Manipulating a message, in a reversible manner, to prevent unauthorized personnel from being able to read the message by making the message incomprehensible (see *cipher*).

Encryption key: See *key*.

Ethernet: A LAN technology used for high-speed computer interconnections. Available in bandwidths of up to 10 Gbps and in wired, fiber-optic, and wireless (WiFi) forms.

Ethical hacker: A computer expert who uses computing/programming talents and skills to identify, report, and correct cyber vulnerabilities, rather than to exploit them (also called a white-hat hacker).

Evil-twin AP: A nonauthorized wireless access point (AP) placed in physical proximity to the real AP, broadcasting a replicated (cloned) identification, so that users log onto the evil-twin AP, rather than the valid AP. The attacker can record packets to get (and spoof) MAC address and WEP authentication-key information.

Extranet: A stand-alone, totally independent, IP-based network that is not interconnected to the Internet.

False negative: Deciding that a person's biometric readings are not sufficient to match that person's recorded readings, thus denying access when this *is* the person in question. (I.e., denying access improperly.)

False positive: Deciding that a person's biometric readings are sufficient to match the recorded readings of the alleged personnel, granting access when this *is not* the person in question. (I.e., granting access improperly.)

FDM: Frequency-division multiplexing. Sharing a single communication channel by breaking it into separate frequency bands or subchannels.

FHSS: Frequency-hopping spread spectrum. See *frequency hopping.*

Firewall: A computer-based security appliance placed between two networks for the purpose of vetting packets going in either direction, blocking those that do not meet predefined rules and guidelines. Firewalls range in capability from simple packet filters to deep inspection (and stateful inspection) versions and even application proxy servers that are protocol aware.

Firmware: The application-specific software that is typically placed into an embedded, special-purpose computer/device and that is never (or rarely) modified or upgraded. Generally, this software is stored in nonvolatile memory, such as Flash or PROM (Programmable Read Only Memory).

FRAD: Frame-relay access device. Router-like networking appliance that makes the physical connection to the frame-relay WAN, and provides serial ports and Ethernet LAN connections to the devices at the particular site. Also used to mean frame-relay assembler/disassembler, one of the internal functions of the FRAD.

Frame relay: A moderate- to high-bandwidth packet switching WAN technology offered by commercial suppliers (usually the telephone companies) that is replacing older, X.25 packet networks.

Frequency hopping: A type of spread spectrum radio in which the transmitter makes channel changes, on a pseudorandom basis, during the transmission of a message, to make monitoring difficult for a receiver not suitably equipped to follow the same pseudorandom channel sequence. This scheme enhances transmission security and allows for better sharing of the available channels among a large group of geographically adjacent users. The primary advantages of frequency hopping radios should be considered as avoiding interference and optimal channel usage, and not increased security.

FTP: File Transfer Protocol. An application-layer protocol in the IP suite. Used to send a copy of a file from one computer to another, over an IP network. It includes error checking and retry logic for transfer reliability.

Full-duplex channel: A communication channel that supports concurrent bidirectional data transmission.

Gateway: A communications appliance used to connect two different types of networks. A gateway deals with issues like the electrical/interface and protocol differences between the two networks.

Generator ramping: Sending control commands to RTUs that are located at generating facilities and interfacing the generating units. Typically, generator ramping provides a stream of momentary contact closures (pulses) to either increase or decrease the speed of the generator.

GMT: Greenwich mean time. A time standard based on the prime meridian (crossing through Greenwich, England) as the starting point for counting time differences between the time zones of the world.

GPS: Global Positioning System. A global network of special-purpose satellites that broadcast signals allowing suitably equipped receivers/computing devices on the surface to make a calculation of their exact latitude and longitude (and altitude), within a few meters of precision.

Hacker: A computer expert who uses computing/programming skills to attempt to obtain unauthorized access to computer systems or to cause damage to those systems. (See also *cracker* and *ethical hacker*)

Hacker tools: Assorted software utilities, developed by hackers and made available over the Internet, that enable users to launch attacks on computer systems. These tools often contain Trojans that infect the systems of those who download and attempt to use them.

Hacker Web sites: Where hackers share information about vulnerabilities in and methods for invading and attacking computer systems and post software utilities (hacker tools) that can be used for staging such attacks.

Half-duplex channel: A communication channel that supports message transmission in both directions, but not concurrently.

Hash code: An algorithm that takes a block of data and produces a unique numeric value, which cannot be used to regenerate the original data and which should never be the same for two differing blocks of data, no matter how slight the difference between the two data blocks.

HIDS: Host-based intrusion detection systems. (See also *NIDS* and *N/ HIDS.*)

HIPPA: Health Insurance Portability Protection Act of 2004. A government regulation that includes provisions regarding the required security and protection of personal information related to health issues, in corporate computer systems.

HMI: Human-machine interface. The displays, keyboard, mouse, touch screen, and other equipment that together present information to and receive commands/data from a human being. (Formerly called *MMI.*)

Hot spot: A WiFi access point (AP) available to the public (possibly for a fee) at such locations as hotels, airports, and shops. (Also called *WiFi hot spot.*)

HTTP: Hypertext Transfer Protocol. A layered protocol in the IP suite that is used for messages between a Web server and a Web client (browser).

HTTP/S: A secure version of HTTP that sets up a session key and encrypts subsequent message traffic between the Web server and Web client (browser). Note that HTTP/S is vulnerable to a man-in-the-middle attack and does not authenticate the browser, only the Web server.

ICCP: Inter–Control Center Communications Protocol (also called UCA1.0 and TASE.2). A layered protocol in the IP suite that is designed for the exchange of many types of simple to complex information, and even commands, between SCADA systems. Primarily used in the electric power industries, but gaining popularity in water/wastewater applications.

ICMP: Internet Control Message Protocol. A set of messages used for management of the traffic across the Internet, including notifications of deleted packets and delivery failures and determining connectivity. Ping is an example of an ICMP message type.

IDS: Intrusion-detection system. Application software that runs in each computer on a monitored network. IDS monitors applications, resources, communications traffic, and other parameters that could indicate anomalous behavior caused by an intrusion. Variations of this are NIDS, HIDS, and N/HIDS.

IEC: International Electrotechnical Committee. An international standards association that deals with electronics and communications technologies.

IEC61131-3: A set of standards that define a series of programming conventions for PLC/DCS control logic, including conventional relay ladder logic, as well as sequential function charts, structured English, and other conventions.

IED: Intelligent electronic device. Electric industry term for microprocessor-based devices used in substations, including RTUs, protective relays, power meters, and fault recorders.

Infinite loop: A program logic error that causes a program to continuously execute a set of instructions that contain no conditions/tests that would cause the program to reach an end point and to terminate.

Integrity scan: A polling request to an RTU requiring a full report of all inputs (and possibly outputs) and other data available within the RTU. Often used when a SCADA system starts up, to refresh its real-time database. Also used on a periodic basis when (unsolicited) report-by-exception polling is used, in case exception messages were missed or lost.

Interoperability: The ability of (different) computer operating systems and/or applications running on different computers to communicate and exchange information.

Interpreter: A program that accepts a data file containing numeric codes defining the actions and operations supported by the program and to be performed in the sequence specified in the data file. The data file can be considered as a program that will be executed by the interpreter program. Scripting languages such as PHP and JavaScript are executed by interpreter programs built into the Web server or browser.

Intranet: An autonomous IP-based network that is interconnected with the actual Internet.

Intrusion detection: Identifying the presence of an unauthorized user, application, or malware, by monitoring of measurable operating system and networking parameters (e.g., message traffic, CPU usage, and file access). (See also *IDS.*)

I/O: Input/output.

I/O hardware: Electronic circuitry that provides an interface between a computer and physical process parameters and equipment, so that the computer can read process parameters and control plant equipment. Usually one of three categories: analog, discrete/digital, or pulse.

IP: Internet Protocol. The actual protocol used to send packets across the Internet.

IP address: The unique 32-bit (IPv4) or 128-bit (IPv6) numeric identifier that is assigned to any computer or computer device (as a router or gateway) that is directly connected to the Internet. IP addresses are registered with regional/national servers that track them and provide URL translation. IP addresses can be static (permanent) or dynamic (temporary.)

IP$_{SEC}$: Internet Protocol security. Authentication and encryption functions embedded within the IP stack at the IP (network) layer, rather than as an add-on like SSL. It makes use of extended versions of the IP message packet that support the required authentication (AH), encryption (ESP), and key-exchange (IKE) functions and protocols.

IP spoofing: A hacker technique of generating IP message packets with a falsified sender IP address, to convince a packet-filtering firewall to allow the messages to pass because the sender appears to be a trusted entity.

ISA: Instruments Systems and Automation (originally the Instrument Society of America but changed in the 1990s to keep up with changes in technology). An organization dedicated to process and plant automation and automated measurement and control.

ISDN: Integrated services digital network. An international communications standard for providing digital data and voice services on a common telecommunication circuit..

ISO: (1) International Standards Organization. The association that develops and issues standards such as the OSI seven-layer model for network architectures. (2) Independent System Operator. A regional organization that manages power markets and buys power from nonregulated electric power generating companies.

ISO/OSI model: A deconstructed computer communications architecture broken into a stack of seven functional layers, each of which performs a specified set of functions and interfaces the adjacent layer(s) via well-defined interfaces.

ISP: Internet service provider. A company that provides a gateway to the Internet, for occasional and permanent users, through dial-up, DSL, satellite, and cable connections. ISPs also provide fixed IP addresses and temporary DHCP-based IP addresses.

IT: Information technology. The group that is responsible for specifying, purchasing, installing, maintaining, and upgrading the computing hardware and software assets of a company, including LANs, WANs, Web sites, portable computing platforms, and business software.

Key: The secret numeric value that is used in a cipher or encryption scheme, to convert plaintext into ciphertext. The encryption scheme can be made known as long as the key is kept secret. (Also called *encryption key*.)

LAN: Local area network. Today LANs are invariably based on Ethernet technology. (See also *PAN, VLAN,* and *WLAN.*)

M2M: Machine to machine. A type of plant/facility networking technology for eliminating sensor and I/O signal wiring in industrial monitoring and control applications.

MAC: (1) Media access control. The hardware and software rules that define how and when a computer may obtain the right to transmit a message onto a shared channel. Part of the layer of the ISO/OSI stack, just above the physical layer. (See also *MAC address.*) (2) Message authentication code. A hash-coded numeric value that is computed from and sent along with a message, to verify that the message has not been modified.

MAC address: The unique 48-bit Ethernet address programmed into every Ethernet controller board and WiFi device. (Currently, computers/ devices are migrating to a 64-bit replacement version called EUI-64.) Although MAC addressing is not specific to Ethernet, this is the most common usage. (See *MAC* [1].)

MAN: Municipal area network. (See also *WAN.*)

Message payload: The data portion of a computer message. That is, the information being transported, separate from header and the routing and validation portions.

Microwave: The portion of the electromagnetic spectrum that sits between infrared radiation and radio waves, spanning 0.3–300 gigahertz (30 cm to 1 mm wavelength).

Middleware: Software used to link (i.e., provide interoperability) disparate applications, by performing the necessary data type conversions and supporting the messages of each connected application. Based on a set of distributed agents or on a central data repository.

MMI: Man-machine interface. See *HMI.*

Modem: Modulator/demodulator. An electronic device that converts binary digits (represented by specific voltage levels on an EIA-232 serial port) into audio tones suitable for transmission through the telephone system or over a voice-grade radio channel.

MP3: A compressed audio file (with encoding that sacrifices some of the audio quality in order to reduce the file size) corresponding to the published standard MPEG-1, audio layer 3.

MTU: Master terminal unit. Either the host computer in a SCADA system or a pre-SCADA electronic device that acted as a data concentrator for the RTUs.

Multi-factor authentication: Verifying a user's identity by requiring two or more sources of identification, such as a password and either an ID card or a biometric measurement or some other form of credential.

NERC 1200/1300: The North American Electric Reliability Council's recommendations for improving the cyber-/overall security of the SCADA infrastructure for electric power generation and transmission.

Network mapper: A utility that sends series of specially crafted IP messages (particularly ICMP messages with increasing TTL values) into a network, in order to identify the various computers through which the packets travel, and to probe the IP address range to see what computers/devices respond.

N/HIDS: A combination of NIDS and HIDS technologies, for broadest range of intrusion detection.

NID: Network intrusion detection. Monitoring the communications traffic on a network, probably with a separate computer appliance on each LAN segment, to identify anomalous message traffic, IP addresses or protocols that could indicate the presence of an attacker attempting to penetrate the network, or malware sending messages across the network. A NID initially develops a characterization of normal network traffic by monitoring the traffic and then begins comparing observed traffic to the characterization, as a way of identifying anomalous traffic.

NIDS: Network-based intrusion-detection systems. (See also *HIDS* and *N/HIDS*.)

Off-line storage: The transfer of bulk data and files to removable media that can be placed into secure storage. Recovery of the information requires that the particular removable media be located and installed into the drive attached to the computer. A scheme often used when the data archive interval desired (and the corresponding data quantity for that interval) greatly exceeds the practical on-line storage capacity of the computer system.

OLE: Object Linking and Embedding. A Microsoft application standard and protocol for distributed objects that allows an application to call on another application to process relevant parts of its data. (E.g., a Microsoft Word document containing a spreadsheet would cause Word to call on Excel to process and render the spreadsheet portion of the Word document.) OLE replaced DDE and has itself been replaced by DCOM and ActiveX controls.

OPC: OLE for Process Control. A standardized mechanism for the exchange of data between programs that produce data (servers) and programs that wish to receive that data (client). Based on the Microsoft OLE architecture and DCOM technology. There are several classes of defined OPC servers, including servers that provide alarm data, historical data, and real-time analog/status values.

Open-loop control: A control sequence, from input measurement to control action, that requires human interaction (as opposed to closed-loop control, in which control actions are automatic and autonomous of human intervention).

Out-of-band signaling: Messages, commands, or data transmitted with the primary data stream that are considered a control signal and demand immediate attention. The receiving side must pass on the out-of-band data to the appropriate software routine in front of any other data that has been buffered and not yet processed, because the command must be executed as soon as possible.

Overview display: The highest-level display (least detail/greatest coverage) in a display hierarchy. Generally, a geographic map–style display with poke points for navigation down to more detailed display levels, as well as indicators/icons with summary information.

Packet: A message sent across a packet switching network with the necessary header/trailer information, per the protocol being used, and carrying a payload of data. (Similar to a *datagram*.)

Packet sniffer: A software package or diagnostic appliance that monitors message traffic over a network (particularly a wired LAN or wireless LAN) and allows the capture and display of messages meeting defined criteria. A packet sniffer can be a useful diagnostic tool but is a dangerous hacker tool as well.

Packet switching: A type of WAN that breaks messages into small, limited-sized pieces and then sends them each as a separate data packet, possibly via different routing, through the network to the destination where they are collected, put into proper order, and delivered as a complete message. X.25 frame relay and IP networks are packet switching networks.

PAN: Personal Area network.

Pass-through mode: Allowing messages on one port of a device such as an RTU to be repeated on a different port, creating the effect of eliminating the device from the resultant circuit. Like a port switch. (Also called *transparent mode*.)

Password cracker: A hacker tool/utility program that attempts to break (guess) a system/user password by sending all possible character variations, one at a time, or by sending character strings selected from any number of word lists (see *dictionary attack*). These programs are effective only against systems that place no limit on the allowable number of login attempts made by a user.

Penetration (pen) testing: Attempting to break into a specified system, using hacker tools and techniques, with the permission of the system owner, to identify security vulnerabilities. Pen testing may be a red team (black box) test or a blue team (gray box) test, based on whether some or no insider information is made available about the system to be tested.

Peripheral transfer switch: An electronic device used to share/switch a peripheral device between a redundant set of computers. Usually part of an automatic "fail-over scheme," transferring peripherals from a previously functioning (now failed) computer to the backup computer. Needed when peripherals cannot be shared on a common bus (as an EIA-232 circuit) or do not support dual connections (as a printer with a parallel port).

PID algorithm: Proportional-integral-derivative calculation. A third-order differential equation used to perform continuous regulatory control in computer-based process automation systems. Emulates the actions of analog circuits used for regulatory control prior to the introduction of digital computers.

Ping: An Internet utility program that verifies whether a specific IP address (or URL) is accessible, uses ICMP messages. Also provides an indication of the time required for a round-trip to/from the specified IP address. Ping will make a URL lookup call to the DNS if given a URL, rather than an IP address.

PKI: Public-key infrastructure. Related to public-key encryption, in which a trusted third party (the CA) issues electronic credentials (digital certificates) that include public keys used for encryption and subsequently validated by the CA.

Plaintext: Original form of a message, prior to conversion into ciphertext.

PLC: (1) Programmable logic controller. A microprocessor-based device with I/O hardware and user-defined control logic that cyclically reads the inputs, computes the resulting logic and then drives the outputs to the desired state. A PLC will generally support some form of communications and various protocols. Widely used in the water/wastewater industry as RTUs. (2) Power line carrier. A low-bandwidth communications technology used by electric utilities, in which messages are sent over the transmission line conductors that carry electric power.

Point: A single physical I/O or calculated value in the real-time database of a SCADA system or DCS. (Also called a *tag.*)

Point tagging: Placement of one or more software flags on a control point in a SCADA system or DCS to inhibit the sending of control commands to (or the discarding of received commands by) that specific output (analog, pulse or contact) analogous to the physical placement of paper tags on the control handles of switch gear in a control room. This safety feature prevents the SCADA system or operator from (de)activating or adjusting a control output while the associated process and/or equipment is in an unsafe condition.

Poke point: A place/area/icon/object on a display screen that, if selected with the pointing device (mouse, touch screen, etc.), will cause a predefined software action to occur.

Polling: Interrogation of RTUs for data updates through the various communication lines and protocol addresses supported, to cycle through all RTUs on a regular basis.

Port scanner: Software utility/hacker tool that sends specially crafted IP messages to a designated IP address, to identify what TCP and/or UDP ports are recognized and supported by the computer system at that IP address. Used to identify known vulnerabilities in various operating system versions.

Port switch: A device that allows a serial communication circuit to be connected to several devices one at a time, through user commands that select the desired device.

Private key: In PKI, the user has a pair of mathematically related keys (a private key and a public key) both of which can be used for encryption and decryption. The public key can (and should) be made available to anyone who needs communications security. The private key must never be revealed, or the security of the encryption scheme will be compromised.

Privatization: Placing the support and maintenance of a formerly governmental/public activity in the hands of a private company that will assume responsibility in exchange for financial compensation.

Protocol: A set of fully specified message formats, data formats, and rules that define the mechanisms for establishing, managing, verifying, and terminating data exchanges between two computers/devices.

Protocol analyzer: A software package that allows a separate computer to be used to monitor, record, and display the messages sent over a serial communication channel or LAN. (See also *packet sniffer* and *protocol test set.*)

Protocol converter: A stand-alone computer, software package, or communications appliance programmed to use one protocol on one port and different protocol(s) on the other port(s) and to unpack and then repack the data and commands passed between the ports. RTU protocol converters allow a different protocol to be used without having to change the protocol running in the existing RTU or host equipment.

Protocol stack: The layers of software that together implement all of the logic necessary to communicate with a similarly equipped computer or communications device running the same protocol. Depending on the protocol, the stack might be only two layers (as in serial Modbus) or up to seven layers (as in the ISO/OSI model).

Protocol test set: Similar to a protocol analyzer except programmed with more specific knowledge of the protocol(s) monitored, with information and displays tailored to the unique features and nomenclature of the particular protocol(s).

Proxy server: A computer used to isolate applications from the actual server they are attempting to access, for security purposes and for performance improvements. If used as a firewall, the proxy server restricts message traffic to a specific set of protocols and processes the protocol messages and then allows their passage if they meet security requirements. The proxy server is protocol-aware meaning that it can check a message for conformance to protocol specifications.

Pseudo I/O point: A point in the real-time database of a SCADA system or DCS whose value is set by manual input or application programs but is processed, alarmed, and treated in the same manner as physical I/O signals.

PSTN: Public switched telephone network. The wires-based dial-up telephone system used for noncellular telephone calls, established by the Bell Telephone Company. A telephone line used to connect to the PSTN may informally be called a POTS (plain old telephone system) line.

Public key: The encryption key, of a PKI key pair, that is disclosed to others so that they may encrypt messages such that only the holder of the corresponding private key can decrypt them. (See also *private key.*)

Publish-subscribe data delivery: An unsolicited report-on-change data-delivery mechanism, allowing producers of information and consumers of that information to be linked for the delivery of new information as it becomes available.

PVC: Permanent virtual circuit. A logical point-to-point communication connection, established across a frame-relay network, that persists between messages and does not have to be reestablished at the start of each transaction.

Raw count: The binary value generated by an A2D circuit for a given value of input voltage. All A2D circuits produce binary values, which need to be translated into the engineering units of the physical parameters measured (pressure, temperature, level, etc.).

Real-time clock: The circuit in a computer that generates a hardware interrupt at a well-defined and consistent time interval. These intervals can be counted and used to compute elapsed time, as well as time of day. The real-time clock in a computer needs to tick at a rate that is substantially faster than the fastest event that must be dealt with by the computer programming (e.g., moving a cursor, detecting keyboard strikes or reading in the next character received on a serial port).

Report by exception: A communications protocol used in RTU polling in which message traffic/time is reduced by allowing the RTU to report only those details that have changed since the prior polling, rather than sending a full report of all data values (many of which may not have changed) with each poll. Since additional identification information is needed, there is a crossover point at which a full report becomes more efficient than report by exception.

RFID: Radio Frequency ID. A bar code like electronic tag that can be attached to items and read from a distance (ranging from inches to almost 100 feet). The tag can contain a simple, fixed numeric code, or it may be rewritable and carry a moderate amount of information. Tags are normally read by activating them with the RF signal of the reader. Noncontact ID badge readers and electronic tool booth scanners are examples of RFID technology. RFID tags are often used for inventory tracking and routing in automated warehouses.

RLL: Relay ladder logic. Graphical Boolean logic, originally designed to describe actual electromechanical relay circuit wiring used for control logic and later adopted as a programming language for use with PLCs (which replaced electromechanical relays).

Rogue AP: An unauthorized WiFi access point attached to a LAN, usually without enabling adequate protective measures.

Rollback: Restoring the prior version of software (or files/data) when installation of an update goes badly or results in performance or reliability reductions. When a SCADA system (or major application) is upgraded to a new version, safety procedures normally include preparing to revert to the previously upgraded version of the software.

Router: A communications appliance that interfaces between a local network and one or more communication links to other networks, for the purpose of sending packets destined for computers on these other networks via the proper link (and receiving packets and placing them onto the local network). Routers usually provide a buffering capability and may perform added functions (e.g., packet filter/firewall).

RTO: Regional Transmission Organization. Under deregulation of electric utilities, these organizations (along with ISOs) were established to ensure a competitive market for power generation and transmission.

RTU: Remote terminal unit. An electronic device (now microprocessor based) with I/O hardware and a communications interface, placed at a remote process location, so that a SCADA system can communicate with the device, to receive updating information about the process and to send commands that effect the process.

SCADA: Supervisory control and data acquisition. A type of computer automation system that uses a central computer system, wide area communications technologies, and a large number of geographically distributed RTUs, to monitor and control geographically distributed processes such as pipelines and electric power transmission.

Script kiddie: A person who lacks the advanced computer expertise and skills of a hacker but employs easy-to-use, readily available hacker tools to launch attacks. A derogatory term used by hackers/crackers, although some use the script kiddies to do their dirty work.

Scripting language: A programming language that is interpretive in nature and that is executed by a suitable application program (an interpreter), rather than being converted into actual computer instructions and executed directly by the computer. VBScript, PHP and JavaScript are prime examples.

Session key: An encryption key generated specifically for on-time use, to protect message traffic during a communications session. A session key strategy prevents an attacker from collecting enough message traffic based on one key to break the encryption. (See also *key*.)

Set point: The numeric value that represents the desired value of a controlled parameter (e.g., flow, level, or pressure) in an automatic control system. The set point defines what the controlled parameter should be, and if it drifts away from the set point, the control system will make control changes to return the parameter to the value of the set point. A PID loop is used for this control purpose.

SFC: Sequential Function Chart. Graphical programming language used to design sequence logic, similar to RLL. SFC is one of the five languages defined by the IEC61131-3 standard. The SFC standard itself is defined in IEC848 ("Preparation of function charts for control systems") and was based on GRAFCET, a graphical programming tool developed in Europe. Most PLCs and many modern RTUs support SFC programming tools.

S-HTTP: Secure Hypertext Transfer Protocol. A secure alternative to the HTTPS protocol that incorporates client-server authentication and message encryption functions.. (See also *HTTP* and *HTTP/S*.)

Simplex channel: A communication channel that supports data transmission only in one direction. Broadcast radio and television are examples of simplex communications.

Smart radio: Radio equipment with integral microprocessor technology such that the radio can be treated as a computer and can communicate via serial or Ethernet interfaces and protocols. The radios in a communicating group can send each other out-of-band messages, for control of the flow of traffic and for error checking, coordination and message transmission retry purposes.

Social engineering: Exploiting typical human behavior to trick people into giving out confidential information, violating security policies and procedures, or providing improper access to secure areas or systems. Social engineering is used by threat agents to gain the insider information they need to launch an attack.

Software library: A set of pretested and documented software modules or utilities that can be used by a programmer as part of an application development. In a SCADA system, such a library might include utilities for sending commands to RTUs, as well as subroutines for presenting information on HMI screens and for manipulating alarm management settings.

Solar panel: A photovoltaic panel that generates electrical power when exposed to sunshine. Solar panels are used to power RTUs in remote locations where no other power source is available. Such RTUs usually include a battery charger that supplies power when sunshine isn't available, and power-down circuitry to minimize power usage between polls from the SCADA system.

Solar powered: Equipment (e.g., RTUs and radios) designed to operate at the low power levels afforded by solar panels.

SONET: Synchronous optical networking. A high-bandwidth telecommunication standard based on fiber-optic transmission, capable of carrying vast numbers of simultaneous telephone conversations or high-speed data. SONET was designed to be highly deterministic and is thus suitable for such data streaming applications as video conferencing. Supported in the United States and Canada but supplanted by SDH in the rest of the world. Can be used as the basis for ATM networking.

SOX: Sarbanes-Oxley Act of 2002. Mandates the accuracy and reliability of corporate financial disclosures and imposes information security and protection measures directly related to corporate cybersecurity issues of information confidentiality, integrity and availability. Extends to any business process related data which can include some of the types of data maintained in SCADA systems.

Spam: Unsolicited (and undesired) e-mails, particularly of a marketing or advertisement nature, that are normally sent out in bulk (to a huge number of recipients), often on a regular basis. The e-mail equivalent of junk mail.

SQL: Standard Query Language. An ANSI/ISO standard language for manipulating relational databases that is supported by all major relational database vendors.

SQL injection: Attacking poorly designed and programmed Web sites with back-end relational databases by entering specially crafted strings into the data entry fields of Web page forms, so that these strings are relayed to the back-end relational database and accepted/executed as valid SQL commands.

SSID: (WiFi) Service Set Identifier. A code (32 characters or less) used by a WiFi access point (AP) and all of the communicating devices to identify them as part of the service set sharing the corresponding AP. Normally, an AP broadcasts its SSID, but this can be disabled as part of an overall security strategy (a strategy that should also include encryption and authentication and possibly MAC address blocking).

Stack overflow: See *buffer overflow.*

Stateful inspection firewall: A firewall that knows the allowed state transitions for IP (as well as the reasonable times allowed for transition between certain states) and the messages expected for each state. A stateful inspection firewall will reject/cancel connections that violate proper message/transition/timing rules, preventing certain types of attacks (e.g., SYN flooding) from being successful. (See also *deep inspection firewall.*)

Strip-chart recorder: An electromechanical recording device that uses a moving strip of paper to record the movement of a pen whose position is controlled by a voltage source that represents a process measurement.

Strong authentication: The use of multiple factors to determine/validate the identity of a user, such as a password and either a magnetic-strip ID card (or RFID) or a biometric measurement.

T1/T3: Telephone system classifications of communication circuits designed to carry a given number of voice telephone channels by being time-division multiplexed. A T1 (or DS1) circuit runs at 1.544 Mbps (24 voice channels). A T3 (or DS3) circuit runs at 43 Mbps (672 voice channels).

Tag: See *point.*

Tag name: The reasonably short descriptive text string assigned to a point (tag) in a SCADA system or DCS, to aid the operator in recognizing that particular point and its physical nature and location. Often based on a standardized company naming scheme or on the naming scheme proposed by the ISA.

TCP: Transmission Control Protocol. A protocol that runs over IP, providing reliable message delivery and stream-like connectivity and allowing the use of ports.

TCP fingerprinting: Identifying an operating system running on a remote computer by analyzing the packets it sends and how it responds to specially crafted packets. Nmap (Network Mapper) is a commonly used Unix tool that performs this function.

TCP/IP: A commonly used conjunction of Transmission Control Protocol and Internet Protocol. Part of the overall IP suite of protocols.

TDM: Time-division multiplexing. Subdividing (sharing) a single communication channel by allocating it on the basis of time slots whereby any application can use the entire bandwidth for a limited amount of time. The telephone companies subdivide their communications systems by using time-division multiplexing.

Thermoelectric generation: Generating electrical power in a device by exploiting the thermoelectric effect, which dictates that physically joined dissimilar metals, when heated, generate a small electrical potential (the principal used in thermocouples). Thermoelectric generation is very reliable, owing to the lack of any moving parts, and is often used as a power source when fuel is available but electricity isn't.

Transport mode: See *pass-through mode.*

Trojan: An apparently useful/benign software applications that contains a set of logic that is triggered under the proper conditions and that may cause damage to a computer system, open up a back door for an attacker, send out confidential information to a remote computer, or perform some other undesirable (and unauthorized) activity. Also called *Trojan horse,* alluding to the tactic used by the Greeks during the Peloponnesian (Trojan) War.

TTL: Time to live. In every IP packet, a counter that was initially intended as an actual time but is now used as a hop counter. Every time a packet goes from one computer to another (in an IP network), the count is decrementally adjusted. If it reaches zero, the packet is discarded and an ICMP message is sent to the sender of the message. Network mapping can be done by sending out IP packets with TTLs that start at one and are adjusted incrementally, tracking each computer that subsequently sends back an ICMP message.

UART: Universal asynchronous receiver transmitter. An electronic circuit that performs all of the hardware tasks required for asynchronous serial transmission or reception of a data octet/character including adding and removing start and stop bits (used to signal the start and end of an octet frame) and bit sampling and storage at the user-specified transmission rate.

UCA2.0: Utility Communications Architecture. An object-based, high-performance architecture originally used within electrical substations for inter-IED communications (on an Ethernet LAN), also used across IP networks and adopted by some municipal water/wastewater utilities.

UDP: User Datagram Protocol. One of the two transport protocols used to connect applications via IP networking (see also *TCP*). Adds the concept of a port to IP networking. A less robust communication transport mechanism than TCP.

UHF: Ultrahigh frequency. Radio frequency band allocated above VHF and below superhigh frequency, with a range of 0.3 to 300 gigahertz. Used for data exchange and wireless communications, as well as cell phones and television.

Unix process: In Unix/Linux, a program or task that is running under the control of the operating system. Assigned a process ID (pid) and allocated resources as required and authorized on the basis of priority.

URL: Universal resource locator. The text string entered into a Web browser or e-mail to direct it to the desired computer, application and network. A URL is more user friendly than remembering an IP address, although a URL is actually converted into an IP address (and port number) by the DNS. A URL has a protocol designation, a resource and domain portion and any added information needed to specifically identify the target.

Validation: Verifying that a user or an application program has the authority to perform a requested operation.

VHF: Very high frequency. Radio frequency band allocated from 30 to 300 megahertz. Used by some radio communications equipment found in older SCADA systems because of superior propagation properties.

Virtual circuit: Simulation of a dedicated, circuit-switched, communication path through a packet switching WAN. A frame-relay network allows for the creation of persistent (permanent) virtual circuits that connect end point equipment.

Virus: Malware that spreads by making copies of itself and appending them to files, documents, and the boot sectors of removable media. A virus may demonstrate multiple phases once activated, the first being self-replication and the next being infliction of damage.

Virus signature: Portions of computer machine code that are part of the overall virus program. A firewall or virus scanner maintains a table of such signatures, which are sufficient to identify particular viruses, and searches for their presence within IP message packets or appended to other programs.

VLAN: Virtual LAN. Subnetwork of interconnected nodes within a larger physical LAN/WAN, with switches and routers configured to restrict routing among only specified sets of end points.

Voice-grade circuit: A communication circuit (e.g., telephone line or radio link) with sufficient continuous bandwidth (typically 64 kbps) to deliver the digitized midrange frequencies of the human voice.

VoIP: Voice over IP. Technology that provides real-time voice-grade telephone communications across an underlying IP network, using protocols designed for such traffic.

VPN: Virtual private network. A set of interacting computers on a larger network that ignore all other computers on that larger network and accept and respond to communications only from those computers that are part of the VPN. Also used to describe the use of authentication and encryption to secure the communications between a central computer and a remote (possibly mobile) PC (see *VPN tunnel*).

VPN tunnel: Establishing a point-to-point connection between two computer devices, or suitably equipped communication devices, such that the two devices can authenticate, exchange encryption keys and then transport all message traffic between these two devices as encrypted packets. This may include taking non-secure IPv4 packets and transporting them as data in encrypted IPv6 packets. The two most common uses are to provide a secure interconnection of two geographically separate LANs and to allow a mobile or remote user secure connectivity to the corporate network, over a dial up or Internet connection.

Wallpaper: A static image placed on the display screen in the background, on which dynamic display elements are placed and updated. In a SCADA HMI, this could be a map image or the top-down architectural layout of a facility.

WAN: Wide area network. A network that spans a geographical area too large to be served by PAN, LAN, or MAN technologies. Where a WAN starts and a MAN ends is not well defined.

War dialing: Using a daemon dialer program to automatically call consecutive telephone numbers within a user-specified range, recording those telephone numbers at which active modems responded.

War driving: Traveling through a geographic area (often an urban or suburban area) with a laptop PC equipped with a WiFi receiver and software that identifies wireless access points (APs) and their characteristics, recording these locations, often to add to a database on a hacker Web site.

Watchdog timer: An electronic circuit designed to send a reset/reboot signal to a computer if the circuit is not sent appropriate commands within a predefined time window. Used to automatically reboot computers that have crashed or are hung (in an infinite loop).

Webcam: Web camera. A self-contained video camera that operates as an autonomous Web site/server and that supplies updating video images as HTML pages to any conventional Web browser program.

Web page: A hypertext document (usually HTML, XHTML, or XML) offered for delivery and display (across a network using HTTP) by a Web server, to any suitably equipped Web client (a Web browser program).

WEP: Wired Equivalent Privacy. A 40-bit encryption scheme that has fallen out of favor due to the ease with which it can be broken by commonly available hacker tools such as AirSnort.

WiFi: Wireless Ethernet technology.

WiFi hot spot: See *hot spot.*

WLAN: Wireless LAN. A LAN based on some version of wireless Ethernet (WiFi/WiMax) technology. Not typically used in reference to other wireless networking technology (e.g., Bluetooth or ZigBee) although that distinction is blurring.

Worm: Malware specifically designed to spread across network connections, rather than by transport through other programs like a virus or Trojan.

X11: The protocol defined at the Massachusetts Institute of Technology for messages sent between an X-Window client/server (X-terminal), describing the display to be rendered and returning keyboard and mouse events for processing.

X.25 packet switching: The earliest type of value-added, commercial, WAN packet switching technology, to network large numbers of dumb terminals to central computers. X.25 packet switching still exists but is being supplanted by frame relay, partly because of the replacement of dumb terminals by computer-based devices.

X.509: An ISO standard that defines the format and information content of a digital certificate for use in a PKI authentication scheme. (The current version is X.509v3.)

XML: The extensible markup language. A very popular markup language in B2B data exchanges, in which users can define their own tags and create self-describing data in the form of a Web page.

X-terminal: A computer display terminal device (or a PC running software emulation) that implements the X-Window standard and supports the X11 protocol. In Unix, this is a dumb terminal but with a graphical, windowed interface, allowing a user to interact with a central server.

ZigBee: Reliable, low-cost, low-power wireless networking technology intended for industrial monitoring and control as an M2M technology.

Zombie computer: A computer (normally with a full-time Internet connection) that has been infected with a Trojan or time bomb such that it can be used (along with thousands of others) to initiate DDoS attacks on designated targets, either at a specific time/date (time bomb) or upon receiving the necessary command (Trojan). It is estimated that there are at least five distinct sets of zombie computers around the Internet, controlled by various hacker groups, that have been used to launch such DDoS attacks.

Index

A

A2D converter, 27
access authority, 115
access control list (ACL), 205, 398
access controls
 electronic, 282–283
 hybrid, 283–285
 manual, 282
 to operating systems, 420
 to SCADA system utilities,
  122–123
 to secure areas, procedures for,
  304–305
accessorization, 431
access rights, 205, 232, 279
access tracking, 285
access verification checks, 126
account, 398
account lockout, 417, 433
account management procedures, 302
accumulator freeze, 49–50
accumulators, 31
acknowledged alarms, 157
Active X Controls, 196, 402
addressing scheme, 95
address mapping, 91
address resolution protocol (ARP), 101
ad hoc operating modes, 204
administrative programs, 113
administrative rights, 398, 417
agents, 196
AirSnort, 185, 202
alarm acknowledgments, 160–161

alarm annunciation, 159–160
alarm filtering, 158–159
alarm history file, 160–161
alarming functions, 156
alarm limit checking, 155
alarm-state visual indication, 161–164
allowable-value range checks, 155–156
alternative (backup) facilities
 application programming done
  on, 420
 for availability, 180
 in centralized architecture design,
  13–16, 400–401
 insider knowledge of, 250
 point-to-point connections with
  SCADA, 252, 390, 423, 436
 restoration from, 257, 311, 337
 X-Window use with, 412
alternative operating site, 390, 423
American Gas Association (AGA)
 volumetric computations, 34
analog circuits, 71
analog circuits vs. digital circuits,
 346–347
analog input point, 155
analog inputs, 27–28
analog modems, 5, 70, 73
analog outputs, 28
analog telephone circuits, 359
analog-to-digital (A2D) converters,
 27, 79
analysis engine, 230
annual review, 311–312
anomalous traffic, 229
anomaly-detection technology, 194

B

D

F

J

K

L

M

T

U

V